BABYLON BERLIN

TITAN
COMICS

ALSO FROM TITAN COMICS AND HARD CASE CRIME

GRAPHIC NOVELS

THE ASSIGNMENT
MILLENNIUM: THE GIRL WITH THE DRAGON TATTOO
MILLENNIUM: THE GIRL WHO PLAYED WITH FIRE
MILLENNIUM: THE GIRL WHO KICKED THE HORNET'S NEST

MINKY WOODCOCK: THE GIRL WHO HANDCUFFED HOUDINI
NORMANDY GOLD
PEEPLAND
QUARRY'S WAR
TRIGGERMAN

NOVELS

361
A DIET OF TREACLE
A TOUCH OF DEATH
A WALK AMONG THE TOMBSTONES
BABY MOLL
BINARY
BLACKMAILER
BLOOD ON THE MINK
BORDERLINE
BRAINQUAKE
BRANDED WOMAN
BUST
CASINO MOON
CHOKE HOLD
THE COCKTAIL WAITRESS
THE COMEDY IS FINISHED
THE CONFESSION
THE CONSUMMATA
THE CORPSE WORE PASTIES
CUT ME IN
THE CUTIE
DEAD STREET
DEADLY BELOVED
THE DEAD MAN'S BROTHER
DRUG OF CHOICE
DUTCH UNCLE
EASY DEATH
EASY GO
FADE TO BLONDE
FAKE I.D.
FALSE NEGATIVE
FIFTY-TO-ONE
FOREVER AND A DEATH
GETTING OFF: A NOVEL OF SEX AND VIOLENCE
THE GIRL WITH THE DEEP BLUE EYES
THE GIRL WITH THE LONG GREEN HEART
GRAVE DESCEND

GRIFTER'S GAME
GUN WORK
THE GUTTER AND THE GRAVE
HELP I AM BEING HELD PRISONER
HOME IS THE SAILOR
HONEY IN HIS MOUTH
HOUSE DICK
JOYLAND
KILL NOW PAY LATER
KILLING CASTRO
THE KNIFE SLIPPED
THE LAST MATCH
THE LAST STAND
LEMONS NEVER LIE
LITTLE GIRL LOST
LOSERS LIVE LONGER
LUCKY AT CARDS
THE MAX
MEMORY
MONEY SHOT
MURDER IS MY BUSINESS
THE MURDERER VINE
THE NICE GUYS
NIGHT WALKER
NO HOUSE LIMIT
NOBODY'S ANGEL
ODDS ON
PASSPORT TO PERIL
THE PEDDLER
PIMP
PLUNDER OF THE SUN
ROBBIE'S WIFE
SAY IT WITH BULLETS
SCRATCH ONE
THE SCRET LIVES OF MARRIED WOMEN
SEDUCTION OF THE INNOCENT
SHOOTING STAR/SPIDERWEB

SINNER MAN
SLIDE
SNATCH
SO NUDE, SO DEAD
SOHO SINS
SOMEBODY OWES ME MONEY
SONGS OF INNOCENCE
STOP THIS MAN!
STRAIGHT CUT
THIEVES FALL OUT
TOP OF THE HEAP
TURN ON THE HEAT
THE TWENTY-YEAR DEATH
TWO FOR THE MONEY
THE VALLEY OF FEAR
THE VENGEFUL VIRGIN
THE VENOM BUSINESS
WEB OF THE CITY
THE WOUNDED AND THE SLAIN
ZERO COOL

QUARRY

THE FIRST QUARRY
THE LAST QUARRY
QUARRY
QUARRY'S CHOICE
QUARRY'S CLIMAX
QUARRY'S CUT
QUARRY'S DEAL
QUARRY'S EX
QUARRY IN THE BLACK
QUARRY IN THE MIDDLE
QUARRY'S LIST
QUARRY'S VOTE
THE WRONG QUARRY

BABYLON BERLIN

TITAN COMICS
COLLECTION EDITOR: JONATHAN STEVENSON
DESIGN: RUSSELL SEAL

Consulting Editor: Charles Ardai
Line Editor: Tom Williams

Managing & Launch Editor: Andrew James
Titan Comics Editorial: Lauren Bowes,
Lauren McPhee, Amoona Saohin
Senior Production Controller: Jackie Flook
Production Supervisor: Maria Pearson
Production Controller: Peter James
Production Assistant: Natalie Bolger
Art Director: Oz Browne
Senior Sales Manager: Steve Tothill
Press Officer: Will O'Mullane
Direct Sales & Marketing Manager: Ricky Claydon
Brand Manager: Lucy Ripper
Commercial Manager: Michelle Fairlamb
Ads & Marketing Assistant: Tom Miller
Publishing Manager: Darryl Tothill
Publishing Director: Chris Teather
Operations Director: Leigh Baulch
Executive Director: Vivian Cheung
Publisher: Nick Landau

BABYLON BERLIN

9781785866357
Published by Titan Comics
A division of Titan Publishing Group Ltd.
144 Southwark St., London, SE1 0UP

A CIP catalogue record for this title is available from the British Library

10 9 8 7 6 5 4 3 2 1
First Published January 2018
Printed in Spain.
Titan Comics.

WWW.TITAN-COMICS.COM
Follow us on Twitter @ComicsTitan
Visit us at facebook.com/comicstitan

BABYLON BERLIN

WRITER & ARTIST

ARNE JYSCH

TRANSLATOR

IVANKA HAHNENBERGER

BASED ON THE NOVEL
BABYLON BERLIN
BY VOLKER KUTSCHER

For
Silvia, Vida
&
Liv

Forensic Director Engelbert Rath
Polizeipräsidium Cologne a. Rhein, 24 January 1929
Krebsgasse 1-3

Mr. Karl Zörgiebel
Chief of Police
Police Headquarters Berlin
Alexanderstraße 2
Berlin C25

Dear Sir,

My dear friend, in a few days Gereon will start at
Alexanderplatz. I can't thank you enough for helping my son
to get the job at police headquarters.

The dirty laundry that was aired after a few unfortunate
situations in Cologne made it impossible for him to work
there anymore. You know how the Cologne press can be. I
don't need to tell you how harsh the articles against him
are, in spite of the fact that he was found not guilty on
all counts. The press is going after him personally and
making him look guilty of everything.

Gereon did the right thing. We cannot allow the Cologne
press to determine his career path.

I know that you were in a hurry to assign him to the Vice
Squad, even though I believe that he is capable of much
more.

My dear Karl, you know Gereon from your Cologne days, and
I am sure that my son will not disappoint you and that he
will soon prove himself capable of greater things.

The next time I come to Berlin I hope that we will be able
to enjoy a Pfälzer wine together.

With kindest regards,

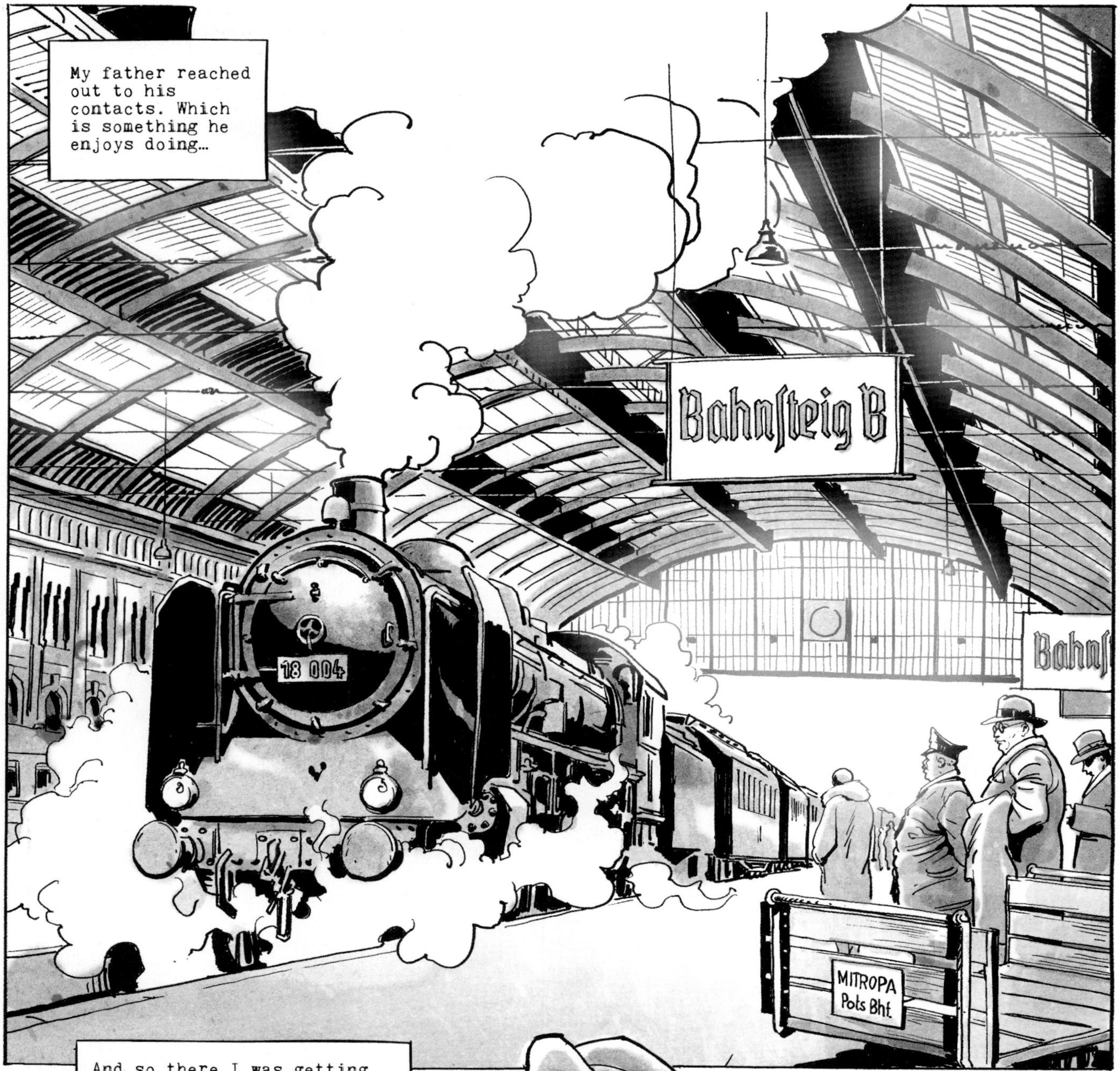
My father reached out to his contacts. Which is something he enjoys doing…
Bahnsteig B
18 004
Bahnſ
MITROPA
Pots Bht.
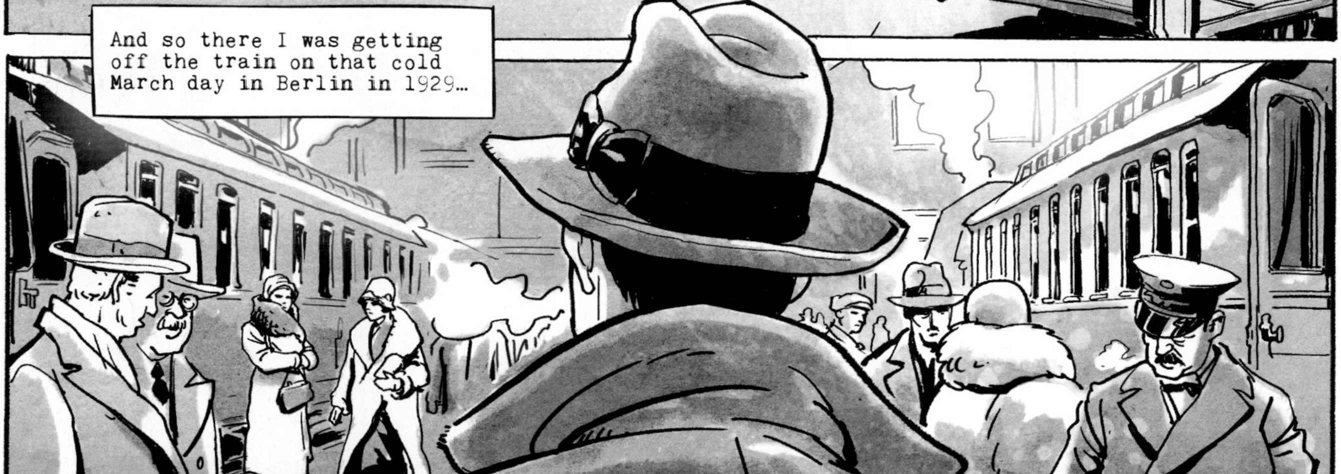
And so there I was getting off the train on that cold March day in Berlin in 1929…

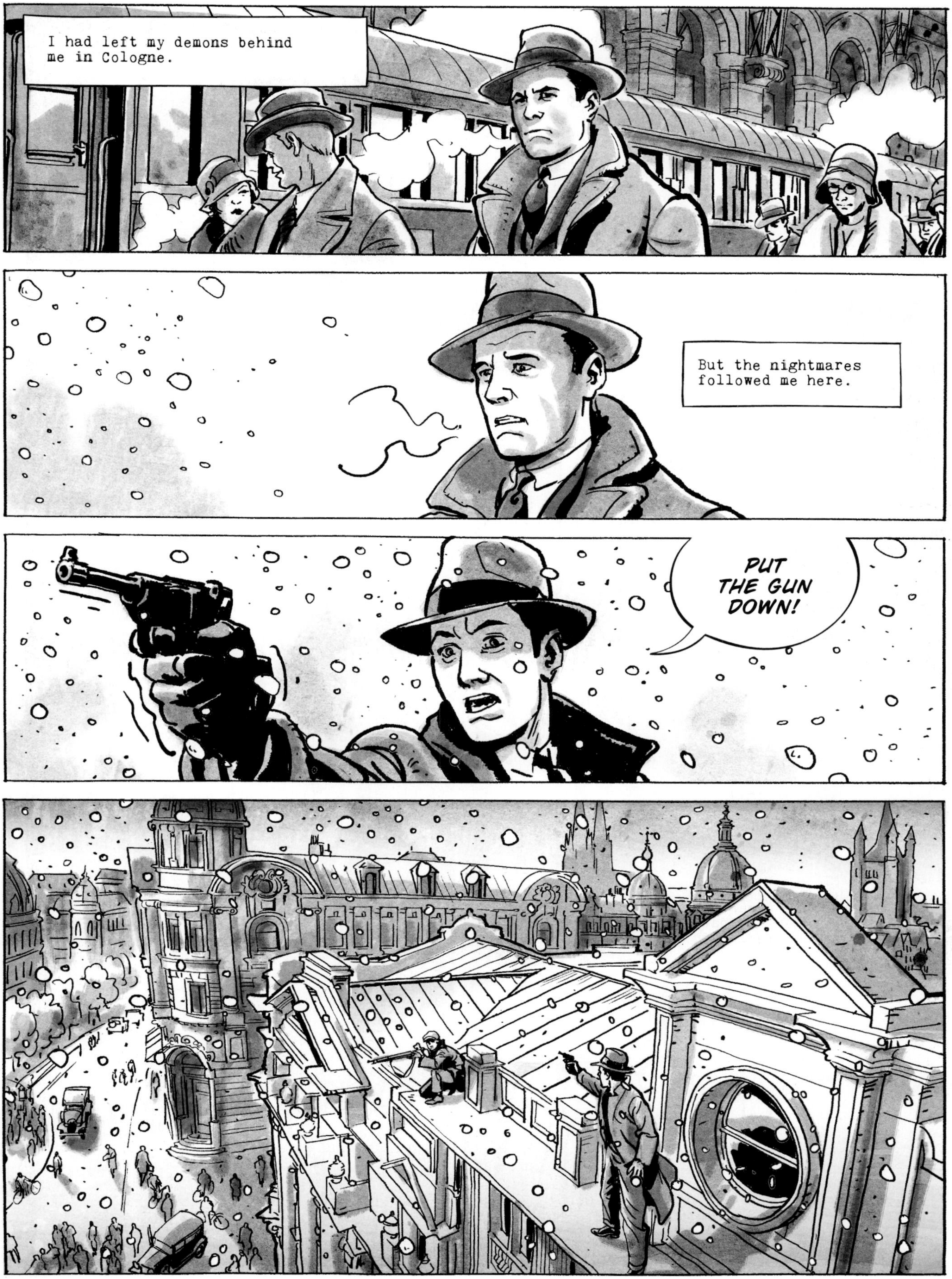
I had left my demons behind me in Cologne.
But the nightmares followed me here.
PUT THE GUN DOWN!

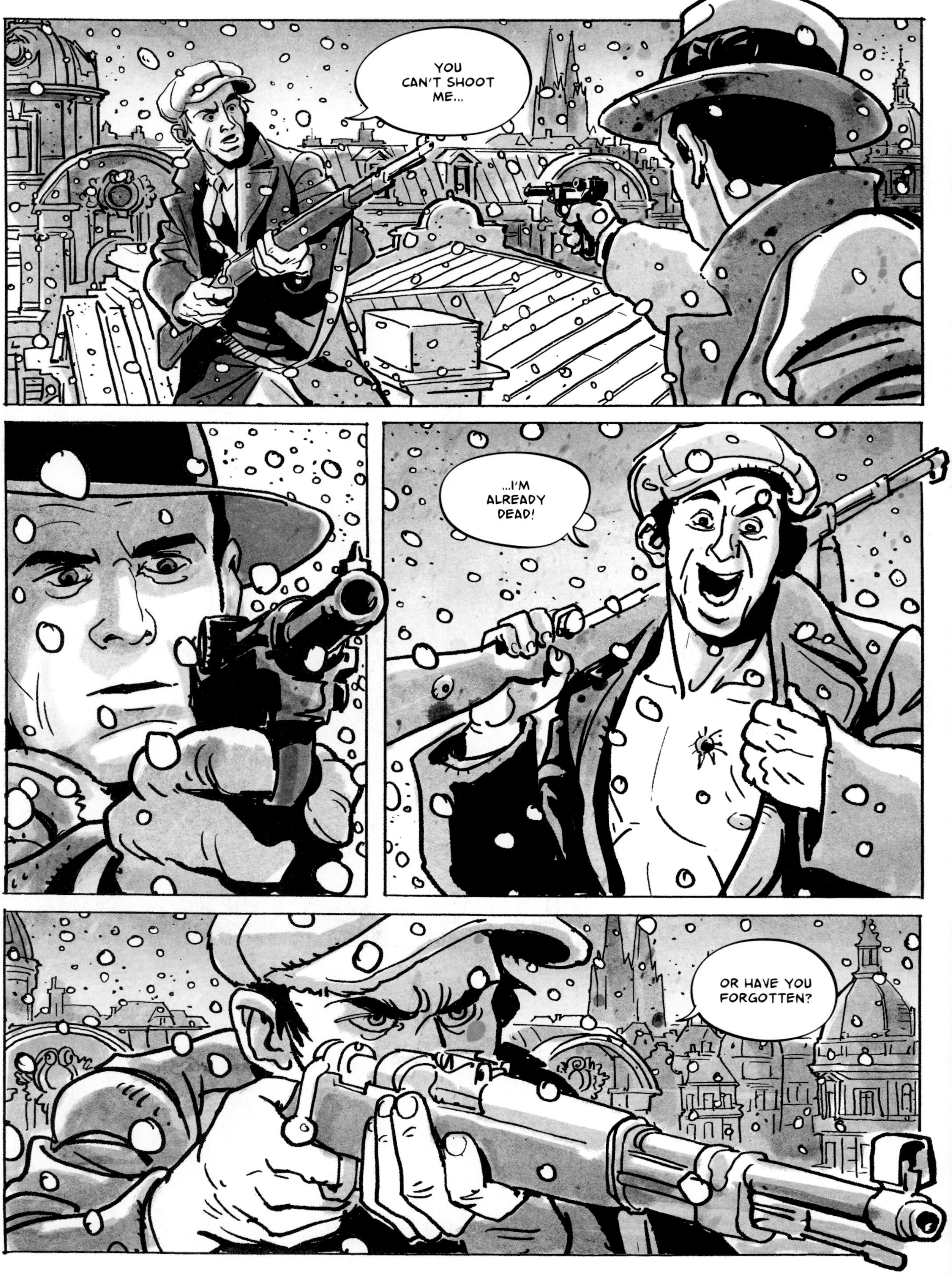
YOU CAN'T SHOOT ME...
...I'M ALREADY DEAD!
OR HAVE YOU FORGOTTEN?

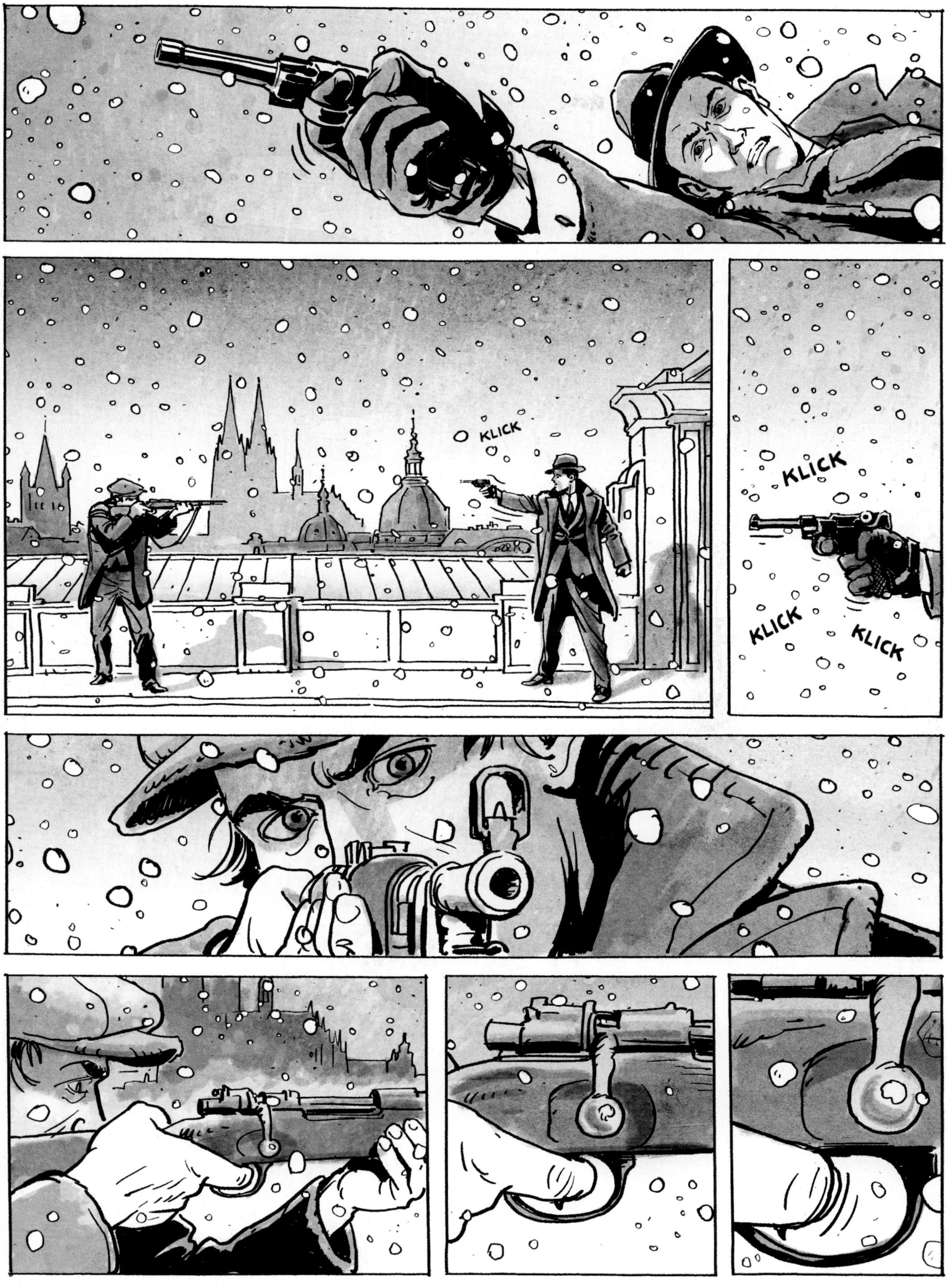
KLICK
KLICK
KLICK
KLICK

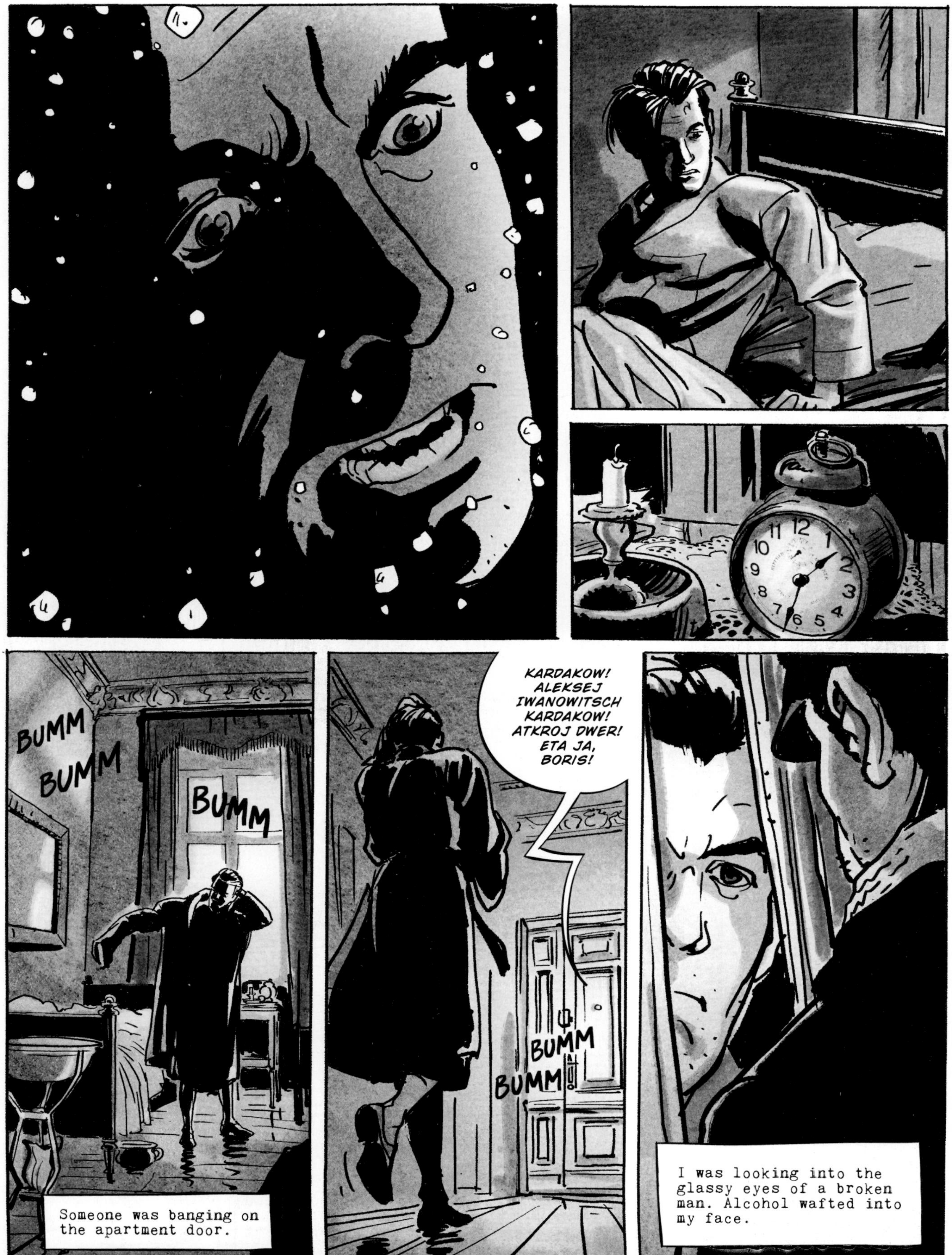
BUMM
BUMM
BUMM
Someone was banging on the apartment door.
KARDAKOW! ALEKSEJ IWANOWITSCH KARDAKOW! ATKROJ DWER! ETA JA, BORIS!
BUMM
BUMM
I was looking into the glassy eyes of a broken man. Alcohol wafted into my face.

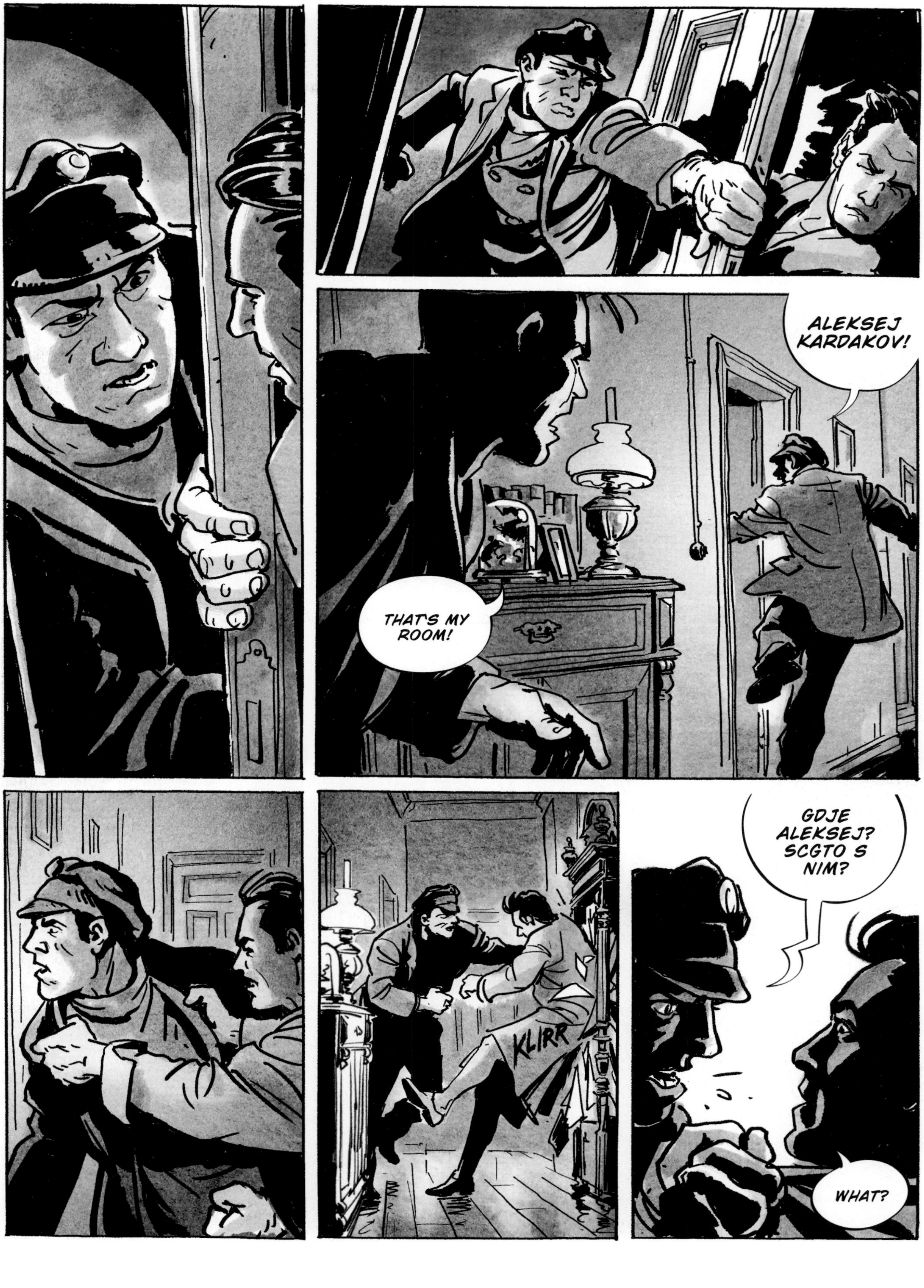
ALEKSEJ KARDAKOV!
THAT'S MY ROOM!
KLIRR
GDJE ALEKSEJ? SCGTO S NIM?
WHAT?

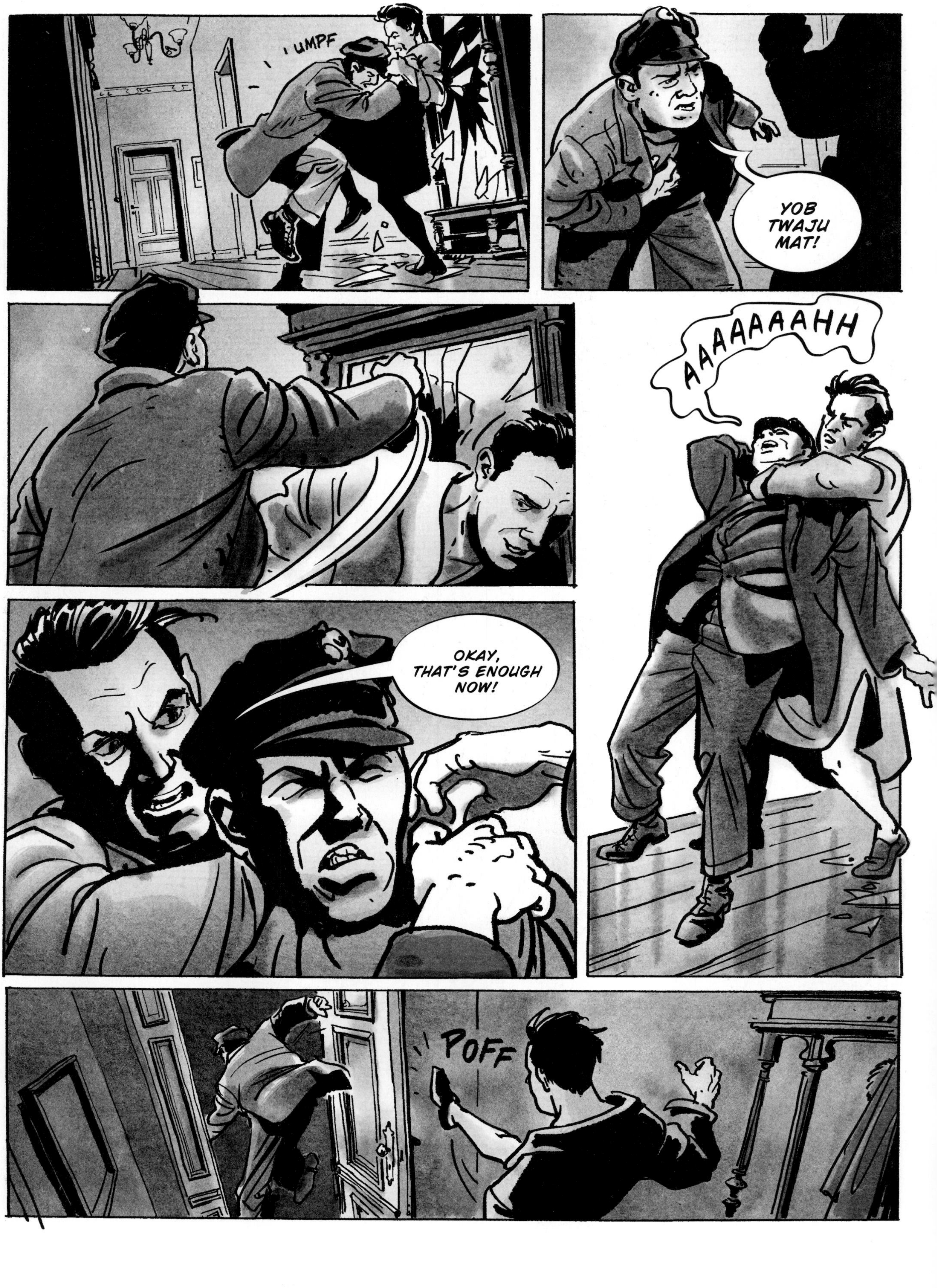
UMPF
YOB TWAJU MAT!
AAAAAAAHH
OKAY, THAT'S ENOUGH NOW!
POFF

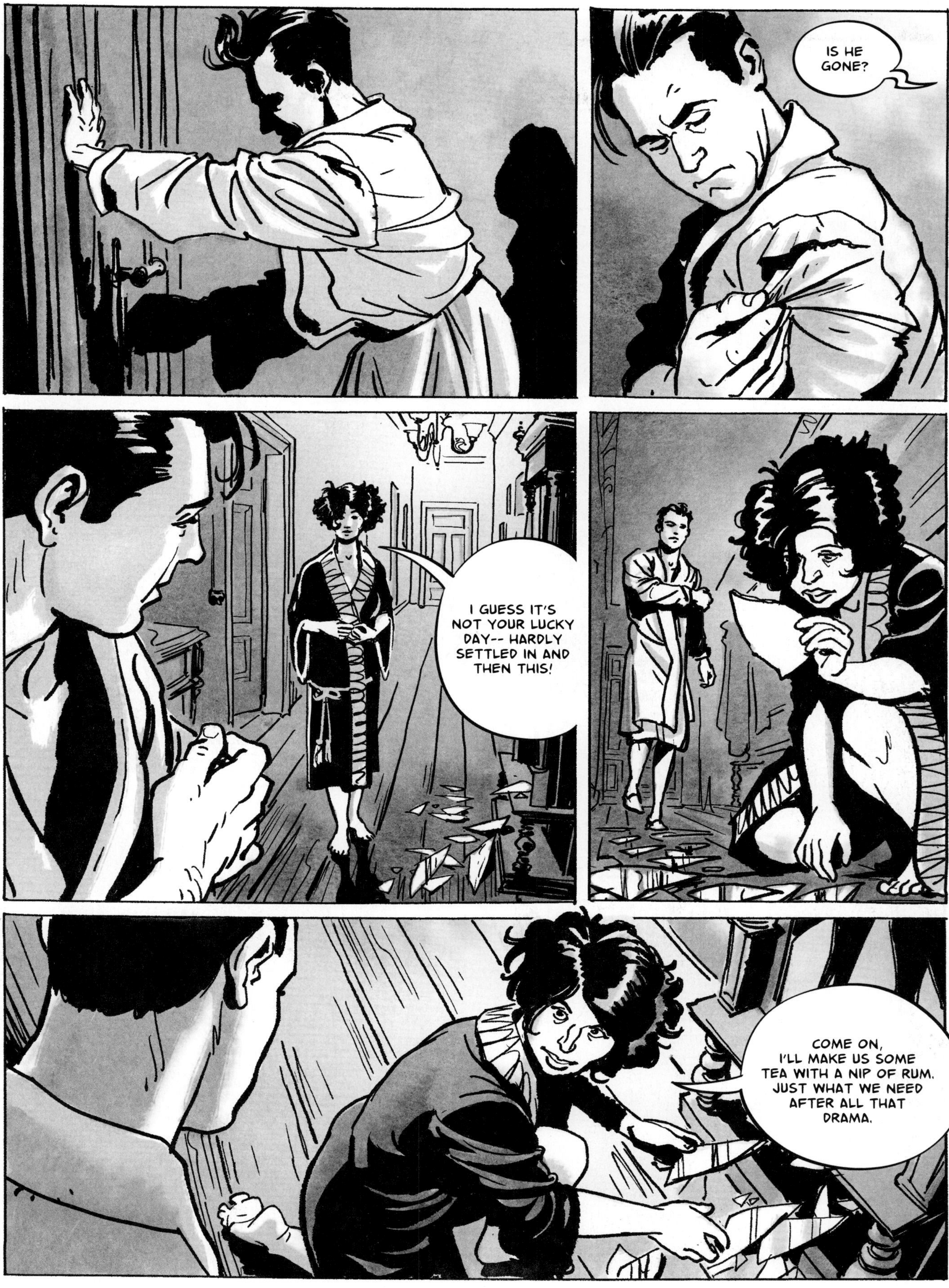
IS HE GONE?
I GUESS IT'S NOT YOUR LUCKY DAY-- HARDLY SETTLED IN AND THEN THIS!
COME ON, I'LL MAKE US SOME TEA WITH A NIP OF RUM. JUST WHAT WE NEED AFTER ALL THAT DRAMA.

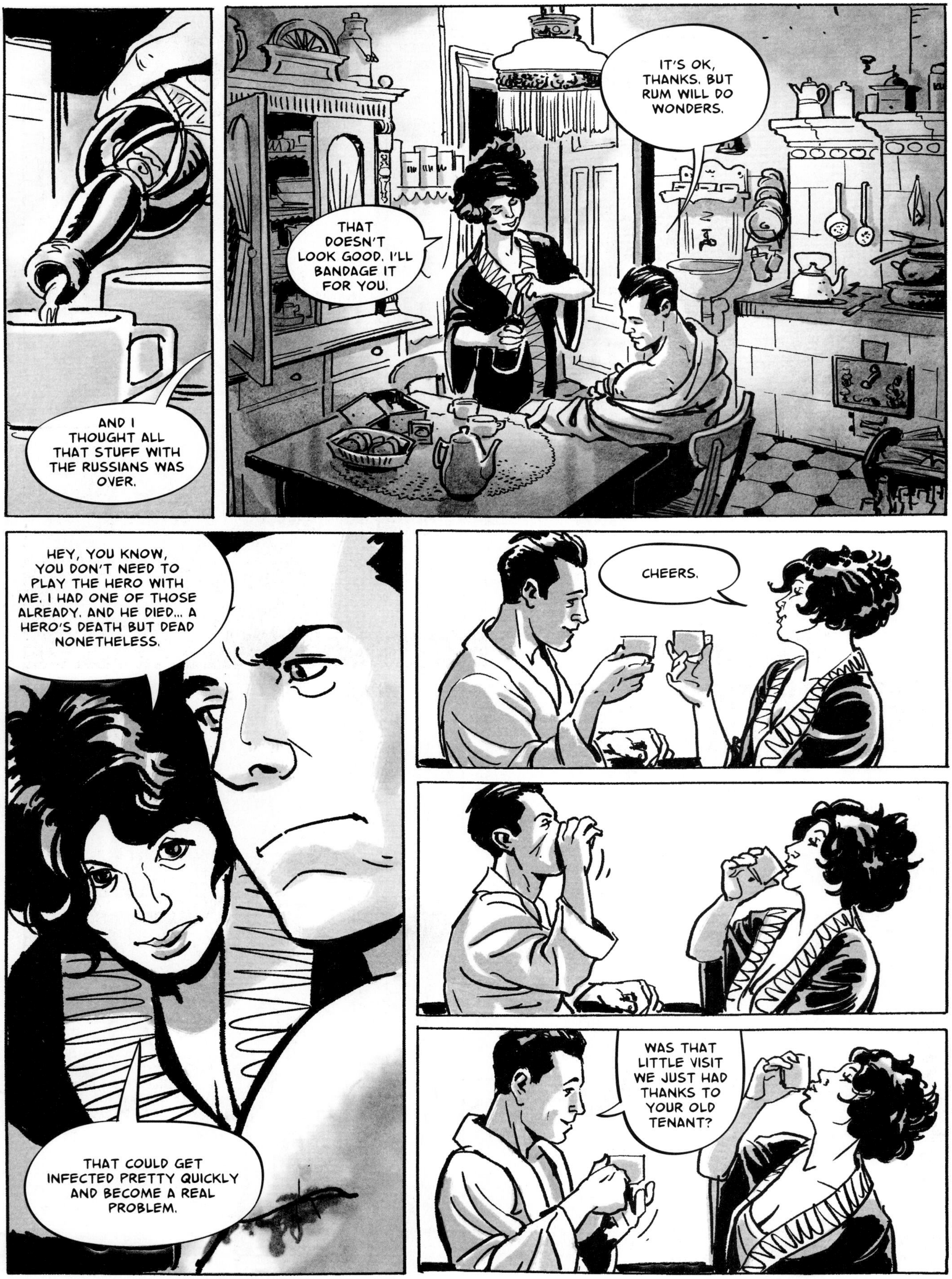
AND I THOUGHT ALL THAT STUFF WITH THE RUSSIANS WAS OVER.
THAT DOESN'T LOOK GOOD. I'LL BANDAGE IT FOR YOU.
IT'S OK, THANKS. BUT RUM WILL DO WONDERS.
HEY, YOU KNOW, YOU DON'T NEED TO PLAY THE HERO WITH ME. I HAD ONE OF THOSE ALREADY. AND HE DIED... A HERO'S DEATH BUT DEAD NONETHELESS.
THAT COULD GET INFECTED PRETTY QUICKLY AND BECOME A REAL PROBLEM.
CHEERS.
WAS THAT LITTLE VISIT WE JUST HAD THANKS TO YOUR OLD TENANT?

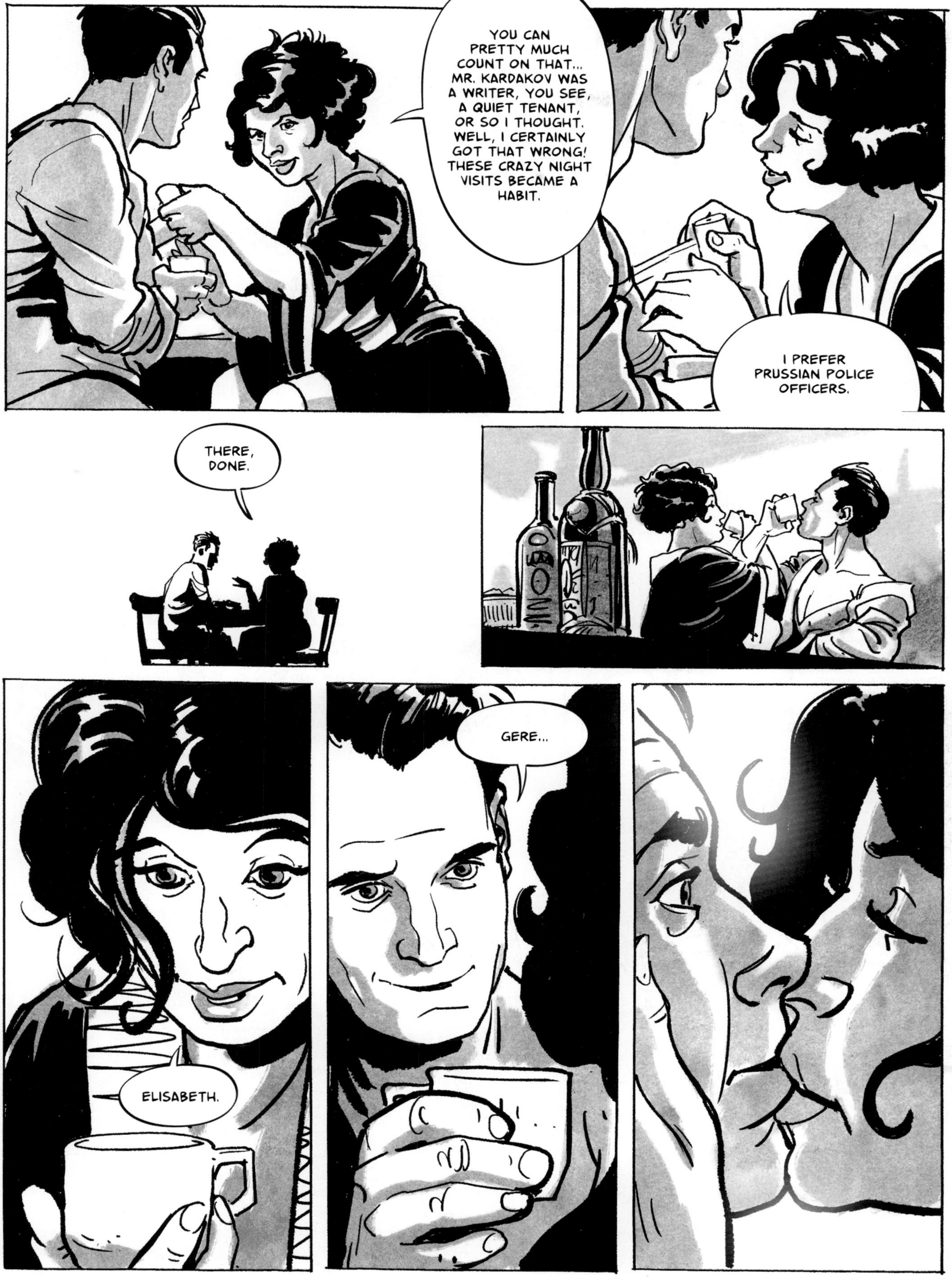
YOU CAN PRETTY MUCH COUNT ON THAT... MR. KARDAKOV WAS A WRITER, YOU SEE, A QUIET TENANT, OR SO I THOUGHT. WELL, I CERTAINLY GOT THAT WRONG! THESE CRAZY NIGHT VISITS BECAME A HABIT.
I PREFER PRUSSIAN POLICE OFFICERS.
THERE, DONE.
ELISABETH.
GERE...

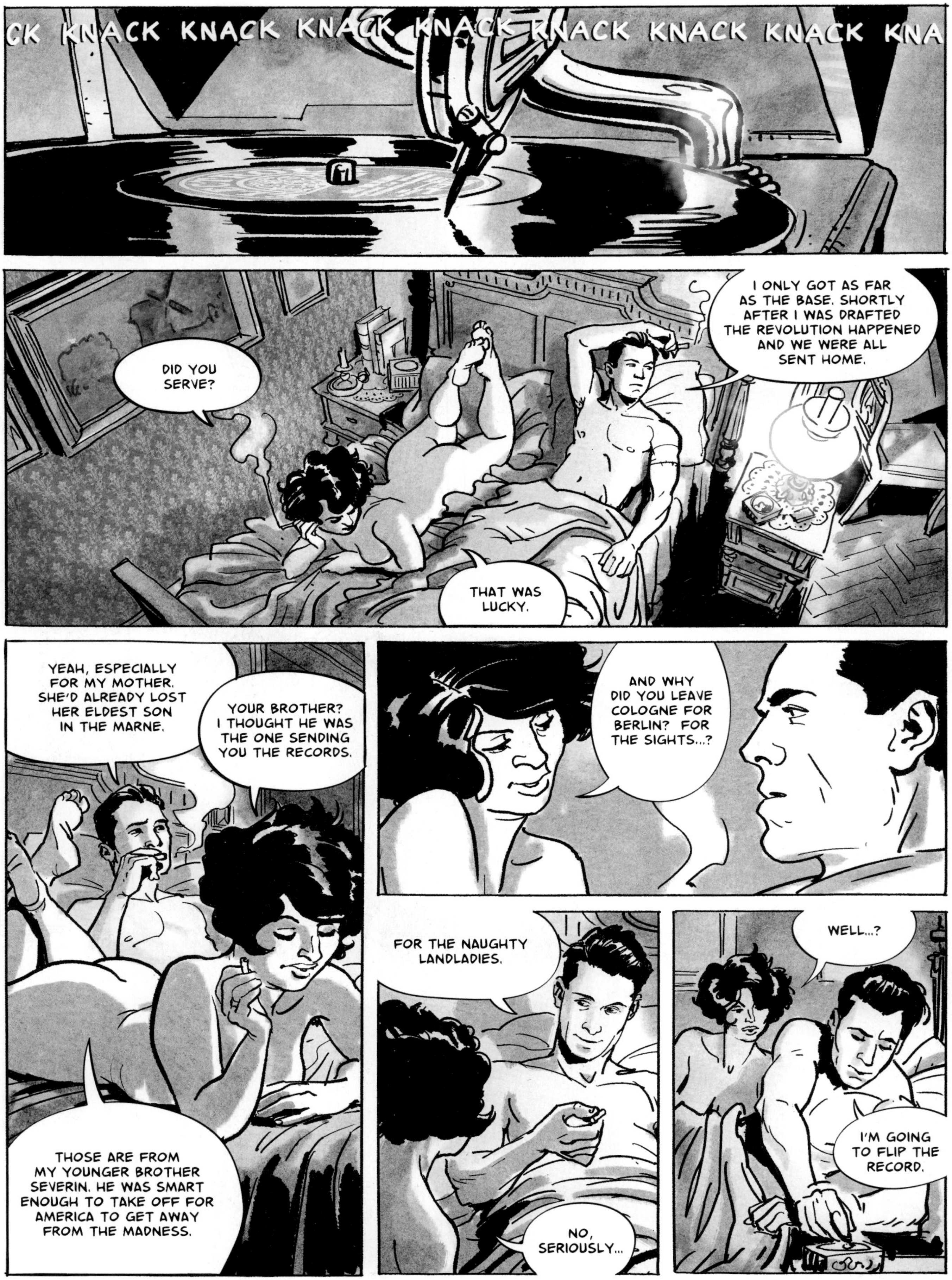
CK KNACK KNACK KNACK KNACK KNACK KNACK KNACK KNA
DID YOU SERVE?
I ONLY GOT AS FAR AS THE BASE. SHORTLY AFTER I WAS DRAFTED THE REVOLUTION HAPPENED AND WE WERE ALL SENT HOME.
THAT WAS LUCKY.
YEAH, ESPECIALLY FOR MY MOTHER. SHE'D ALREADY LOST HER ELDEST SON IN THE MARNE.
YOUR BROTHER? I THOUGHT HE WAS THE ONE SENDING YOU THE RECORDS.
THOSE ARE FROM MY YOUNGER BROTHER SEVERIN. HE WAS SMART ENOUGH TO TAKE OFF FOR AMERICA TO GET AWAY FROM THE MADNESS.
AND WHY DID YOU LEAVE COLOGNE FOR BERLIN? FOR THE SIGHTS...?
FOR THE NAUGHTY LANDLADIES.
NO, SERIOUSLY...
WELL...?
I'M GOING TO FLIP THE RECORD.

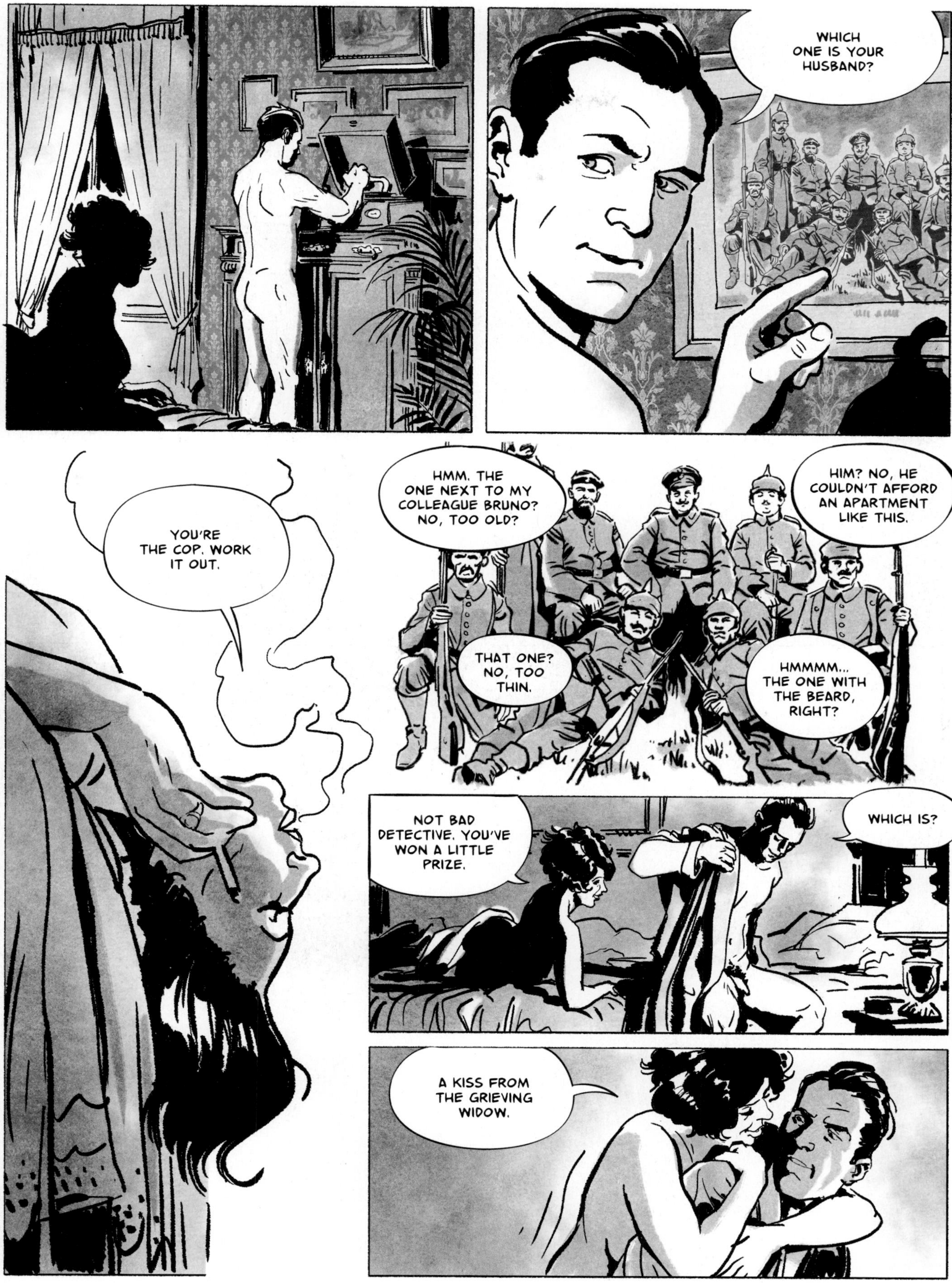
WHICH ONE IS YOUR HUSBAND?
YOU'RE THE COP. WORK IT OUT.
HMM. THE ONE NEXT TO MY COLLEAGUE BRUNO? NO, TOO OLD?
HIM? NO, HE COULDN'T AFFORD AN APARTMENT LIKE THIS.
THAT ONE? NO, TOO THIN.
HMMMM... THE ONE WITH THE BEARD, RIGHT?
NOT BAD DETECTIVE. YOU'VE WON A LITTLE PRIZE.
WHICH IS?
A KISS FROM THE GRIEVING WIDOW.

PART I
The Body In The Landwehr Canal

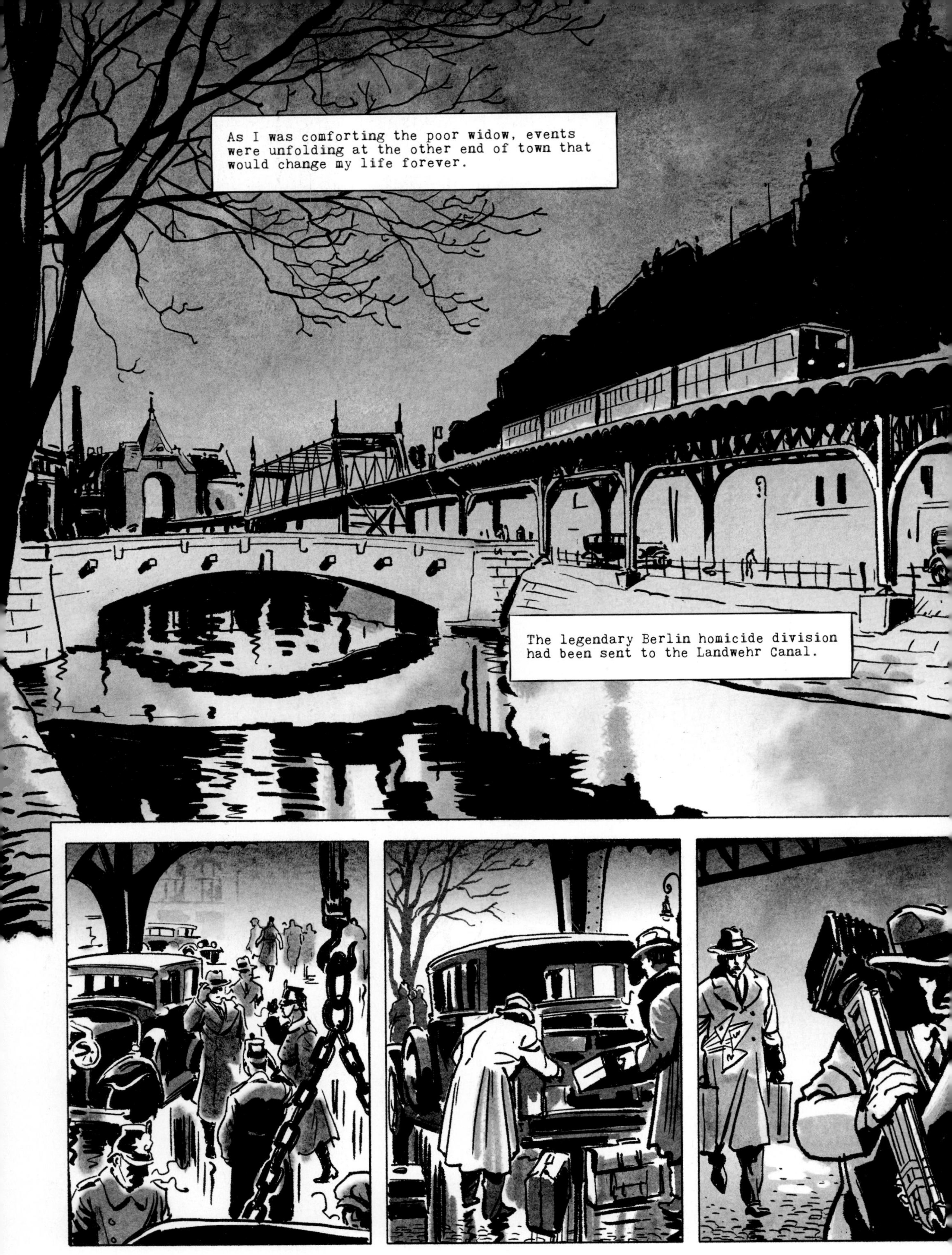
As I was comforting the poor widow, events were unfolding at the other end of town that would change my life forever.
The legendary Berlin homicide division had been sent to the Landwehr Canal.

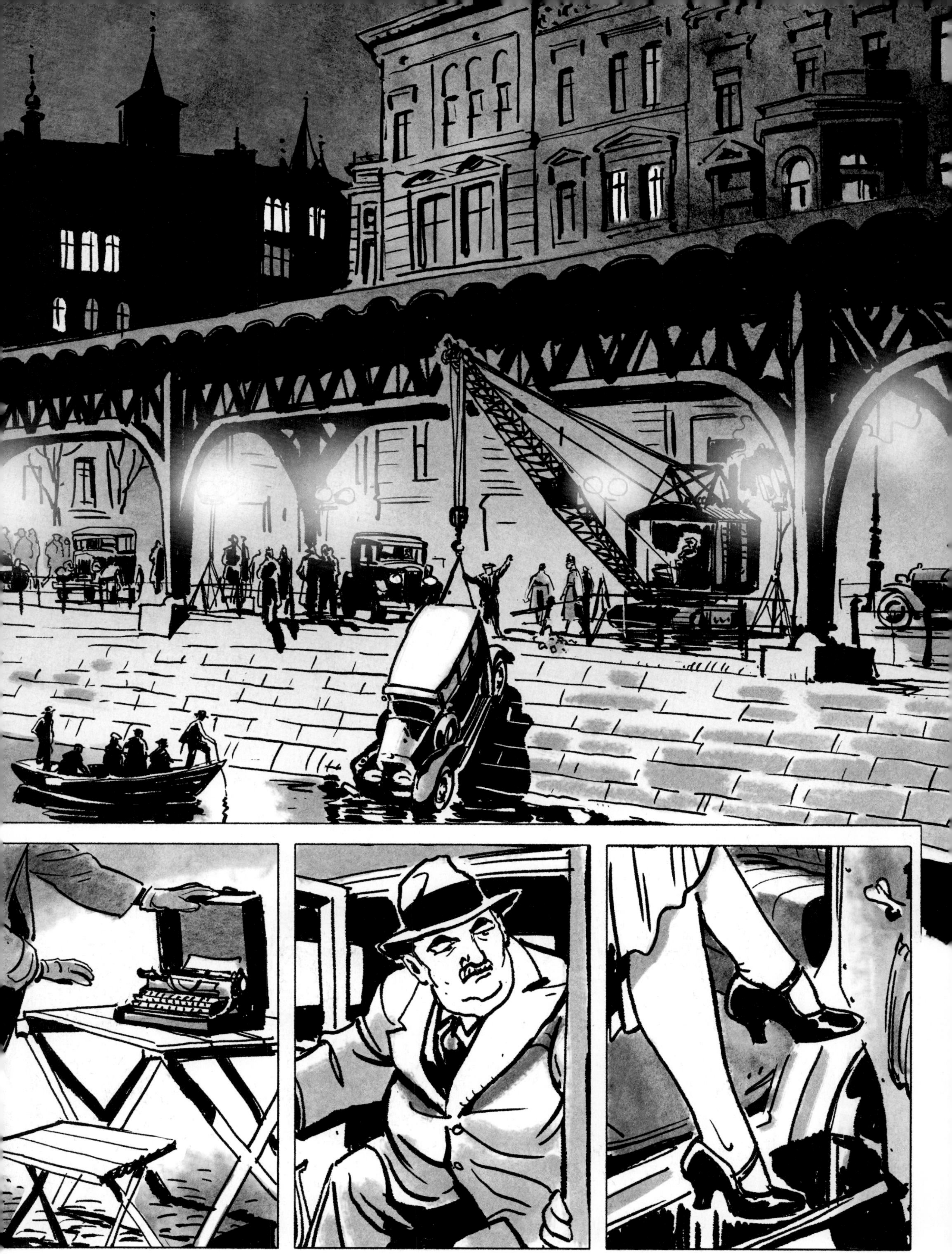

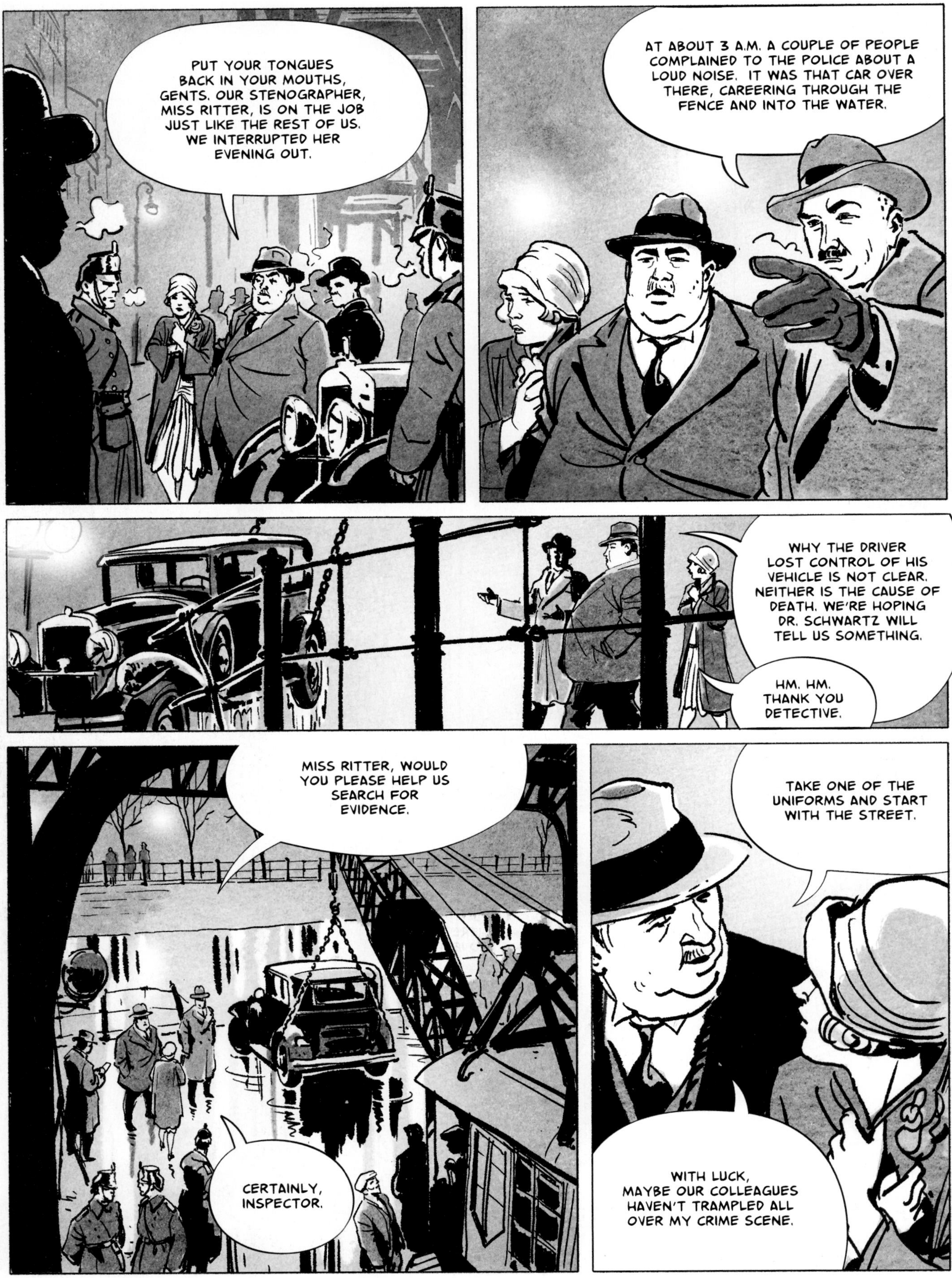
PUT YOUR TONGUES BACK IN YOUR MOUTHS, GENTS. OUR STENOGRAPHER, MISS RITTER, IS ON THE JOB JUST LIKE THE REST OF US. WE INTERRUPTED HER EVENING OUT.
AT ABOUT 3 A.M. A COUPLE OF PEOPLE COMPLAINED TO THE POLICE ABOUT A LOUD NOISE. IT WAS THAT CAR OVER THERE, CAREERING THROUGH THE FENCE AND INTO THE WATER.
WHY THE DRIVER LOST CONTROL OF HIS VEHICLE IS NOT CLEAR. NEITHER IS THE CAUSE OF DEATH. WE'RE HOPING DR. SCHWARTZ WILL TELL US SOMETHING.
HM. HM. THANK YOU DETECTIVE.
MISS RITTER, WOULD YOU PLEASE HELP US SEARCH FOR EVIDENCE.
CERTAINLY, INSPECTOR.
TAKE ONE OF THE UNIFORMS AND START WITH THE STREET.
WITH LUCK, MAYBE OUR COLLEAGUES HAVEN'T TRAMPLED ALL OVER MY CRIME SCENE.

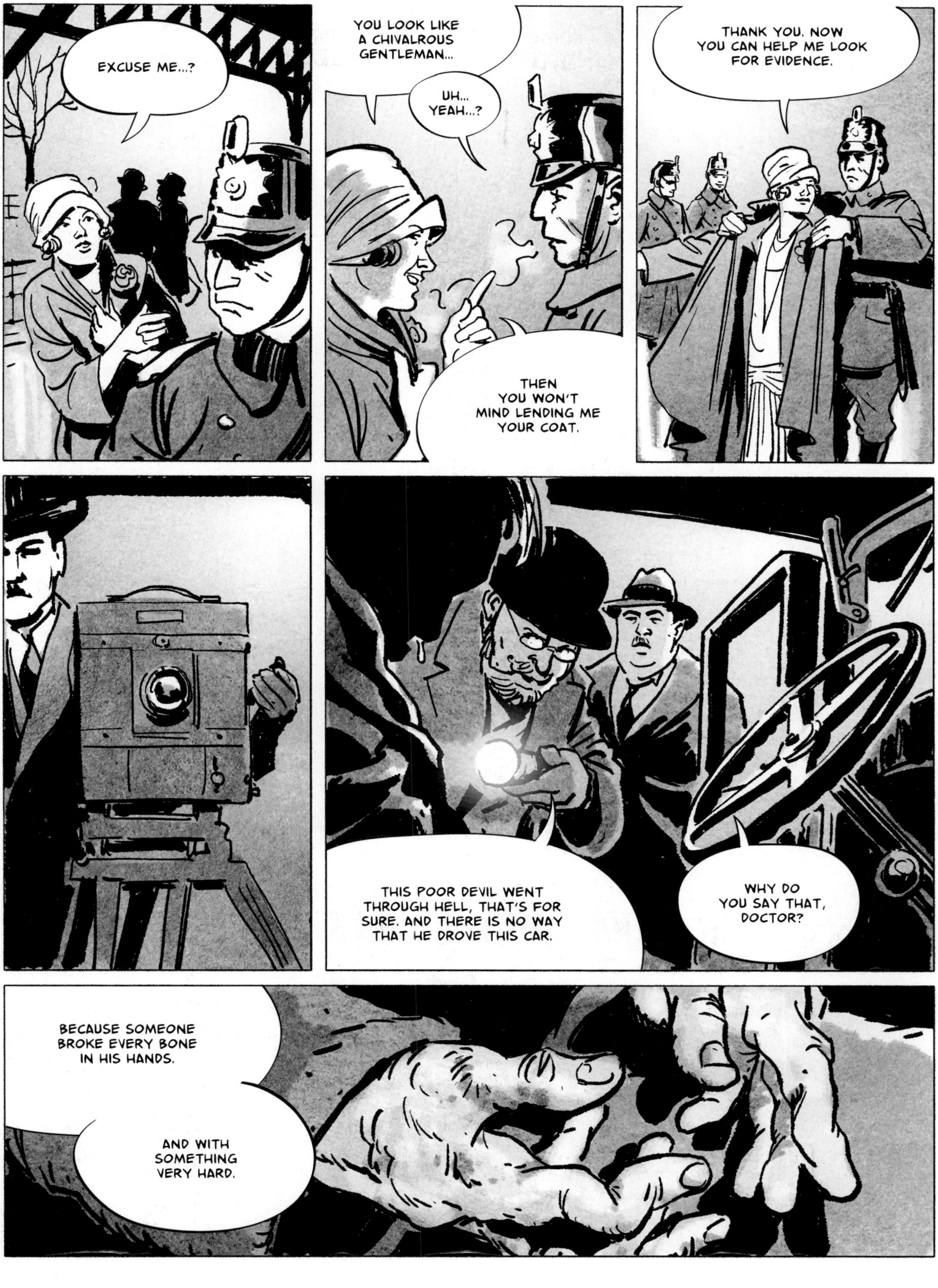
EXCUSE ME...?
YOU LOOK LIKE A CHIVALROUS GENTLEMAN...
UH... YEAH...?
THEN YOU WON'T MIND LENDING ME YOUR COAT.
THANK YOU. NOW YOU CAN HELP ME LOOK FOR EVIDENCE.
THIS POOR DEVIL WENT THROUGH HELL, THAT'S FOR SURE. AND THERE IS NO WAY THAT HE DROVE THIS CAR.
WHY DO YOU SAY THAT, DOCTOR?
BECAUSE SOMEONE BROKE EVERY BONE IN HIS HANDS.
AND WITH SOMETHING VERY HARD.

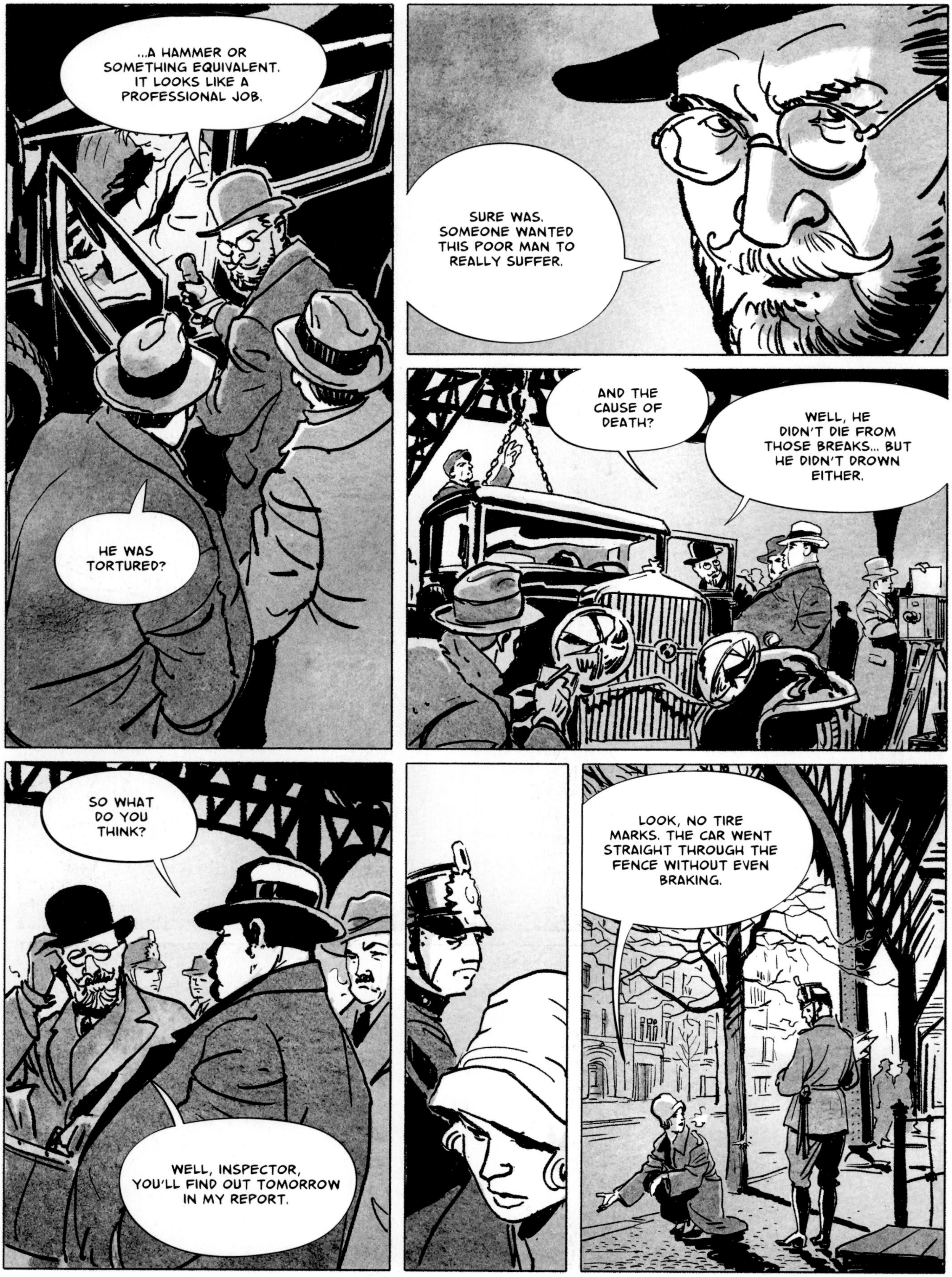
...A HAMMER OR SOMETHING EQUIVALENT. IT LOOKS LIKE A PROFESSIONAL JOB.
HE WAS TORTURED?
SURE WAS. SOMEONE WANTED THIS POOR MAN TO REALLY SUFFER.
AND THE CAUSE OF DEATH?
WELL, HE DIDN'T DIE FROM THOSE BREAKS... BUT HE DIDN'T DROWN EITHER.
SO WHAT DO YOU THINK?
WELL, INSPECTOR, YOU'LL FIND OUT TOMORROW IN MY REPORT.
LOOK, NO TIRE MARKS. THE CAR WENT STRAIGHT THROUGH THE FENCE WITHOUT EVEN BRAKING.

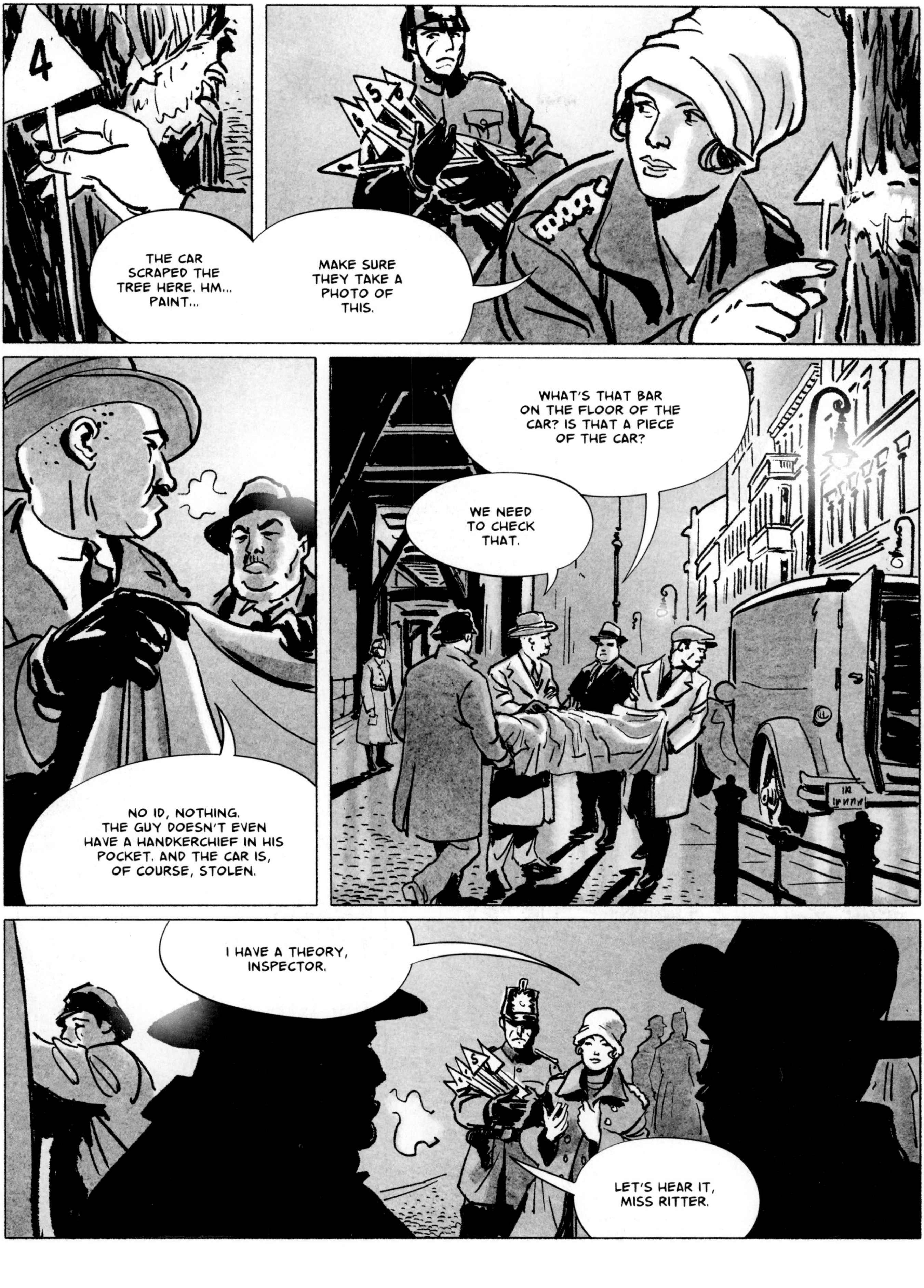

THE CAR SCRAPED THE TREE HERE. HM... PAINT...
MAKE SURE THEY TAKE A PHOTO OF THIS.
NO ID, NOTHING. THE GUY DOESN'T EVEN HAVE A HANDKERCHIEF IN HIS POCKET. AND THE CAR IS, OF COURSE, STOLEN.
WHAT'S THAT BAR ON THE FLOOR OF THE CAR? IS THAT A PIECE OF THE CAR?
WE NEED TO CHECK THAT.
I HAVE A THEORY, INSPECTOR.
LET'S HEAR IT, MISS RITTER.

SOMEONE WANTED TO GET RID OF A BODY AND MAKE IT LOOK LIKE AN ACCIDENT.

THAT'S RIDICULOUS. WHY GO TO SO MUCH TROUBLE WHEN WE'D OBVIOUSLY FIND OUT THAT HE WAS DEAD BEFORE HE WENT INTO THE CANAL?

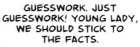

BECAUSE, IF THE CAR HAD GONE HEAD ON INTO A TREE WE WOULD NOT HAVE BEEN ABLE TO FIGURE IT OUT THAT EASILY.

I DON'T THINK IT WENT AS PLANNED. THERE ARE MARKS ON THE TREE OVER THERE...

GUESSWORK. JUST GUESSWORK! YOUNG LADY, WE SHOULD STICK TO THE FACTS.

IT'S ONLY A THEORY, RIGHT MISS RITTER? LET'S WAIT AND SEE WHAT THE GOOD DOCTOR SCHWARTZ CAN BRING TO LIGHT.

AND KEEP YOUR WILD SPECULATIONS TO YOURSELF FOR THE TIME BEING, MISS!

QUIT BICKERING, THE TWO OF YOU. I'LL SEE YOU BOTH BACK AT THE STATION.

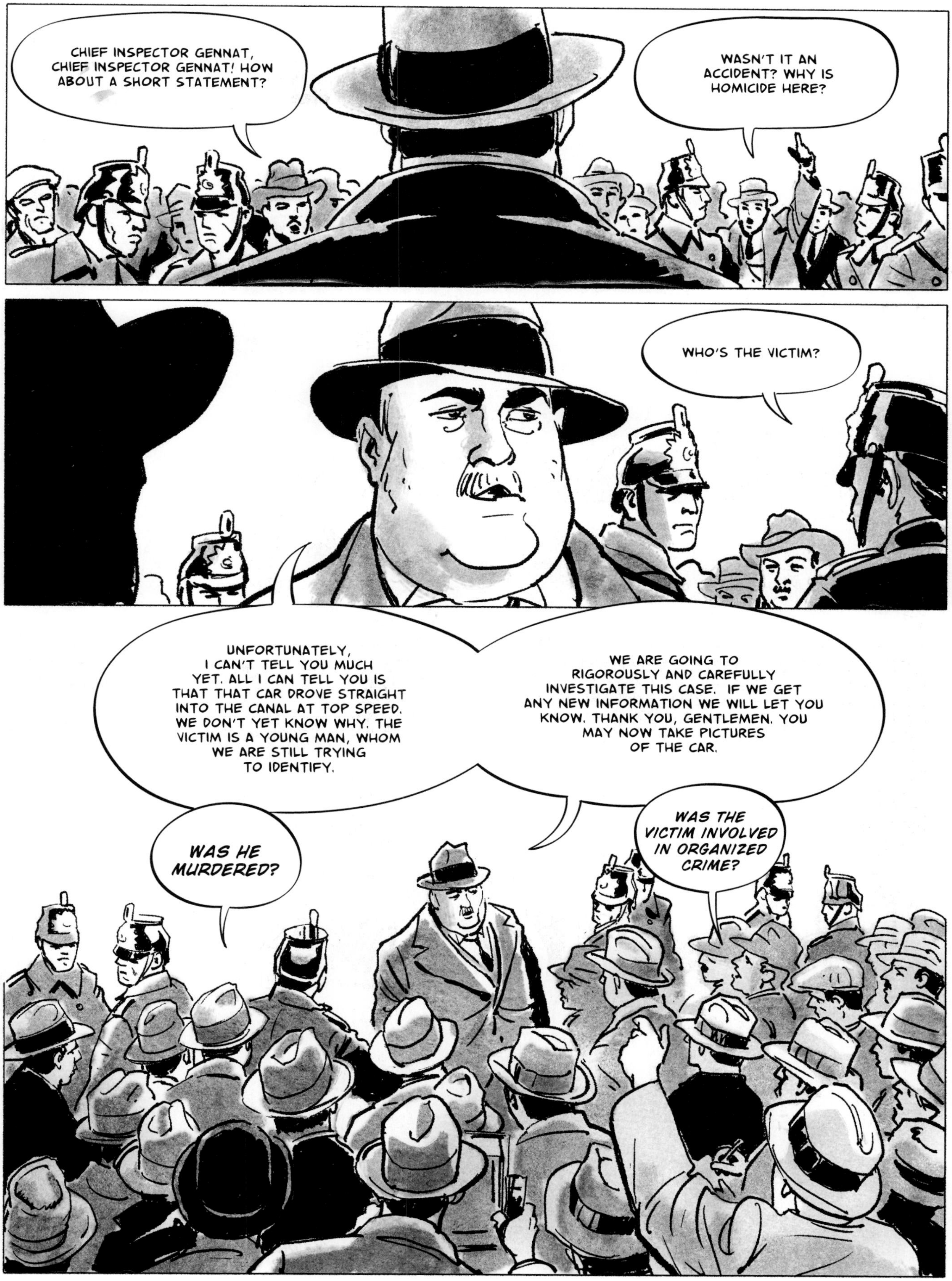
CHIEF INSPECTOR GENNAT, CHIEF INSPECTOR GENNAT! HOW ABOUT A SHORT STATEMENT?
WASN'T IT AN ACCIDENT? WHY IS HOMICIDE HERE?
WHO'S THE VICTIM?
UNFORTUNATELY, I CAN'T TELL YOU MUCH YET. ALL I CAN TELL YOU IS THAT THAT CAR DROVE STRAIGHT INTO THE CANAL AT TOP SPEED. WE DON'T YET KNOW WHY. THE VICTIM IS A YOUNG MAN, WHOM WE ARE STILL TRYING TO IDENTIFY.
WE ARE GOING TO RIGOROUSLY AND CAREFULLY INVESTIGATE THIS CASE. IF WE GET ANY NEW INFORMATION WE WILL LET YOU KNOW. THANK YOU, GENTLEMEN. YOU MAY NOW TAKE PICTURES OF THE CAR.
WAS HE MURDERED?
WAS THE VICTIM INVOLVED IN ORGANIZED CRIME?

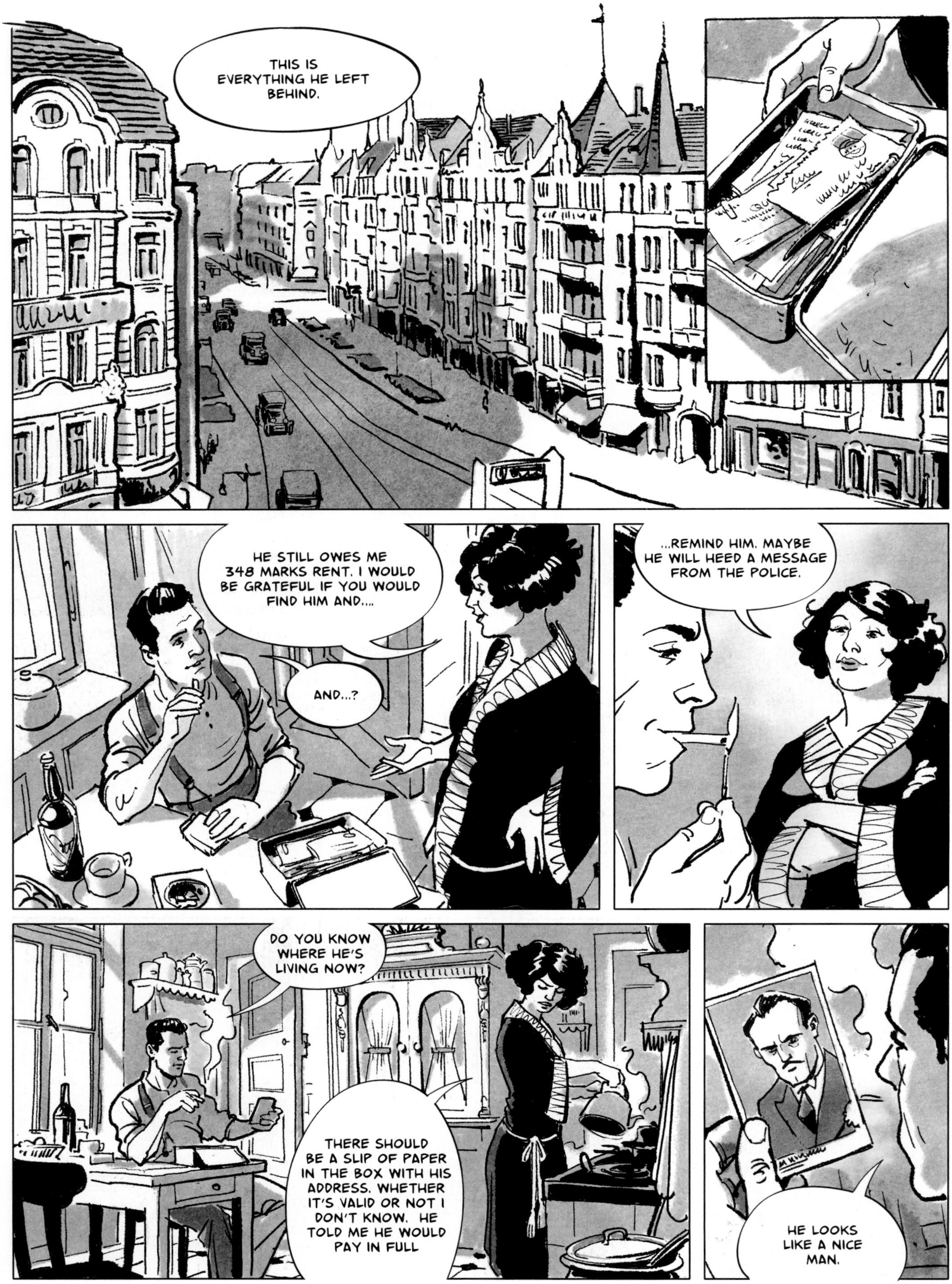
THIS IS EVERYTHING HE LEFT BEHIND.
HE STILL OWES ME 348 MARKS RENT. I WOULD BE GRATEFUL IF YOU WOULD FIND HIM AND....
AND...?
...REMIND HIM. MAYBE HE WILL HEED A MESSAGE FROM THE POLICE.
DO YOU KNOW WHERE HE'S LIVING NOW?
THERE SHOULD BE A SLIP OF PAPER IN THE BOX WITH HIS ADDRESS. WHETHER IT'S VALID OR NOT I DON'T KNOW. HE TOLD ME HE WOULD PAY IN FULL
HE LOOKS LIKE A NICE MAN.

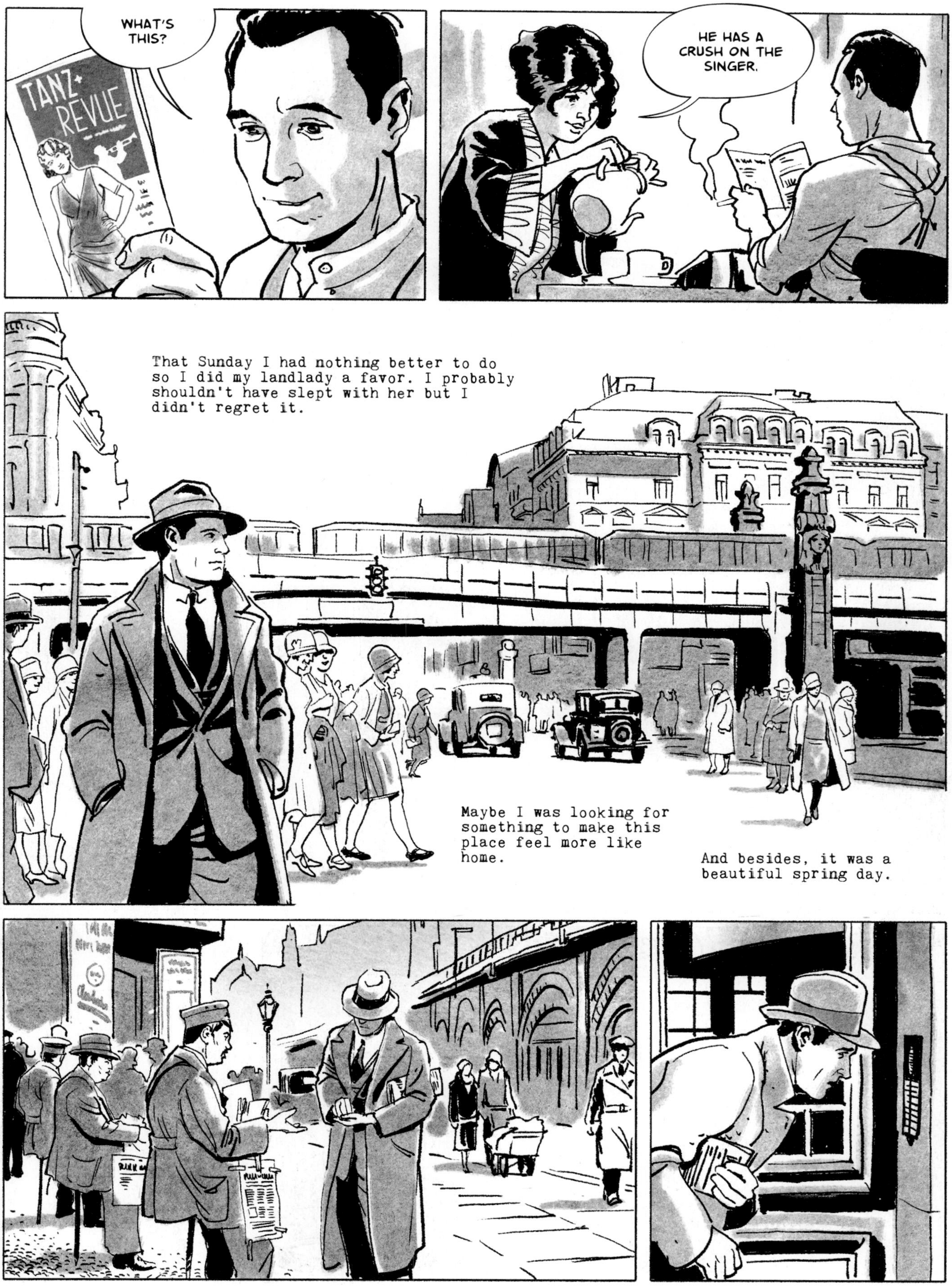
TANZ+ REVUE
WHAT'S THIS?
HE HAS A CRUSH ON THE SINGER.
That Sunday I had nothing better to do so I did my landlady a favor. I probably shouldn't have slept with her but I didn't regret it.
Maybe I was looking for something to make this place feel more like home.
And besides, it was a beautiful spring day.

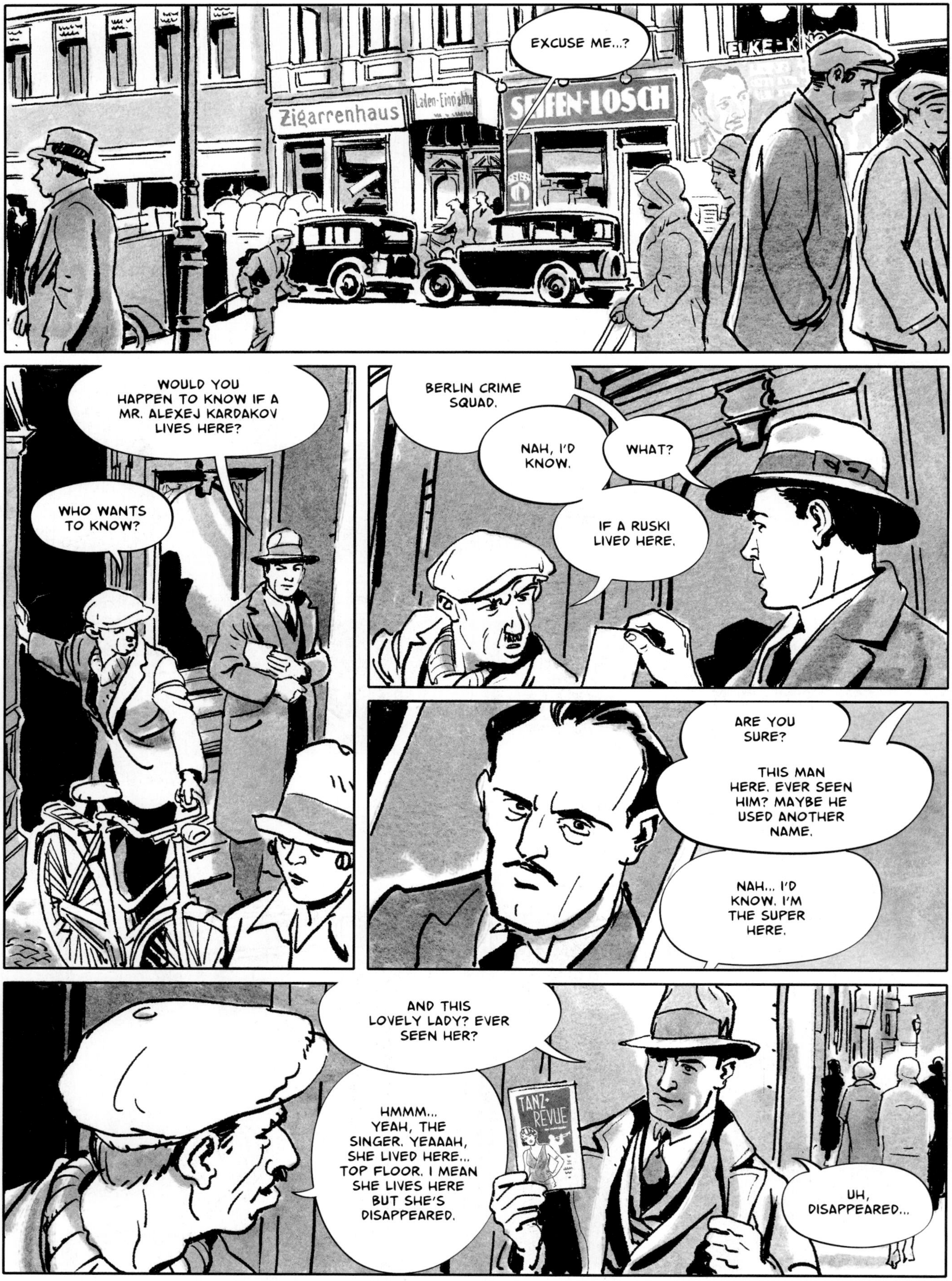
ZIGARRENHAUS
SEIFEN-LOSCH
EXCUSE ME...?
WOULD YOU HAPPEN TO KNOW IF A MR. ALEXEJ KARDAKOV LIVES HERE?
WHO WANTS TO KNOW?
BERLIN CRIME SQUAD.
WHAT?
IF A RUSKI LIVED HERE.
NAH, I'D KNOW.
ARE YOU SURE?
THIS MAN HERE. EVER SEEN HIM? MAYBE HE USED ANOTHER NAME.
NAH... I'D KNOW. I'M THE SUPER HERE.
AND THIS LOVELY LADY? EVER SEEN HER?
HMMM... YEAH, THE SINGER. YEAAAH, SHE LIVED HERE... TOP FLOOR. I MEAN SHE LIVES HERE BUT SHE'S DISAPPEARED.
TANZ-REVUE
UH, DISAPPEARED...

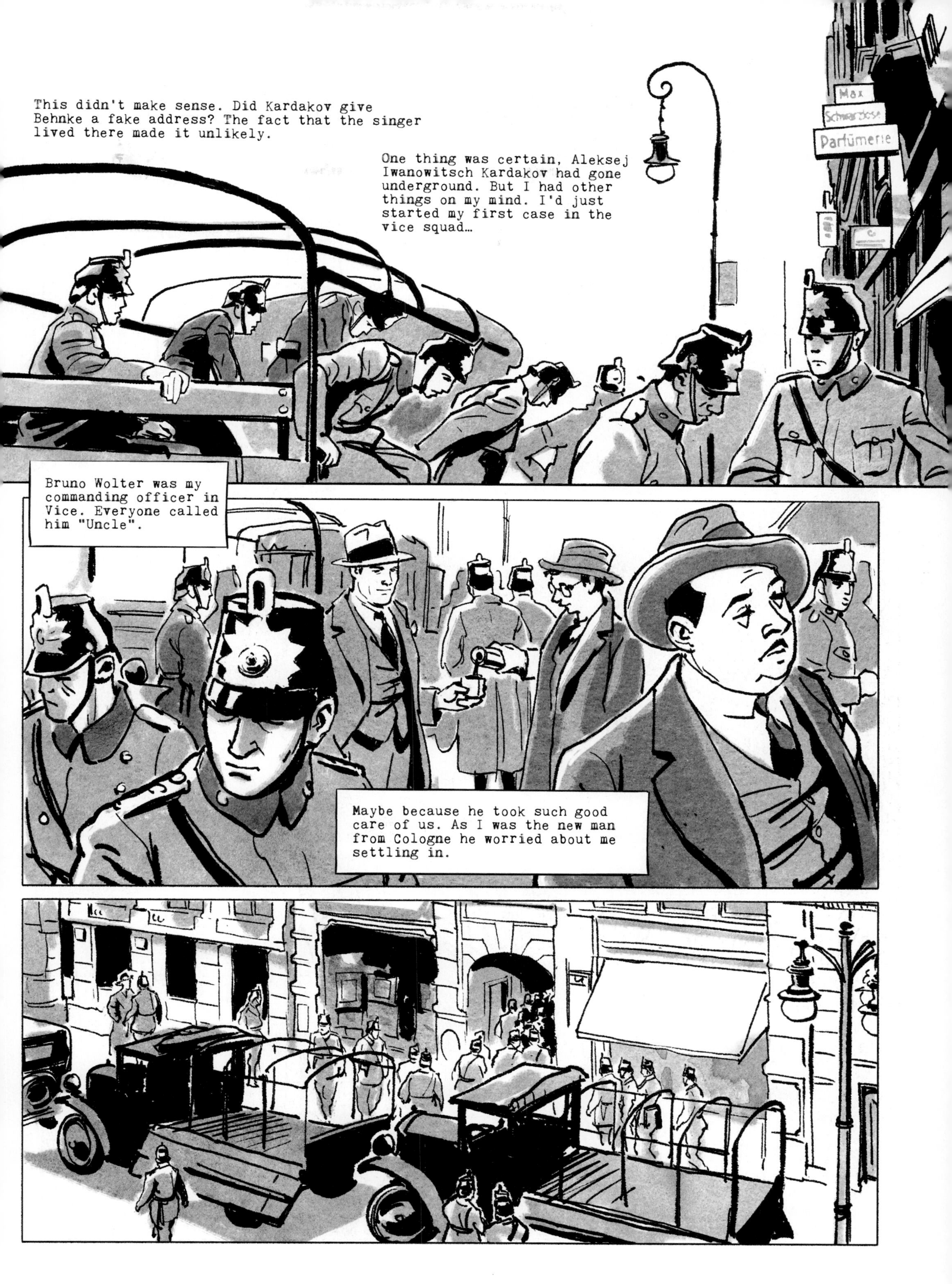
This didn't make sense. Did Kardakov give Behnke a fake address? The fact that the singer lived there made it unlikely.
One thing was certain, Aleksej Iwanowitsch Kardakov had gone underground. But I had other things on my mind. I'd just started my first case in the vice squad…
Max
Schwarzlose
Parfümerie
Bruno Wolter was my commanding officer in Vice. Everyone called him "Uncle".
Maybe because he took such good care of us. As I was the new man from Cologne he worried about me settling in.

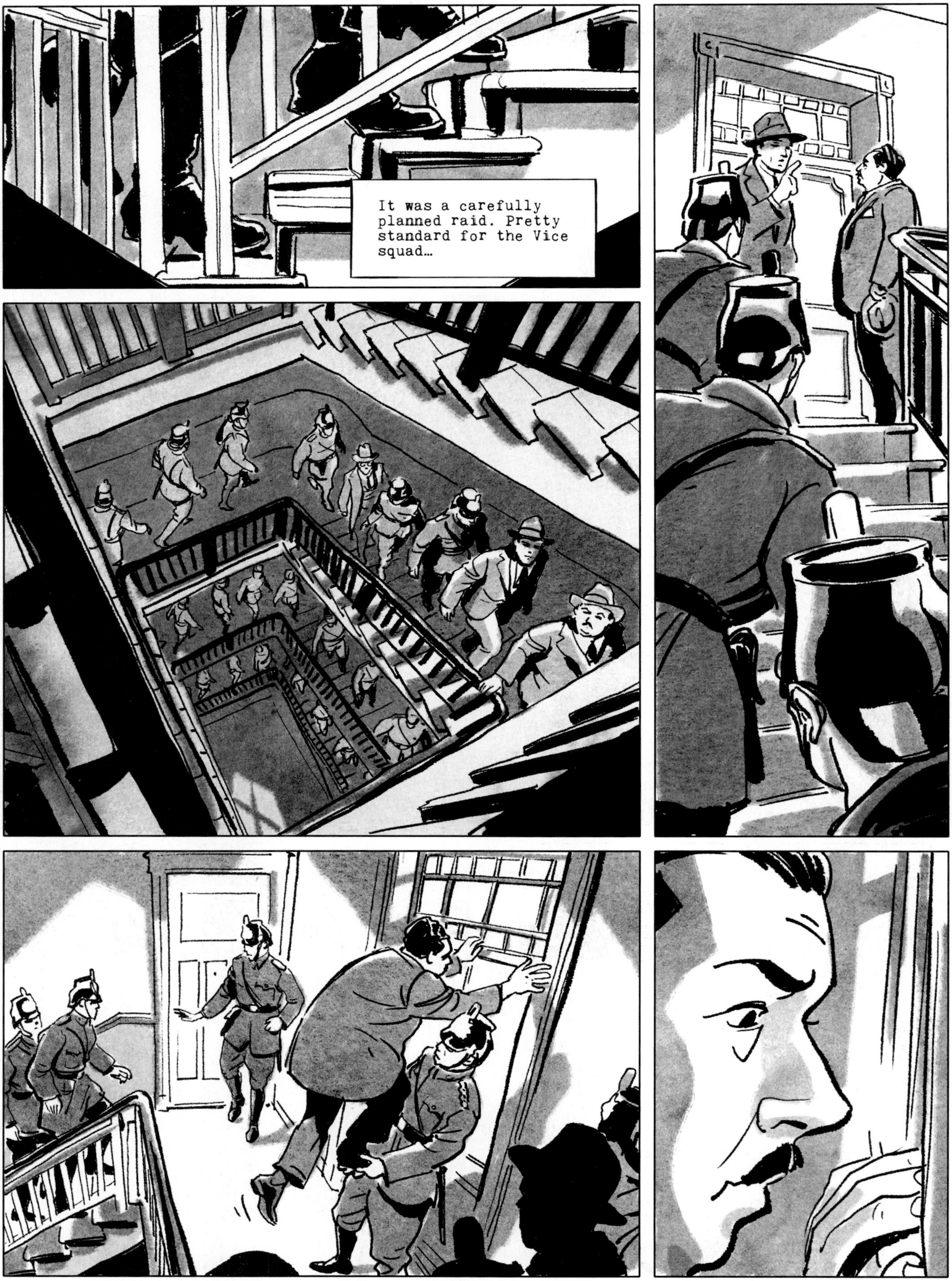
It was a carefully planned raid. Pretty standard for the Vice squad…

TRRIIIII

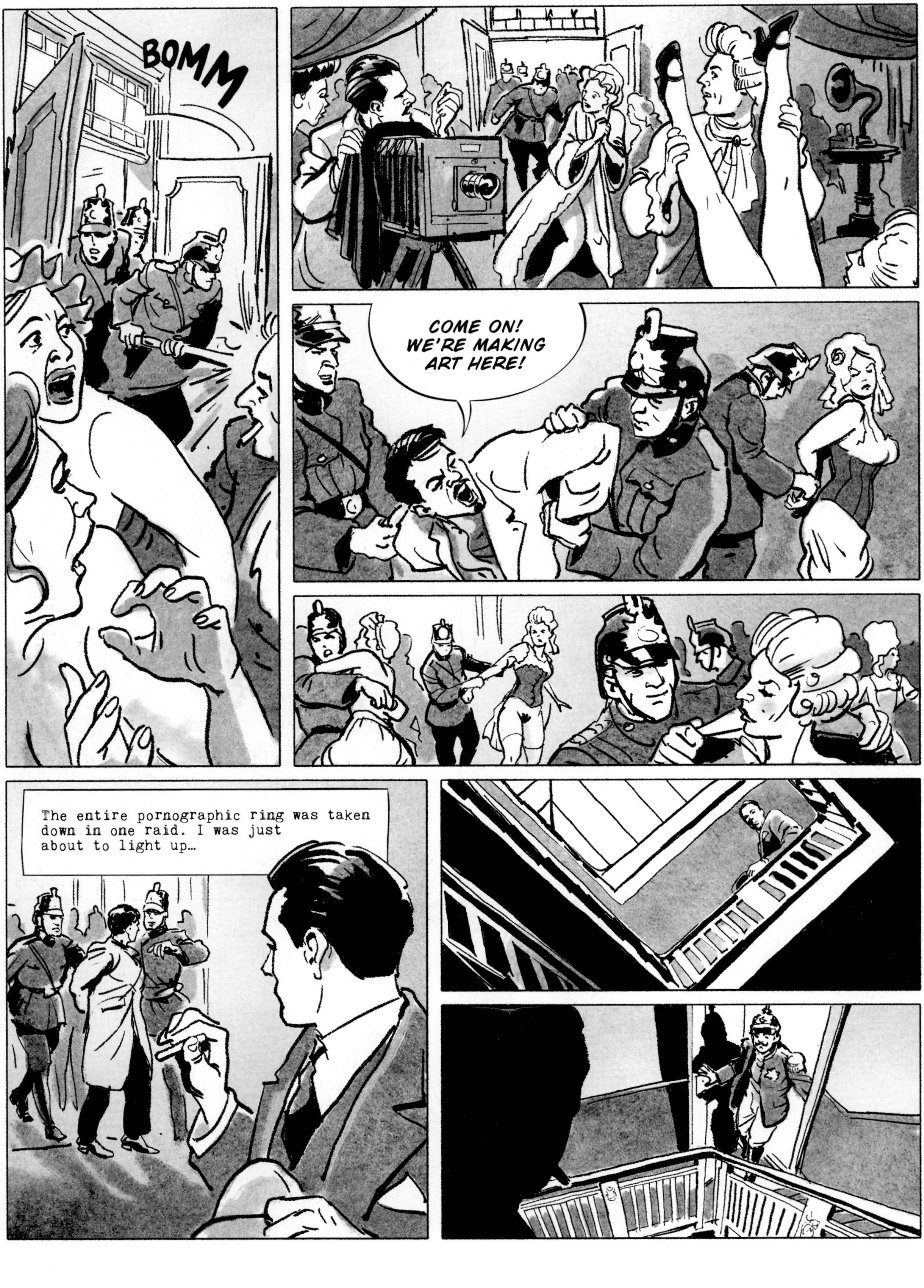
BOMM
COME ON! WE'RE MAKING ART HERE!
The entire pornographic ring was taken down in one raid. I was just about to light up...

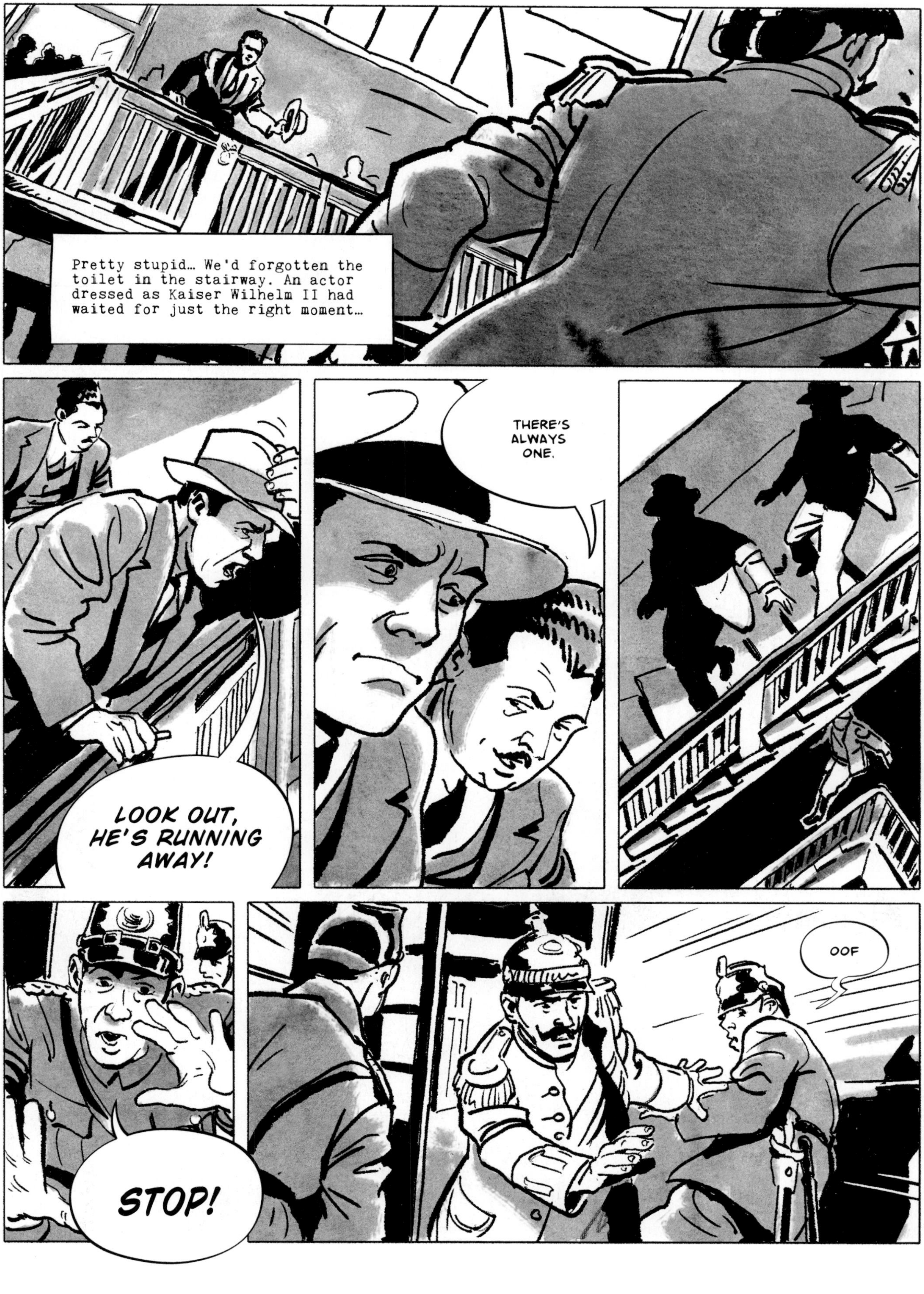
Pretty stupid… We'd forgotten the toilet in the stairway. An actor dressed as Kaiser Wilhelm II had waited for just the right moment…
LOOK OUT, HE'S RUNNING AWAY!
THERE'S ALWAYS ONE.
STOP!
OOF

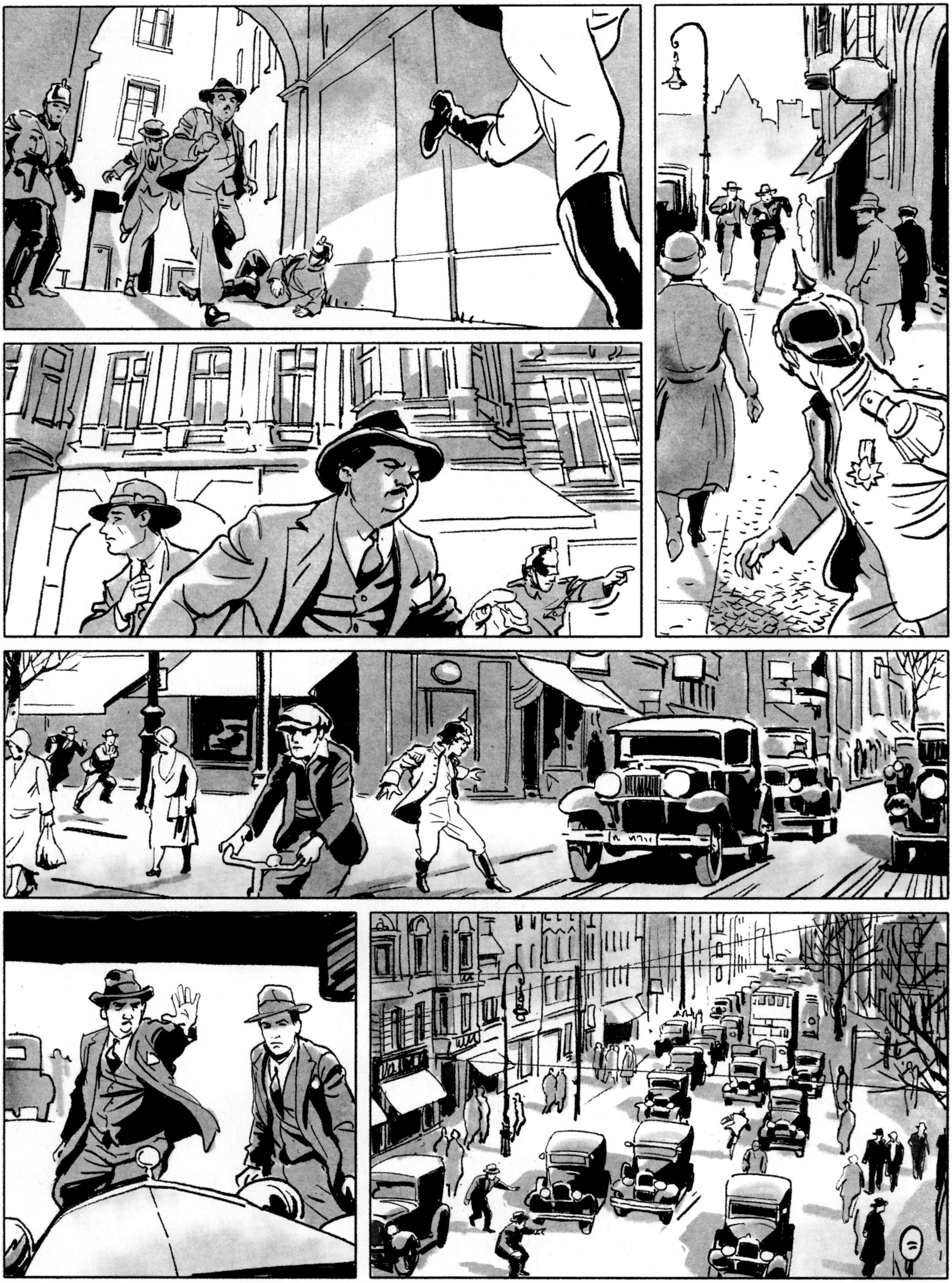

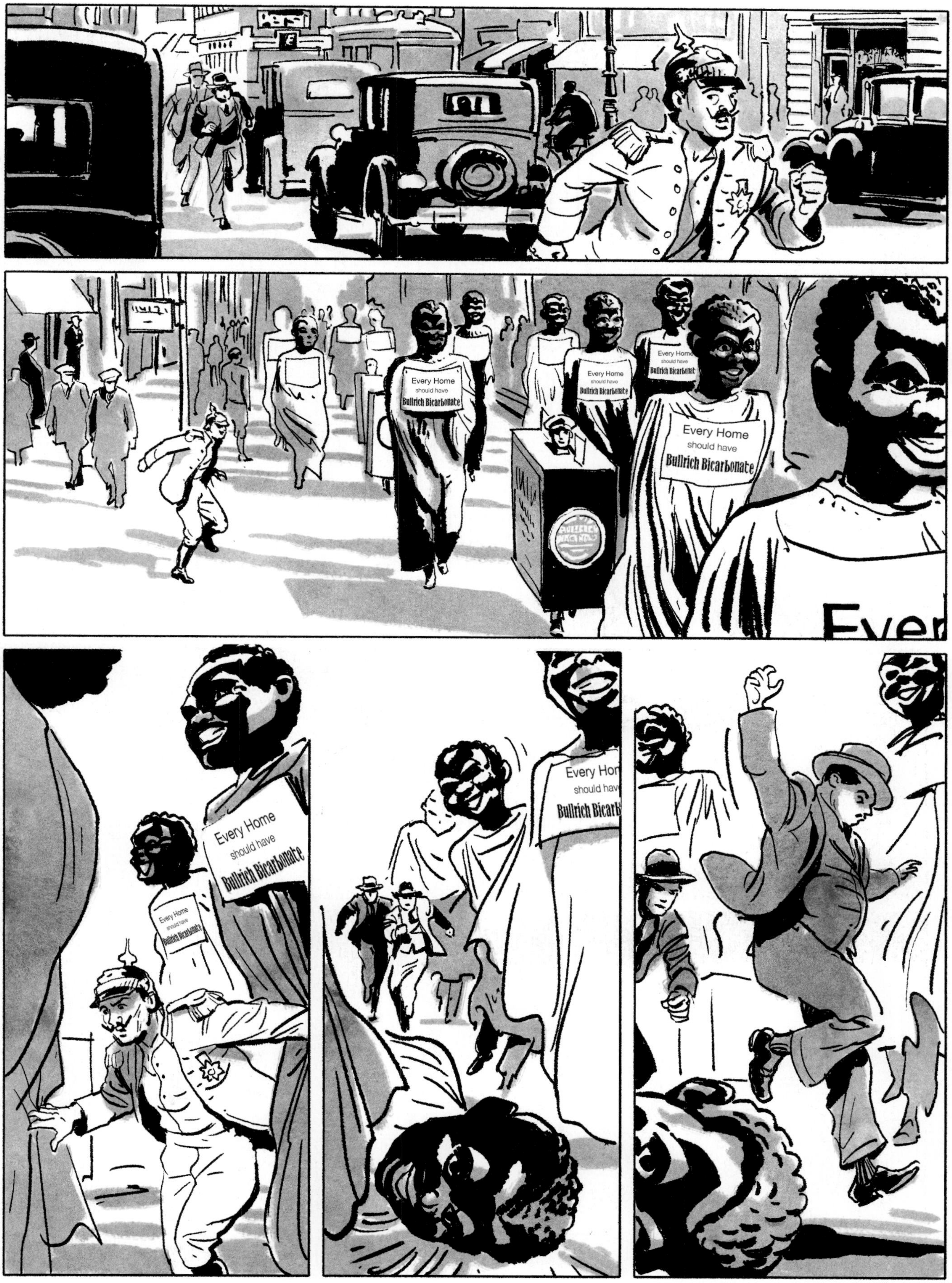
Every Home
should have
Bullrich Bicarbonate
Every Home
should have
Bullrich Bicarbonate
Every Home
should have
Bullrich Bicarbonate
Every Home
should have
Bullrich Bicarbonate
Ever
Every Home
should have
Bullrich Bicarbonate
Every Home
should have
Bullrich Bicarbonate
Every Hom
should hav
Bullrich Bicarb

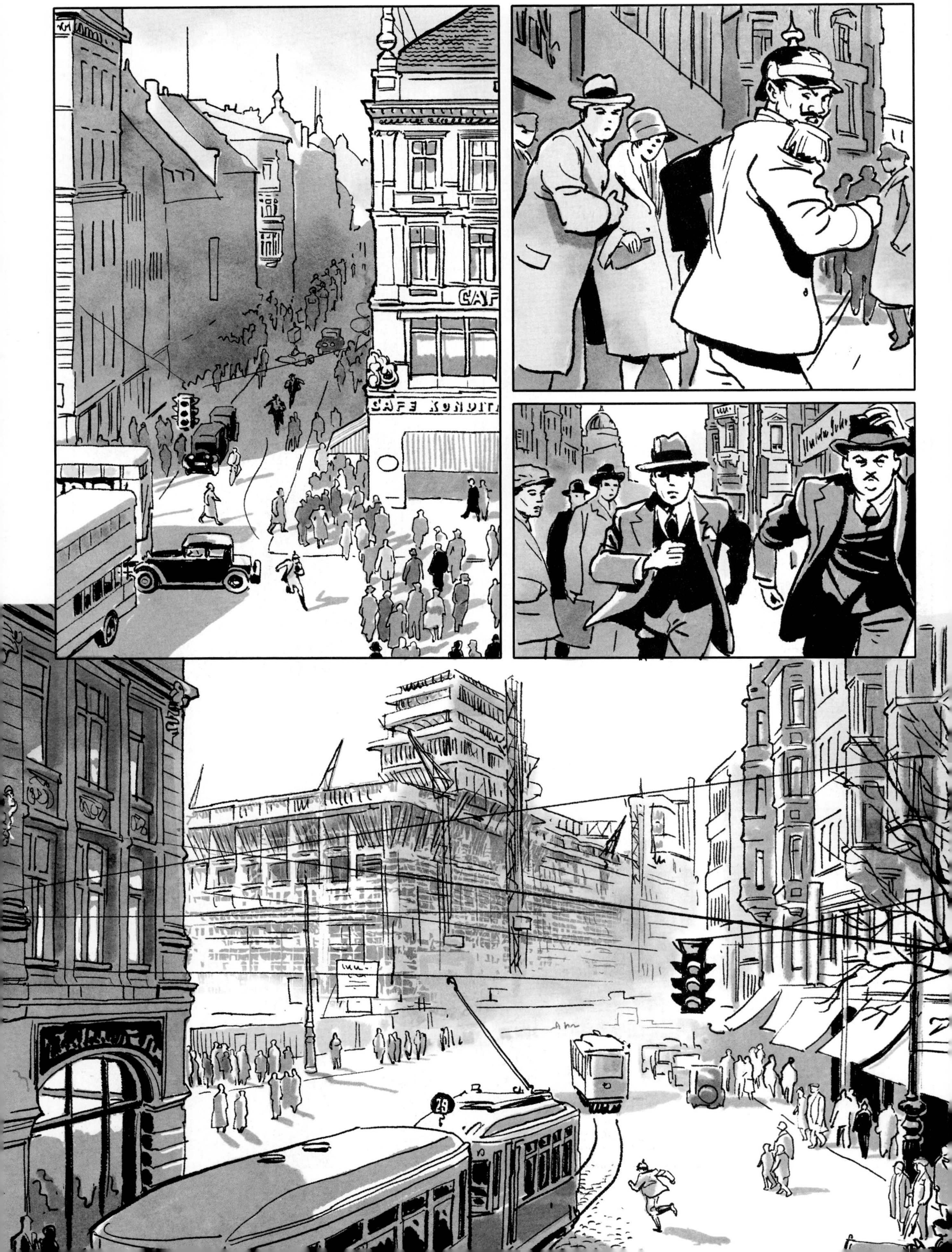
CAF
CAFE KONDIT
29

DRRRRRRRRRRRIIIING

SHIT!

WHERE'D HE GO?

NBAU
BERLIN

HE CAN'T HAVE JUST VANISHED!

Das Be
Rauste
verb

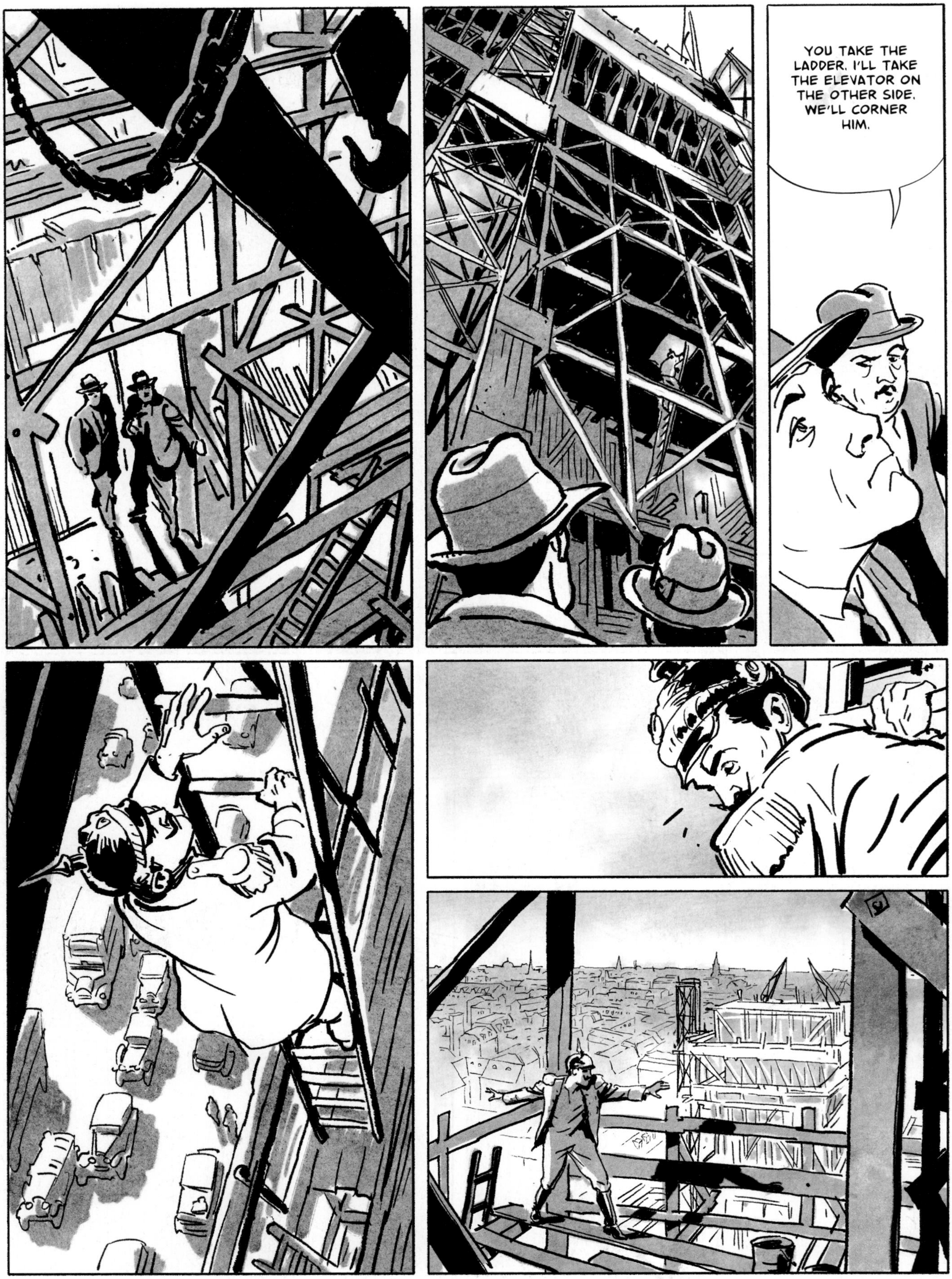
YOU TAKE THE LADDER. I'LL TAKE THE ELEVATOR ON THE OTHER SIDE. WE'LL CORNER HIM.

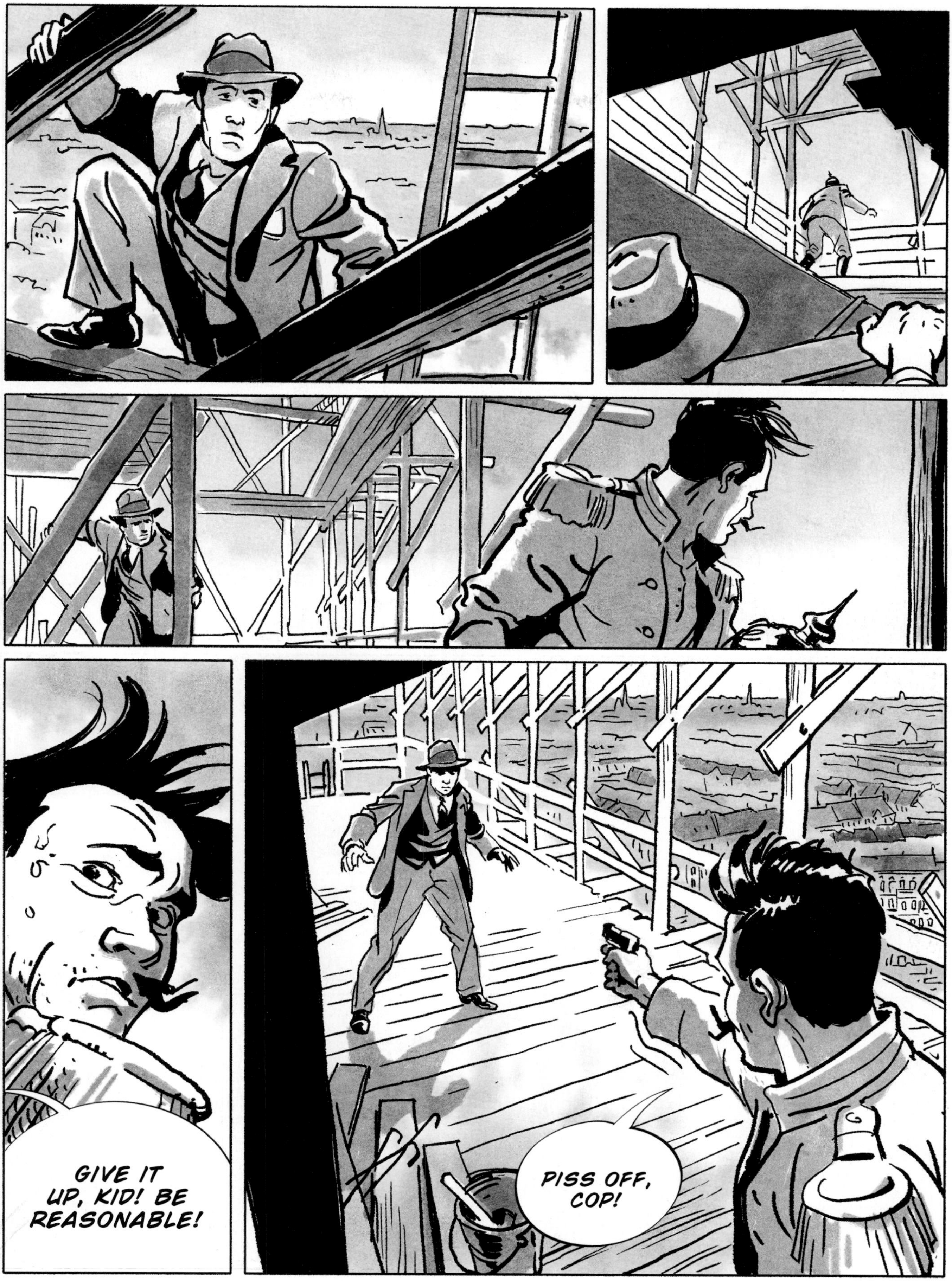
GIVE IT UP, KID! BE REASONABLE!
PISS OFF, COP!

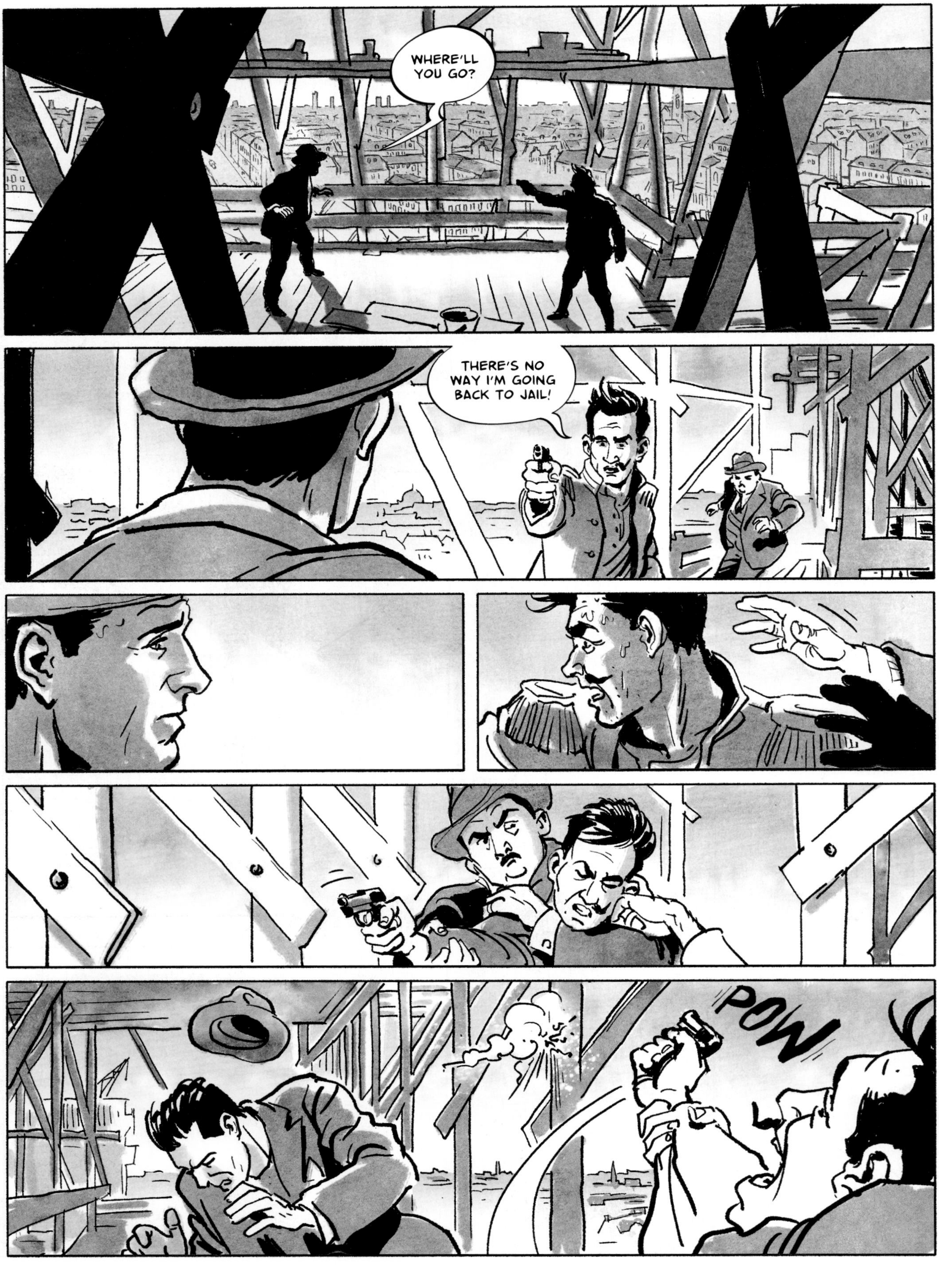
WHERE'LL YOU GO?
THERE'S NO WAY I'M GOING BACK TO JAIL!
POW

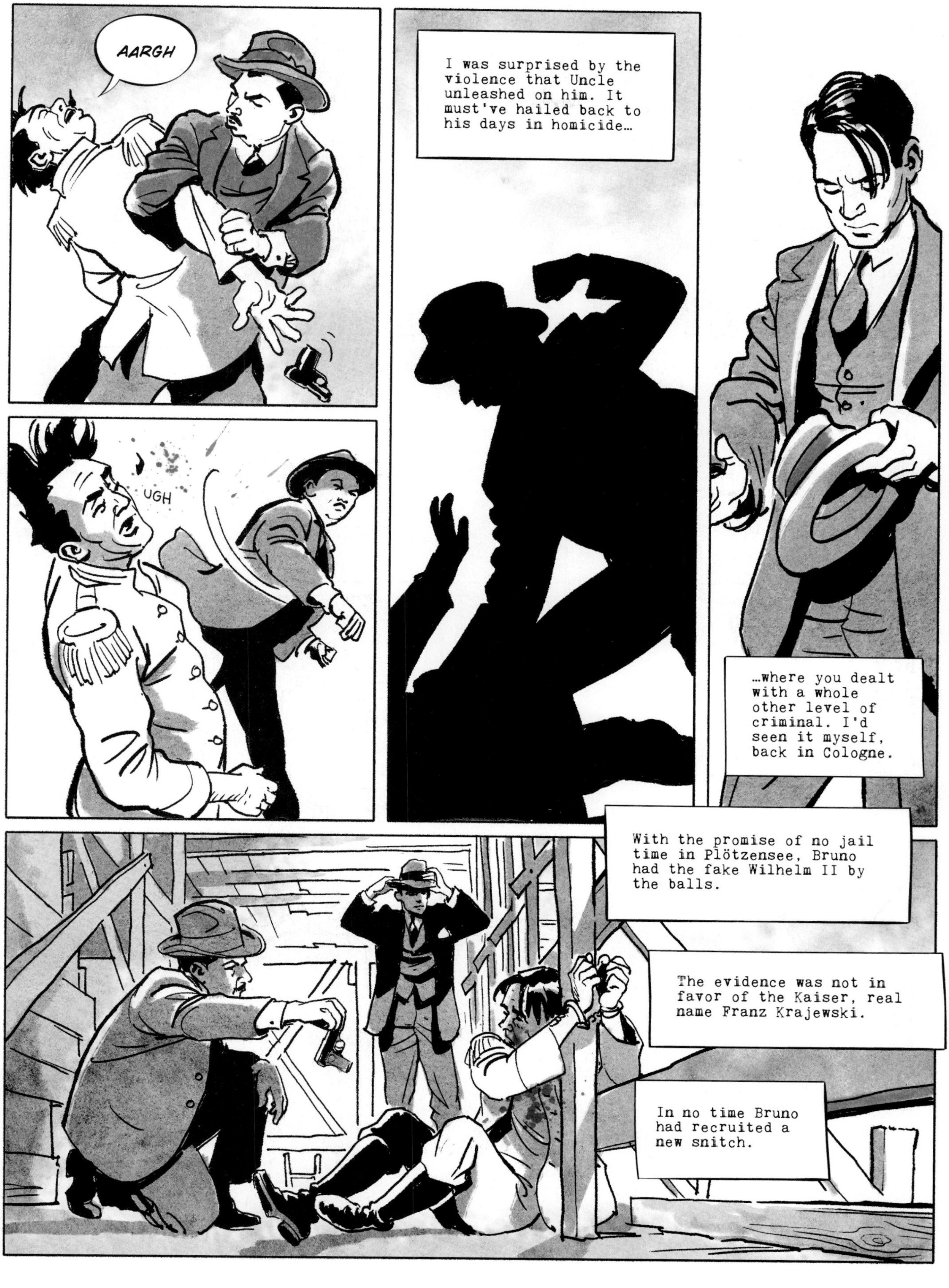
AARGH
UGH
I was surprised by the violence that Uncle unleashed on him. It must've hailed back to his days in homicide…
…where you dealt with a whole other level of criminal. I'd seen it myself, back in Cologne.
With the promise of no jail time in Plötzensee, Bruno had the fake Wilhelm II by the balls.
The evidence was not in favor of the Kaiser, real name Franz Krajewski.
In no time Bruno had recruited a new snitch.

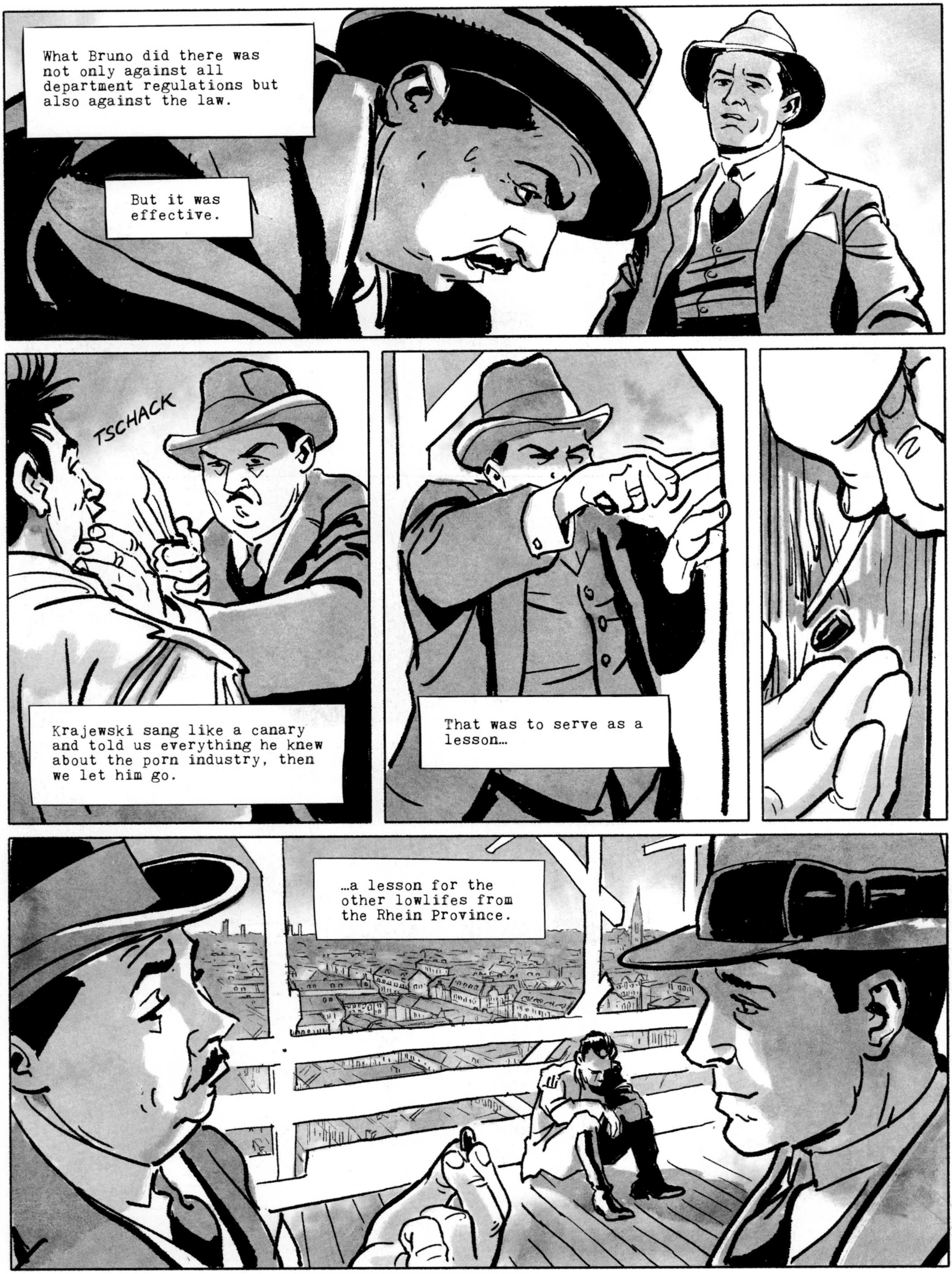

What Bruno did there was not only against all department regulations but also against the law.
But it was effective.
TSCHACK
Krajewski sang like a canary and told us everything he knew about the porn industry, then we let him go.
That was to serve as a lesson…
…a lesson for the other lowlifes from the Rhein Province.

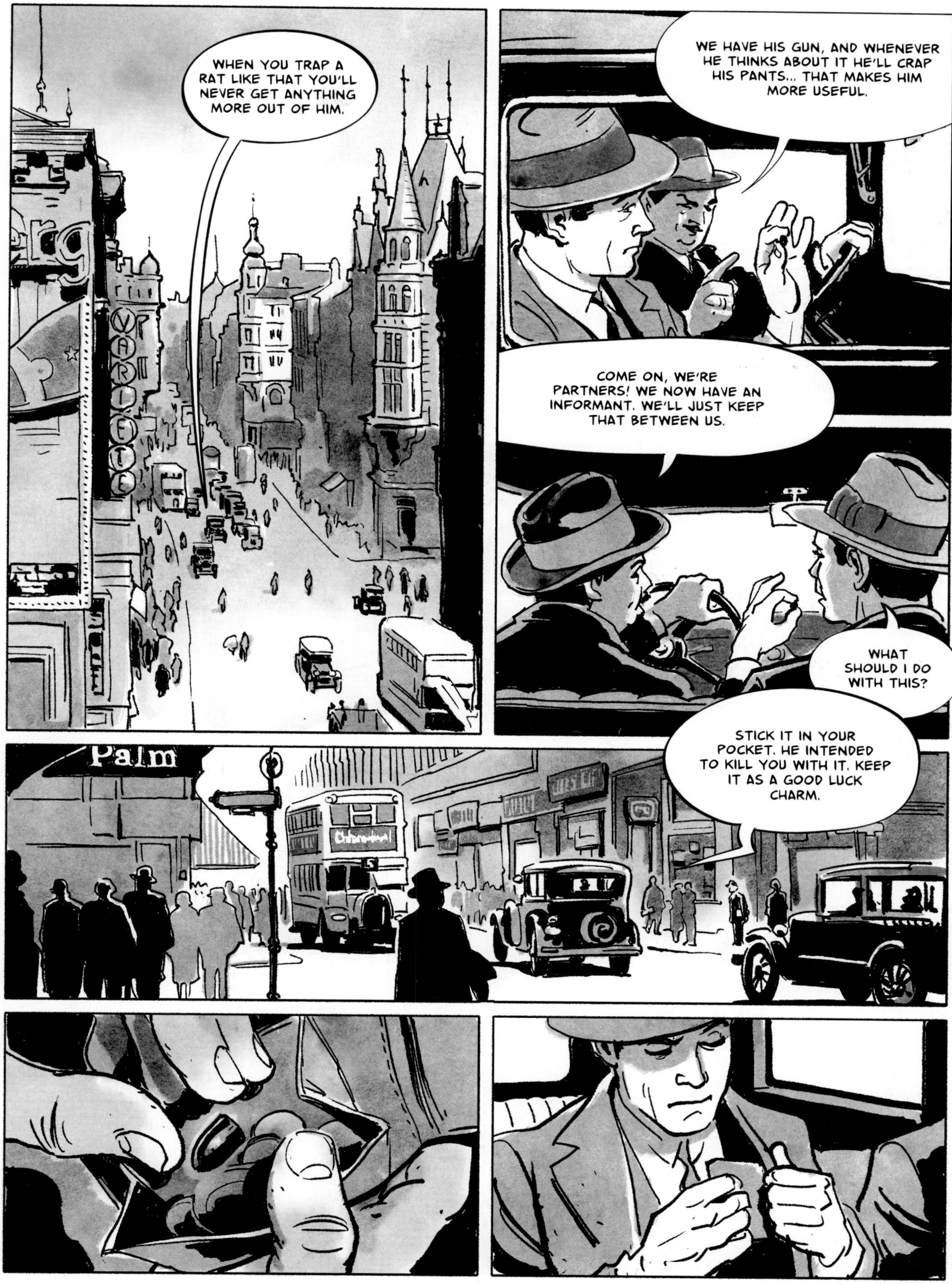
WHEN YOU TRAP A RAT LIKE THAT YOU'LL NEVER GET ANYTHING MORE OUT OF HIM.
WE HAVE HIS GUN, AND WHENEVER HE THINKS ABOUT IT HE'LL CRAP HIS PANTS... THAT MAKES HIM MORE USEFUL.
COME ON, WE'RE PARTNERS! WE NOW HAVE AN INFORMANT. WE'LL JUST KEEP THAT BETWEEN US.
WHAT SHOULD I DO WITH THIS?
STICK IT IN YOUR POCKET. HE INTENDED TO KILL YOU WITH IT. KEEP IT AS A GOOD LUCK CHARM.
Palm

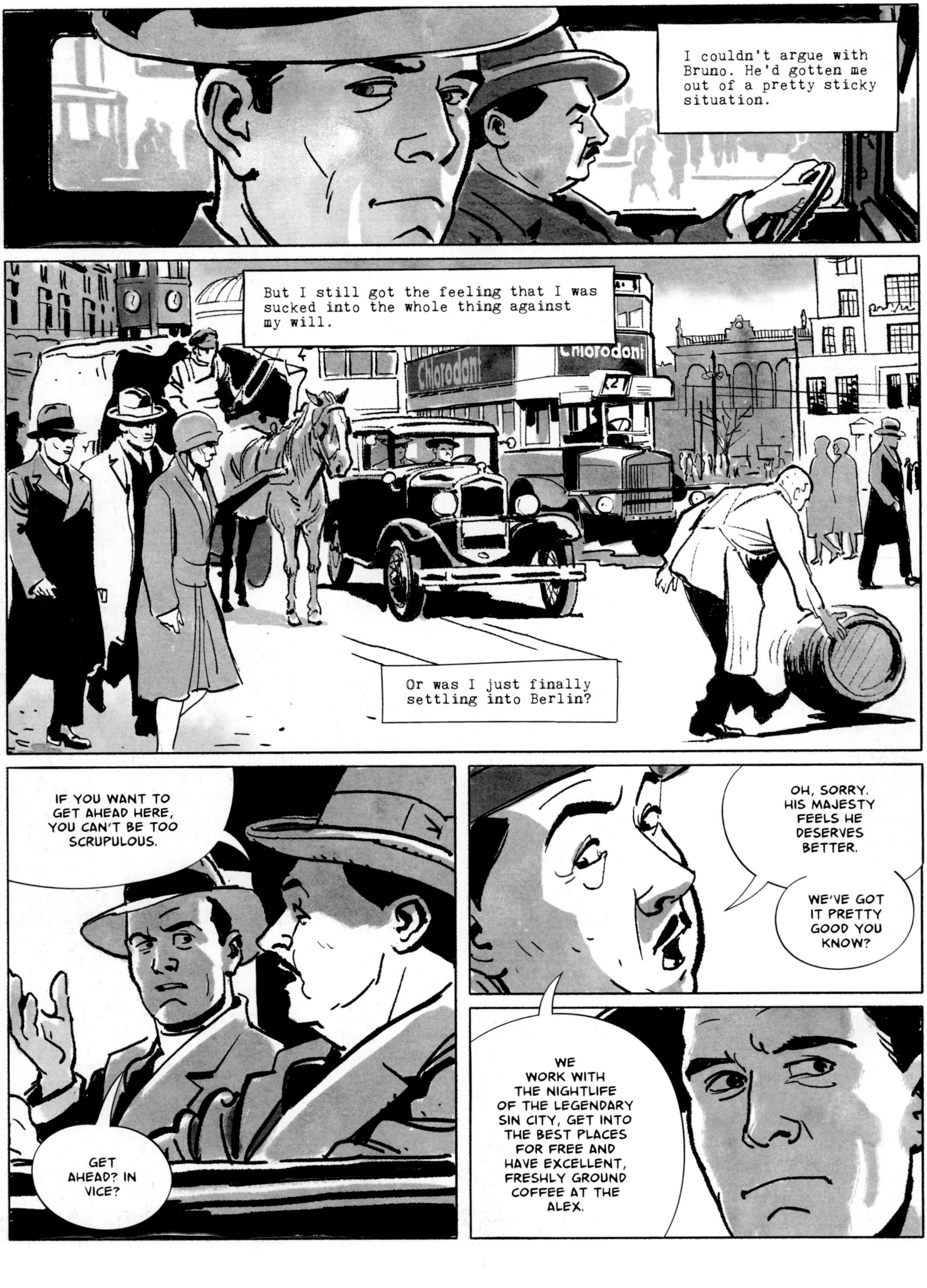
I couldn't argue with Bruno. He'd gotten me out of a pretty sticky situation.
But I still got the feeling that I was sucked into the whole thing against my will.
Chlorodont
Chlorodont
Or was I just finally settling into Berlin?
IF YOU WANT TO GET AHEAD HERE, YOU CAN'T BE TOO SCRUPULOUS.
GET AHEAD? IN VICE?
OH, SORRY. HIS MAJESTY FEELS HE DESERVES BETTER.
WE'VE GOT IT PRETTY GOOD YOU KNOW?
WE WORK WITH THE NIGHTLIFE OF THE LEGENDARY SIN CITY, GET INTO THE BEST PLACES FOR FREE AND HAVE EXCELLENT, FRESHLY GROUND COFFEE AT THE ALEX.

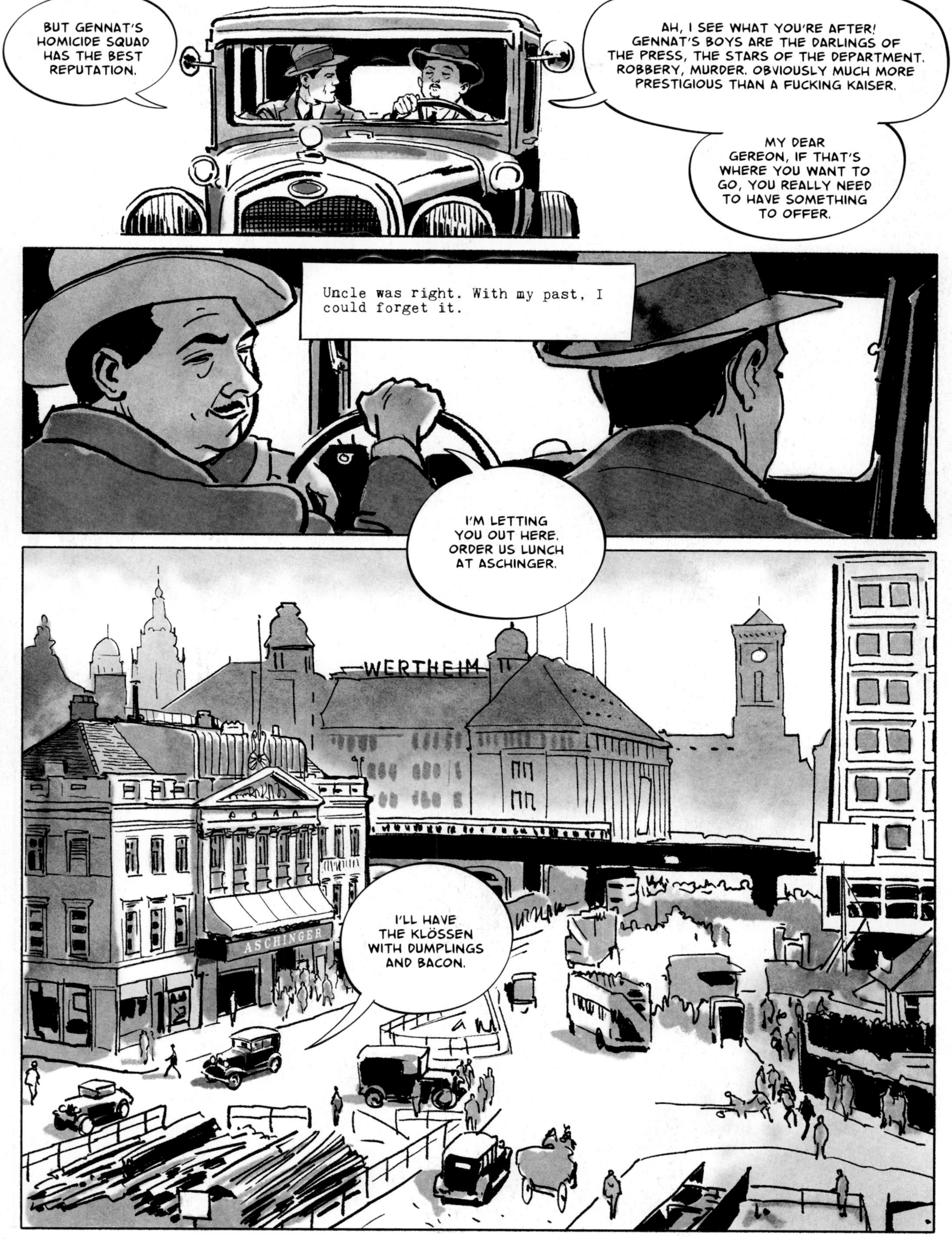
BUT GENNAT'S HOMICIDE SQUAD HAS THE BEST REPUTATION.
AH, I SEE WHAT YOU'RE AFTER! GENNAT'S BOYS ARE THE DARLINGS OF THE PRESS, THE STARS OF THE DEPARTMENT. ROBBERY, MURDER. OBVIOUSLY MUCH MORE PRESTIGIOUS THAN A FUCKING KAISER.
MY DEAR GEREON, IF THAT'S WHERE YOU WANT TO GO, YOU REALLY NEED TO HAVE SOMETHING TO OFFER.
Uncle was right. With my past, I could forget it.
I'M LETTING YOU OUT HERE. ORDER US LUNCH AT ASCHINGER.
WERTHEIM
ASCHINGER
I'LL HAVE THE KLÖSSEN WITH DUMPLINGS AND BACON.

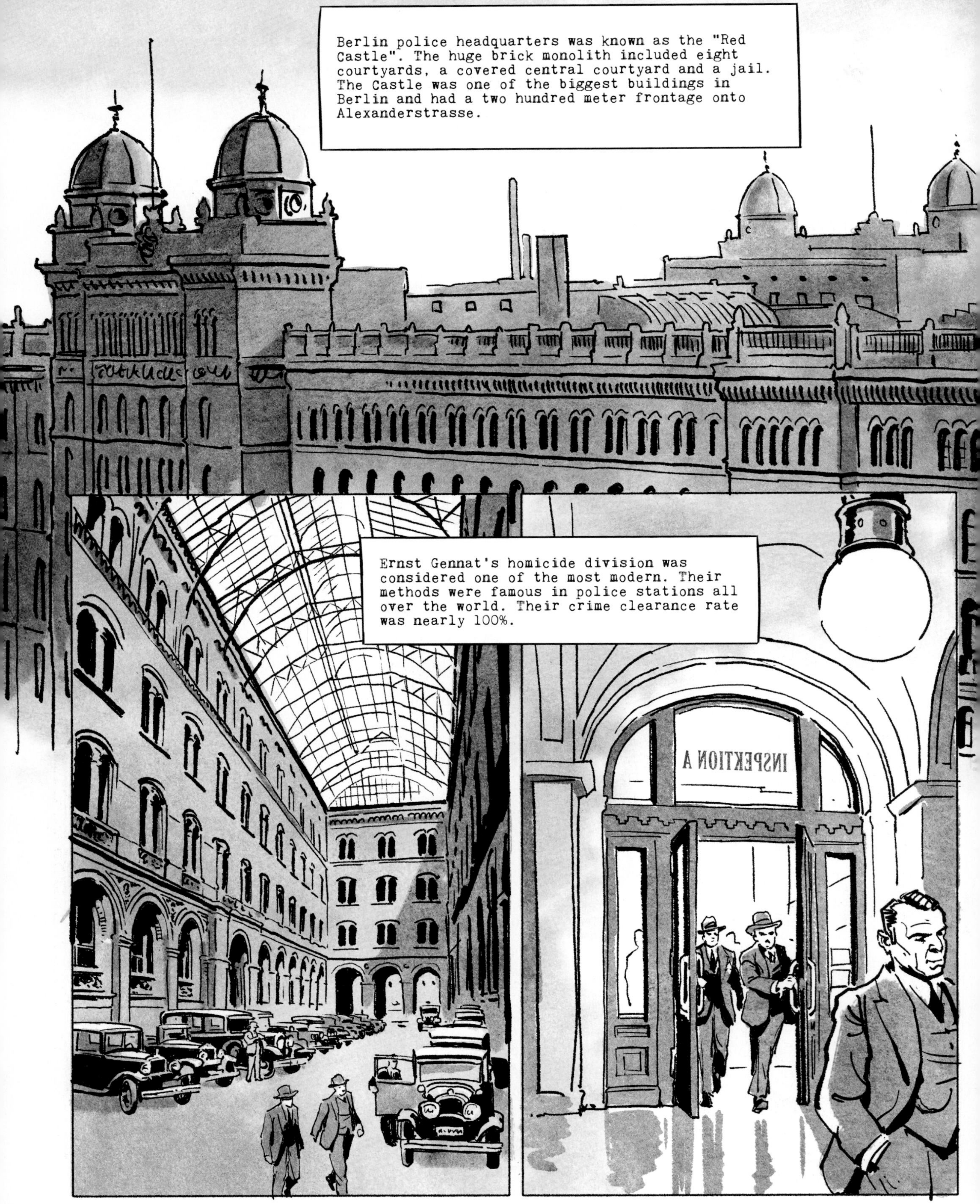
Berlin police headquarters was known as the "Red Castle". The huge brick monolith included eight courtyards, a covered central courtyard and a jail. The Castle was one of the biggest buildings in Berlin and had a two hundred meter frontage onto Alexanderstrasse.
Ernst Gennat's homicide division was considered one of the most modern. Their methods were famous in police stations all over the world. Their crime clearance rate was nearly 100%.
INSPEKTION A

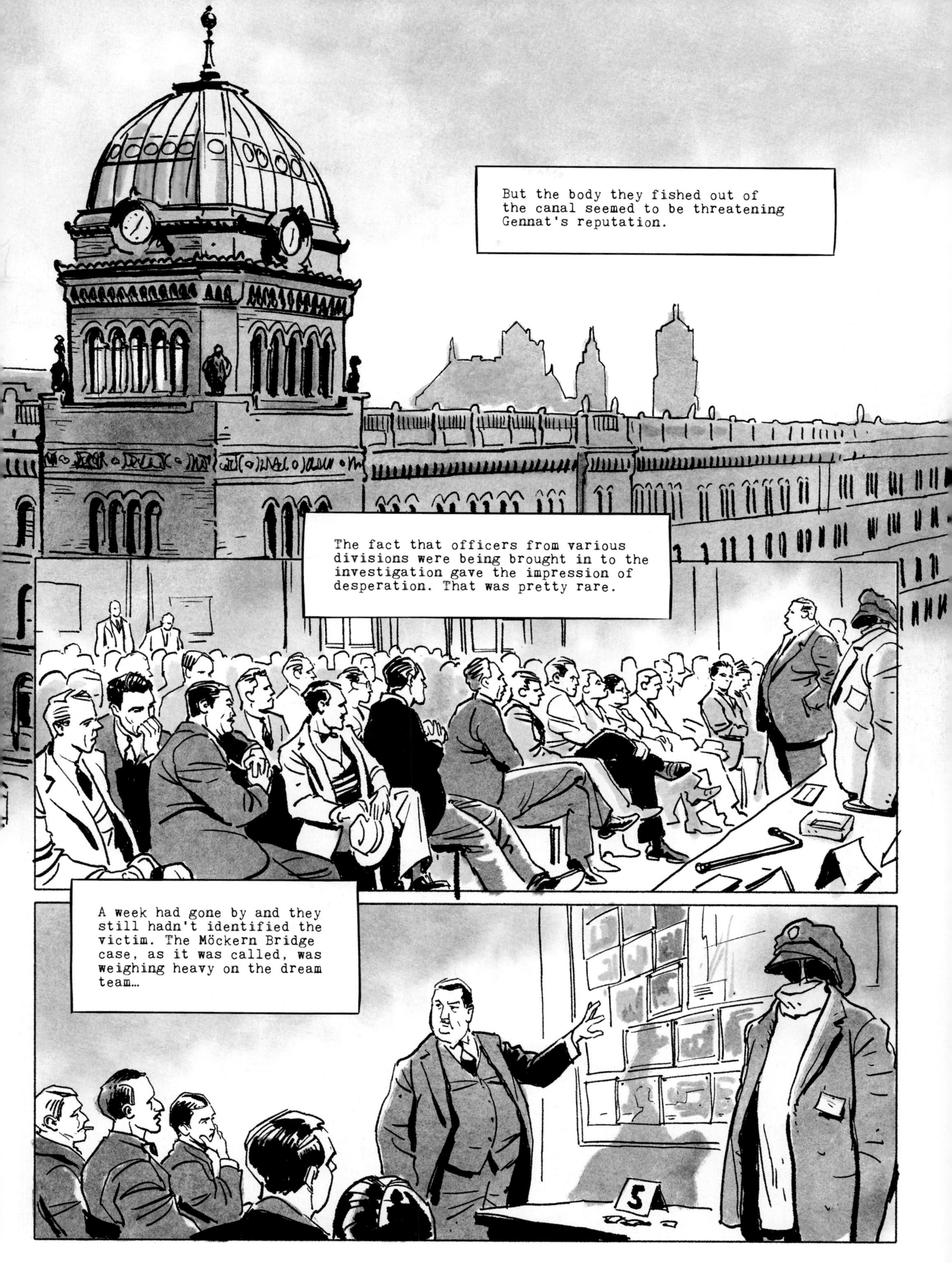
But the body they fished out of the canal seemed to be threatening Gennat's reputation.
The fact that officers from various divisions were being brought in to the investigation gave the impression of desperation. That was pretty rare.
A week had gone by and they still hadn't identified the victim. The Möckern Bridge case, as it was called, was weighing heavy on the dream team…
5

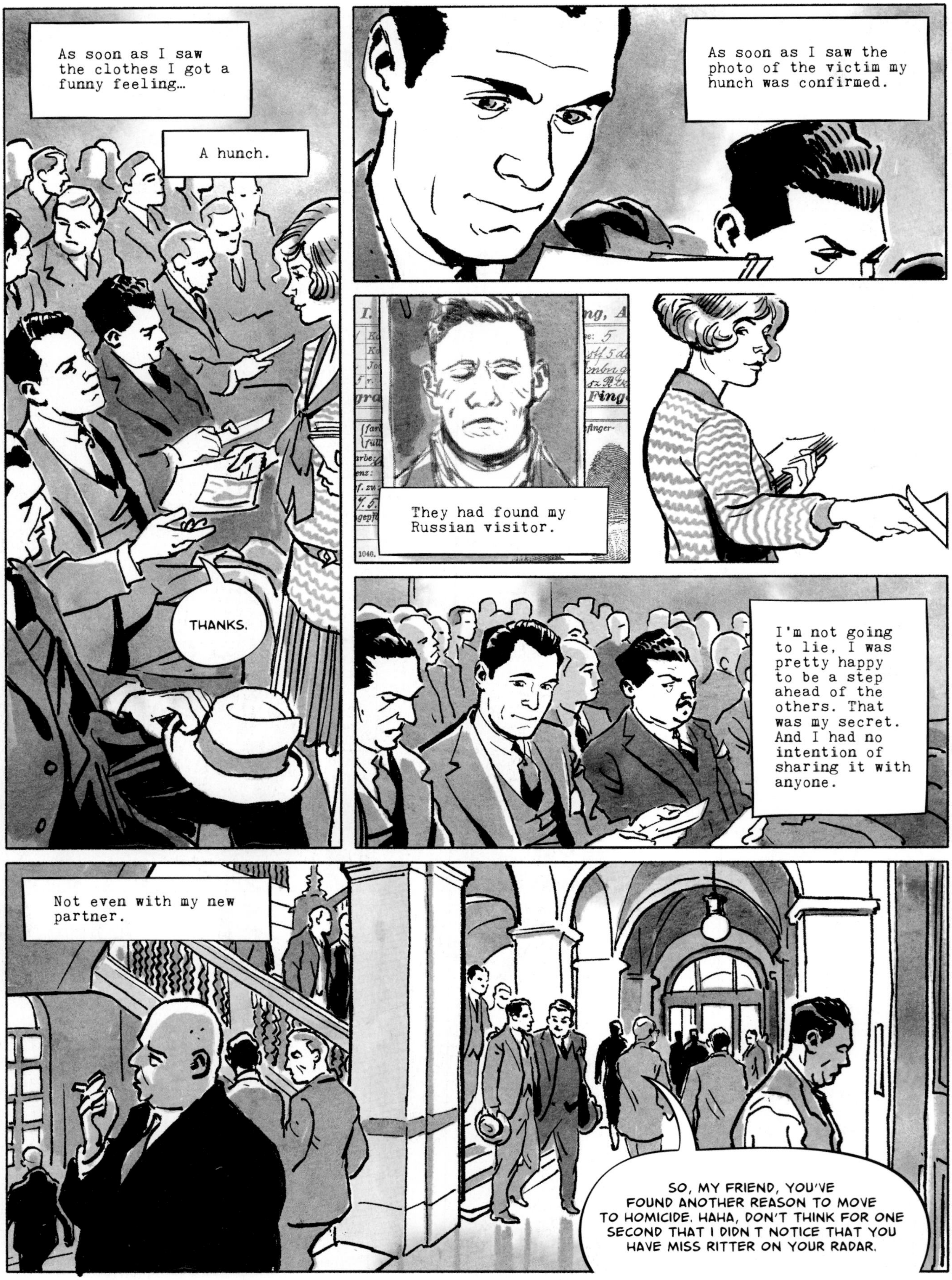
As soon as I saw the clothes I got a funny feeling...
A hunch.
THANKS.
As soon as I saw the photo of the victim my hunch was confirmed.
They had found my Russian visitor.
I'm not going to lie, I was pretty happy to be a step ahead of the others. That was my secret. And I had no intention of sharing it with anyone.
Not even with my new partner.
SO, MY FRIEND, YOU'VE FOUND ANOTHER REASON TO MOVE TO HOMICIDE. HAHA, DON'T THINK FOR ONE SECOND THAT I DIDN T NOTICE THAT YOU HAVE MISS RITTER ON YOUR RADAR.

12. Jahrg. / Nr. 93 / Preis für Groß-Berlin 20 Pfennig
Auswärts 25 Pf.

Berlin, Sonntag, 21. April 1929

Die Rote Fahne

Zentralorgan der Kommunistischen Partei Deutschlands (Sektion der Kommunistischen Internationale)

Begründet von
Karl Liebknecht und Rosa Luxemburg

Zörgiebel will am 1. Mai schießen!

sagt das sozialdemokratische „Sächsische Volksblatt"

MAI 1

Many workers thought that the police chief, their comrade Zörgiebel, a social democrat, would suspend the ban on the right to demonstrate on May 1...

But in fact, he reconfirmed it.

Make Way! The Red Wave is Coming!

It looked like there were going to be riots on the streets...

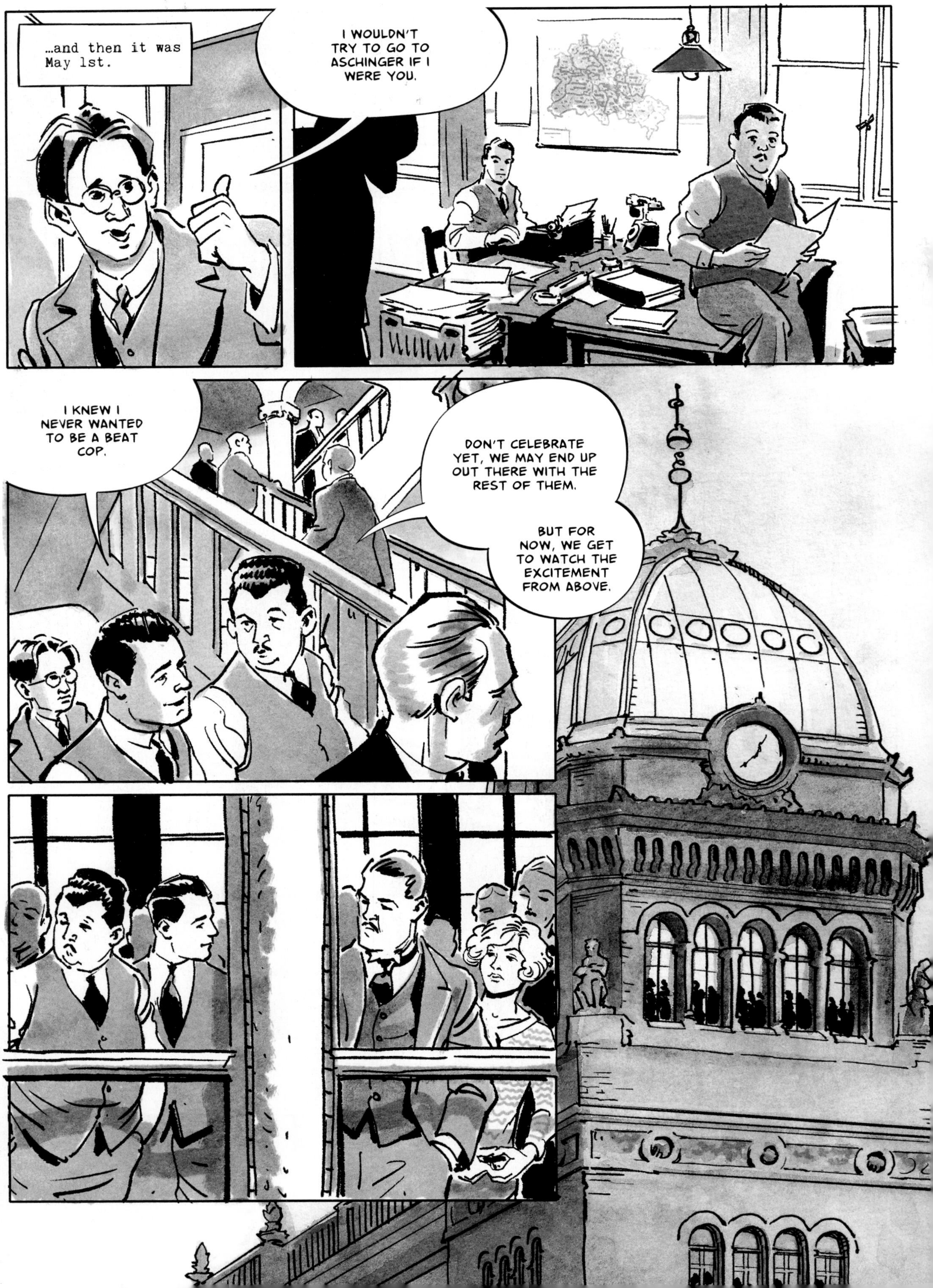
...and then it was May 1st.
I WOULDN'T TRY TO GO TO ASCHINGER IF I WERE YOU.
I KNEW I NEVER WANTED TO BE A BEAT COP.
DON'T CELEBRATE YET, WE MAY END UP OUT THERE WITH THE REST OF THEM.
BUT FOR NOW, WE GET TO WATCH THE EXCITEMENT FROM ABOVE.

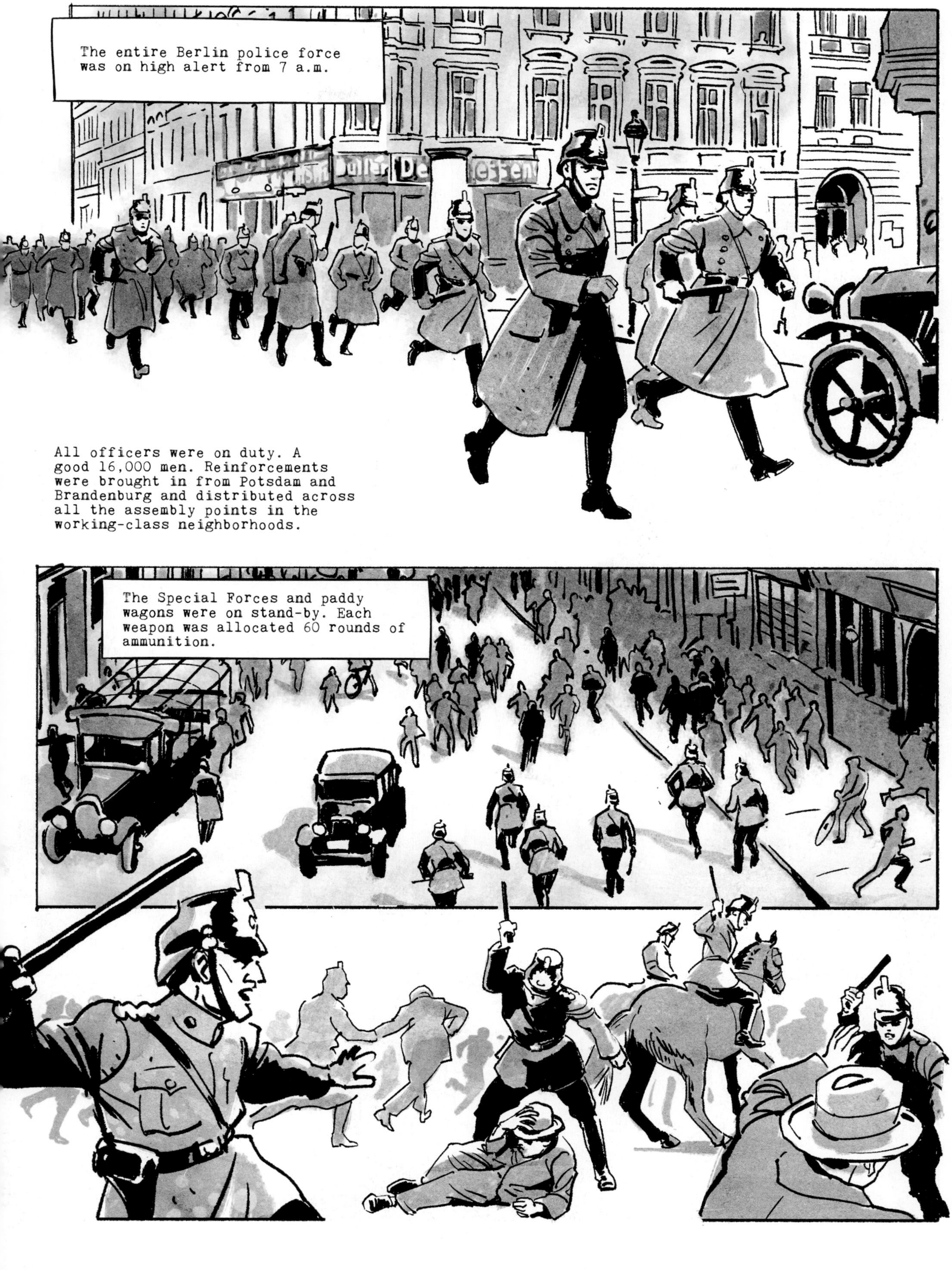
The entire Berlin police force was on high alert from 7 a.m.
All officers were on duty. A good 16,000 men. Reinforcements were brought in from Potsdam and Brandenburg and distributed across all the assembly points in the working-class neighborhoods.
The Special Forces and paddy wagons were on stand-by. Each weapon was allocated 60 rounds of ammunition.

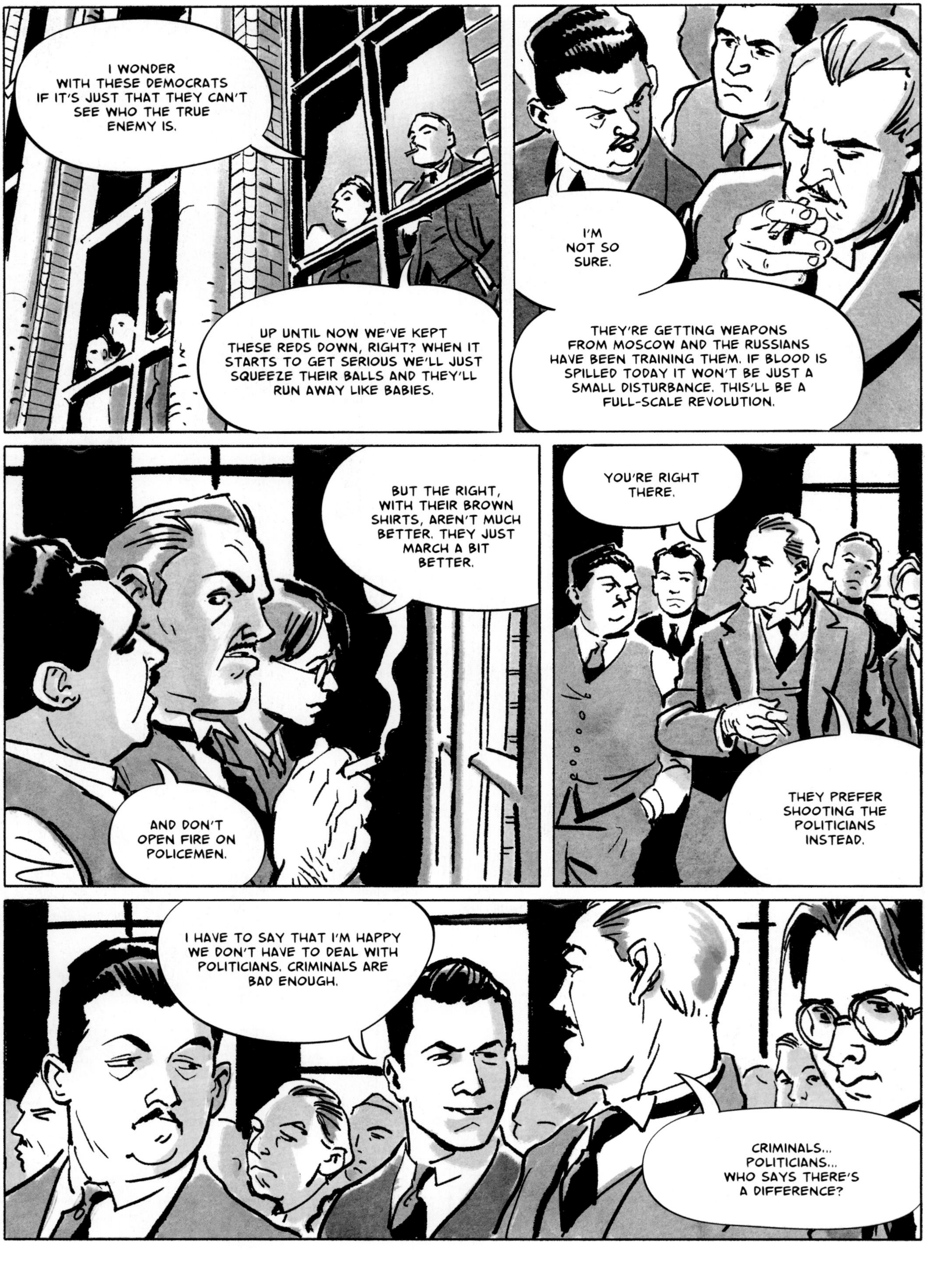
I WONDER WITH THESE DEMOCRATS IF IT'S JUST THAT THEY CAN'T SEE WHO THE TRUE ENEMY IS.
UP UNTIL NOW WE'VE KEPT THESE REDS DOWN, RIGHT? WHEN IT STARTS TO GET SERIOUS WE'LL JUST SQUEEZE THEIR BALLS AND THEY'LL RUN AWAY LIKE BABIES.
I'M NOT SO SURE.
THEY'RE GETTING WEAPONS FROM MOSCOW AND THE RUSSIANS HAVE BEEN TRAINING THEM. IF BLOOD IS SPILLED TODAY IT WON'T BE JUST A SMALL DISTURBANCE. THIS'LL BE A FULL-SCALE REVOLUTION.
BUT THE RIGHT, WITH THEIR BROWN SHIRTS, AREN'T MUCH BETTER. THEY JUST MARCH A BIT BETTER.
AND DON'T OPEN FIRE ON POLICEMEN.
YOU'RE RIGHT THERE.
THEY PREFER SHOOTING THE POLITICIANS INSTEAD.
I HAVE TO SAY THAT I'M HAPPY WE DON'T HAVE TO DEAL WITH POLITICIANS. CRIMINALS ARE BAD ENOUGH.
CRIMINALS... POLITICIANS... WHO SAYS THERE'S A DIFFERENCE?

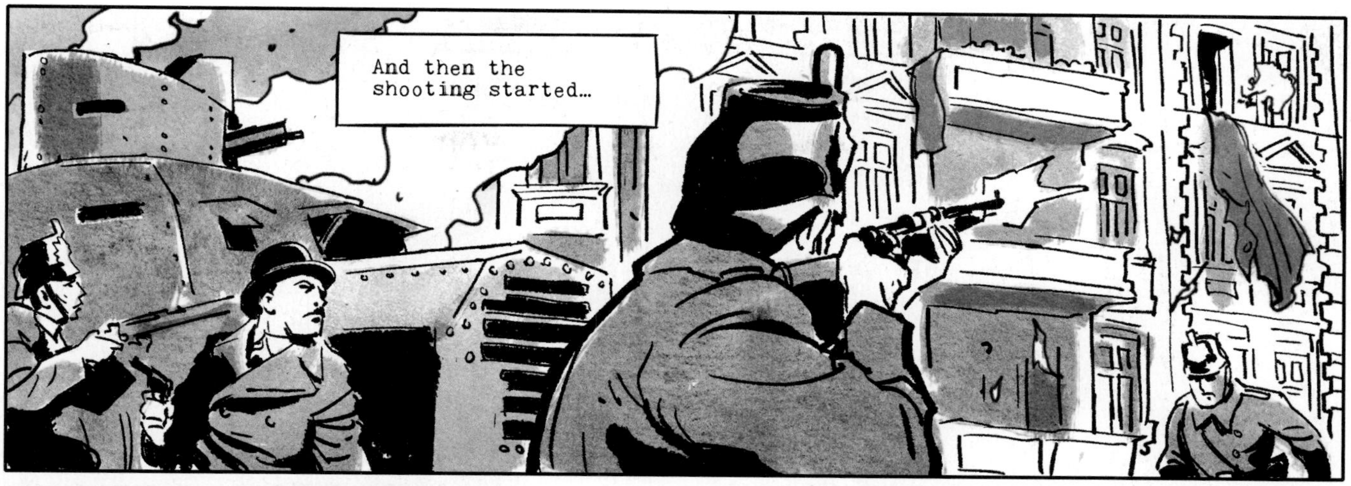
And then the shooting started...

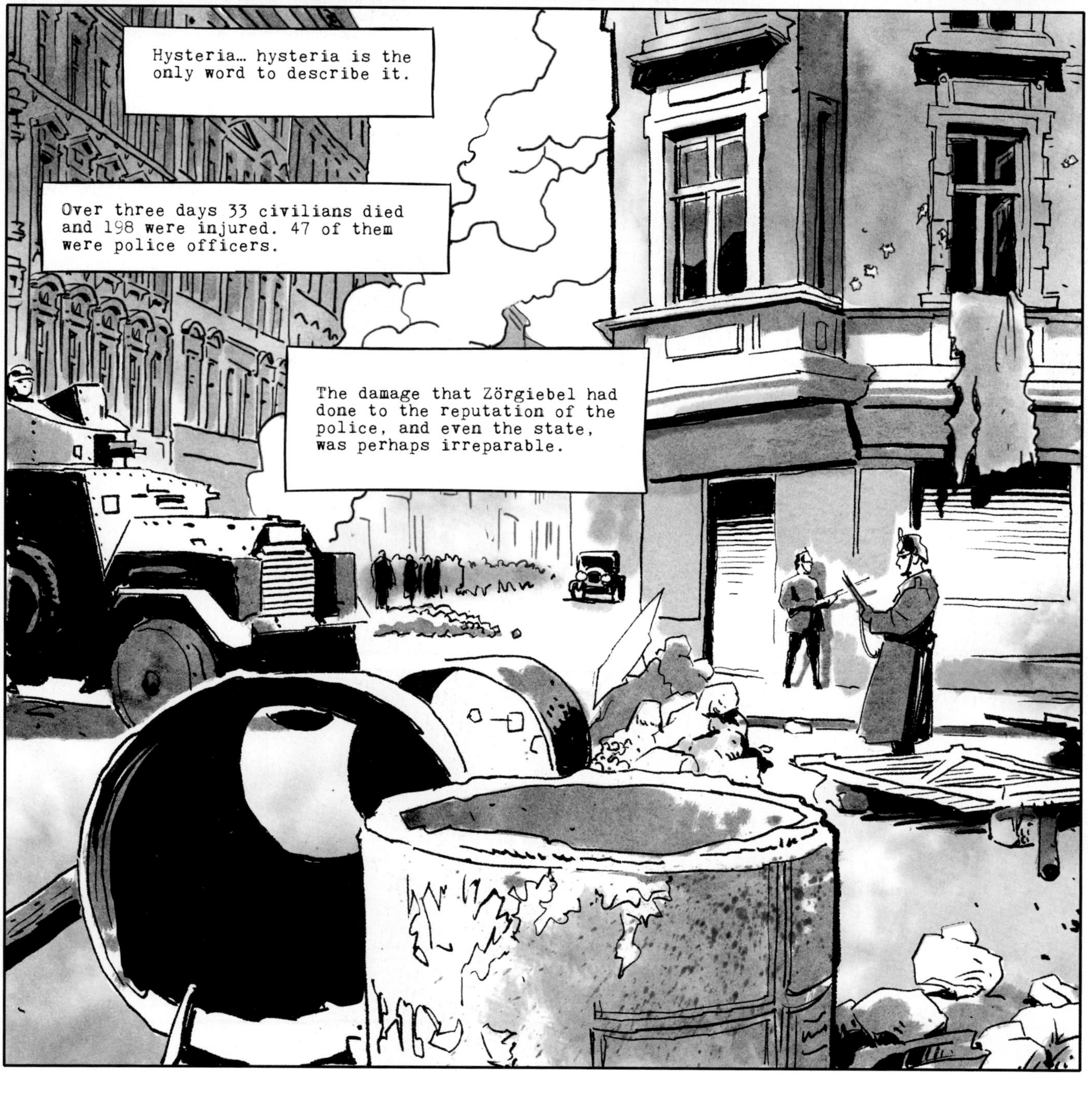
Hysteria... hysteria is the only word to describe it.
Over three days 33 civilians died and 198 were injured. 47 of them were police officers.
The damage that Zörgiebel had done to the reputation of the police, and even the state, was perhaps irreparable.

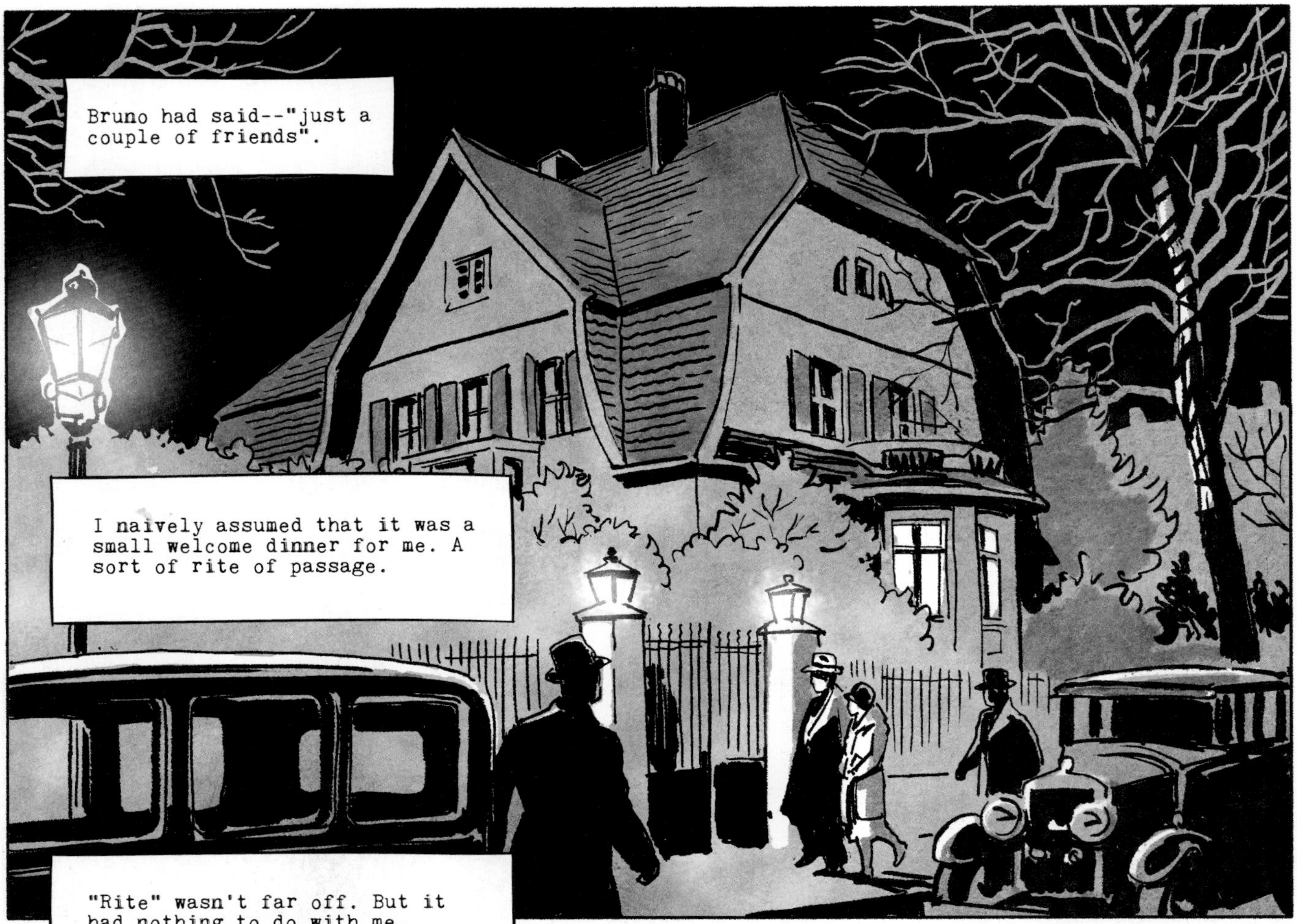
Bruno had said--"just a couple of friends".
I naively assumed that it was a small welcome dinner for me. A sort of rite of passage.
"Rite" wasn't far off. But it had nothing to do with me…

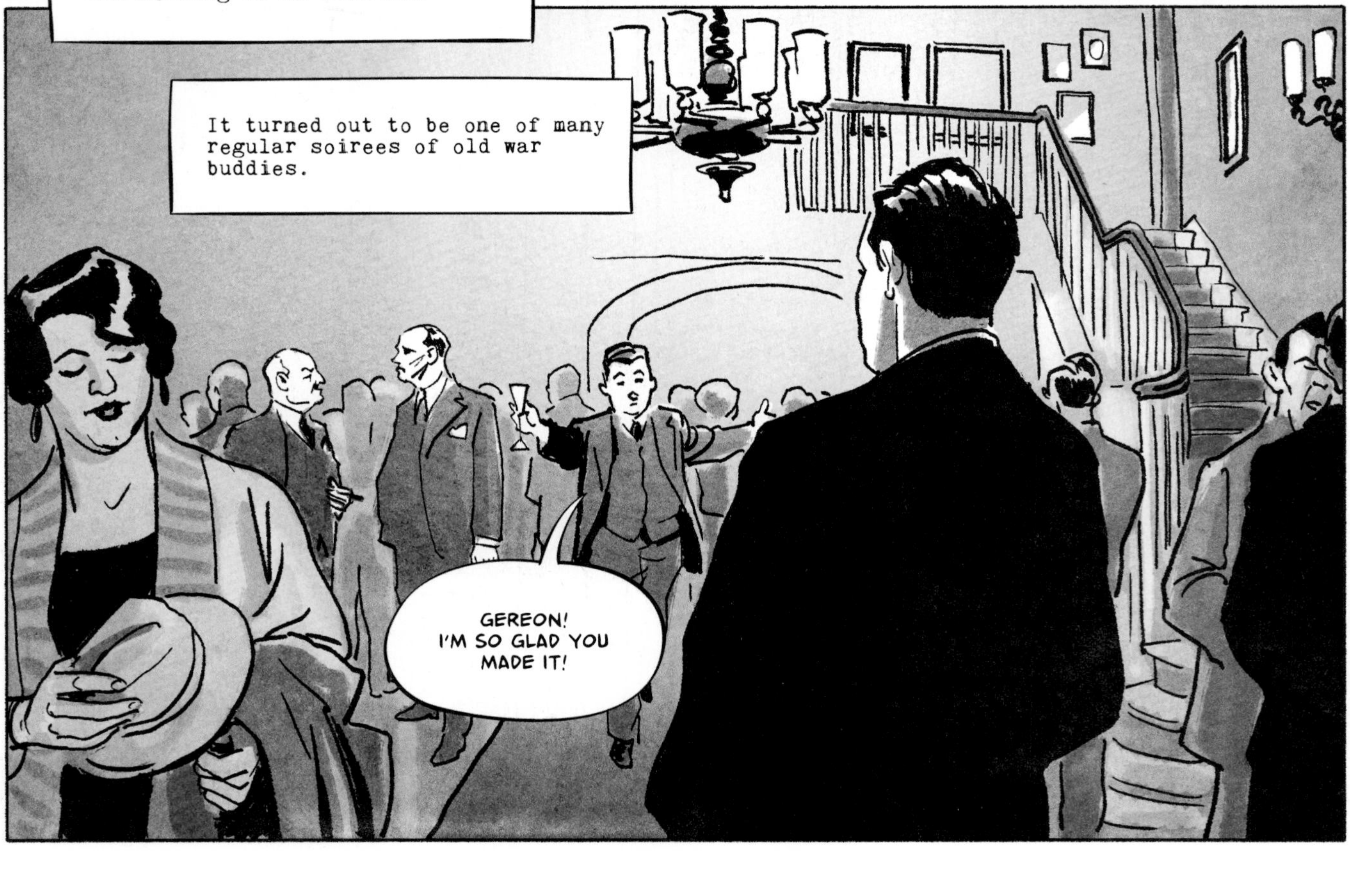
It turned out to be one of many regular soirees of old war buddies.
GEREON! I'M SO GLAD YOU MADE IT!

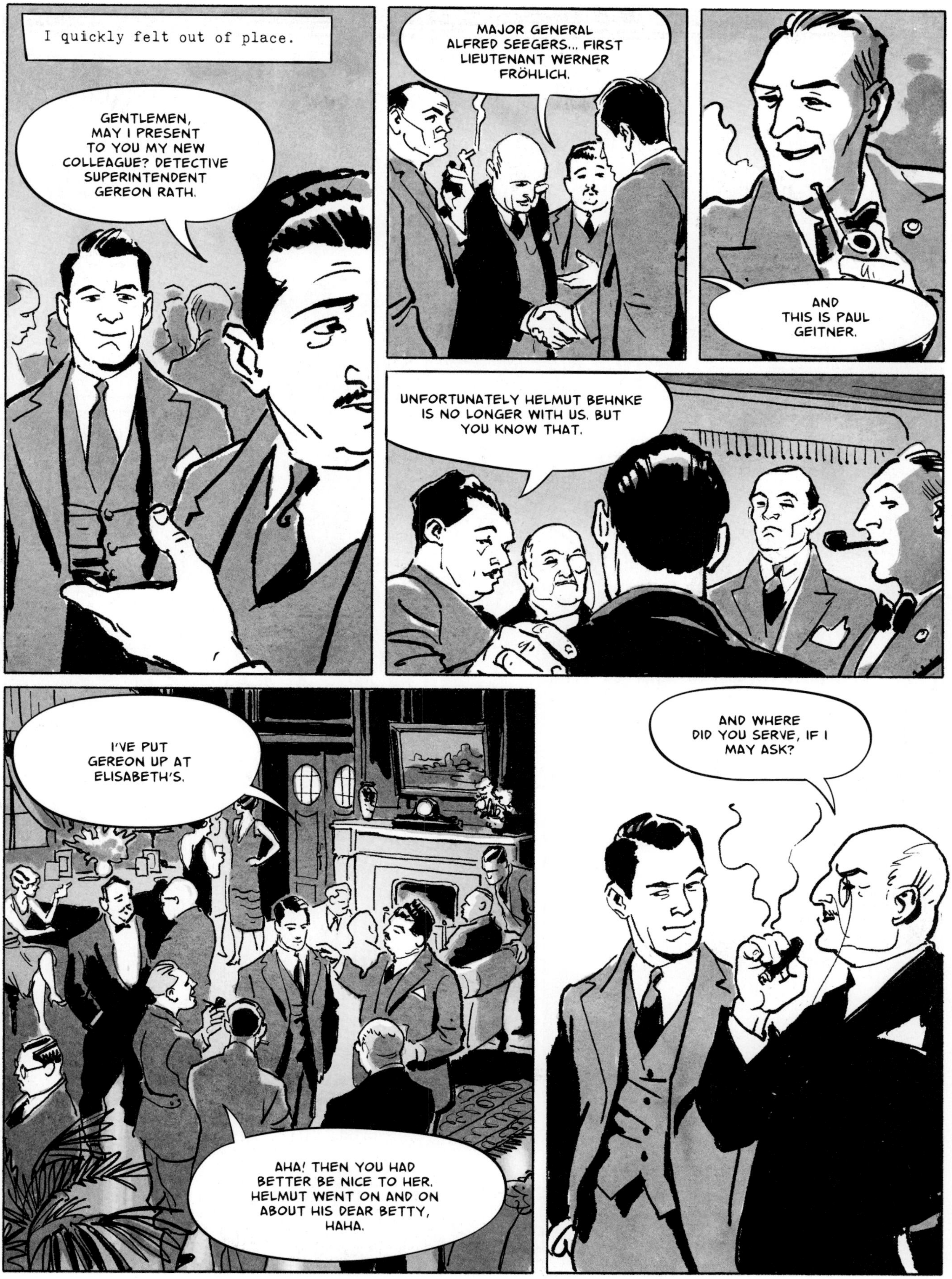
I quickly felt out of place.
GENTLEMEN, MAY I PRESENT TO YOU MY NEW COLLEAGUE? DETECTIVE SUPERINTENDENT GEREON RATH.
MAJOR GENERAL ALFRED SEEGERS... FIRST LIEUTENANT WERNER FRÖHLICH.
AND THIS IS PAUL GEITNER.
UNFORTUNATELY HELMUT BEHNKE IS NO LONGER WITH US. BUT YOU KNOW THAT.
I'VE PUT GEREON UP AT ELISABETH'S.
AHA! THEN YOU HAD BETTER BE NICE TO HER. HELMUT WENT ON AND ON ABOUT HIS DEAR BETTY, HAHA.
AND WHERE DID YOU SERVE, IF I MAY ASK?

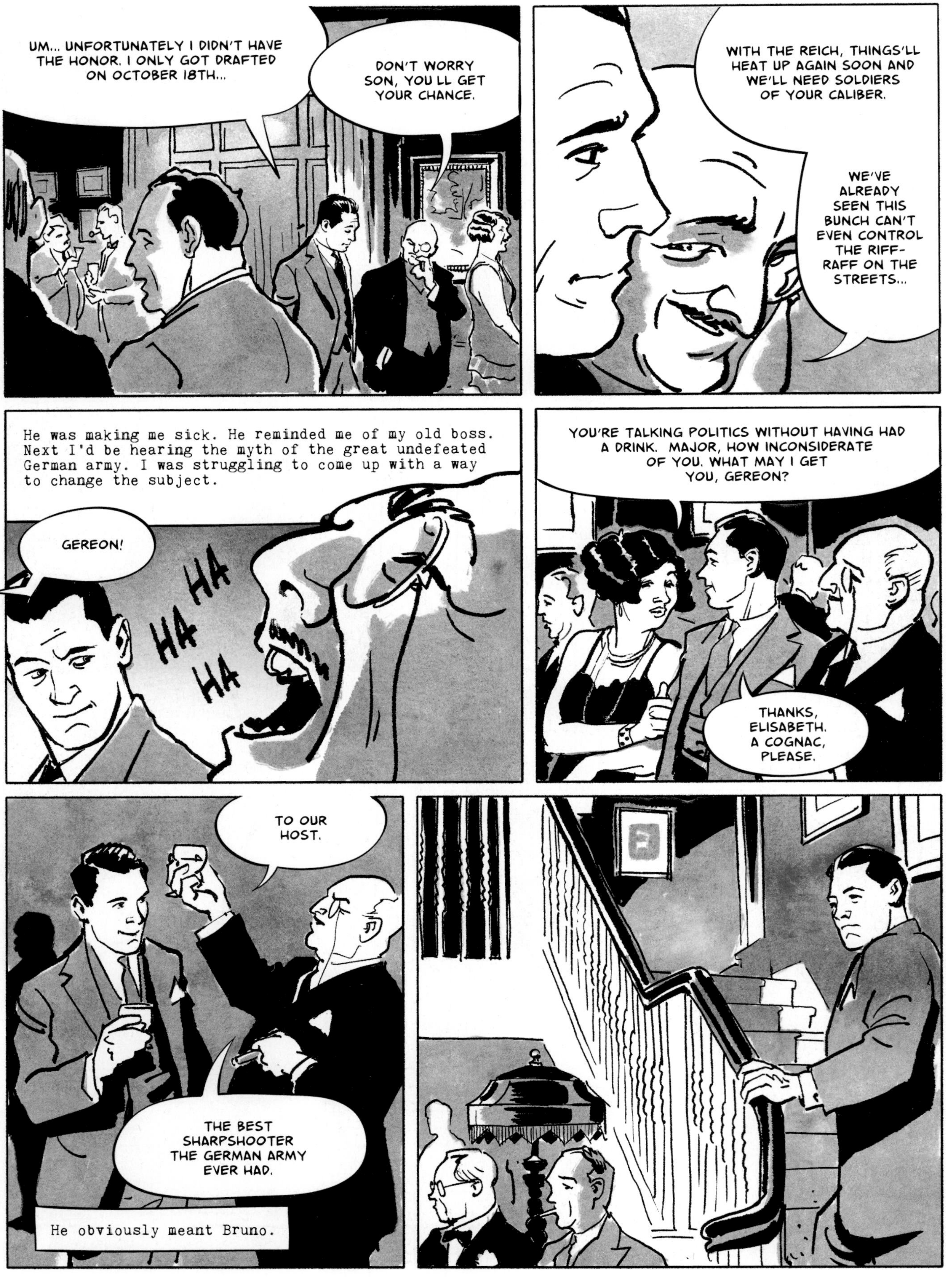
UM... UNFORTUNATELY I DIDN'T HAVE THE HONOR. I ONLY GOT DRAFTED ON OCTOBER 18TH...
DON'T WORRY SON, YOU'LL GET YOUR CHANCE.
WITH THE REICH, THINGS'LL HEAT UP AGAIN SOON AND WE'LL NEED SOLDIERS OF YOUR CALIBER.
WE'VE ALREADY SEEN THIS BUNCH CAN'T EVEN CONTROL THE RIFF-RAFF ON THE STREETS...
He was making me sick. He reminded me of my old boss. Next I'd be hearing the myth of the great undefeated German army. I was struggling to come up with a way to change the subject.
GEREON!
HA HA HA HA
YOU'RE TALKING POLITICS WITHOUT HAVING HAD A DRINK. MAJOR, HOW INCONSIDERATE OF YOU. WHAT MAY I GET YOU, GEREON?
THANKS, ELISABETH. A COGNAC, PLEASE.
TO OUR HOST.
THE BEST SHARPSHOOTER THE GERMAN ARMY EVER HAD.
He obviously meant Bruno.

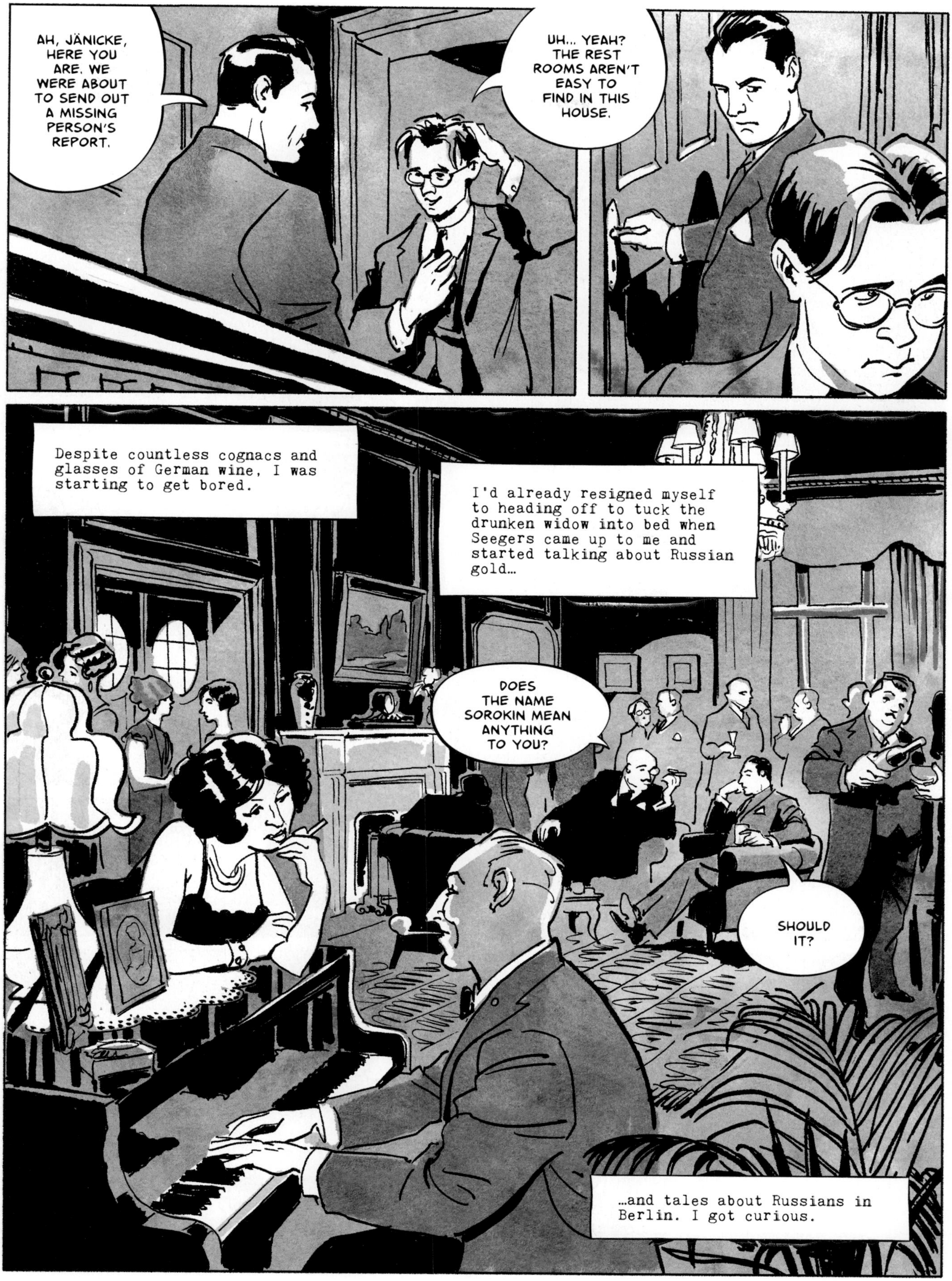
AH, JÄNICKE, HERE YOU ARE. WE WERE ABOUT TO SEND OUT A MISSING PERSON'S REPORT.
UH... YEAH? THE REST ROOMS AREN'T EASY TO FIND IN THIS HOUSE.
Despite countless cognacs and glasses of German wine, I was starting to get bored.
I'd already resigned myself to heading off to tuck the drunken widow into bed when Seegers came up to me and started talking about Russian gold...
DOES THE NAME SOROKIN MEAN ANYTHING TO YOU?
SHOULD IT?
...and tales about Russians in Berlin. I got curious.

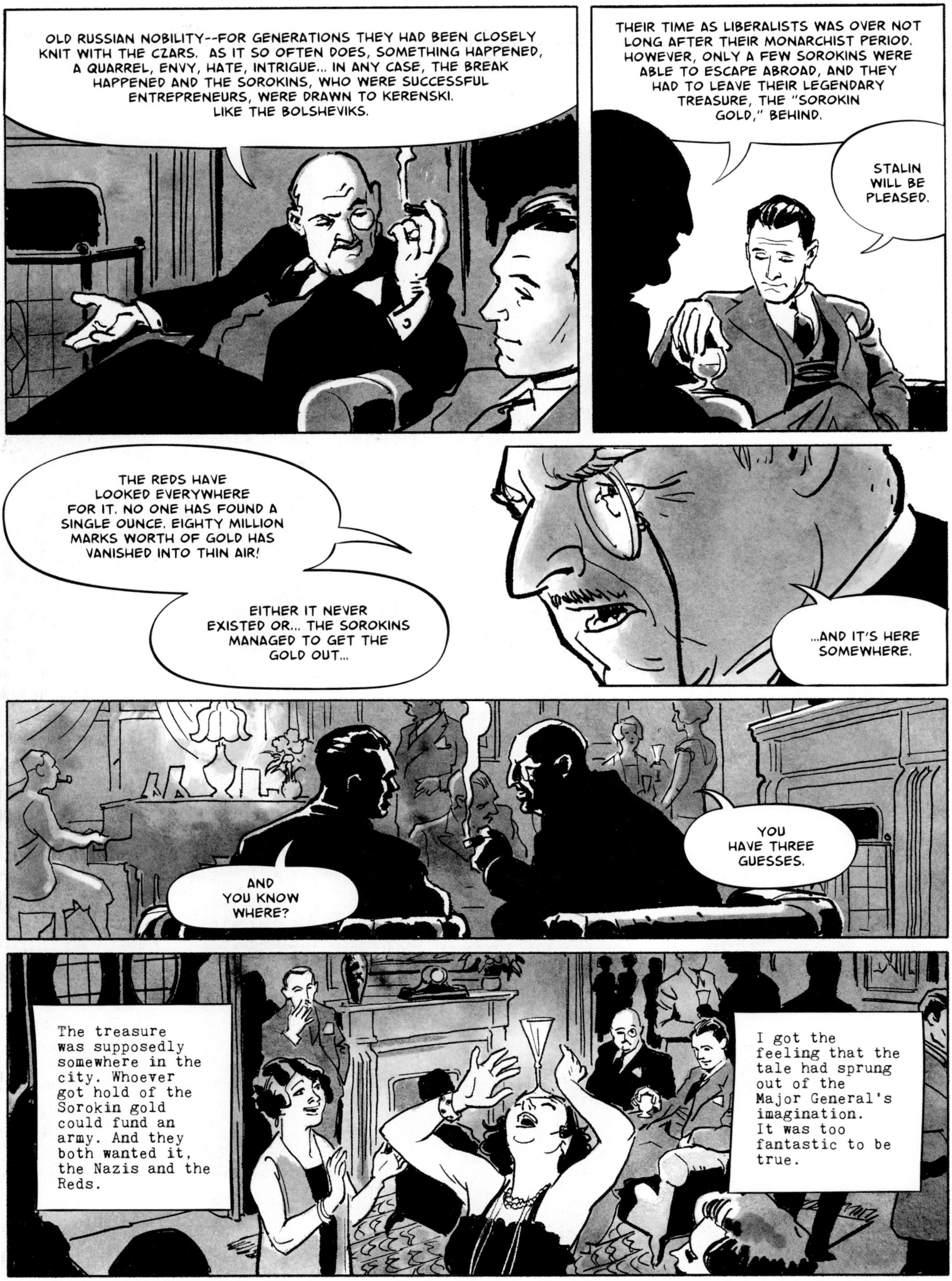
OLD RUSSIAN NOBILITY--FOR GENERATIONS THEY HAD BEEN CLOSELY KNIT WITH THE CZARS. AS IT SO OFTEN DOES, SOMETHING HAPPENED, A QUARREL, ENVY, HATE, INTRIGUE... IN ANY CASE, THE BREAK HAPPENED AND THE SOROKINS, WHO WERE SUCCESSFUL ENTREPRENEURS, WERE DRAWN TO KERENSKI. LIKE THE BOLSHEVIKS.
THEIR TIME AS LIBERALISTS WAS OVER NOT LONG AFTER THEIR MONARCHIST PERIOD. HOWEVER, ONLY A FEW SOROKINS WERE ABLE TO ESCAPE ABROAD, AND THEY HAD TO LEAVE THEIR LEGENDARY TREASURE, THE "SOROKIN GOLD," BEHIND.
STALIN WILL BE PLEASED.
THE REDS HAVE LOOKED EVERYWHERE FOR IT. NO ONE HAS FOUND A SINGLE OUNCE. EIGHTY MILLION MARKS WORTH OF GOLD HAS VANISHED INTO THIN AIR!
EITHER IT NEVER EXISTED OR... THE SOROKINS MANAGED TO GET THE GOLD OUT...
...AND IT'S HERE SOMEWHERE.
AND YOU KNOW WHERE?
YOU HAVE THREE GUESSES.
The treasure was supposedly somewhere in the city. Whoever got hold of the Sorokin gold could fund an army. And they both wanted it, the Nazis and the Reds.
I got the feeling that the tale had sprung out of the Major General's imagination. It was too fantastic to be true.

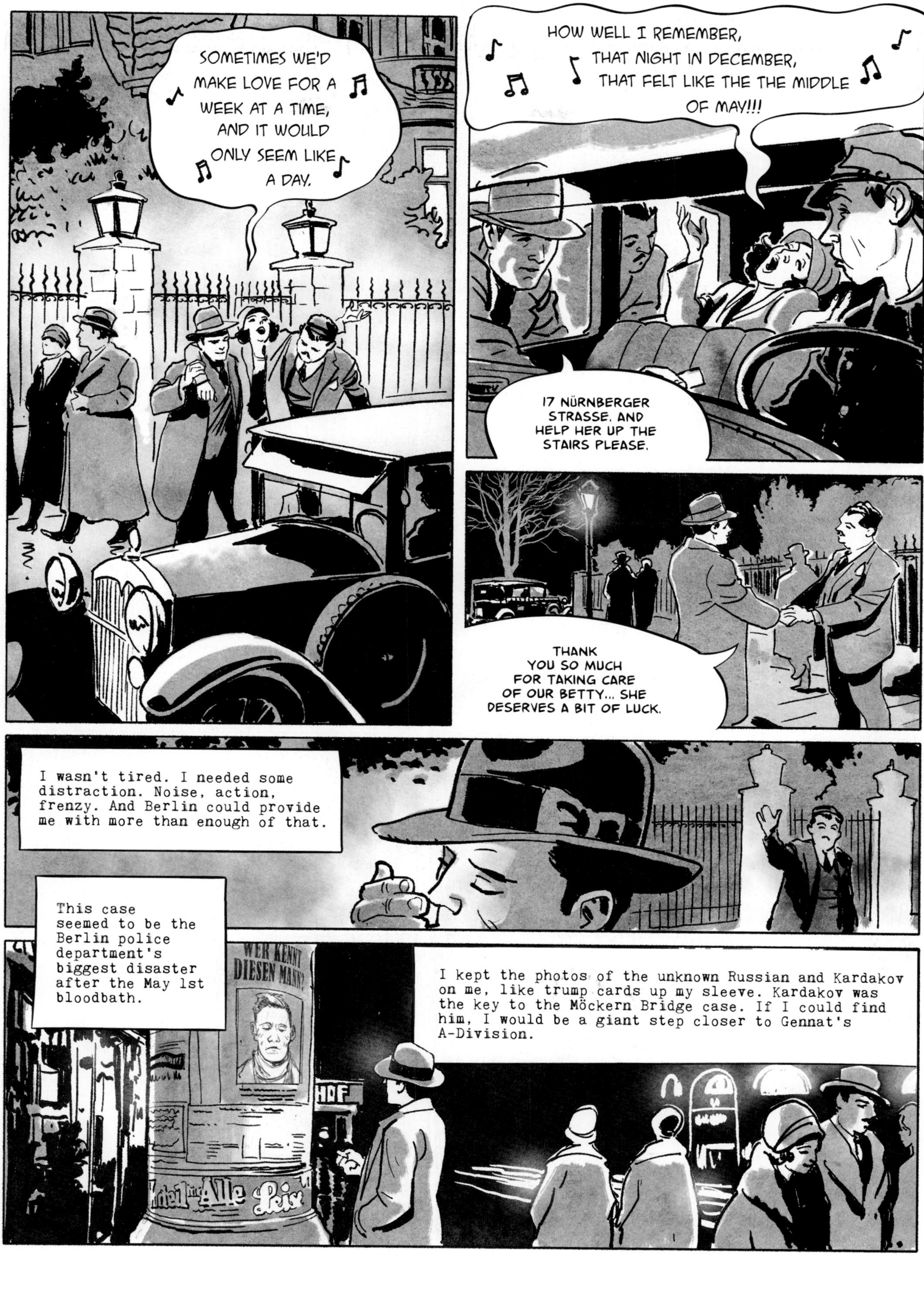
SOMETIMES WE'D MAKE LOVE FOR A WEEK AT A TIME, AND IT WOULD ONLY SEEM LIKE A DAY.
HOW WELL I REMEMBER, THAT NIGHT IN DECEMBER, THAT FELT LIKE THE THE MIDDLE OF MAY!!!
17 NÜRNBERGER STRASSE. AND HELP HER UP THE STAIRS PLEASE.
THANK YOU SO MUCH FOR TAKING CARE OF OUR BETTY... SHE DESERVES A BIT OF LUCK.
I wasn't tired. I needed some distraction. Noise, action, frenzy. And Berlin could provide me with more than enough of that.
This case seemed to be the Berlin police department's biggest disaster after the May 1st bloodbath.
WER KENNT DIESEN MANN?
I kept the photos of the unknown Russian and Kardakov on me, like trump cards up my sleeve. Kardakov was the key to the Möckern Bridge case. If I could find him, I would be a giant step closer to Gennat's A-Division.

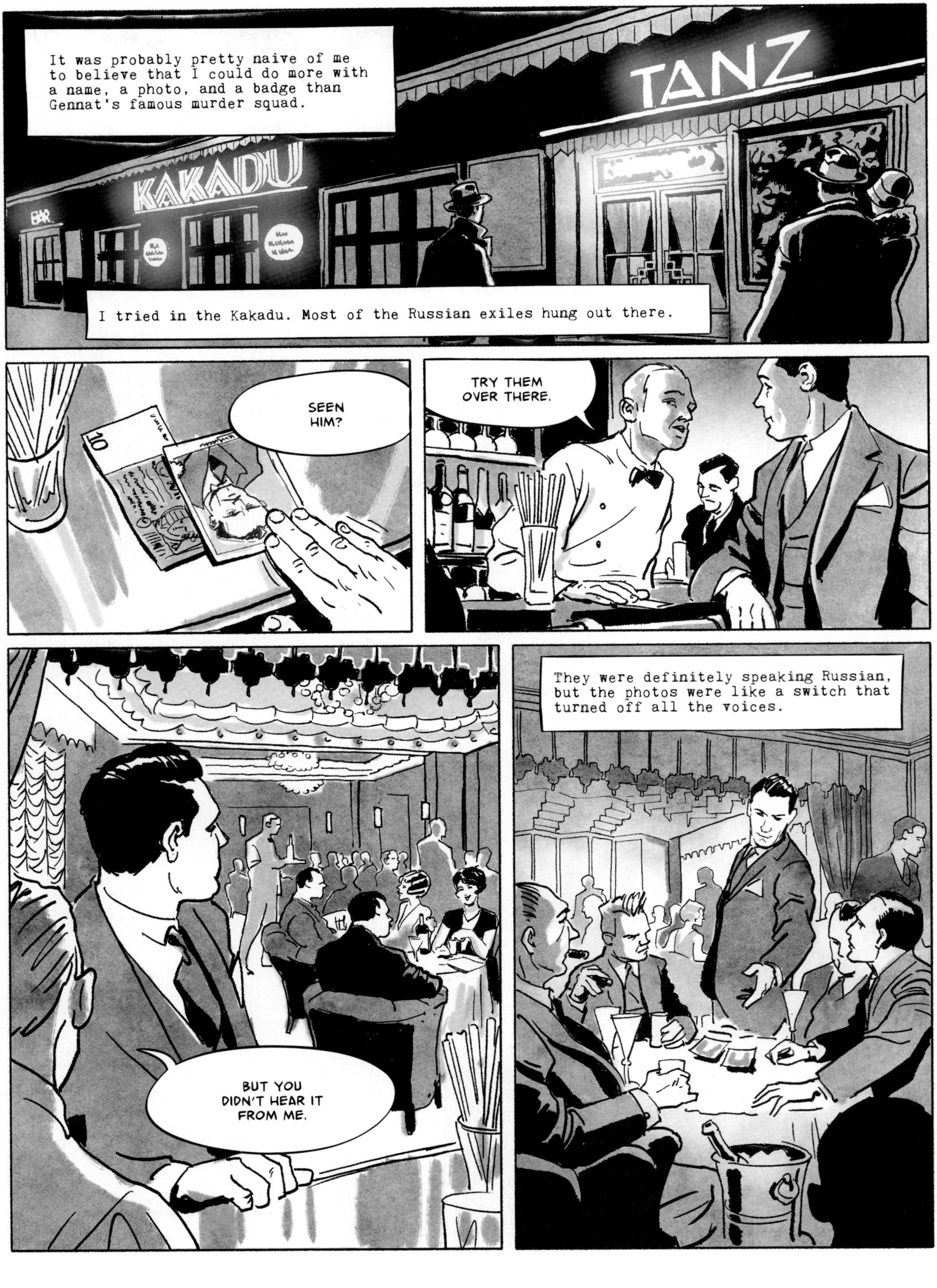
It was probably pretty naive of me to believe that I could do more with a name, a photo, and a badge than Gennat's famous murder squad.
TANZ
KAKADU
BAR
I tried in the Kakadu. Most of the Russian exiles hung out there.
SEEN HIM?
TRY THEM OVER THERE.
BUT YOU DIDN'T HEAR IT FROM ME.
They were definitely speaking Russian, but the photos were like a switch that turned off all the voices.

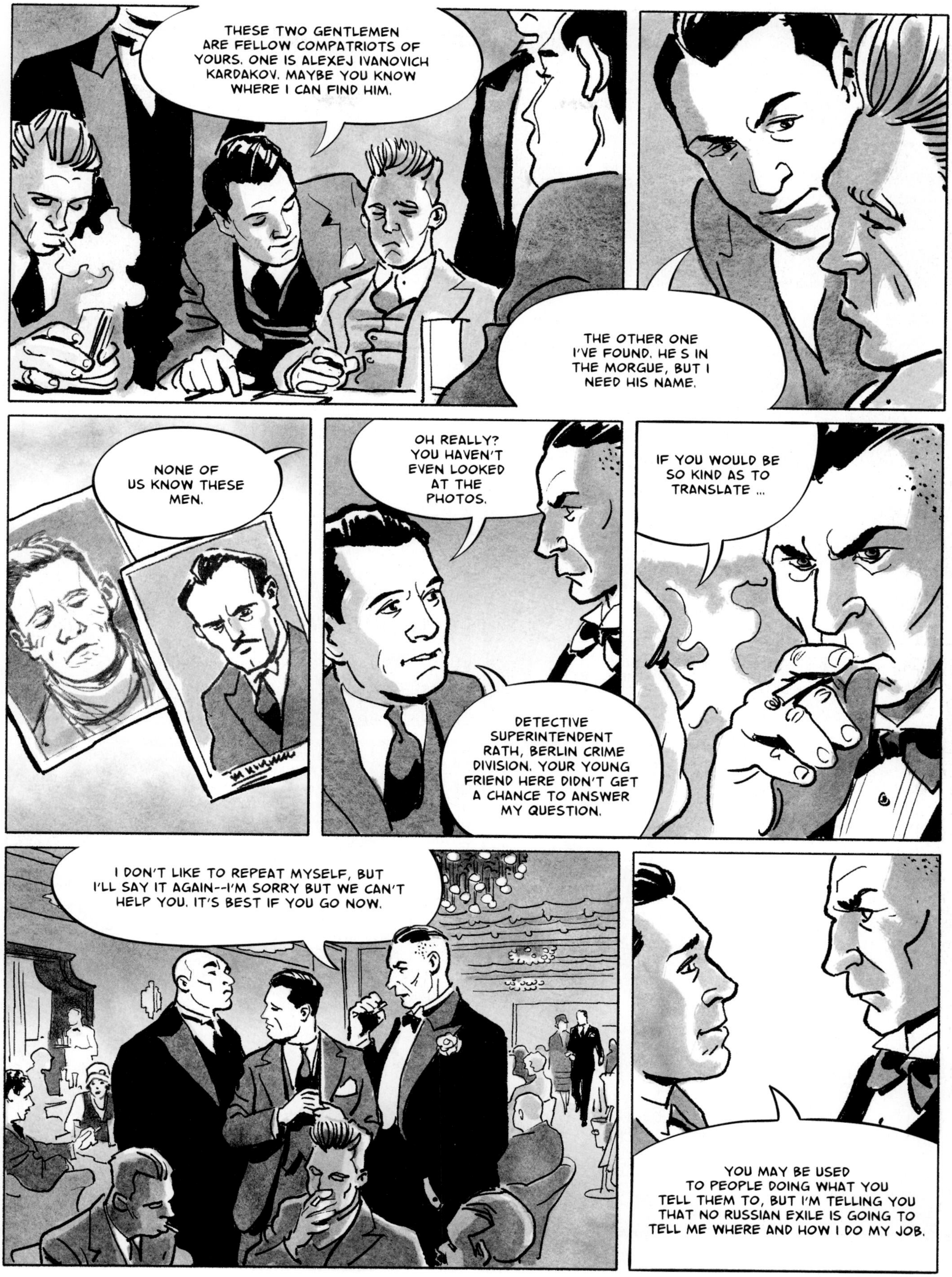
THESE TWO GENTLEMEN ARE FELLOW COMPATRIOTS OF YOURS. ONE IS ALEXEJ IVANOVICH KARDAKOV. MAYBE YOU KNOW WHERE I CAN FIND HIM.
THE OTHER ONE I'VE FOUND. HE S IN THE MORGUE, BUT I NEED HIS NAME.
NONE OF US KNOW THESE MEN.
OH REALLY? YOU HAVEN'T EVEN LOOKED AT THE PHOTOS.
DETECTIVE SUPERINTENDENT RATH, BERLIN CRIME DIVISION. YOUR YOUNG FRIEND HERE DIDN'T GET A CHANCE TO ANSWER MY QUESTION.
IF YOU WOULD BE SO KIND AS TO TRANSLATE ...
I DON'T LIKE TO REPEAT MYSELF, BUT I'LL SAY IT AGAIN--I'M SORRY BUT WE CAN'T HELP YOU. IT'S BEST IF YOU GO NOW.
YOU MAY BE USED TO PEOPLE DOING WHAT YOU TELL THEM TO, BUT I'M TELLING YOU THAT NO RUSSIAN EXILE IS GOING TO TELL ME WHERE AND HOW I DO MY JOB.

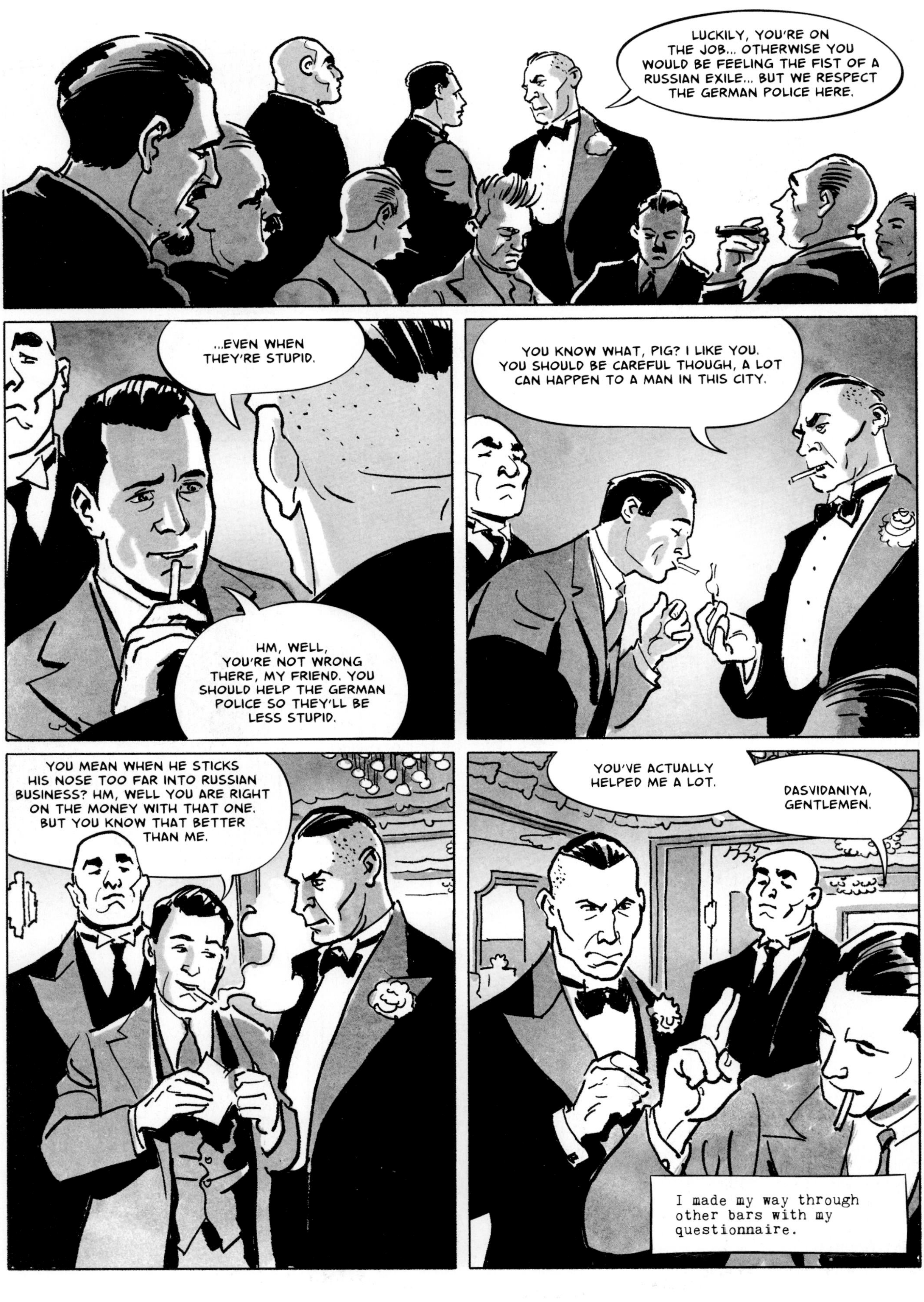
LUCKILY, YOU'RE ON THE JOB... OTHERWISE YOU WOULD BE FEELING THE FIST OF A RUSSIAN EXILE... BUT WE RESPECT THE GERMAN POLICE HERE.
...EVEN WHEN THEY'RE STUPID.
HM, WELL, YOU'RE NOT WRONG THERE, MY FRIEND. YOU SHOULD HELP THE GERMAN POLICE SO THEY'LL BE LESS STUPID.
YOU KNOW WHAT, PIG? I LIKE YOU. YOU SHOULD BE CAREFUL THOUGH, A LOT CAN HAPPEN TO A MAN IN THIS CITY.
YOU MEAN WHEN HE STICKS HIS NOSE TOO FAR INTO RUSSIAN BUSINESS? HM, WELL YOU ARE RIGHT ON THE MONEY WITH THAT ONE. BUT YOU KNOW THAT BETTER THAN ME.
YOU'VE ACTUALLY HELPED ME A LOT.
DASVIDANIYA, GENTLEMEN.
I made my way through other bars with my questionnaire.

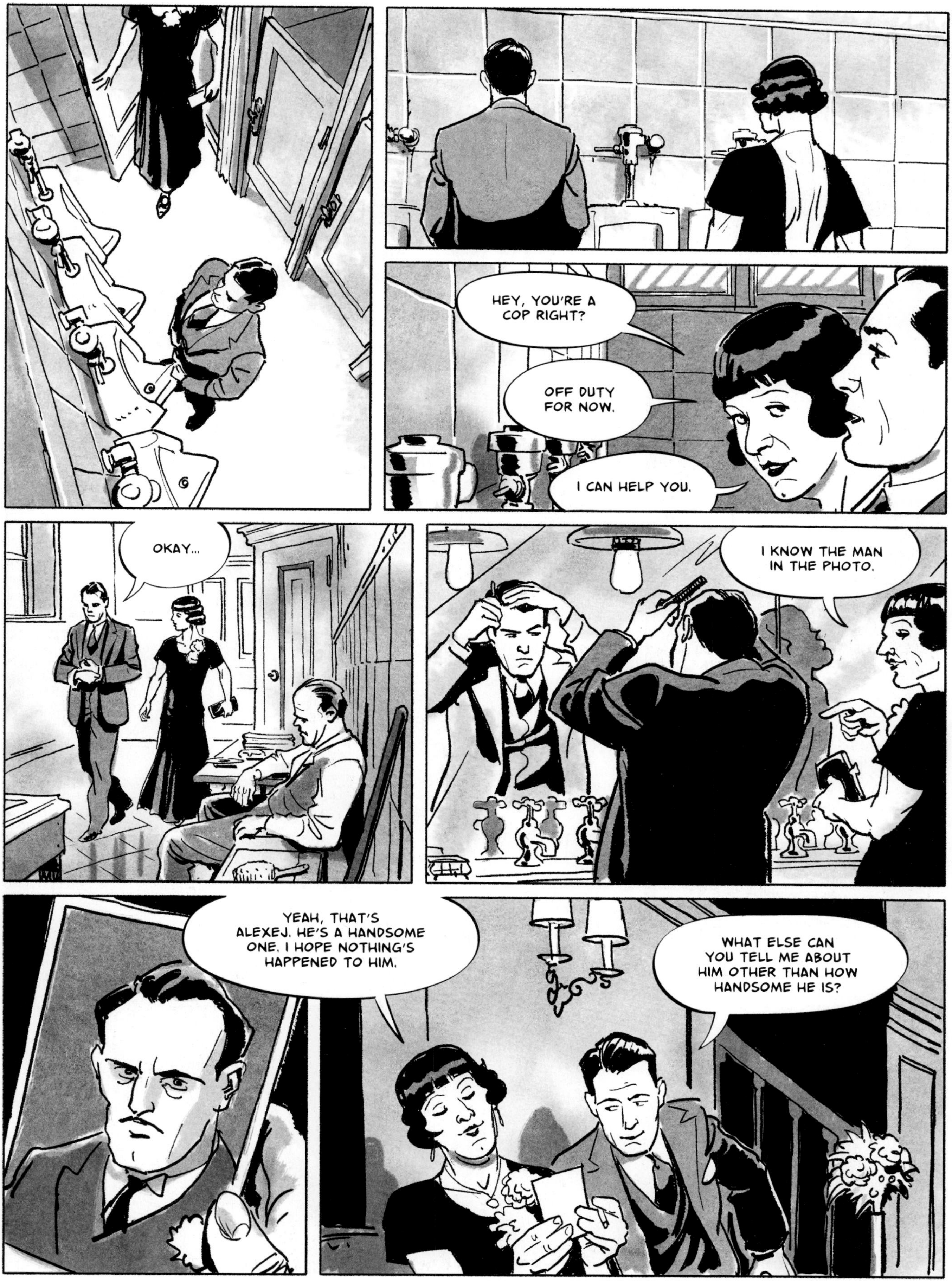
HEY, YOU'RE A COP RIGHT?
OFF DUTY FOR NOW.
I CAN HELP YOU.
OKAY...
I KNOW THE MAN IN THE PHOTO.
YEAH, THAT'S ALEXEJ. HE'S A HANDSOME ONE. I HOPE NOTHING'S HAPPENED TO HIM.
WHAT ELSE CAN YOU TELL ME ABOUT HIM OTHER THAN HOW HANDSOME HE IS?

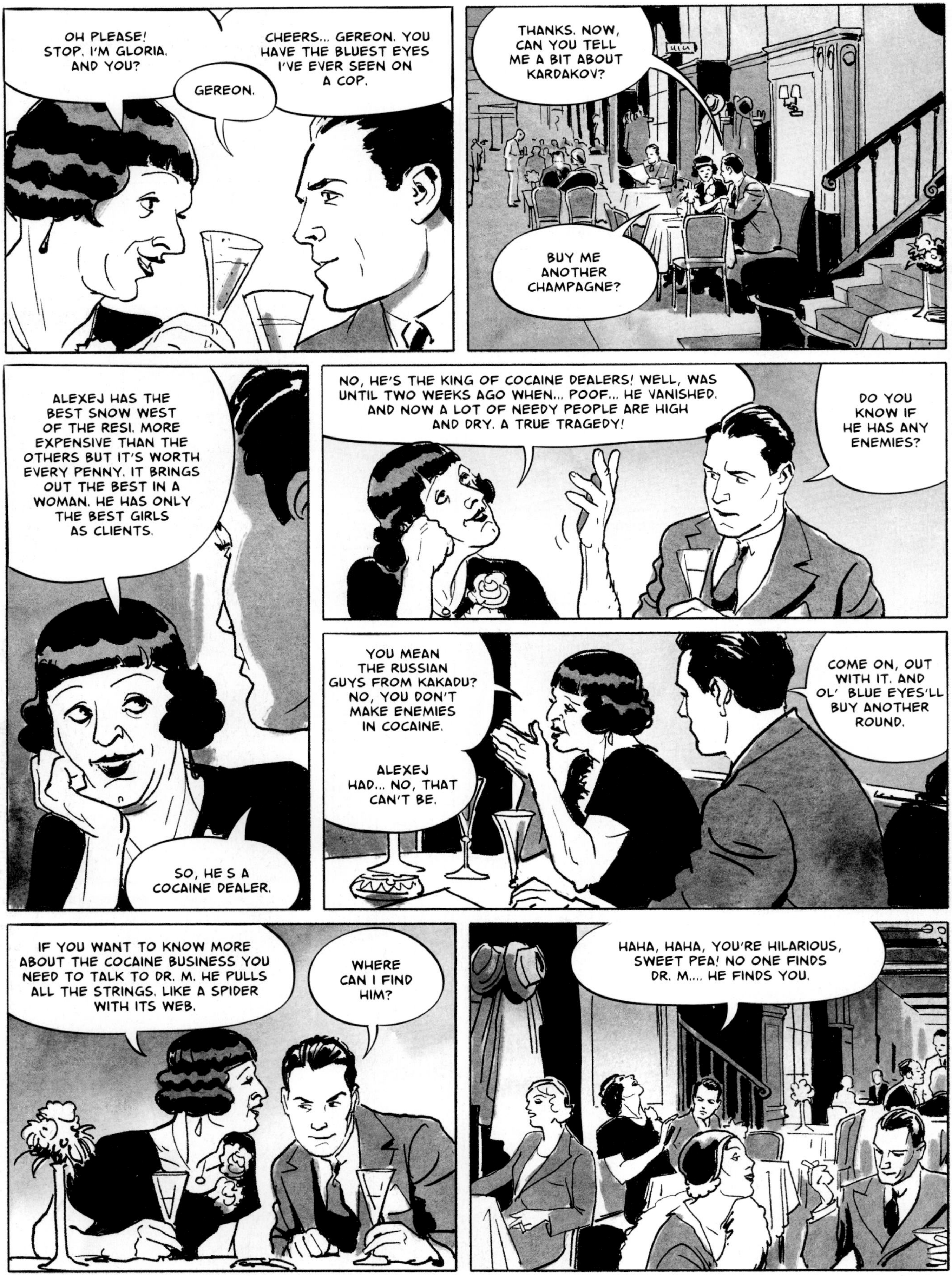

OH PLEASE! STOP. I'M GLORIA. AND YOU?
GEREON.
CHEERS... GEREON. YOU HAVE THE BLUEST EYES I'VE EVER SEEN ON A COP.
THANKS. NOW, CAN YOU TELL ME A BIT ABOUT KARDAKOV?
BUY ME ANOTHER CHAMPAGNE?
ALEXEJ HAS THE BEST SNOW WEST OF THE RESI. MORE EXPENSIVE THAN THE OTHERS BUT IT'S WORTH EVERY PENNY. IT BRINGS OUT THE BEST IN A WOMAN. HE HAS ONLY THE BEST GIRLS AS CLIENTS.
SO, HE S A COCAINE DEALER.
NO, HE'S THE KING OF COCAINE DEALERS! WELL, WAS UNTIL TWO WEEKS AGO WHEN... POOF... HE VANISHED. AND NOW A LOT OF NEEDY PEOPLE ARE HIGH AND DRY. A TRUE TRAGEDY!
DO YOU KNOW IF HE HAS ANY ENEMIES?
YOU MEAN THE RUSSIAN GUYS FROM KAKADU? NO, YOU DON'T MAKE ENEMIES IN COCAINE.
ALEXEJ HAD... NO, THAT CAN'T BE.
COME ON, OUT WITH IT. AND OL' BLUE EYES'LL BUY ANOTHER ROUND.
IF YOU WANT TO KNOW MORE ABOUT THE COCAINE BUSINESS YOU NEED TO TALK TO DR. M. HE PULLS ALL THE STRINGS. LIKE A SPIDER WITH ITS WEB.
WHERE CAN I FIND HIM?
HAHA, HAHA, YOU'RE HILARIOUS, SWEET PEA! NO ONE FINDS DR. M.... HE FINDS YOU.

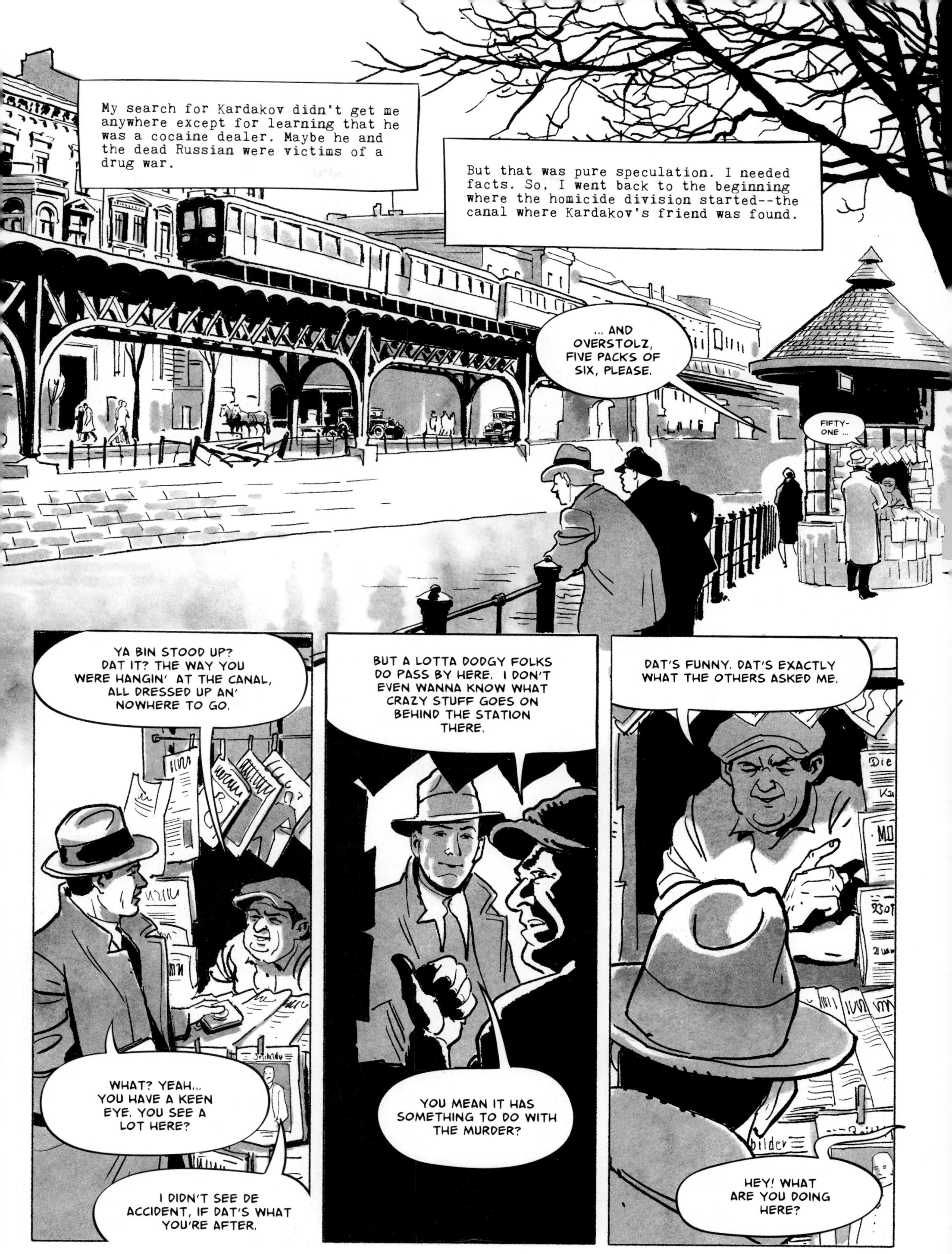
My search for Kardakov didn't get me anywhere except for learning that he was a cocaine dealer. Maybe he and the dead Russian were victims of a drug war.
But that was pure speculation. I needed facts. So, I went back to the beginning where the homicide division started--the canal where Kardakov's friend was found.
... AND OVERSTOLZ, FIVE PACKS OF SIX, PLEASE.
FIFTY-ONE ...
YA BIN STOOD UP? DAT IT? THE WAY YOU WERE HANGIN' AT THE CANAL, ALL DRESSED UP AN' NOWHERE TO GO.
WHAT? YEAH... YOU HAVE A KEEN EYE. YOU SEE A LOT HERE?
I DIDN'T SEE DE ACCIDENT, IF DAT'S WHAT YOU'RE AFTER.
BUT A LOTTA DODGY FOLKS DO PASS BY HERE. I DON'T EVEN WANNA KNOW WHAT CRAZY STUFF GOES ON BEHIND THE STATION THERE.
YOU MEAN IT HAS SOMETHING TO DO WITH THE MURDER?
DAT'S FUNNY. DAT'S EXACTLY WHAT THE OTHERS ASKED ME.
HEY! WHAT ARE YOU DOING HERE?

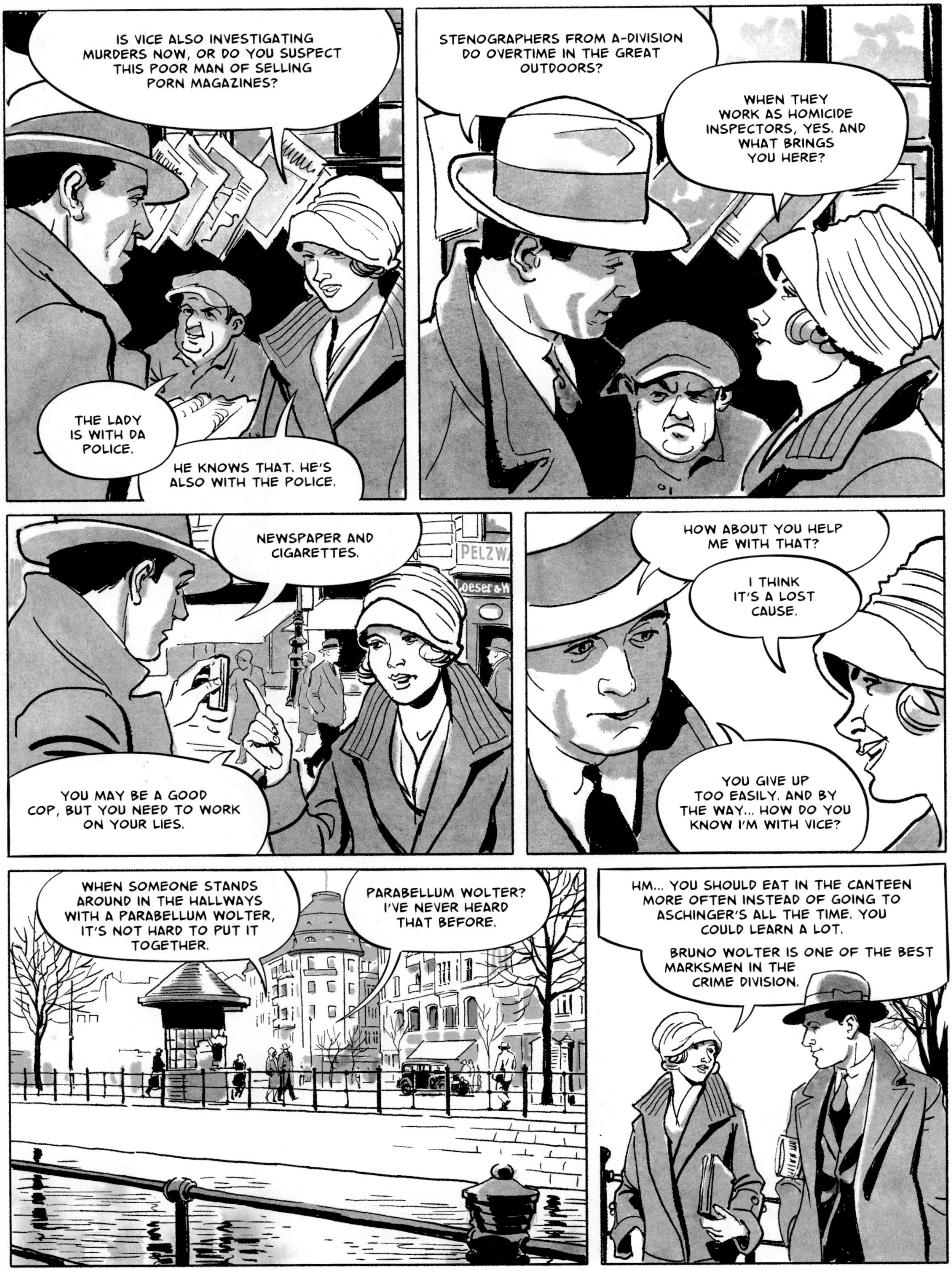
IS VICE ALSO INVESTIGATING MURDERS NOW, OR DO YOU SUSPECT THIS POOR MAN OF SELLING PORN MAGAZINES?
THE LADY IS WITH DA POLICE.
HE KNOWS THAT. HE'S ALSO WITH THE POLICE.
STENOGRAPHERS FROM A-DIVISION DO OVERTIME IN THE GREAT OUTDOORS?
WHEN THEY WORK AS HOMICIDE INSPECTORS, YES. AND WHAT BRINGS YOU HERE?
NEWSPAPER AND CIGARETTES.
PELZW
Loeser & W
YOU MAY BE A GOOD COP, BUT YOU NEED TO WORK ON YOUR LIES.
HOW ABOUT YOU HELP ME WITH THAT?
I THINK IT'S A LOST CAUSE.
YOU GIVE UP TOO EASILY. AND BY THE WAY... HOW DO YOU KNOW I'M WITH VICE?
WHEN SOMEONE STANDS AROUND IN THE HALLWAYS WITH A PARABELLUM WOLTER, IT'S NOT HARD TO PUT IT TOGETHER.
PARABELLUM WOLTER? I'VE NEVER HEARD THAT BEFORE.
HM... YOU SHOULD EAT IN THE CANTEEN MORE OFTEN INSTEAD OF GOING TO ASCHINGER'S ALL THE TIME. YOU COULD LEARN A LOT.
BRUNO WOLTER IS ONE OF THE BEST MARKSMEN IN THE CRIME DIVISION.

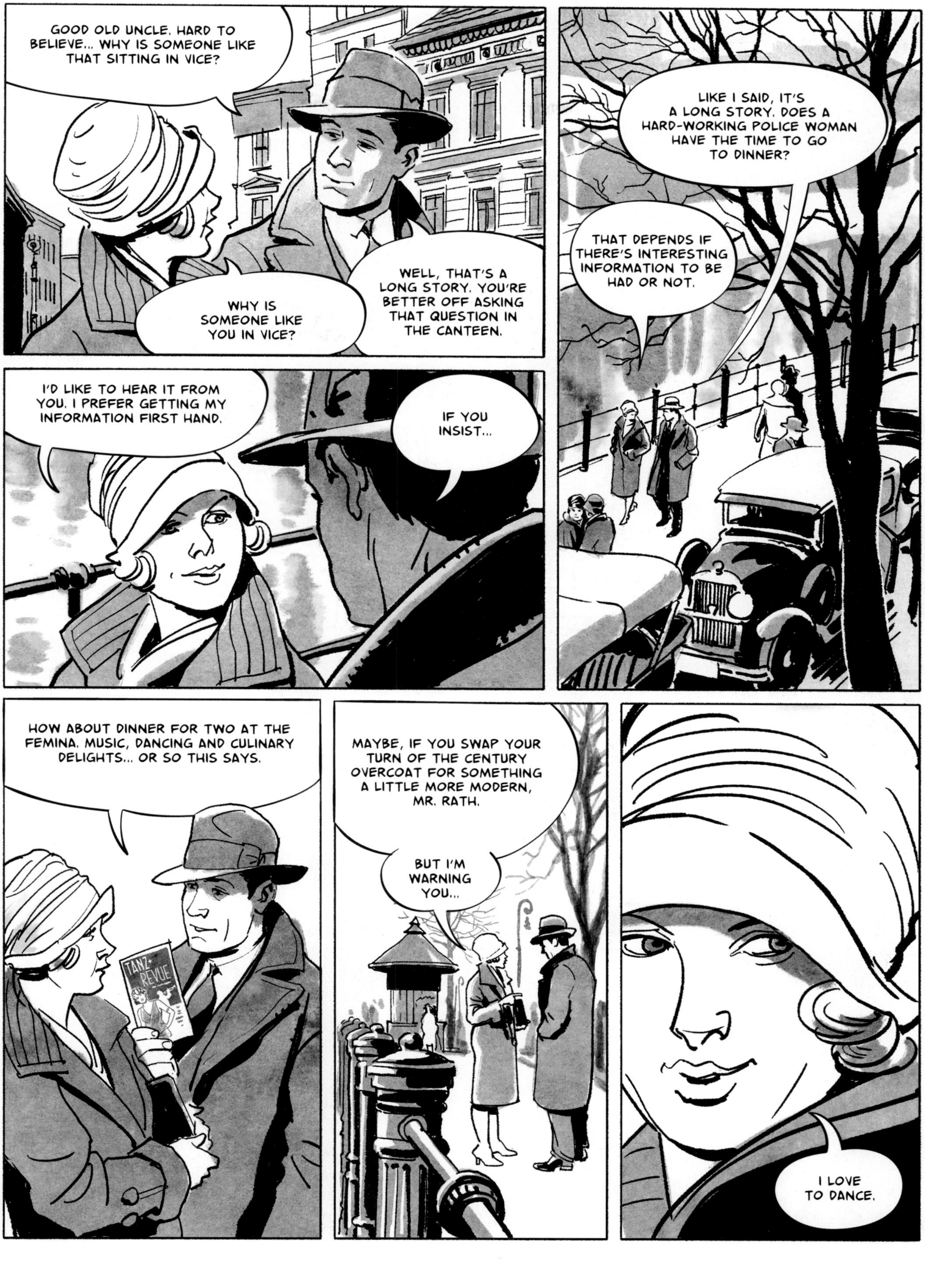
GOOD OLD UNCLE. HARD TO BELIEVE... WHY IS SOMEONE LIKE THAT SITTING IN VICE?
WHY IS SOMEONE LIKE YOU IN VICE?
WELL, THAT'S A LONG STORY. YOU'RE BETTER OFF ASKING THAT QUESTION IN THE CANTEEN.
LIKE I SAID, IT'S A LONG STORY. DOES A HARD-WORKING POLICE WOMAN HAVE THE TIME TO GO TO DINNER?
THAT DEPENDS IF THERE'S INTERESTING INFORMATION TO BE HAD OR NOT.
I'D LIKE TO HEAR IT FROM YOU. I PREFER GETTING MY INFORMATION FIRST HAND.
IF YOU INSIST...
HOW ABOUT DINNER FOR TWO AT THE FEMINA. MUSIC, DANCING AND CULINARY DELIGHTS... OR SO THIS SAYS.
TANZ-REVUE
MAYBE, IF YOU SWAP YOUR TURN OF THE CENTURY OVERCOAT FOR SOMETHING A LITTLE MORE MODERN, MR. RATH.
BUT I'M WARNING YOU...
I LOVE TO DANCE.

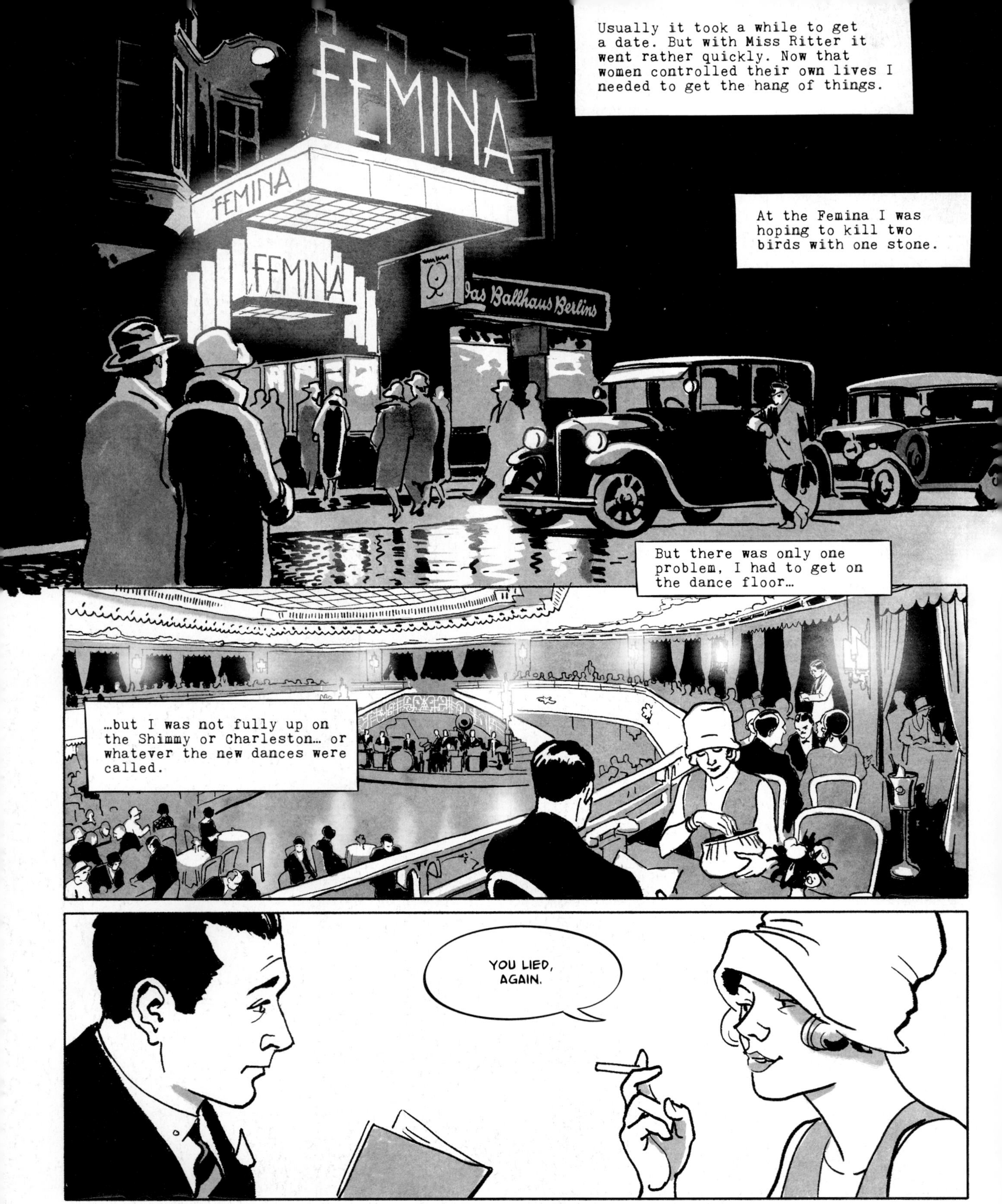
Usually it took a while to get a date. But with Miss Ritter it went rather quickly. Now that women controlled their own lives I needed to get the hang of things.
FEMINA
FEMINA
FEMINA
Das Ballhaus Berlins
At the Femina I was hoping to kill two birds with one stone.
But there was only one problem, I had to get on the dance floor…
…but I was not fully up on the Shimmy or Charleston… or whatever the new dances were called.
YOU LIED, AGAIN.

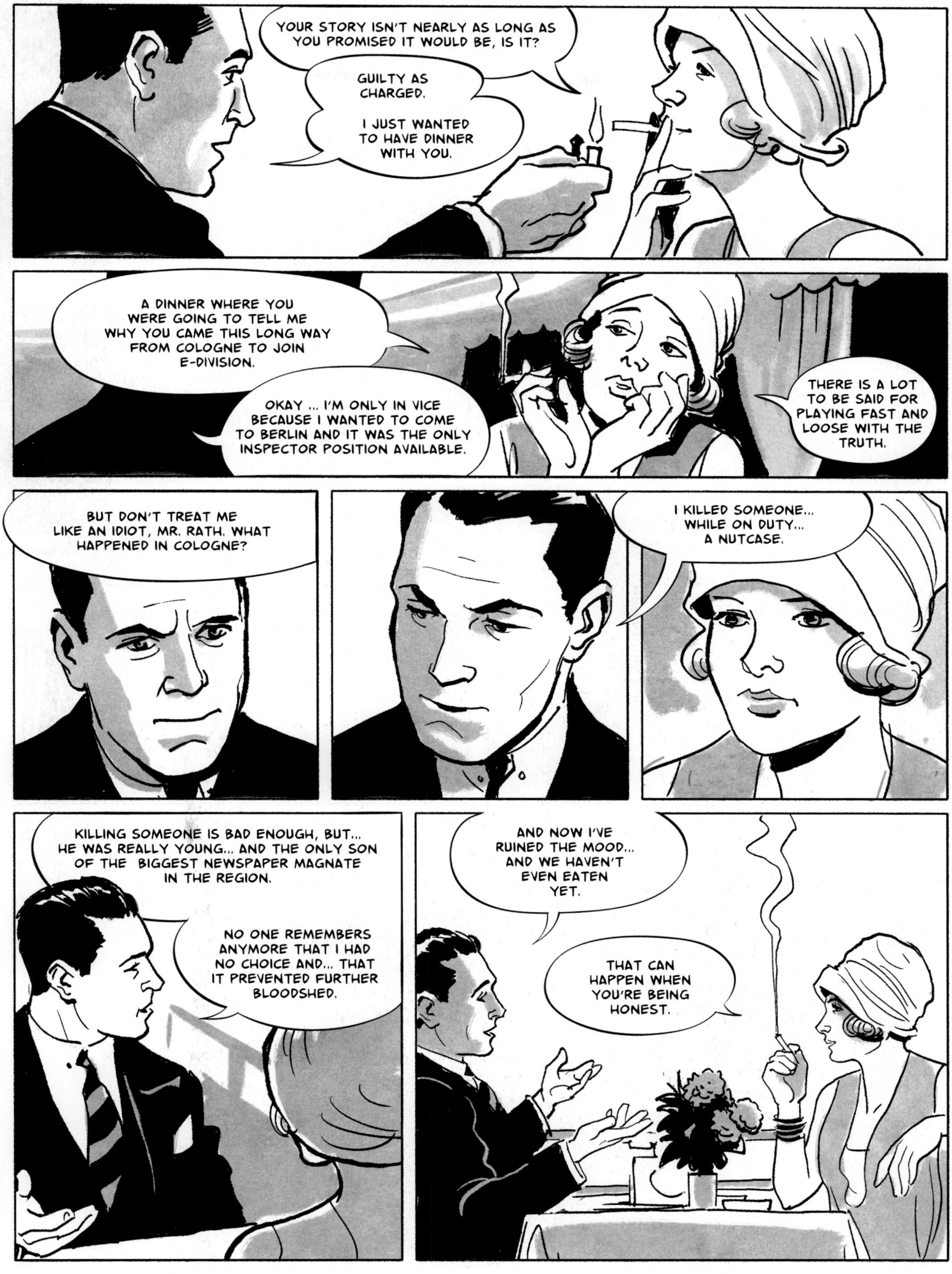
YOUR STORY ISN'T NEARLY AS LONG AS YOU PROMISED IT WOULD BE, IS IT?
GUILTY AS CHARGED.
I JUST WANTED TO HAVE DINNER WITH YOU.
A DINNER WHERE YOU WERE GOING TO TELL ME WHY YOU CAME THIS LONG WAY FROM COLOGNE TO JOIN E-DIVISION.
OKAY ... I'M ONLY IN VICE BECAUSE I WANTED TO COME TO BERLIN AND IT WAS THE ONLY INSPECTOR POSITION AVAILABLE.
THERE IS A LOT TO BE SAID FOR PLAYING FAST AND LOOSE WITH THE TRUTH.
BUT DON'T TREAT ME LIKE AN IDIOT, MR. RATH. WHAT HAPPENED IN COLOGNE?
I KILLED SOMEONE... WHILE ON DUTY... A NUTCASE.
KILLING SOMEONE IS BAD ENOUGH, BUT... HE WAS REALLY YOUNG... AND THE ONLY SON OF THE BIGGEST NEWSPAPER MAGNATE IN THE REGION.
NO ONE REMEMBERS ANYMORE THAT I HAD NO CHOICE AND... THAT IT PREVENTED FURTHER BLOODSHED.
AND NOW I'VE RUINED THE MOOD... AND WE HAVEN'T EVEN EATEN YET.
THAT CAN HAPPEN WHEN YOU'RE BEING HONEST.

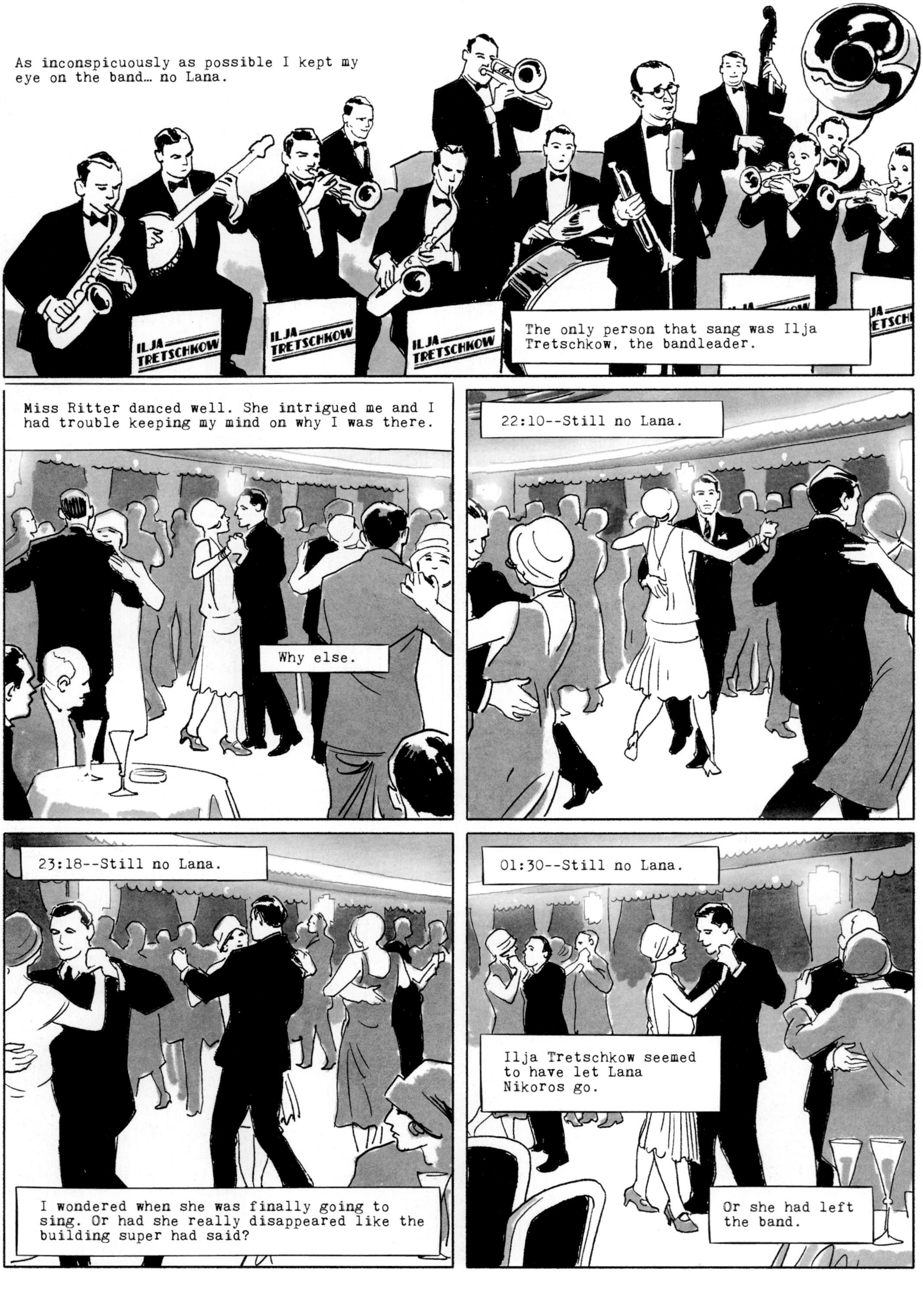
As inconspicuously as possible I kept my eye on the band… no Lana.
ILJA TRETSCHKOW
ILJA TRETSCHKOW
ILJA TRETSCHKOW
The only person that sang was Ilja Tretschkow, the bandleader.
Miss Ritter danced well. She intrigued me and I had trouble keeping my mind on why I was there.
Why else.
22:10--Still no Lana.
23:18--Still no Lana.
I wondered when she was finally going to sing. Or had she really disappeared like the building super had said?
01:30--Still no Lana.
Ilja Tretschkow seemed to have let Lana Nikoros go.
Or she had left the band.

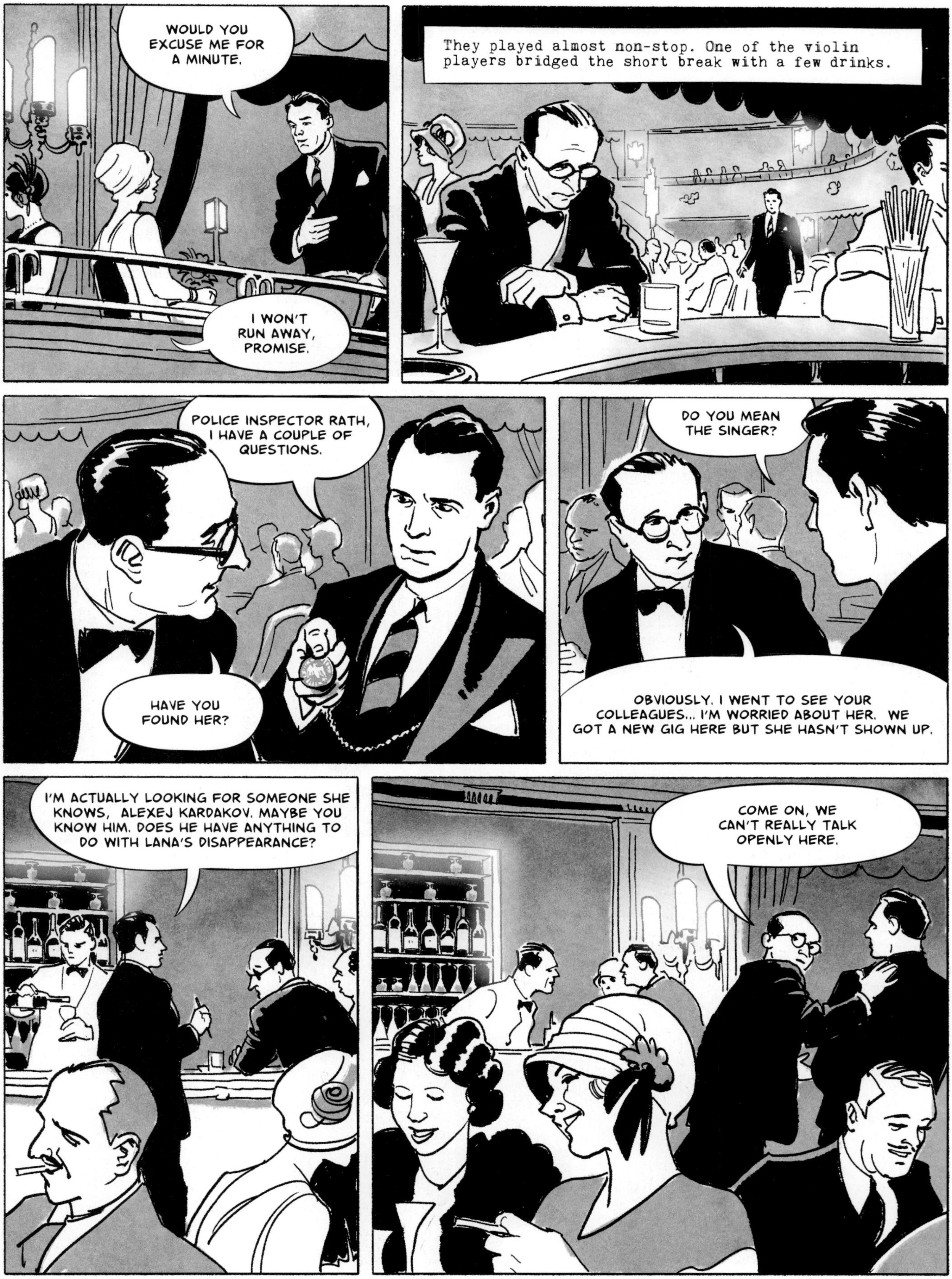
WOULD YOU EXCUSE ME FOR A MINUTE.
I WON'T RUN AWAY, PROMISE.
They played almost non-stop. One of the violin players bridged the short break with a few drinks.
POLICE INSPECTOR RATH, I HAVE A COUPLE OF QUESTIONS.
HAVE YOU FOUND HER?
DO YOU MEAN THE SINGER?
OBVIOUSLY. I WENT TO SEE YOUR COLLEAGUES... I'M WORRIED ABOUT HER. WE GOT A NEW GIG HERE BUT SHE HASN'T SHOWN UP.
I'M ACTUALLY LOOKING FOR SOMEONE SHE KNOWS, ALEXEJ KARDAKOV. MAYBE YOU KNOW HIM. DOES HE HAVE ANYTHING TO DO WITH LANA'S DISAPPEARANCE?
COME ON, WE CAN'T REALLY TALK OPENLY HERE.

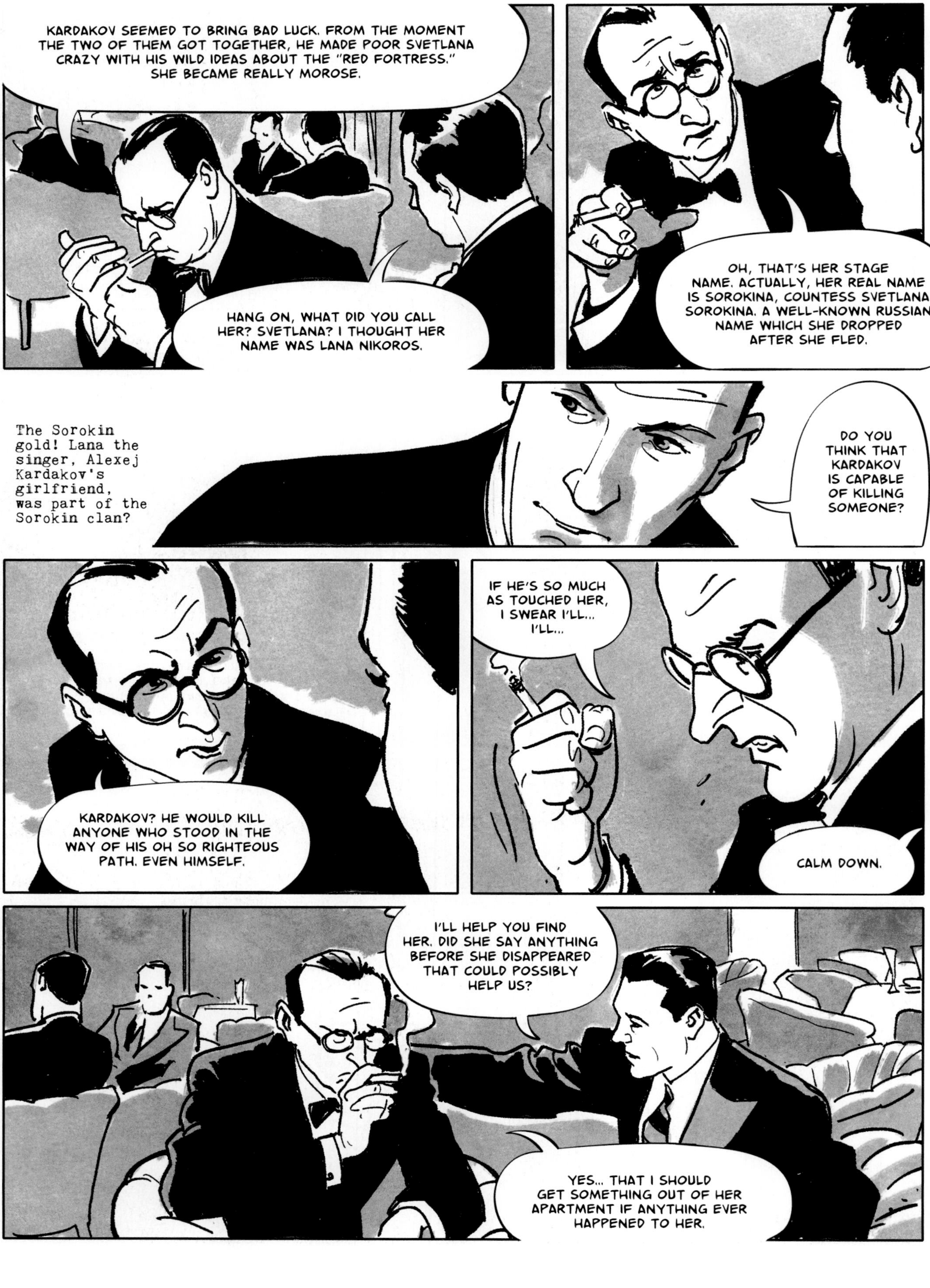
KARDAKOV SEEMED TO BRING BAD LUCK. FROM THE MOMENT THE TWO OF THEM GOT TOGETHER, HE MADE POOR SVETLANA CRAZY WITH HIS WILD IDEAS ABOUT THE "RED FORTRESS." SHE BECAME REALLY MOROSE.
HANG ON, WHAT DID YOU CALL HER? SVETLANA? I THOUGHT HER NAME WAS LANA NIKOROS.
OH, THAT'S HER STAGE NAME. ACTUALLY, HER REAL NAME IS SOROKINA, COUNTESS SVETLANA SOROKINA. A WELL-KNOWN RUSSIAN NAME WHICH SHE DROPPED AFTER SHE FLED.
The Sorokin gold! Lana the singer, Alexej Kardakov's girlfriend, was part of the Sorokin clan?
DO YOU THINK THAT KARDAKOV IS CAPABLE OF KILLING SOMEONE?
KARDAKOV? HE WOULD KILL ANYONE WHO STOOD IN THE WAY OF HIS OH SO RIGHTEOUS PATH. EVEN HIMSELF.
IF HE'S SO MUCH AS TOUCHED HER, I SWEAR I'LL... I'LL...
CALM DOWN.
I'LL HELP YOU FIND HER. DID SHE SAY ANYTHING BEFORE SHE DISAPPEARED THAT COULD POSSIBLY HELP US?
YES... THAT I SHOULD GET SOMETHING OUT OF HER APARTMENT IF ANYTHING EVER HAPPENED TO HER.

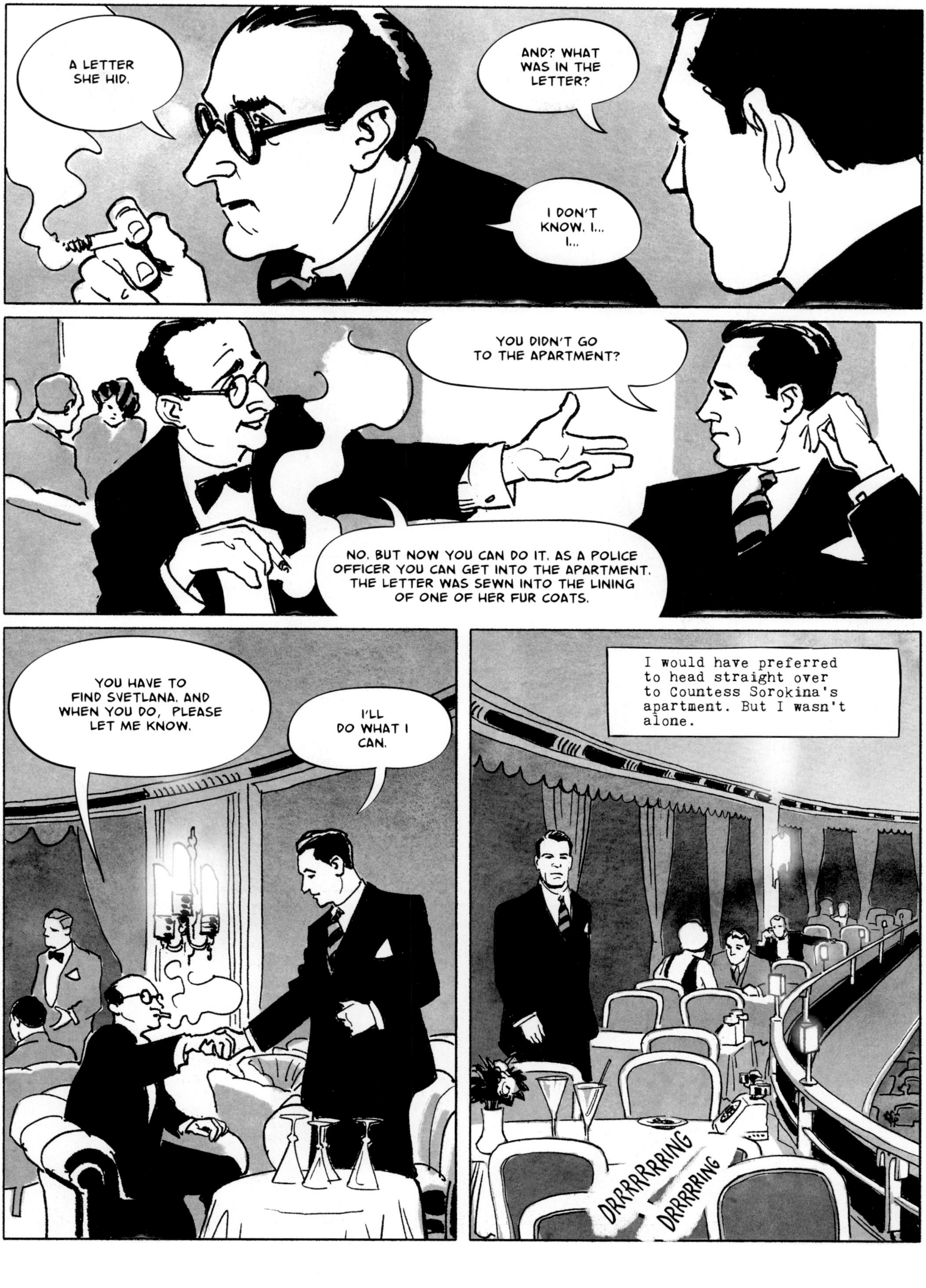

A LETTER SHE HID.
AND? WHAT WAS IN THE LETTER?
I DON'T KNOW. I... I...
YOU DIDN'T GO TO THE APARTMENT?
NO. BUT NOW YOU CAN DO IT. AS A POLICE OFFICER YOU CAN GET INTO THE APARTMENT. THE LETTER WAS SEWN INTO THE LINING OF ONE OF HER FUR COATS.
YOU HAVE TO FIND SVETLANA. AND WHEN YOU DO, PLEASE LET ME KNOW.
I'LL DO WHAT I CAN.
I would have preferred to head straight over to Countess Sorokina's apartment. But I wasn't alone.
DRRRRRRRING
DRRRRRING

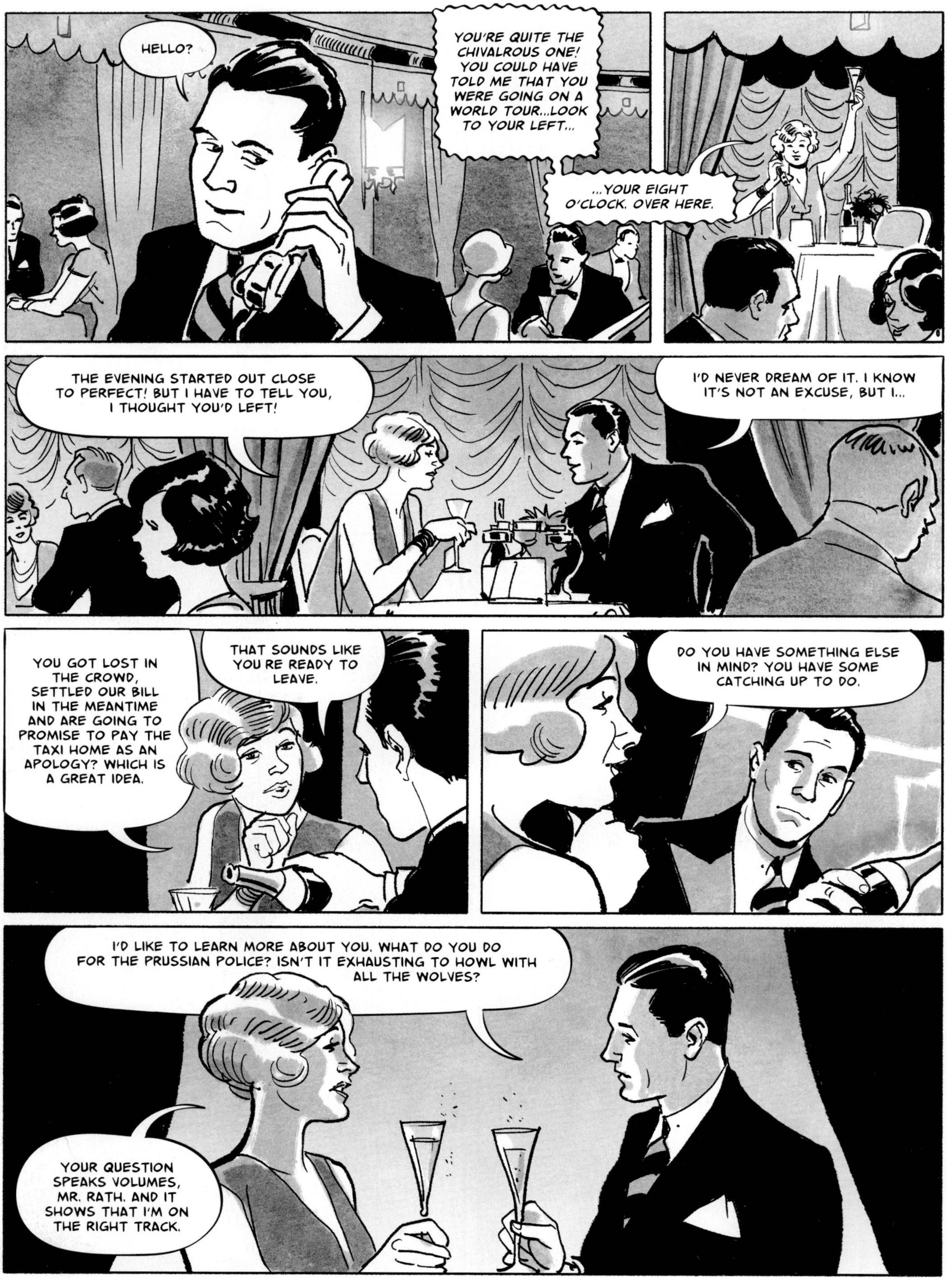
HELLO?
YOU'RE QUITE THE CHIVALROUS ONE! YOU COULD HAVE TOLD ME THAT YOU WERE GOING ON A WORLD TOUR...LOOK TO YOUR LEFT...
...YOUR EIGHT O'CLOCK. OVER HERE.
THE EVENING STARTED OUT CLOSE TO PERFECT! BUT I HAVE TO TELL YOU, I THOUGHT YOU'D LEFT!
I'D NEVER DREAM OF IT. I KNOW IT'S NOT AN EXCUSE, BUT I...
YOU GOT LOST IN THE CROWD, SETTLED OUR BILL IN THE MEANTIME AND ARE GOING TO PROMISE TO PAY THE TAXI HOME AS AN APOLOGY? WHICH IS A GREAT IDEA.
THAT SOUNDS LIKE YOU'RE READY TO LEAVE.
DO YOU HAVE SOMETHING ELSE IN MIND? YOU HAVE SOME CATCHING UP TO DO.
I'D LIKE TO LEARN MORE ABOUT YOU. WHAT DO YOU DO FOR THE PRUSSIAN POLICE? ISN'T IT EXHAUSTING TO HOWL WITH ALL THE WOLVES?
YOUR QUESTION SPEAKS VOLUMES, MR. RATH. AND IT SHOWS THAT I'M ON THE RIGHT TRACK.

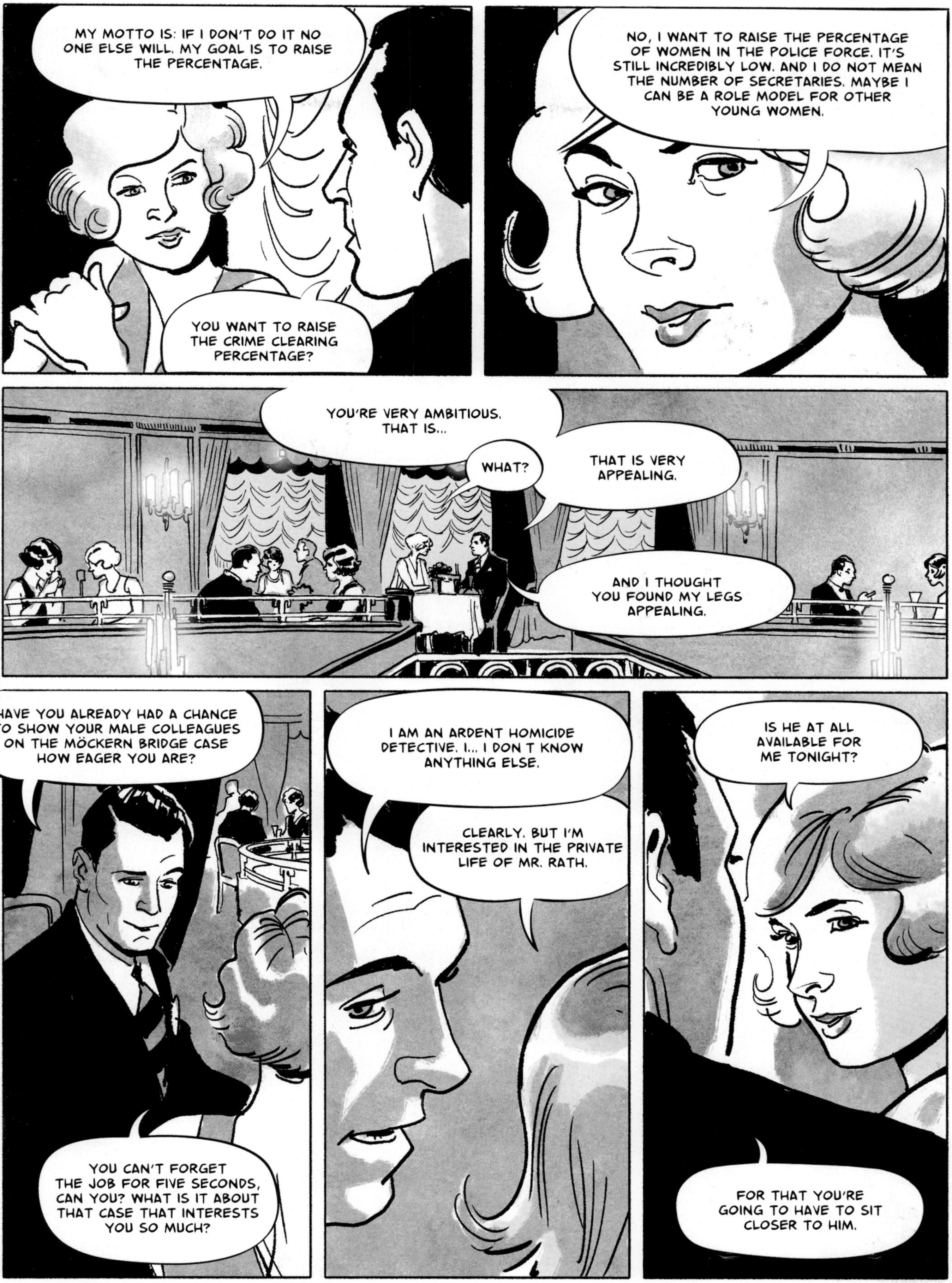

MY MOTTO IS: IF I DON'T DO IT NO ONE ELSE WILL. MY GOAL IS TO RAISE THE PERCENTAGE.
YOU WANT TO RAISE THE CRIME CLEARING PERCENTAGE?
NO, I WANT TO RAISE THE PERCENTAGE OF WOMEN IN THE POLICE FORCE. IT'S STILL INCREDIBLY LOW. AND I DO NOT MEAN THE NUMBER OF SECRETARIES. MAYBE I CAN BE A ROLE MODEL FOR OTHER YOUNG WOMEN.
YOU'RE VERY AMBITIOUS. THAT IS...
WHAT?
THAT IS VERY APPEALING.
AND I THOUGHT YOU FOUND MY LEGS APPEALING.
HAVE YOU ALREADY HAD A CHANCE TO SHOW YOUR MALE COLLEAGUES ON THE MÖCKERN BRIDGE CASE HOW EAGER YOU ARE?
YOU CAN'T FORGET THE JOB FOR FIVE SECONDS, CAN YOU? WHAT IS IT ABOUT THAT CASE THAT INTERESTS YOU SO MUCH?
I AM AN ARDENT HOMICIDE DETECTIVE. I... I DON T KNOW ANYTHING ELSE.
CLEARLY. BUT I'M INTERESTED IN THE PRIVATE LIFE OF MR. RATH.
IS HE AT ALL AVAILABLE FOR ME TONIGHT?
FOR THAT YOU'RE GOING TO HAVE TO SIT CLOSER TO HIM.

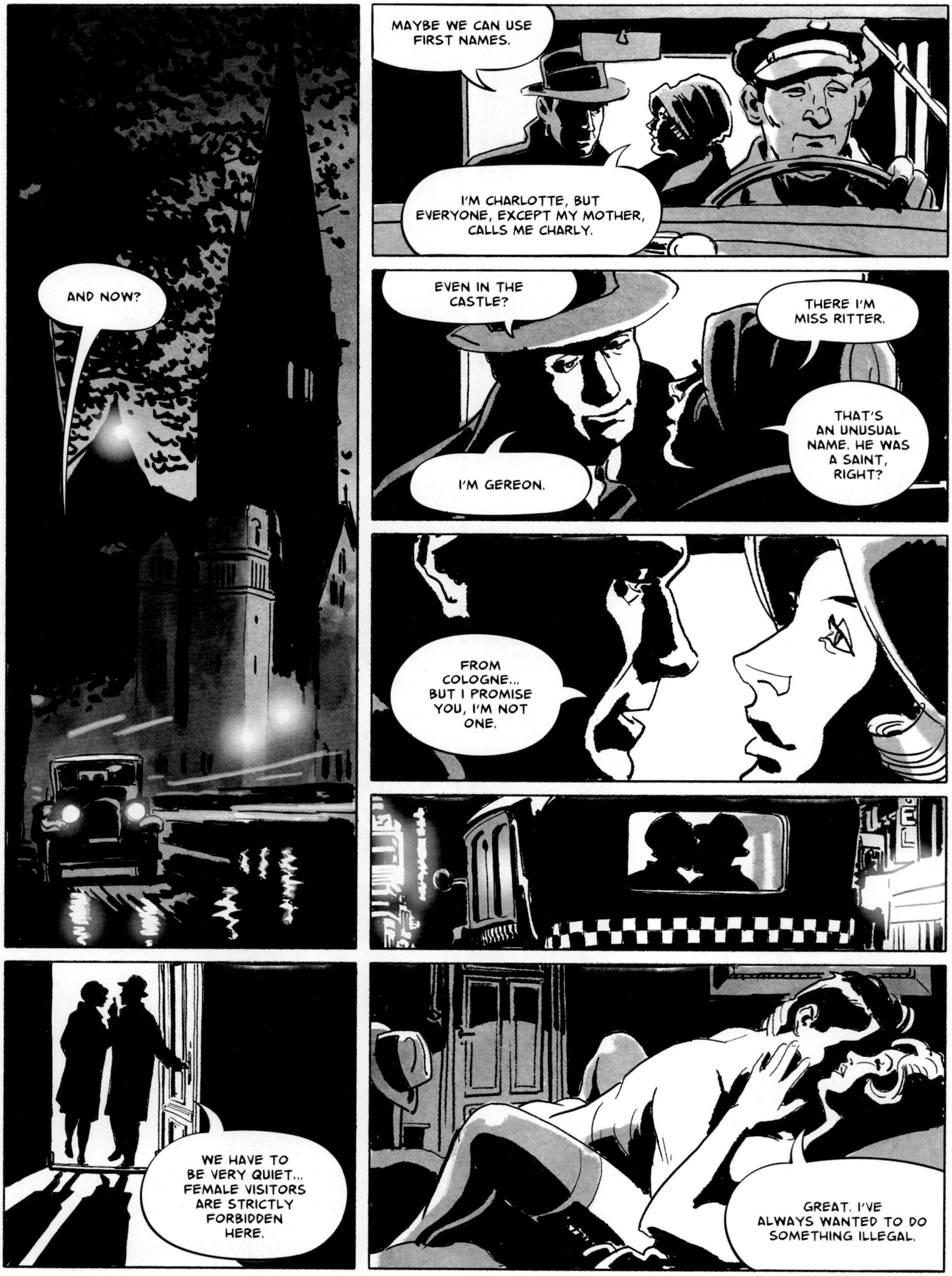
AND NOW?
MAYBE WE CAN USE FIRST NAMES.
I'M CHARLOTTE, BUT EVERYONE, EXCEPT MY MOTHER, CALLS ME CHARLY.
EVEN IN THE CASTLE?
THERE I'M MISS RITTER.
I'M GEREON.
THAT'S AN UNUSUAL NAME. HE WAS A SAINT, RIGHT?
FROM COLOGNE... BUT I PROMISE YOU, I'M NOT ONE.
WE HAVE TO BE VERY QUIET... FEMALE VISITORS ARE STRICTLY FORBIDDEN HERE.
GREAT. I'VE ALWAYS WANTED TO DO SOMETHING ILLEGAL.

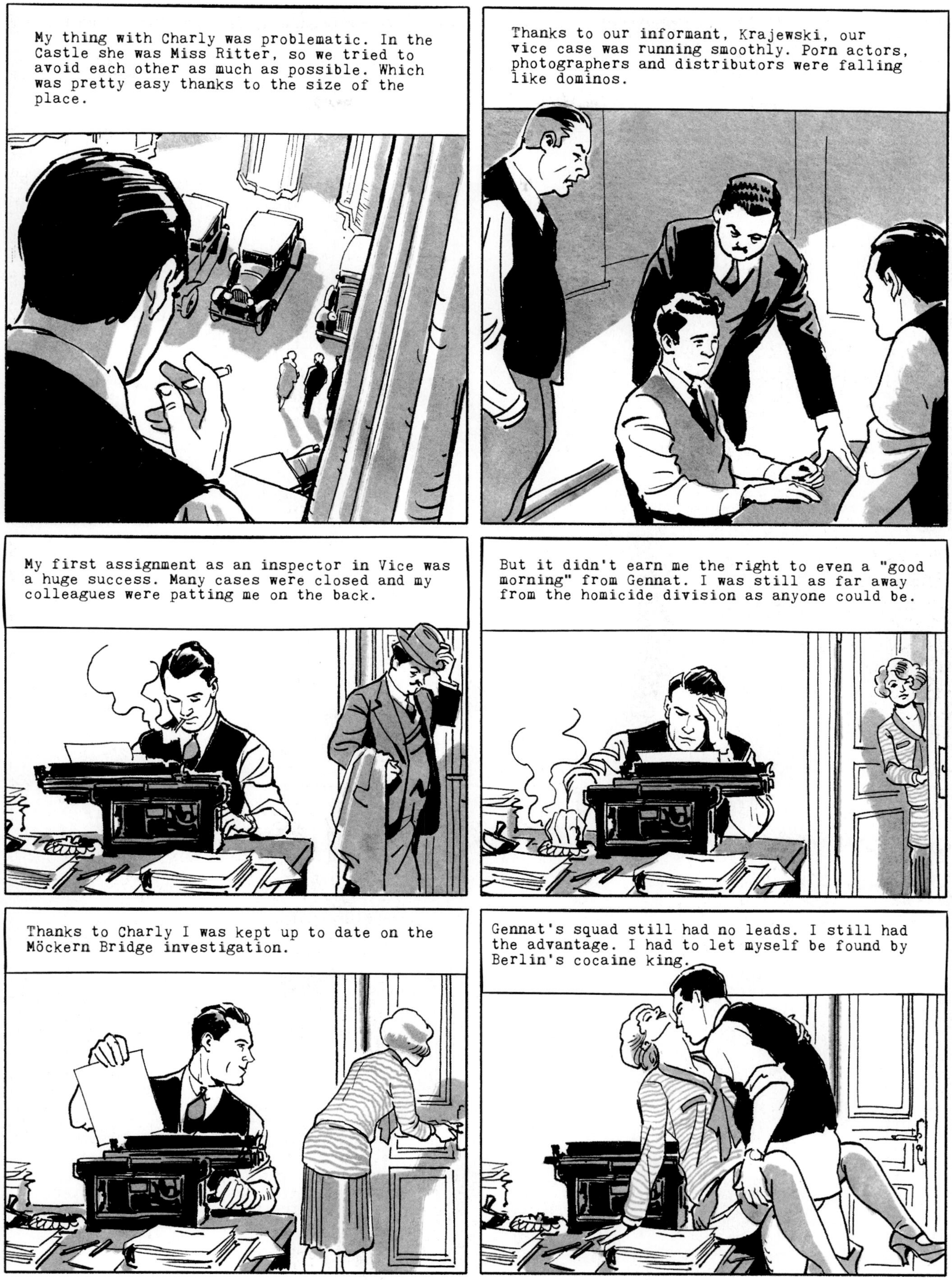
My thing with Charly was problematic. In the Castle she was Miss Ritter, so we tried to avoid each other as much as possible. Which was pretty easy thanks to the size of the place.
Thanks to our informant, Krajewski, our vice case was running smoothly. Porn actors, photographers and distributors were falling like dominos.
My first assignment as an inspector in Vice was a huge success. Many cases were closed and my colleagues were patting me on the back.
But it didn't earn me the right to even a "good morning" from Gennat. I was still as far away from the homicide division as anyone could be.
Thanks to Charly I was kept up to date on the Möckern Bridge investigation.
Gennat's squad still had no leads. I still had the advantage. I had to let myself be found by Berlin's cocaine king.

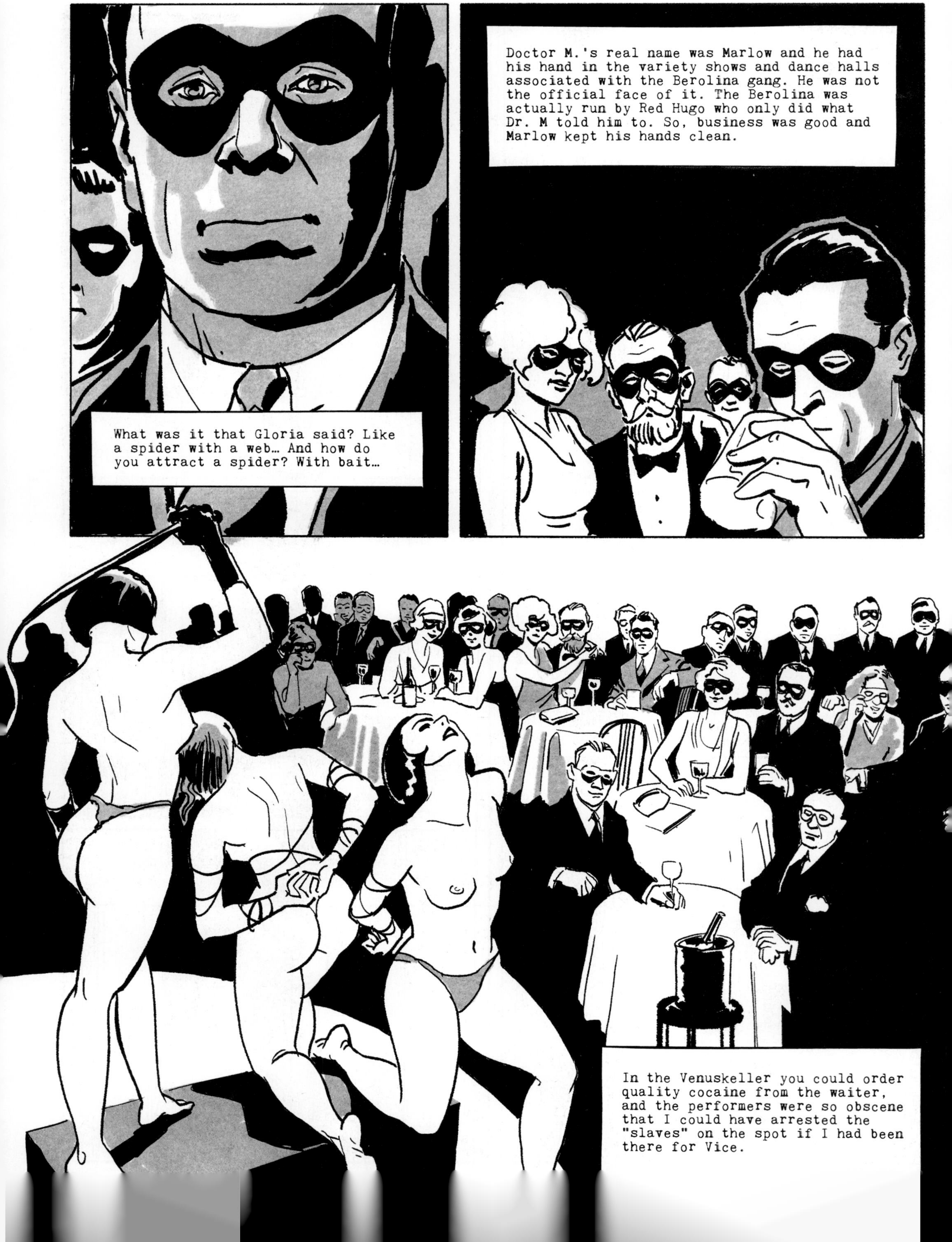
What was it that Gloria said? Like a spider with a web… And how do you attract a spider? With bait…
Doctor M.'s real name was Marlow and he had his hand in the variety shows and dance halls associated with the Berolina gang. He was not the official face of it. The Berolina was actually run by Red Hugo who only did what Dr. M told him to. So, business was good and Marlow kept his hands clean.
In the Venuskeller you could order quality cocaine from the waiter, and the performers were so obscene that I could have arrested the "slaves" on the spot if I had been there for Vice.

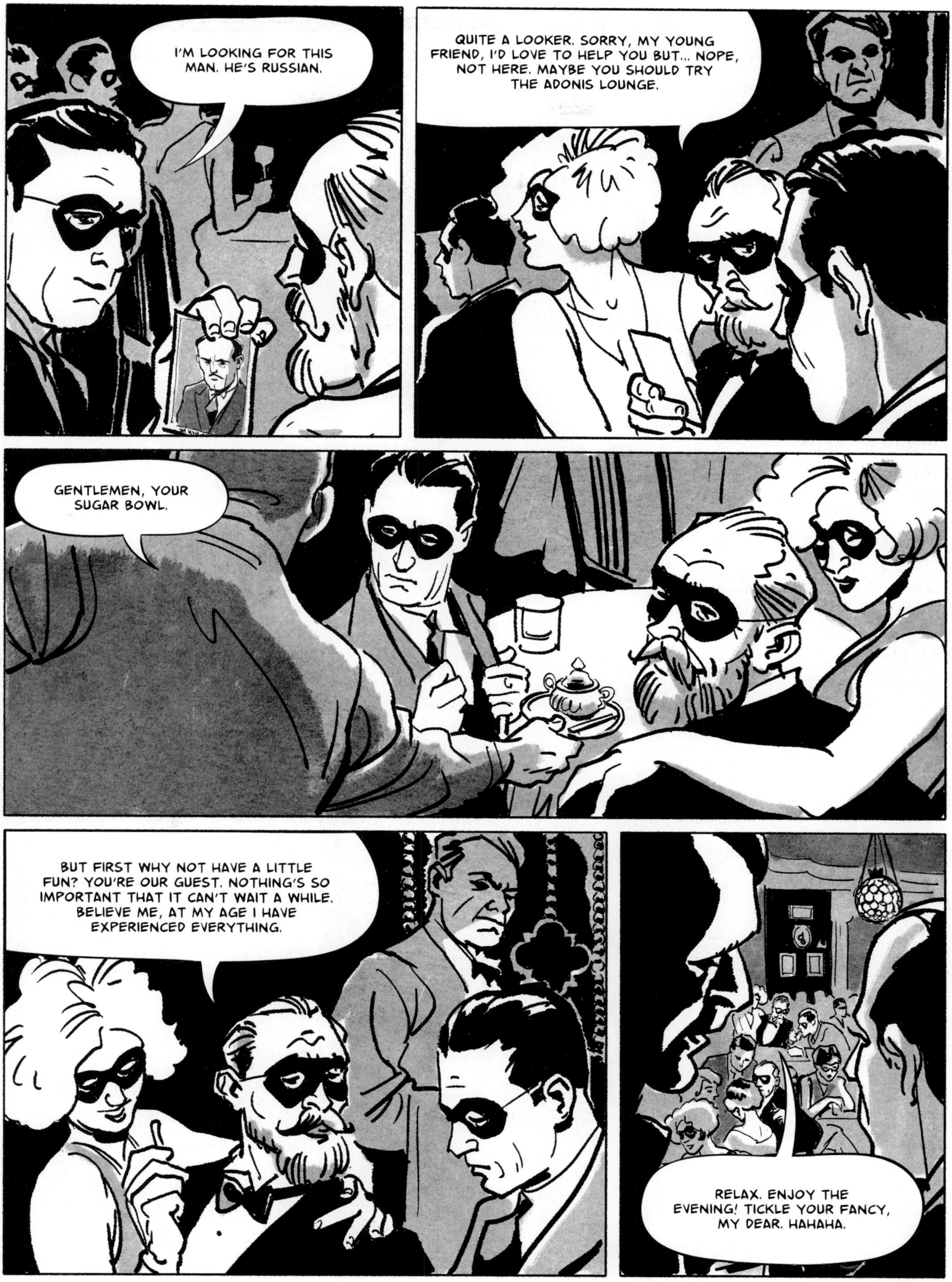
I'M LOOKING FOR THIS MAN. HE'S RUSSIAN.
QUITE A LOOKER. SORRY, MY YOUNG FRIEND, I'D LOVE TO HELP YOU BUT... NOPE, NOT HERE. MAYBE YOU SHOULD TRY THE ADONIS LOUNGE.
GENTLEMEN, YOUR SUGAR BOWL.
BUT FIRST WHY NOT HAVE A LITTLE FUN? YOU'RE OUR GUEST. NOTHING'S SO IMPORTANT THAT IT CAN'T WAIT A WHILE. BELIEVE ME, AT MY AGE I HAVE EXPERIENCED EVERYTHING.
RELAX. ENJOY THE EVENING! TICKLE YOUR FANCY, MY DEAR. HAHAHA.

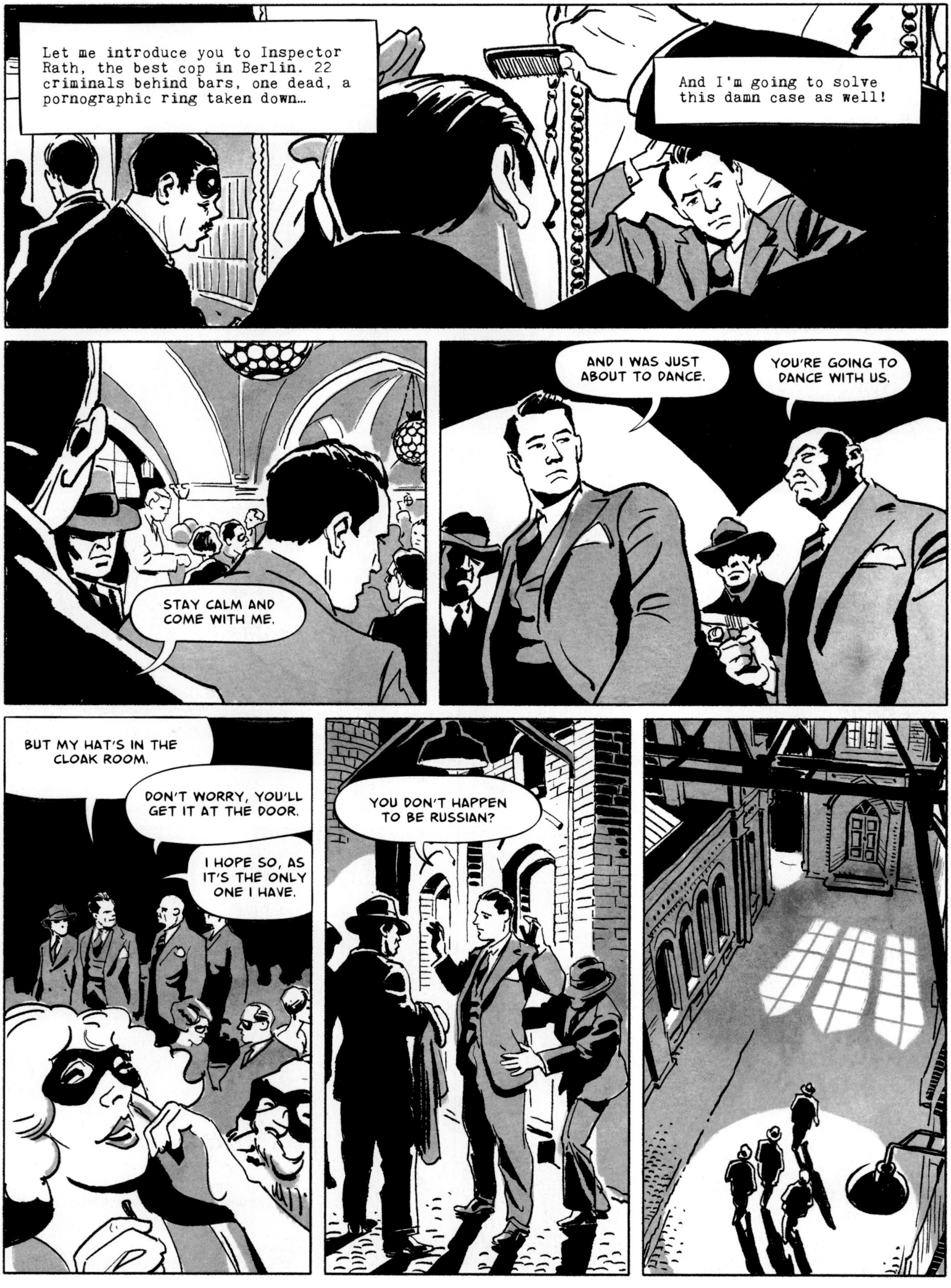
Let me introduce you to Inspector Rath, the best cop in Berlin. 22 criminals behind bars, one dead, a pornographic ring taken down…
And I'm going to solve this damn case as well!
STAY CALM AND COME WITH ME.
AND I WAS JUST ABOUT TO DANCE.
YOU'RE GOING TO DANCE WITH US.
BUT MY HAT'S IN THE CLOAK ROOM.
DON'T WORRY, YOU'LL GET IT AT THE DOOR.
I HOPE SO, AS IT'S THE ONLY ONE I HAVE.
YOU DON'T HAPPEN TO BE RUSSIAN?

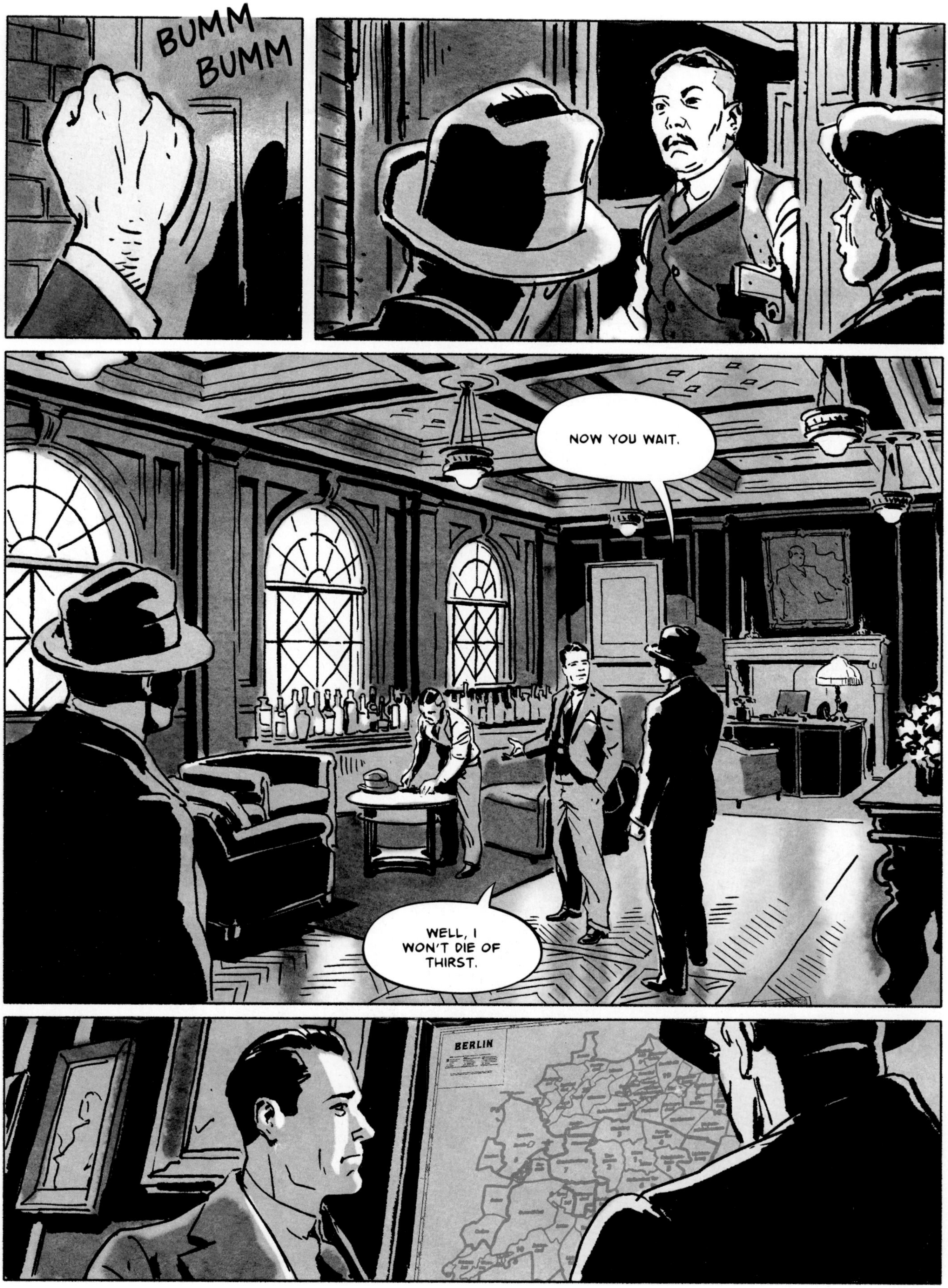
BUMM
BUMM
NOW YOU WAIT.
WELL, I WON'T DIE OF THIRST.
BERLIN

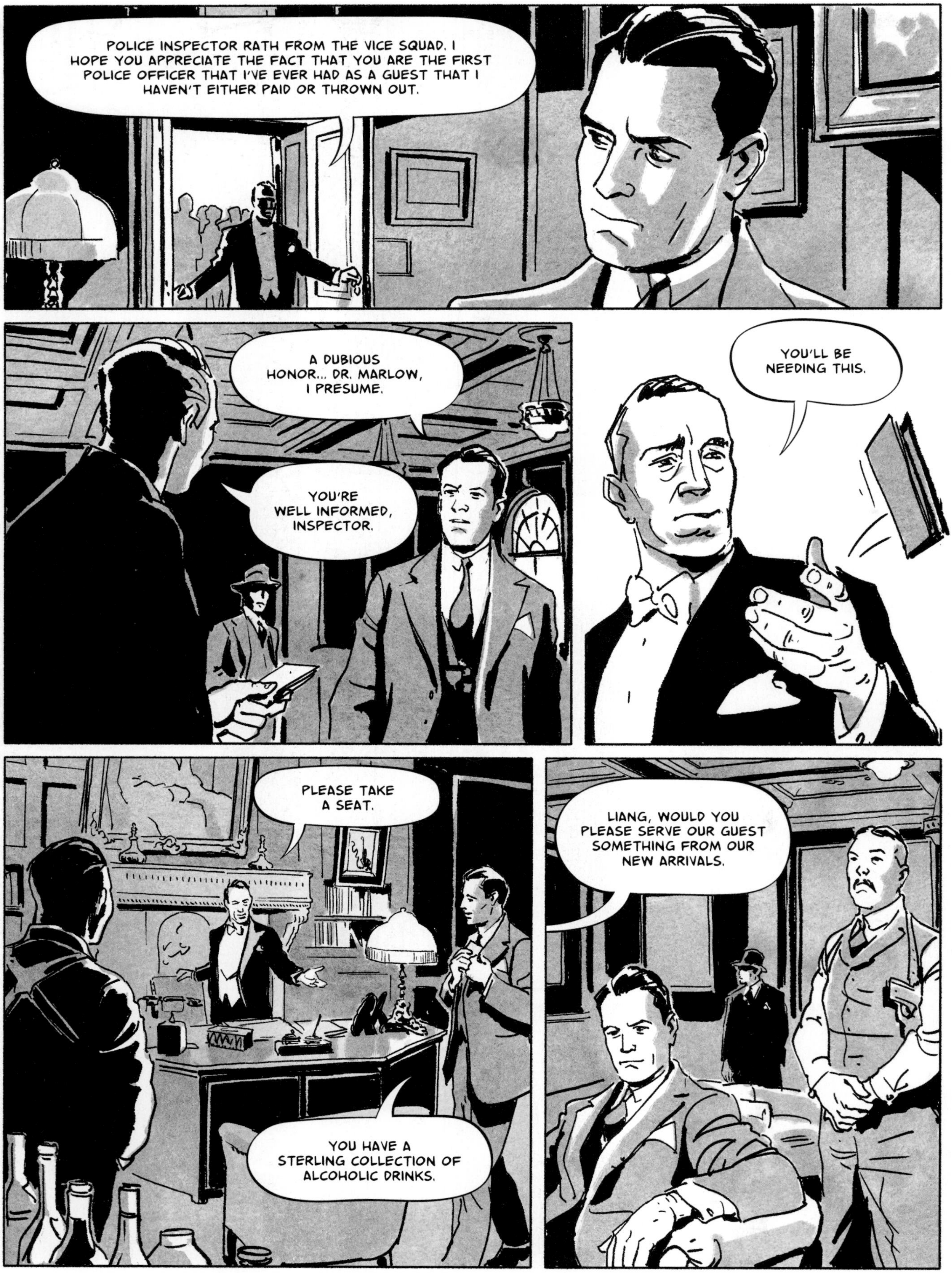
POLICE INSPECTOR RATH FROM THE VICE SQUAD. I HOPE YOU APPRECIATE THE FACT THAT YOU ARE THE FIRST POLICE OFFICER THAT I'VE EVER HAD AS A GUEST THAT I HAVEN'T EITHER PAID OR THROWN OUT.
A DUBIOUS HONOR... DR. MARLOW, I PRESUME.
YOU'RE WELL INFORMED, INSPECTOR.
YOU'LL BE NEEDING THIS.
PLEASE TAKE A SEAT.
YOU HAVE A STERLING COLLECTION OF ALCOHOLIC DRINKS.
LIANG, WOULD YOU PLEASE SERVE OUR GUEST SOMETHING FROM OUR NEW ARRIVALS.

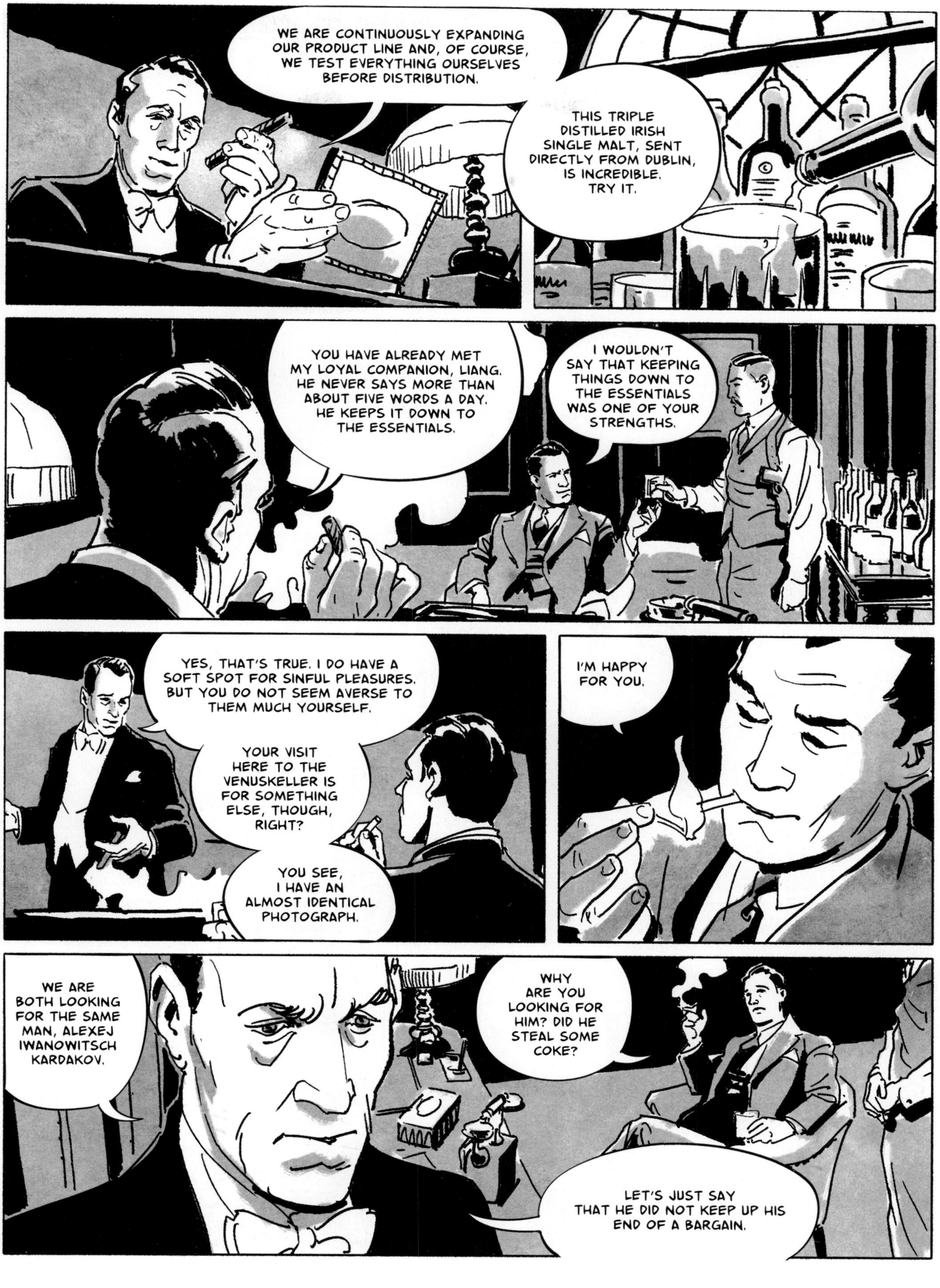
WE ARE CONTINUOUSLY EXPANDING OUR PRODUCT LINE AND, OF COURSE, WE TEST EVERYTHING OURSELVES BEFORE DISTRIBUTION.
THIS TRIPLE DISTILLED IRISH SINGLE MALT, SENT DIRECTLY FROM DUBLIN, IS INCREDIBLE. TRY IT.
YOU HAVE ALREADY MET MY LOYAL COMPANION, LIANG. HE NEVER SAYS MORE THAN ABOUT FIVE WORDS A DAY. HE KEEPS IT DOWN TO THE ESSENTIALS.
I WOULDN'T SAY THAT KEEPING THINGS DOWN TO THE ESSENTIALS WAS ONE OF YOUR STRENGTHS.
YES, THAT'S TRUE. I DO HAVE A SOFT SPOT FOR SINFUL PLEASURES. BUT YOU DO NOT SEEM AVERSE TO THEM MUCH YOURSELF.
YOUR VISIT HERE TO THE VENUSKELLER IS FOR SOMETHING ELSE, THOUGH, RIGHT?
YOU SEE, I HAVE AN ALMOST IDENTICAL PHOTOGRAPH.
I'M HAPPY FOR YOU.
WE ARE BOTH LOOKING FOR THE SAME MAN, ALEXEJ IWANOWITSCH KARDAKOV.
WHY ARE YOU LOOKING FOR HIM? DID HE STEAL SOME COKE?
LET'S JUST SAY THAT HE DID NOT KEEP UP HIS END OF A BARGAIN.

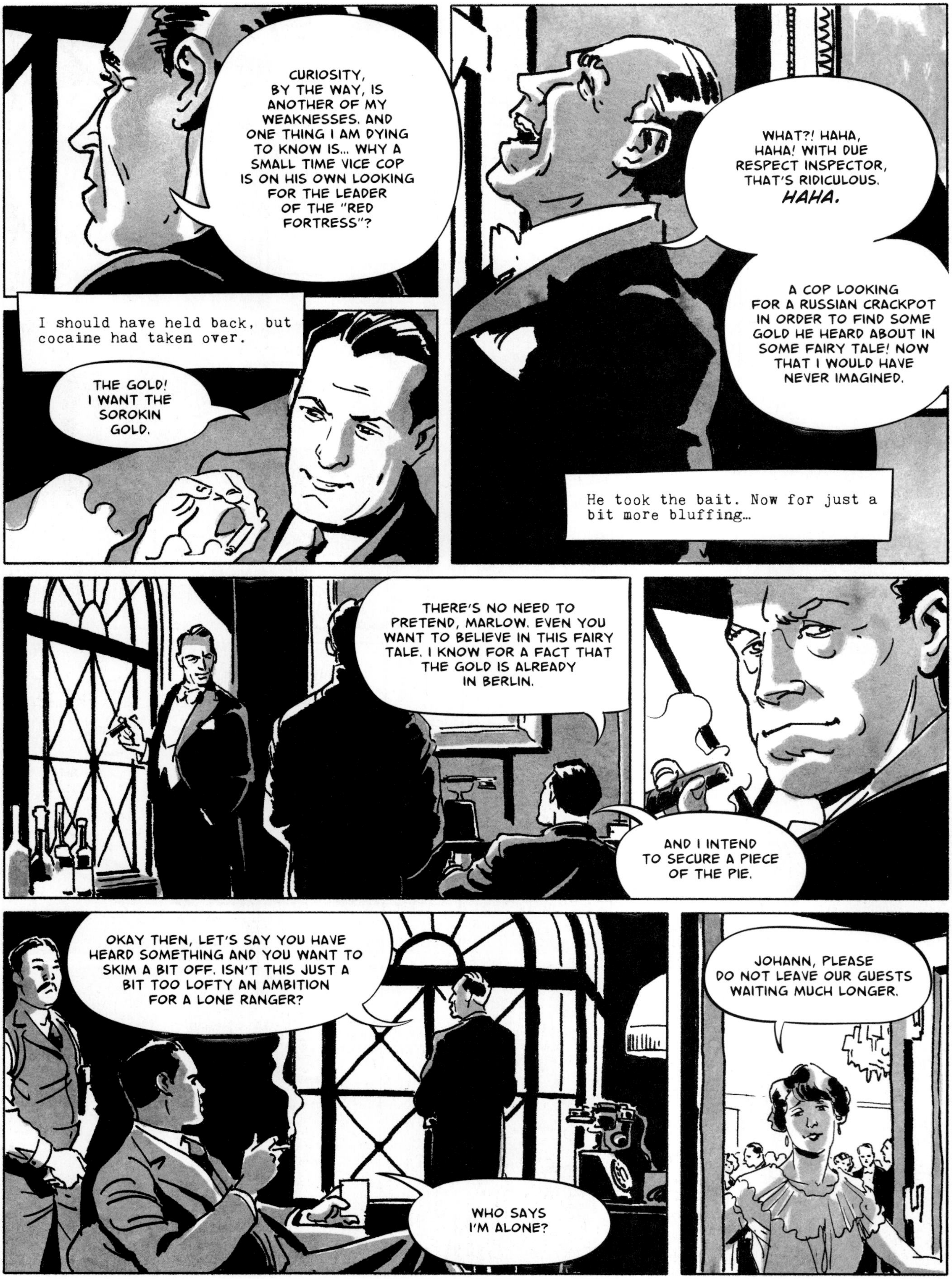
CURIOSITY, BY THE WAY, IS ANOTHER OF MY WEAKNESSES. AND ONE THING I AM DYING TO KNOW IS... WHY A SMALL TIME VICE COP IS ON HIS OWN LOOKING FOR THE LEADER OF THE "RED FORTRESS"?
I should have held back, but cocaine had taken over.
THE GOLD! I WANT THE SOROKIN GOLD.
WHAT?! HAHA, HAHA! WITH DUE RESPECT INSPECTOR, THAT'S RIDICULOUS. HAHA.
A COP LOOKING FOR A RUSSIAN CRACKPOT IN ORDER TO FIND SOME GOLD HE HEARD ABOUT IN SOME FAIRY TALE! NOW THAT I WOULD HAVE NEVER IMAGINED.
He took the bait. Now for just a bit more bluffing...
THERE'S NO NEED TO PRETEND, MARLOW. EVEN YOU WANT TO BELIEVE IN THIS FAIRY TALE. I KNOW FOR A FACT THAT THE GOLD IS ALREADY IN BERLIN.
AND I INTEND TO SECURE A PIECE OF THE PIE.
OKAY THEN, LET'S SAY YOU HAVE HEARD SOMETHING AND YOU WANT TO SKIM A BIT OFF. ISN'T THIS JUST A BIT TOO LOFTY AN AMBITION FOR A LONE RANGER?
WHO SAYS I'M ALONE?
JOHANN, PLEASE DO NOT LEAVE OUR GUESTS WAITING MUCH LONGER.

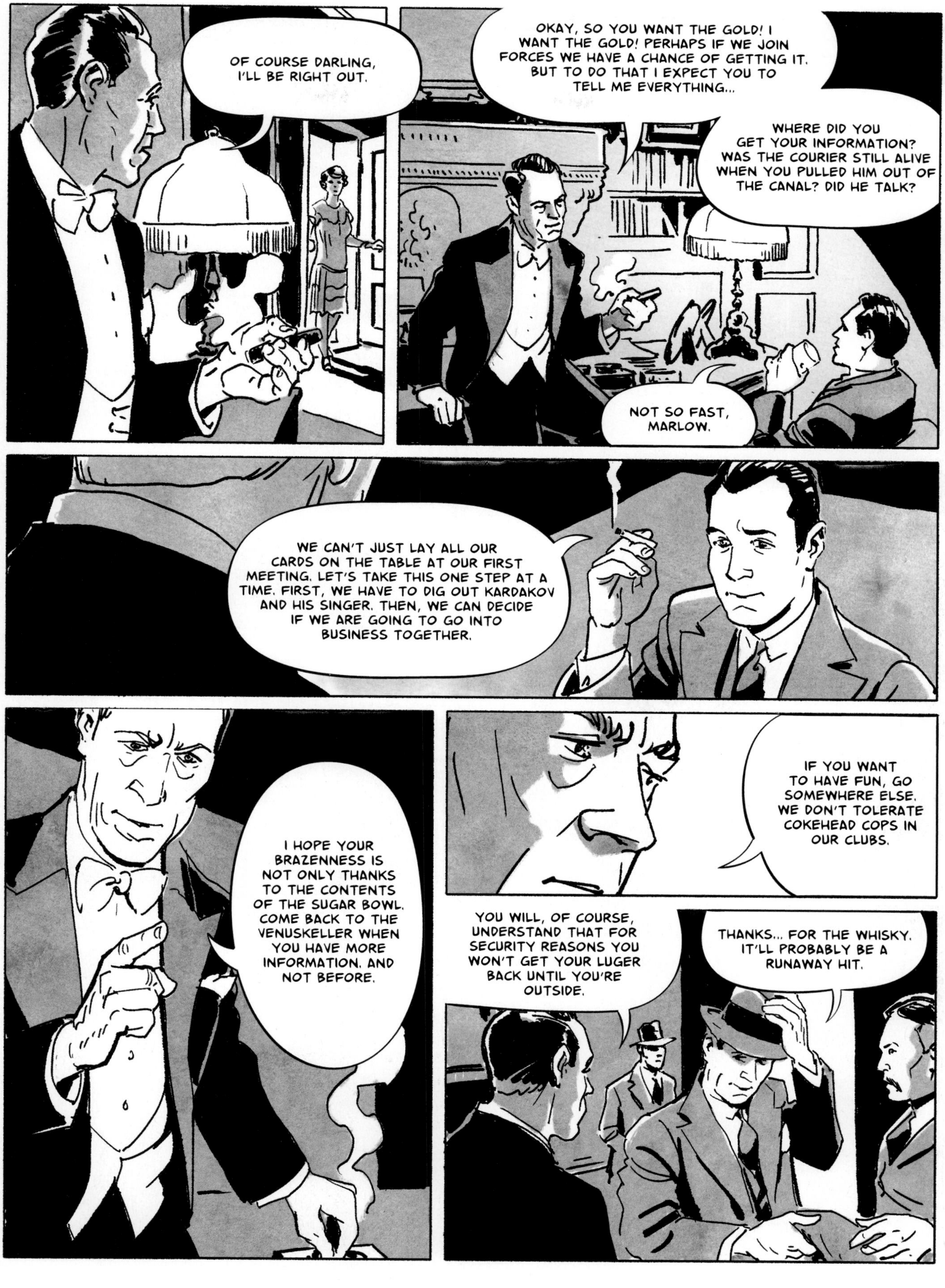
OF COURSE DARLING, I'LL BE RIGHT OUT.
OKAY, SO YOU WANT THE GOLD! I WANT THE GOLD! PERHAPS IF WE JOIN FORCES WE HAVE A CHANCE OF GETTING IT. BUT TO DO THAT I EXPECT YOU TO TELL ME EVERYTHING...
WHERE DID YOU GET YOUR INFORMATION? WAS THE COURIER STILL ALIVE WHEN YOU PULLED HIM OUT OF THE CANAL? DID HE TALK?
NOT SO FAST, MARLOW.
WE CAN'T JUST LAY ALL OUR CARDS ON THE TABLE AT OUR FIRST MEETING. LET'S TAKE THIS ONE STEP AT A TIME. FIRST, WE HAVE TO DIG OUT KARDAKOV AND HIS SINGER. THEN, WE CAN DECIDE IF WE ARE GOING TO GO INTO BUSINESS TOGETHER.
I HOPE YOUR BRAZENNESS IS NOT ONLY THANKS TO THE CONTENTS OF THE SUGAR BOWL. COME BACK TO THE VENUSKELLER WHEN YOU HAVE MORE INFORMATION. AND NOT BEFORE.
IF YOU WANT TO HAVE FUN, GO SOMEWHERE ELSE. WE DON'T TOLERATE COKEHEAD COPS IN OUR CLUBS.
YOU WILL, OF COURSE, UNDERSTAND THAT FOR SECURITY REASONS YOU WON'T GET YOUR LUGER BACK UNTIL YOU'RE OUTSIDE.
THANKS... FOR THE WHISKY. IT'LL PROBABLY BE A RUNAWAY HIT.

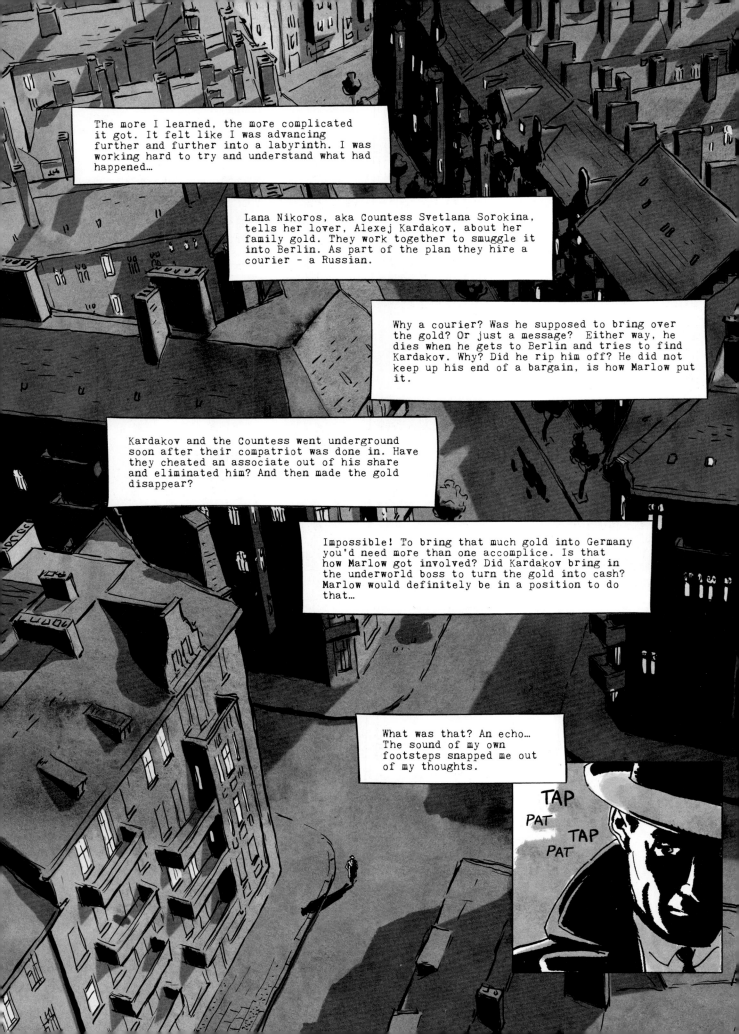

The more I learned, the more complicated it got. It felt like I was advancing further and further into a labyrinth. I was working hard to try and understand what had happened…

Lana Nikoros, aka Countess Svetlana Sorokina, tells her lover, Alexej Kardakov, about her family gold. They work together to smuggle it into Berlin. As part of the plan they hire a courier - a Russian.

Why a courier? Was he supposed to bring over the gold? Or just a message? Either way, he dies when he gets to Berlin and tries to find Kardakov. Why? Did he rip him off? He did not keep up his end of a bargain, is how Marlow put it.

Kardakov and the Countess went underground soon after their compatriot was done in. Have they cheated an associate out of his share and eliminated him? And then made the gold disappear?

Impossible! To bring that much gold into Germany you'd need more than one accomplice. Is that how Marlow got involved? Did Kardakov bring in the underworld boss to turn the gold into cash? Marlow would definitely be in a position to do that…

What was that? An echo… The sound of my own footsteps snapped me out of my thoughts.

TAP
PAT
TAP
PAT

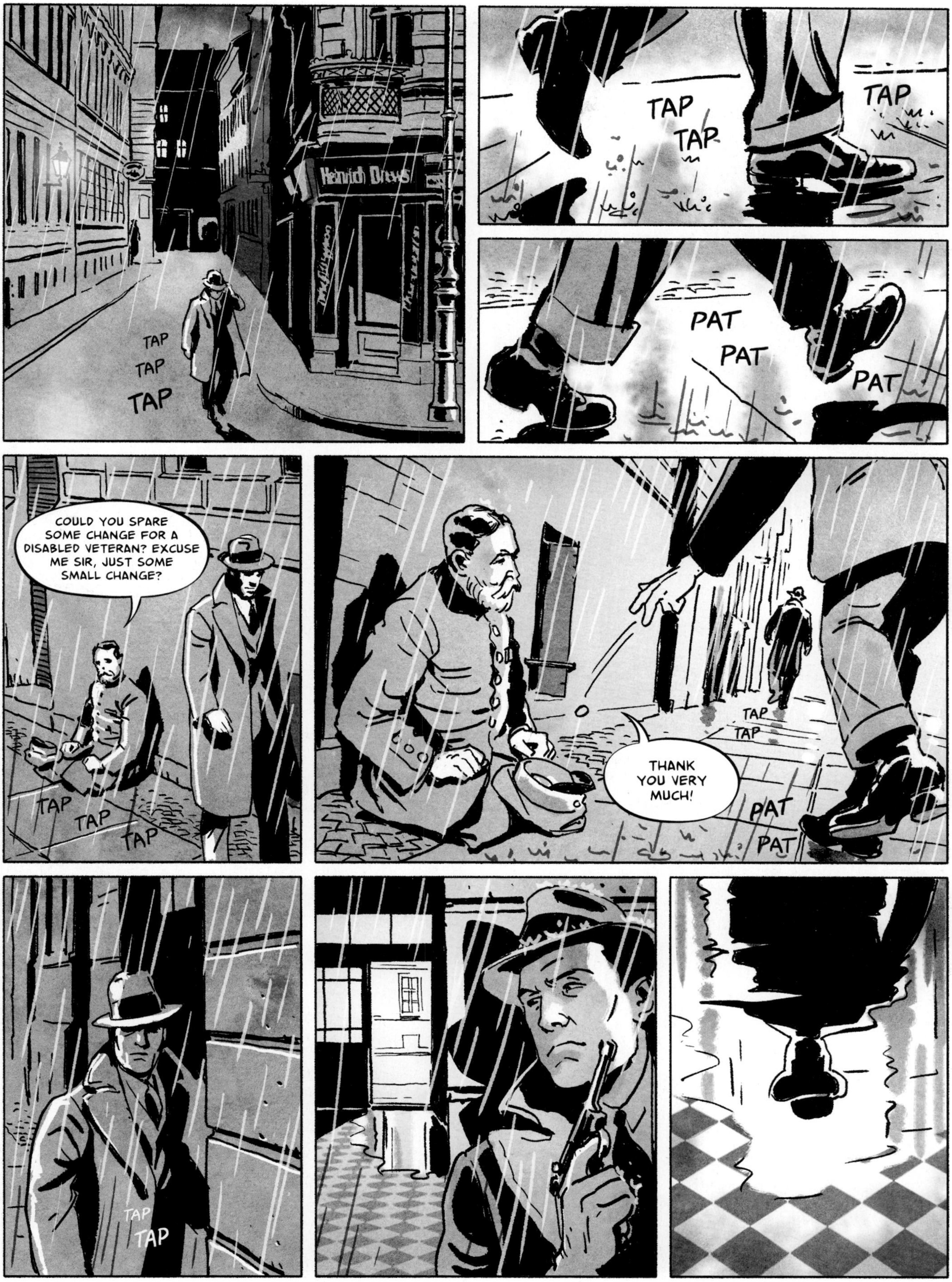
Heinrich Drews
TAP
TAP
TAP
TAP
TAP
TAP
PAT
PAT
PAT
COULD YOU SPARE SOME CHANGE FOR A DISABLED VETERAN? EXCUSE ME SIR, JUST SOME SMALL CHANGE?
TAP
TAP
TAP
TAP
TAP
THANK YOU VERY MUCH!
PAT
PAT
TAP
TAP

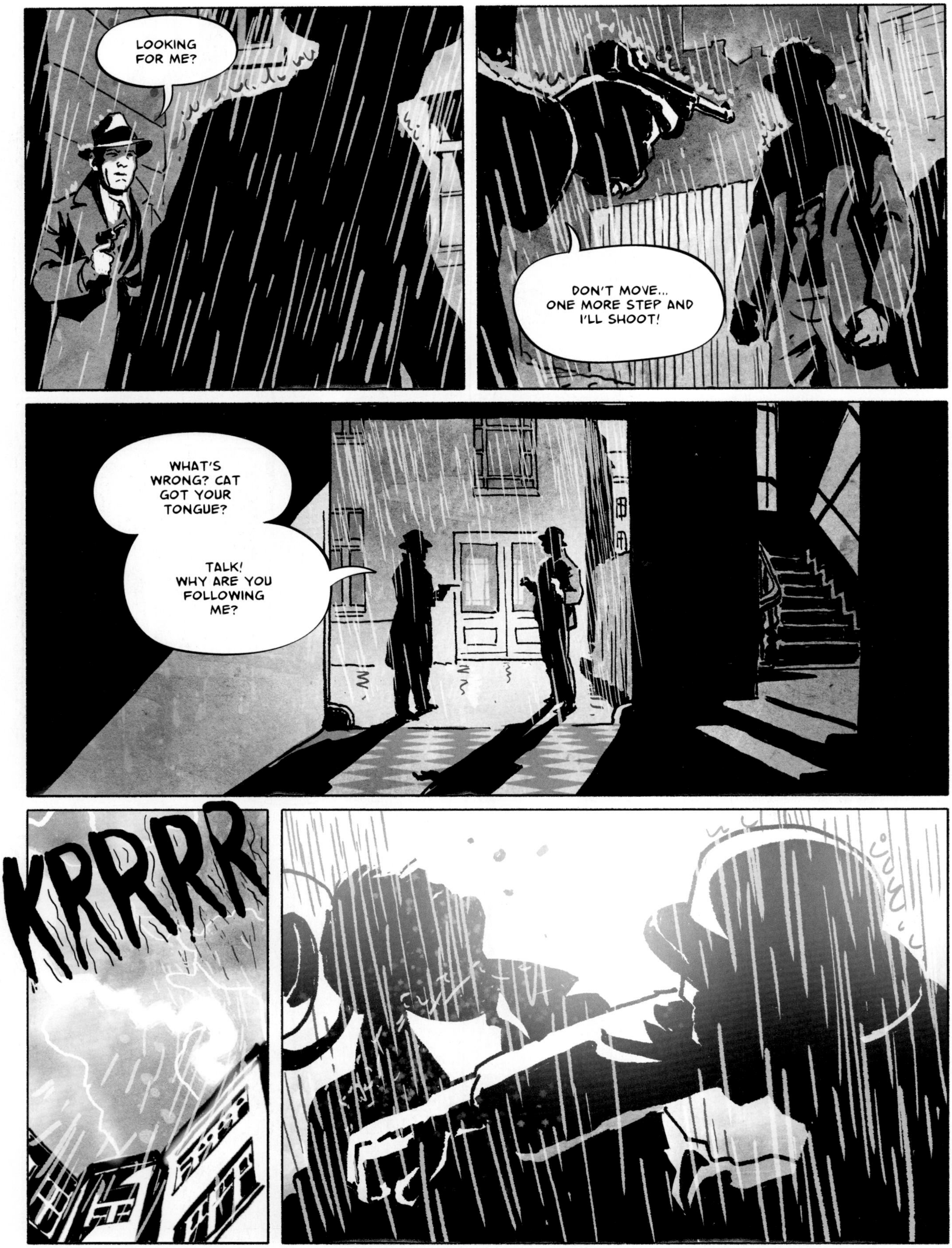
LOOKING FOR ME?
DON'T MOVE... ONE MORE STEP AND I'LL SHOOT!
WHAT'S WRONG? CAT GOT YOUR TONGUE?
TALK! WHY ARE YOU FOLLOWING ME?
KRRRR

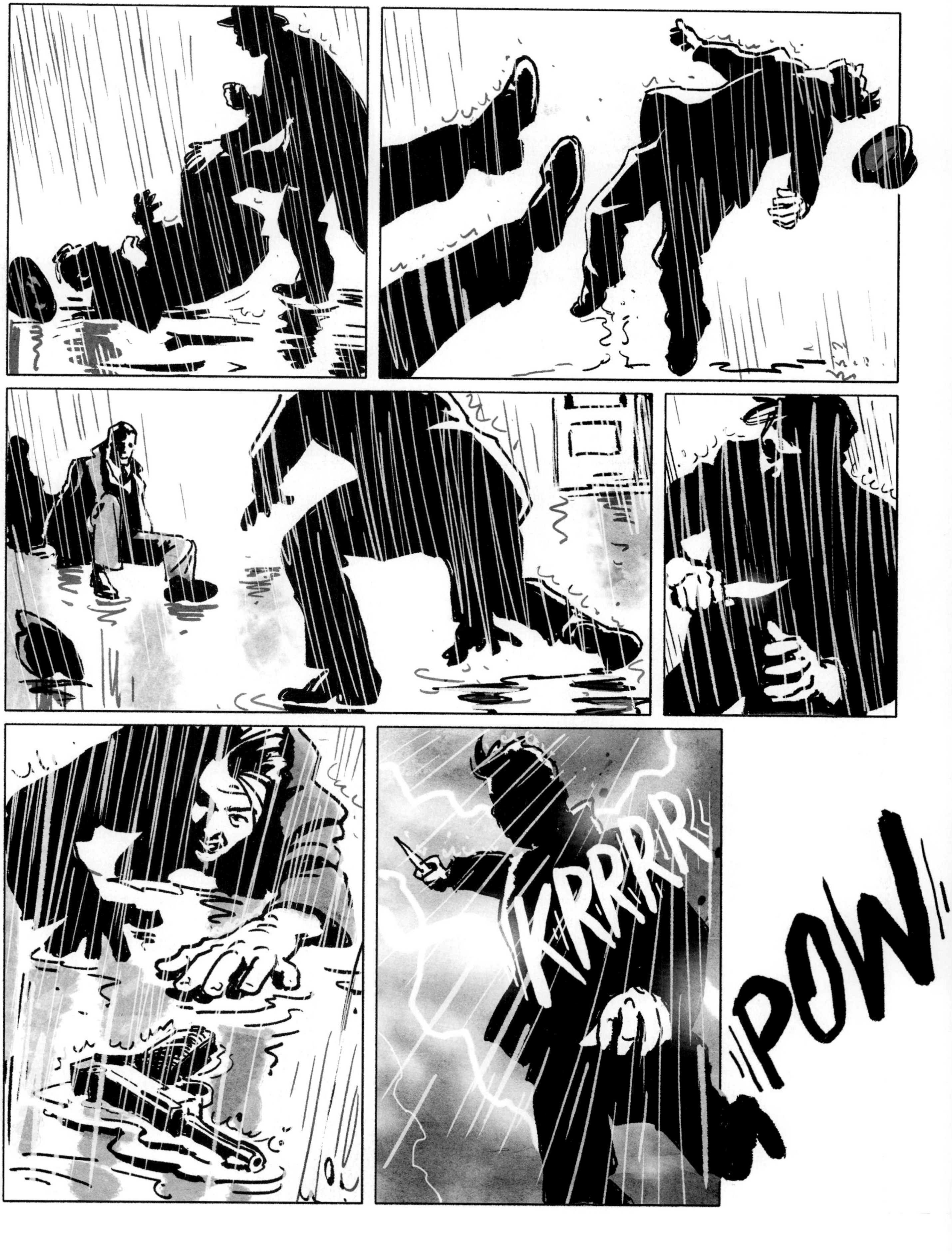
KRRRR
POW

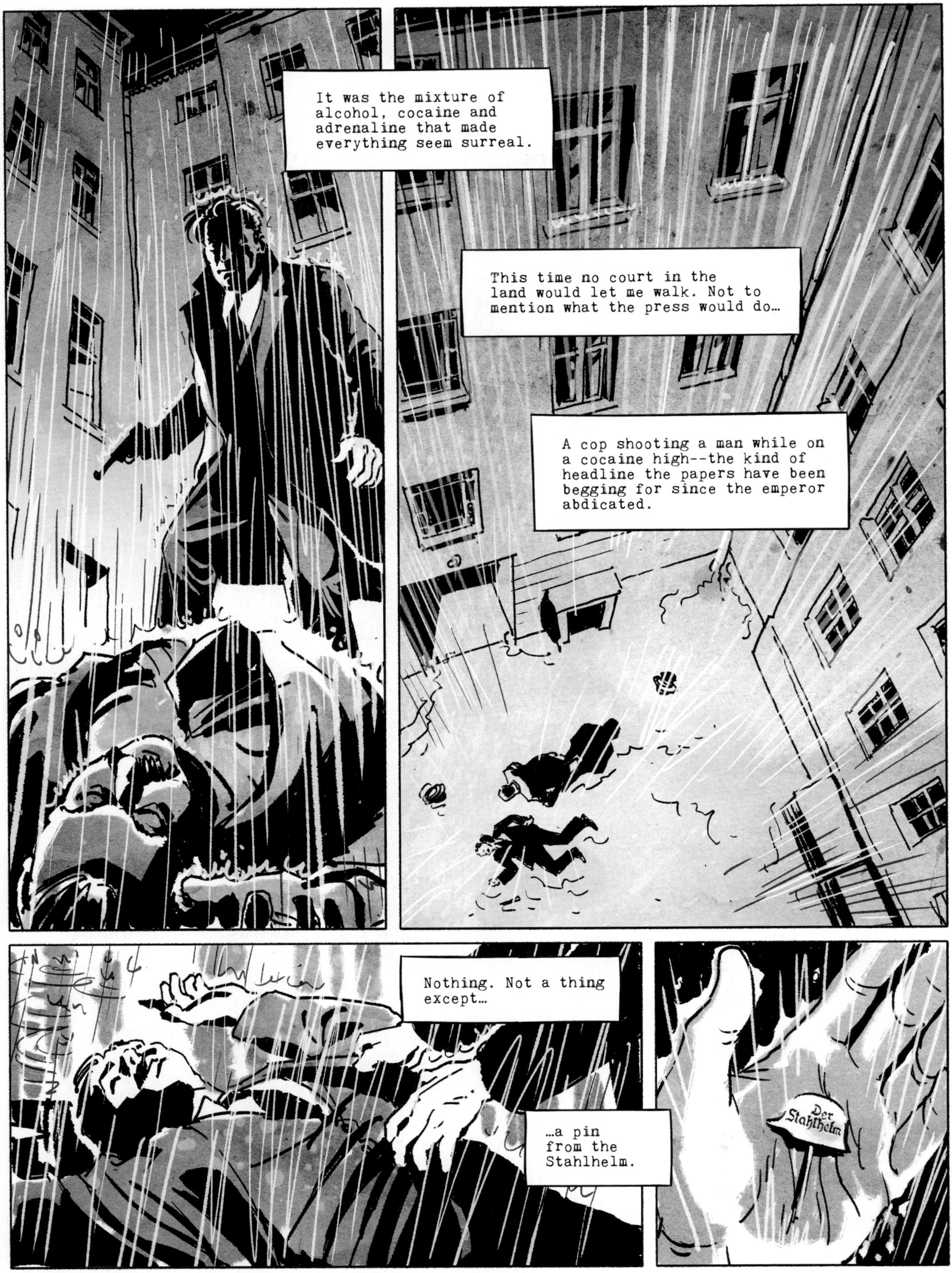
It was the mixture of alcohol, cocaine and adrenaline that made everything seem surreal.
This time no court in the land would let me walk. Not to mention what the press would do…
A cop shooting a man while on a cocaine high--the kind of headline the papers have been begging for since the emperor abdicated.
Nothing. Not a thing except…
…a pin from the Stahlhelm.
Der Stahlhelm

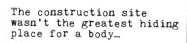
The construction site wasn't the greatest hiding place for a body...

But it was the best I could do under the circumstances.

I got lucky--the shot was covered by thunder and the blood was washed away by the rain.

It was just a way...

...to buy me some time.

PART II
A-Division

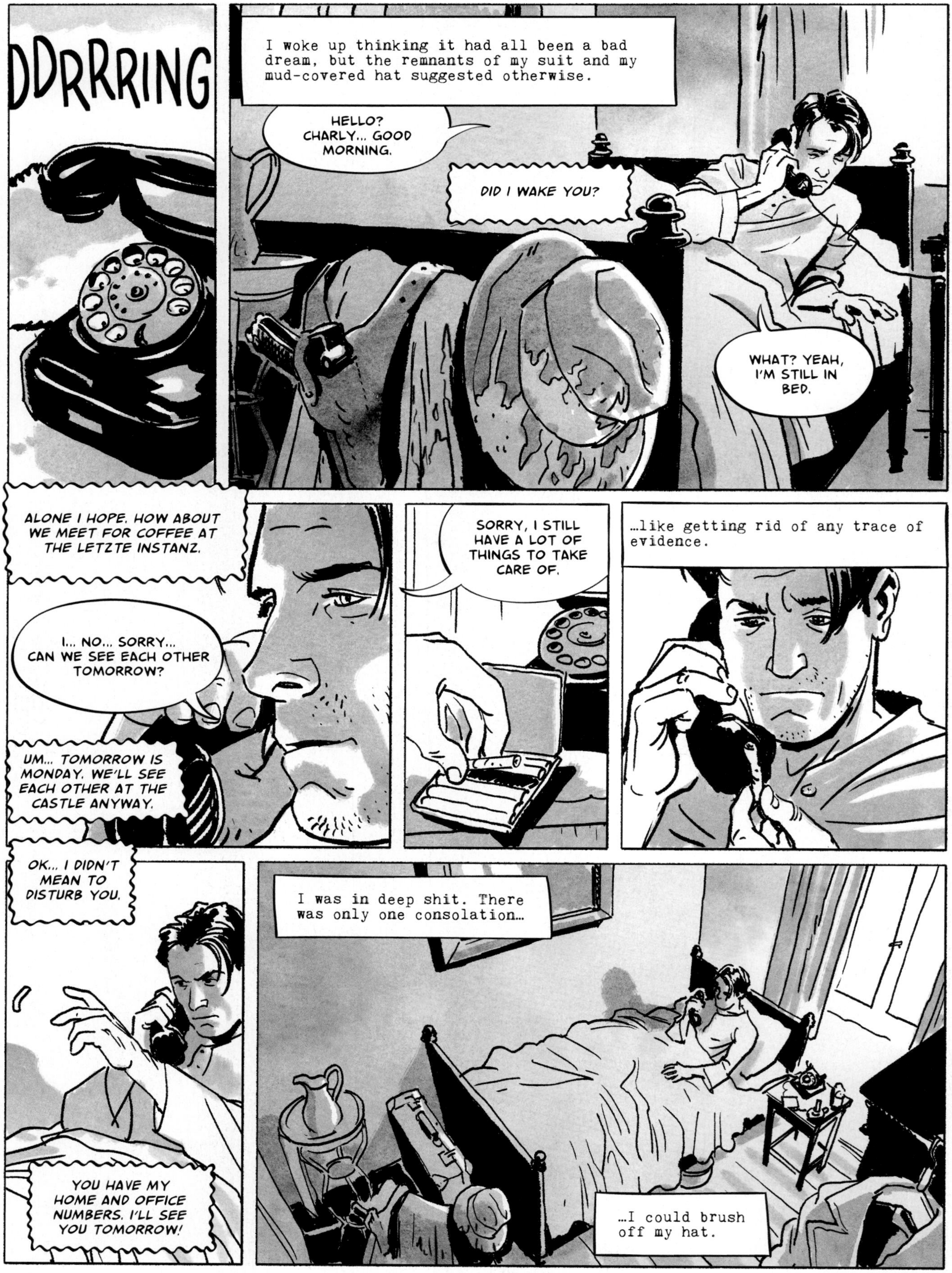
DDRRRING
I woke up thinking it had all been a bad dream, but the remnants of my suit and my mud-covered hat suggested otherwise.
HELLO? CHARLY... GOOD MORNING.
DID I WAKE YOU?
WHAT? YEAH, I'M STILL IN BED.
ALONE I HOPE. HOW ABOUT WE MEET FOR COFFEE AT THE LETZTE INSTANZ.
I... NO... SORRY... CAN WE SEE EACH OTHER TOMORROW?
UM... TOMORROW IS MONDAY. WE'LL SEE EACH OTHER AT THE CASTLE ANYWAY.
SORRY, I STILL HAVE A LOT OF THINGS TO TAKE CARE OF.
...like getting rid of any trace of evidence.
OK... I DIDN'T MEAN TO DISTURB YOU.
YOU HAVE MY HOME AND OFFICE NUMBERS. I'LL SEE YOU TOMORROW!
I was in deep shit. There was only one consolation...
...I could brush off my hat.

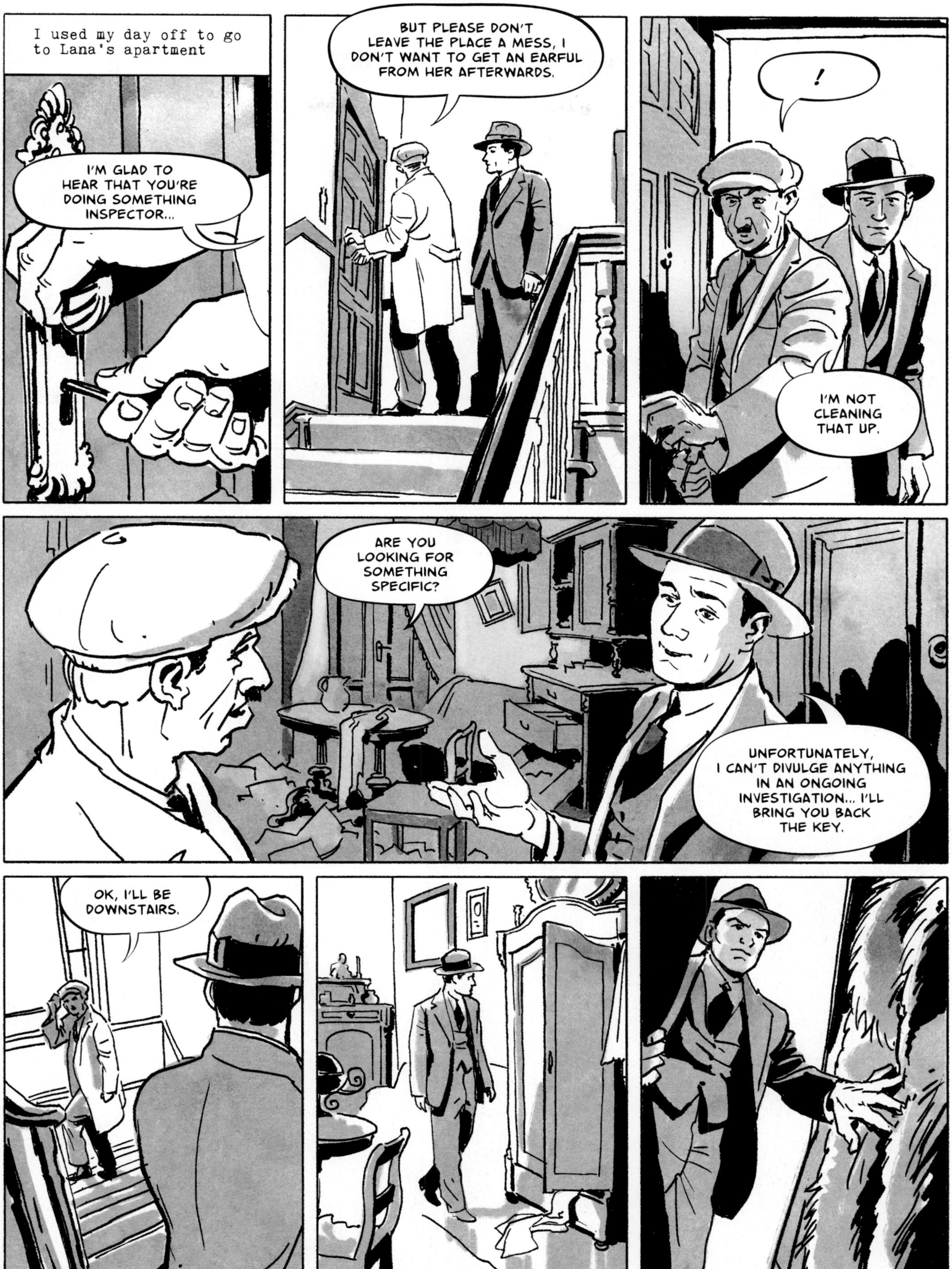
I used my day off to go to Lana's apartment
I'M GLAD TO HEAR THAT YOU'RE DOING SOMETHING INSPECTOR...
BUT PLEASE DON'T LEAVE THE PLACE A MESS, I DON'T WANT TO GET AN EARFUL FROM HER AFTERWARDS.
!
I'M NOT CLEANING THAT UP.
ARE YOU LOOKING FOR SOMETHING SPECIFIC?
UNFORTUNATELY, I CAN'T DIVULGE ANYTHING IN AN ONGOING INVESTIGATION... I'LL BRING YOU BACK THE KEY.
OK, I'LL BE DOWNSTAIRS.

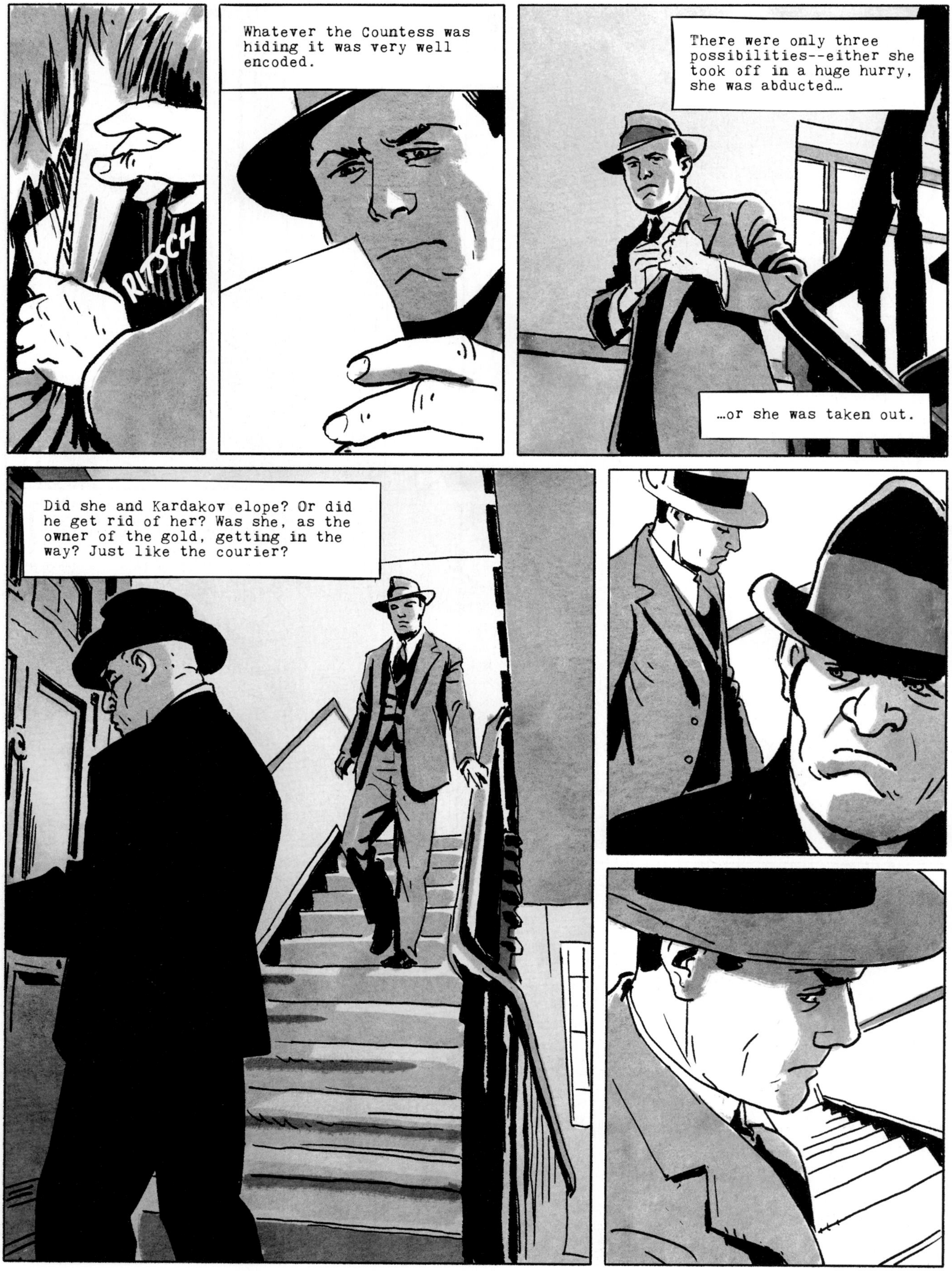
RITSCH
Whatever the Countess was hiding it was very well encoded.
There were only three possibilities--either she took off in a huge hurry, she was abducted...
...or she was taken out.
Did she and Kardakov elope? Or did he get rid of her? Was she, as the owner of the gold, getting in the way? Just like the courier?

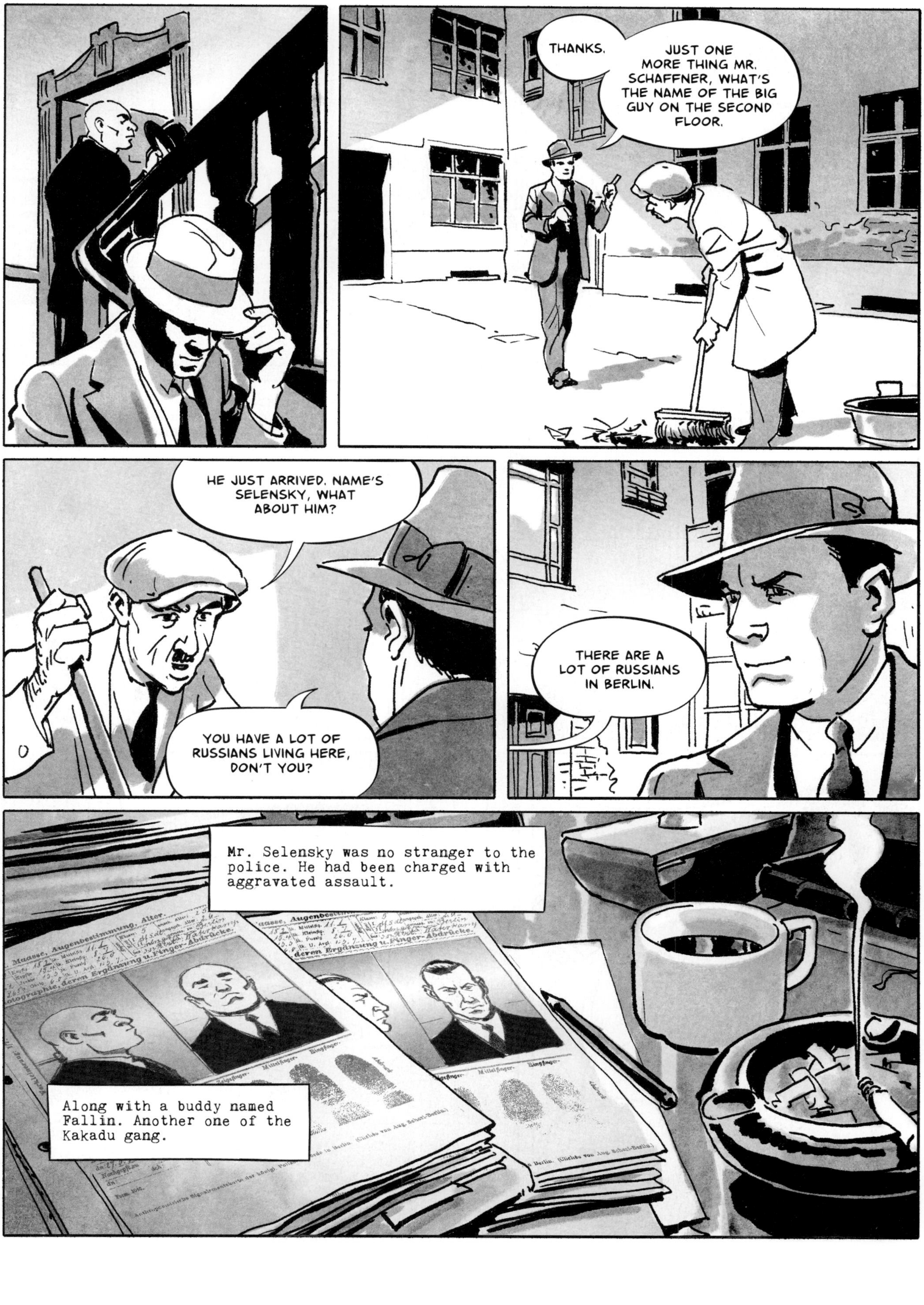
THANKS.
JUST ONE MORE THING MR. SCHAFFNER, WHAT'S THE NAME OF THE BIG GUY ON THE SECOND FLOOR.
HE JUST ARRIVED. NAME'S SELENSKY, WHAT ABOUT HIM?
YOU HAVE A LOT OF RUSSIANS LIVING HERE, DON'T YOU?
THERE ARE A LOT OF RUSSIANS IN BERLIN.
Mr. Selensky was no stranger to the police. He had been charged with aggravated assault.
Along with a buddy named Fallin. Another one of the Kakadu gang.

The two didn't hold back. In a fight with a fellow countryman they had gone too far and the victim died. In the end there was too little evidence for a conviction...

What the files unfortunately did not provide, was an answer to the question of why Selensky lived in the same place as the countess.

The same address as the one Kardakov had written down as his new place of residence. Definitely not a coincidence. But what did the two thugs have to do with Kardakov and his singer?

DDRRRRR RRING

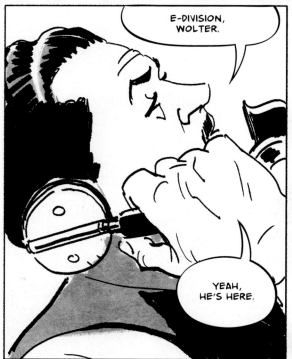

E-DIVISION, WOLTER.

YEAH, HE'S HERE.

IT'S FOR YOU... THE CALL YOU'VE BEEN WAITING FOR.

I knew Charly would never call me at the office. But this call was even more unexpected.

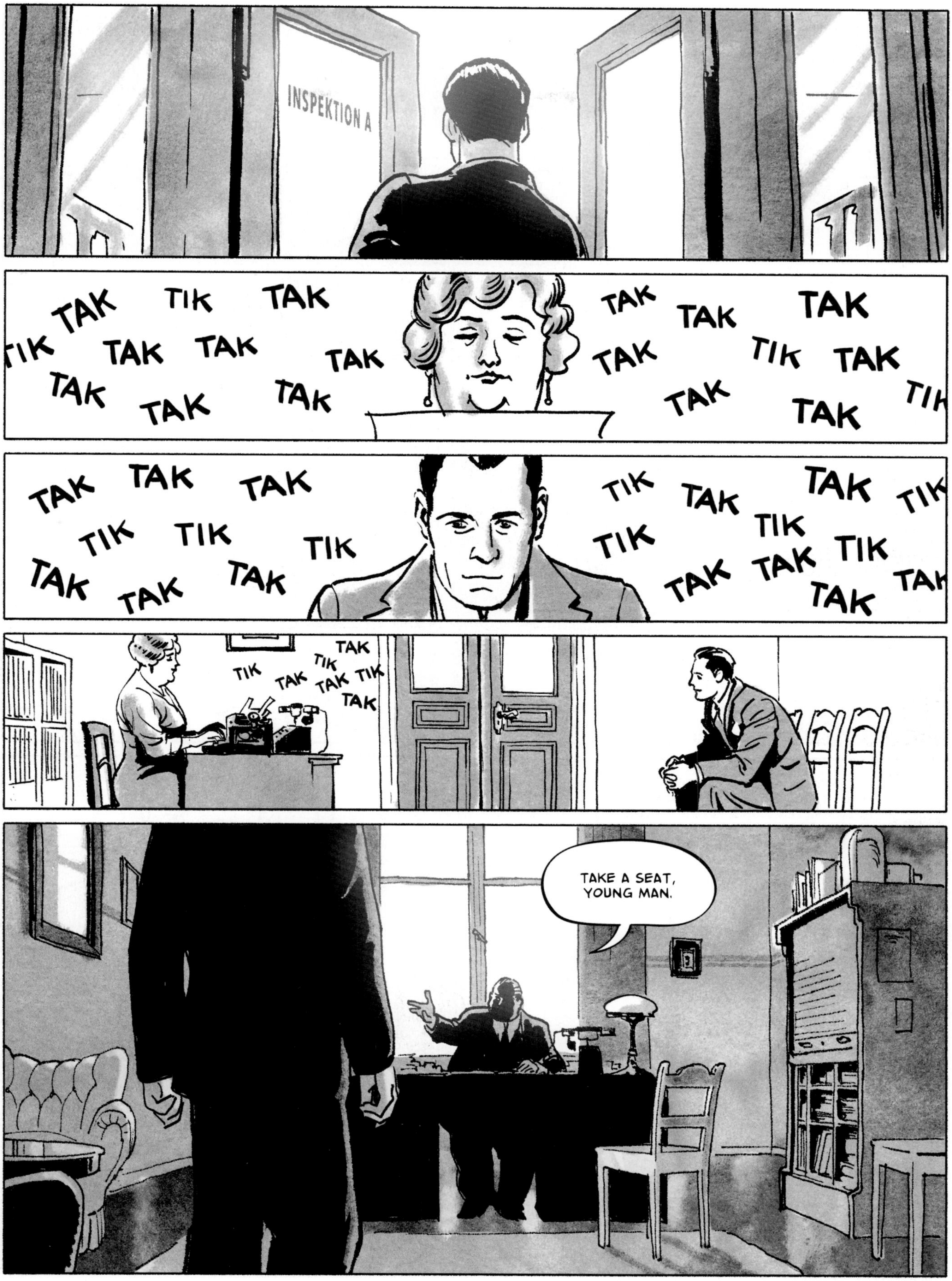
INSPEKTION A
TIK TAK TIK TAK TAK TAK TAK TAK TAK TAK
TAK TAK TAK TAK TIK TAK TAK TAK TIK
TAK TAK TAK TIK TIK TIK TAK TAK TAK
TIK TAK TAK TIK TIK TAK TAK TIK TAK TAK TAK
TIK TIK TAK TAK TAK TIK TAK
TAKE A SEAT, YOUNG MAN.

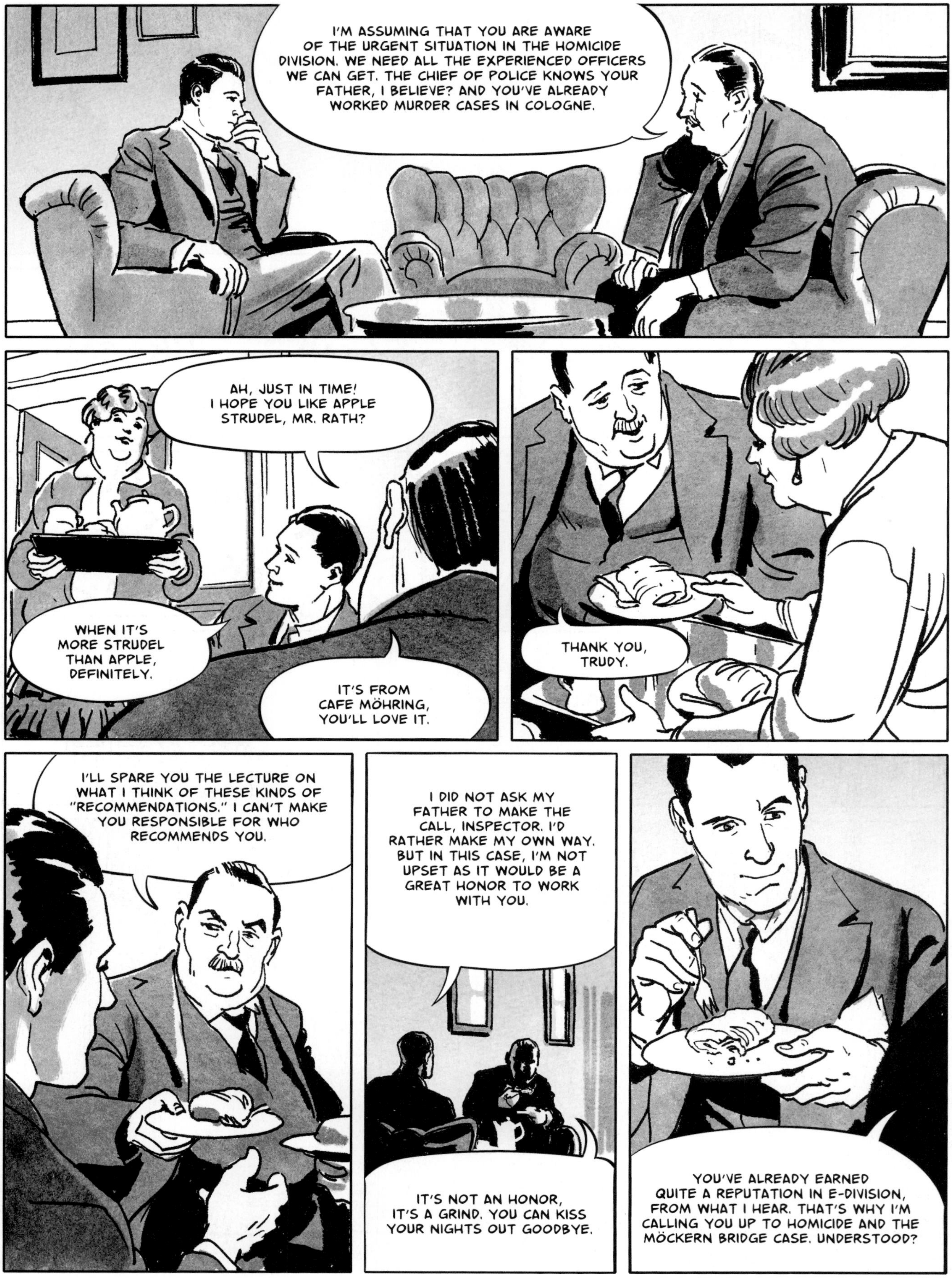
I'M ASSUMING THAT YOU ARE AWARE OF THE URGENT SITUATION IN THE HOMICIDE DIVISION. WE NEED ALL THE EXPERIENCED OFFICERS WE CAN GET. THE CHIEF OF POLICE KNOWS YOUR FATHER, I BELIEVE? AND YOU'VE ALREADY WORKED MURDER CASES IN COLOGNE.
AH, JUST IN TIME! I HOPE YOU LIKE APPLE STRUDEL, MR. RATH?
WHEN IT'S MORE STRUDEL THAN APPLE, DEFINITELY.
IT'S FROM CAFE MÖHRING, YOU'LL LOVE IT.
THANK YOU, TRUDY.
I'LL SPARE YOU THE LECTURE ON WHAT I THINK OF THESE KINDS OF "RECOMMENDATIONS." I CAN'T MAKE YOU RESPONSIBLE FOR WHO RECOMMENDS YOU.
I DID NOT ASK MY FATHER TO MAKE THE CALL, INSPECTOR. I'D RATHER MAKE MY OWN WAY. BUT IN THIS CASE, I'M NOT UPSET AS IT WOULD BE A GREAT HONOR TO WORK WITH YOU.
IT'S NOT AN HONOR, IT'S A GRIND. YOU CAN KISS YOUR NIGHTS OUT GOODBYE.
YOU'VE ALREADY EARNED QUITE A REPUTATION IN E-DIVISION, FROM WHAT I HEAR. THAT'S WHY I'M CALLING YOU UP TO HOMICIDE AND THE MÖCKERN BRIDGE CASE. UNDERSTOOD?

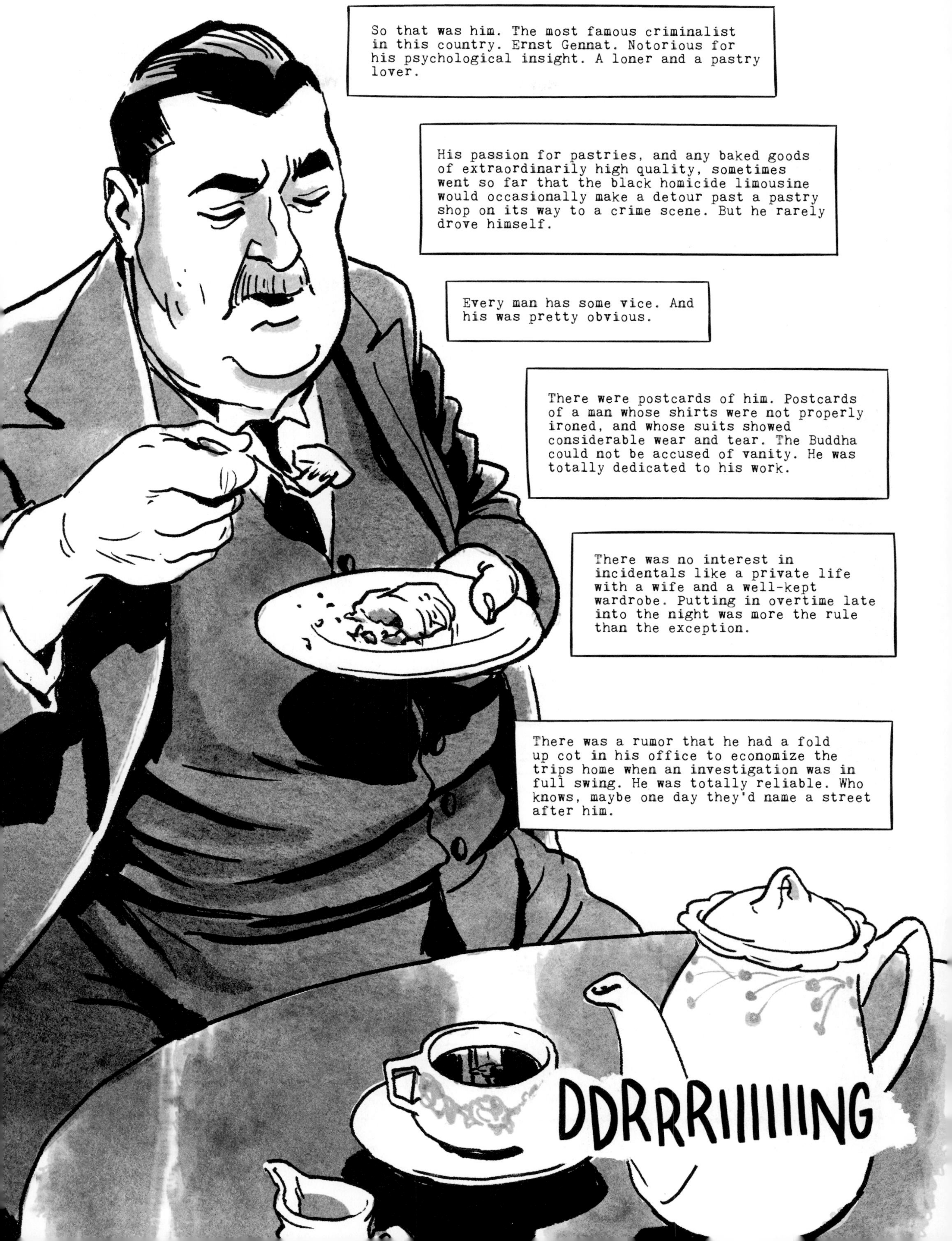
So that was him. The most famous criminalist in this country. Ernst Gennat. Notorious for his psychological insight. A loner and a pastry lover.
His passion for pastries, and any baked goods of extraordinarily high quality, sometimes went so far that the black homicide limousine would occasionally make a detour past a pastry shop on its way to a crime scene. But he rarely drove himself.
Every man has some vice. And his was pretty obvious.
There were postcards of him. Postcards of a man whose shirts were not properly ironed, and whose suits showed considerable wear and tear. The Buddha could not be accused of vanity. He was totally dedicated to his work.
There was no interest in incidentals like a private life with a wife and a well-kept wardrobe. Putting in overtime late into the night was more the rule than the exception.
There was a rumor that he had a fold up cot in his office to economize the trips home when an investigation was in full swing. He was totally reliable. Who knows, maybe one day they'd name a street after him.
DDRRRRIIIIIING

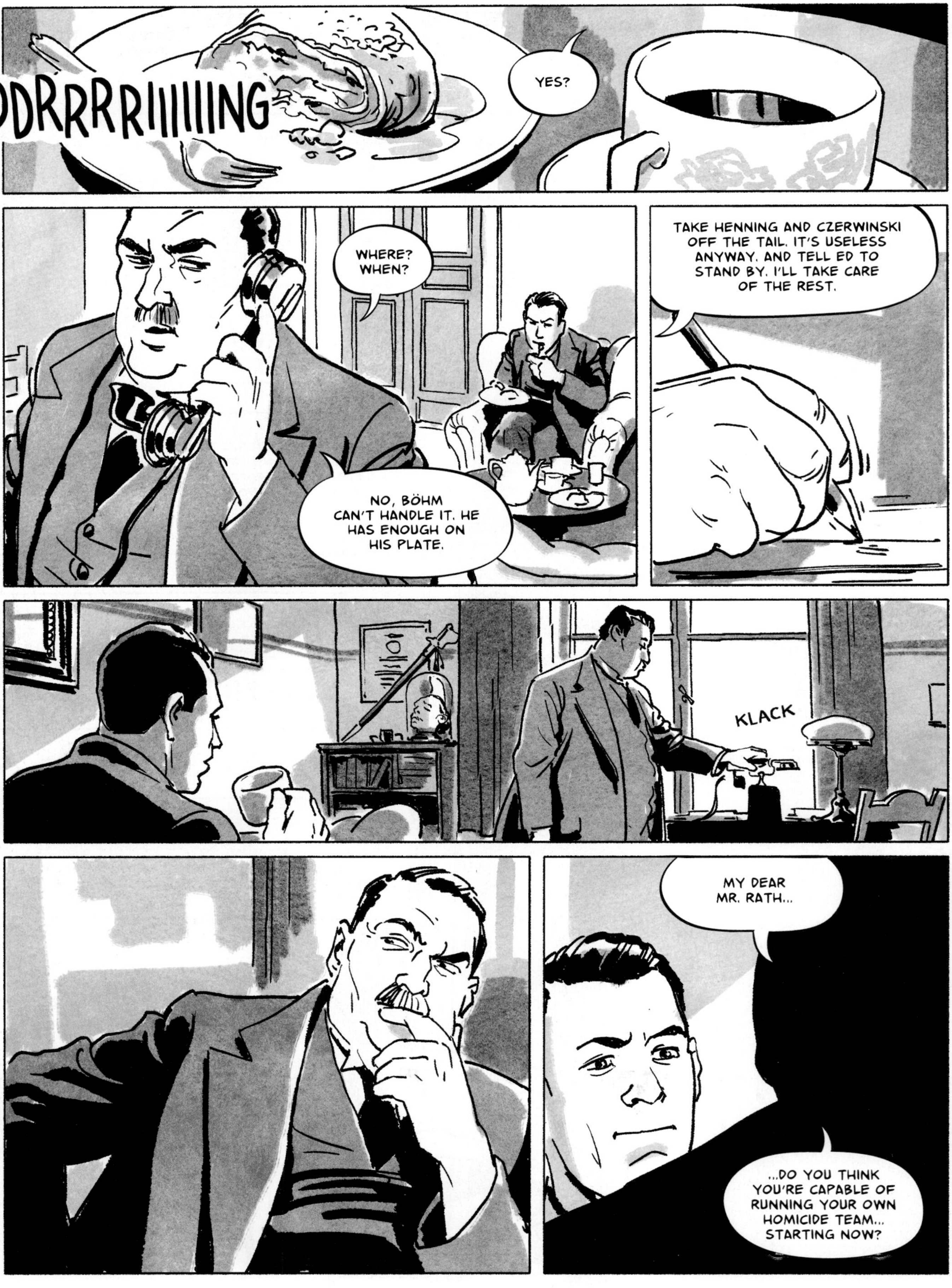
DDRRRRIIIIIIING
YES?
WHERE? WHEN?
NO, BÖHM CAN'T HANDLE IT. HE HAS ENOUGH ON HIS PLATE.
TAKE HENNING AND CZERWINSKI OFF THE TAIL. IT'S USELESS ANYWAY. AND TELL ED TO STAND BY. I'LL TAKE CARE OF THE REST.
KLACK
MY DEAR MR. RATH...
...DO YOU THINK YOU'RE CAPABLE OF RUNNING YOUR OWN HOMICIDE TEAM... STARTING NOW?

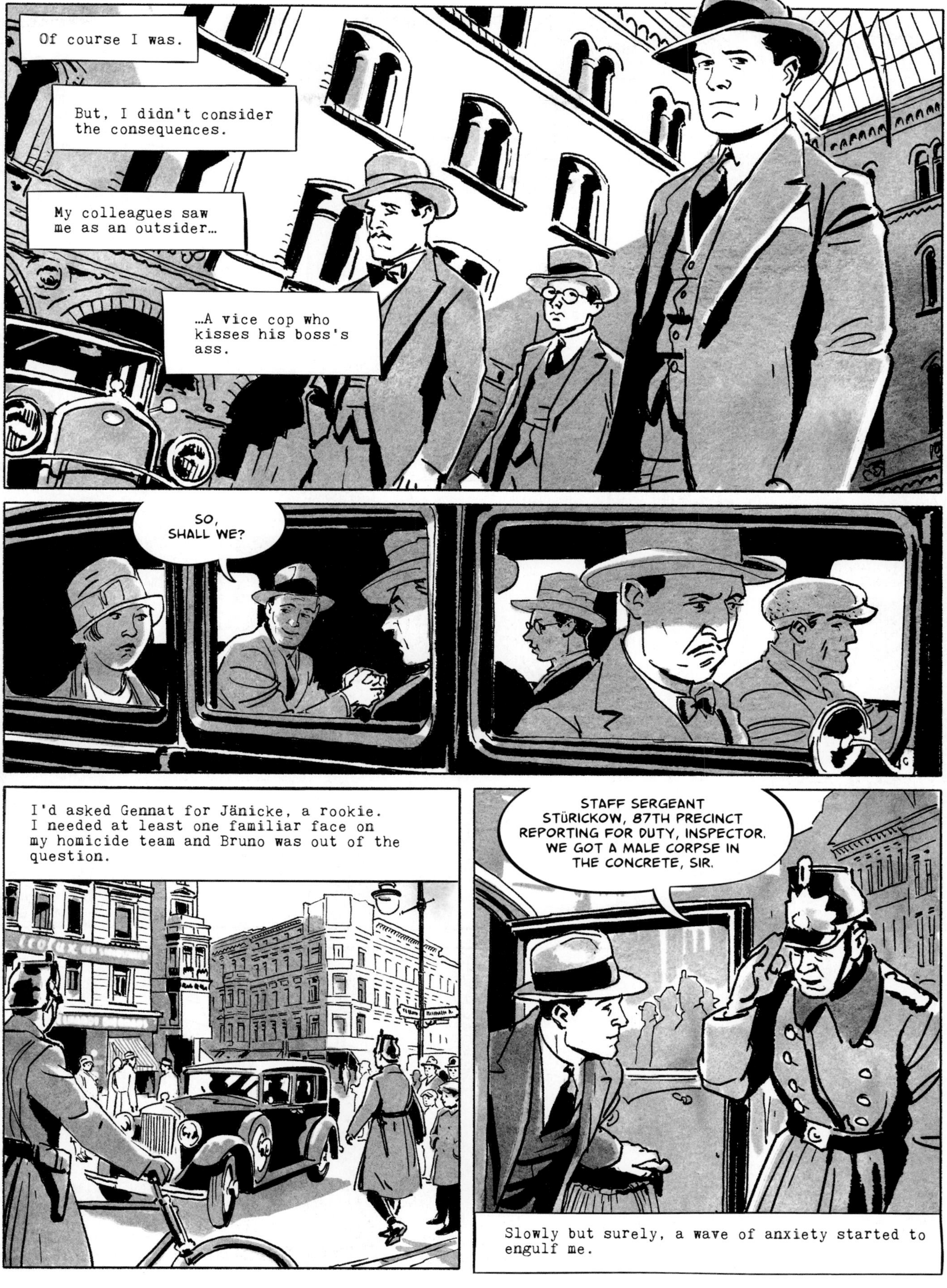
Of course I was.
But, I didn't consider the consequences.
My colleagues saw me as an outsider…
…A vice cop who kisses his boss's ass.
SO, SHALL WE?
I'd asked Gennat for Jänicke, a rookie. I needed at least one familiar face on my homicide team and Bruno was out of the question.
STAFF SERGEANT STÜRICKOW, 87TH PRECINCT REPORTING FOR DUTY, INSPECTOR. WE GOT A MALE CORPSE IN THE CONCRETE, SIR.
Slowly but surely, a wave of anxiety started to engulf me.

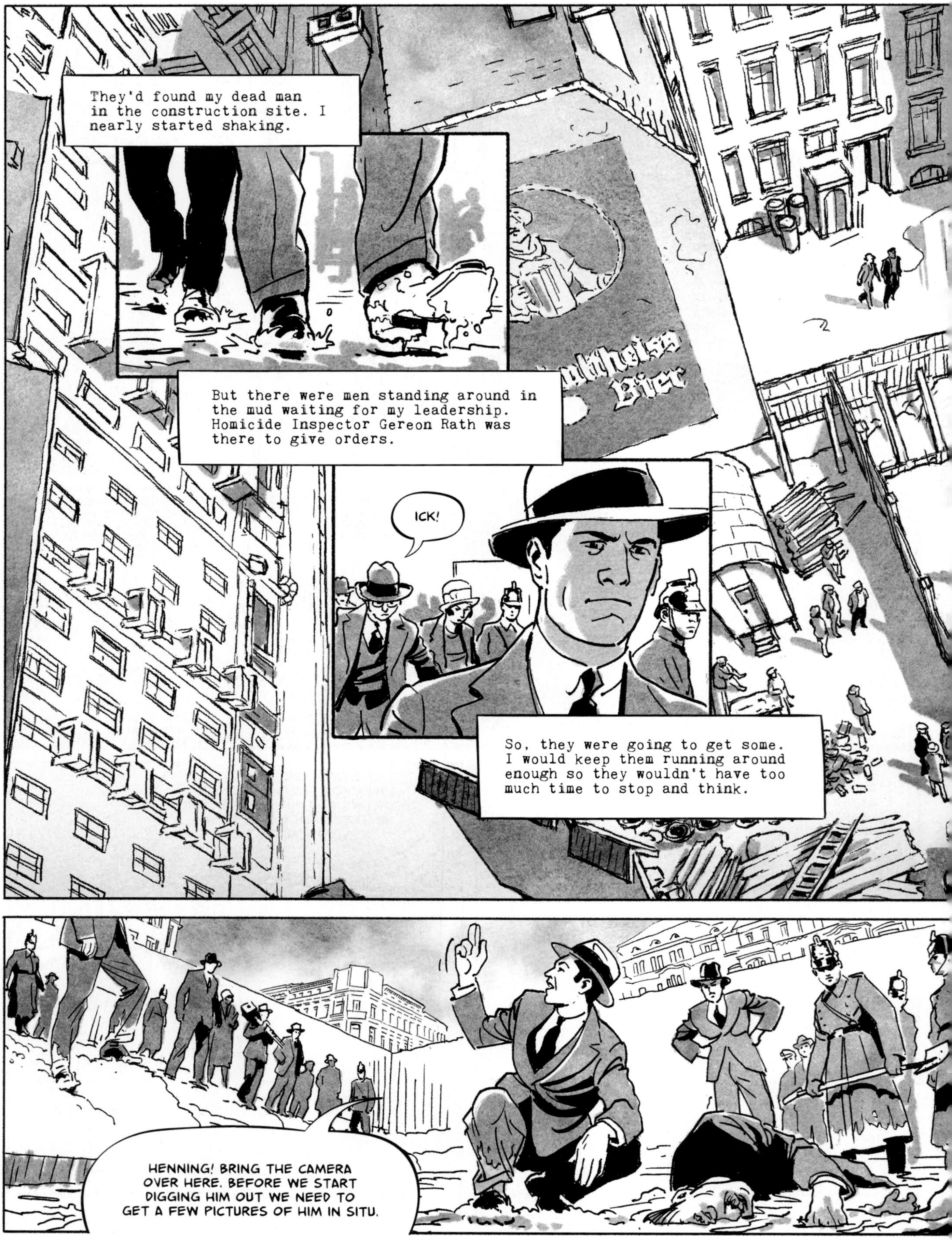
They'd found my dead man in the construction site. I nearly started shaking.
But there were men standing around in the mud waiting for my leadership. Homicide Inspector Gereon Rath was there to give orders.
ICK!
So, they were going to get some. I would keep them running around enough so they wouldn't have too much time to stop and think.
HENNING! BRING THE CAMERA OVER HERE. BEFORE WE START DIGGING HIM OUT WE NEED TO GET A FEW PICTURES OF HIM IN SITU.

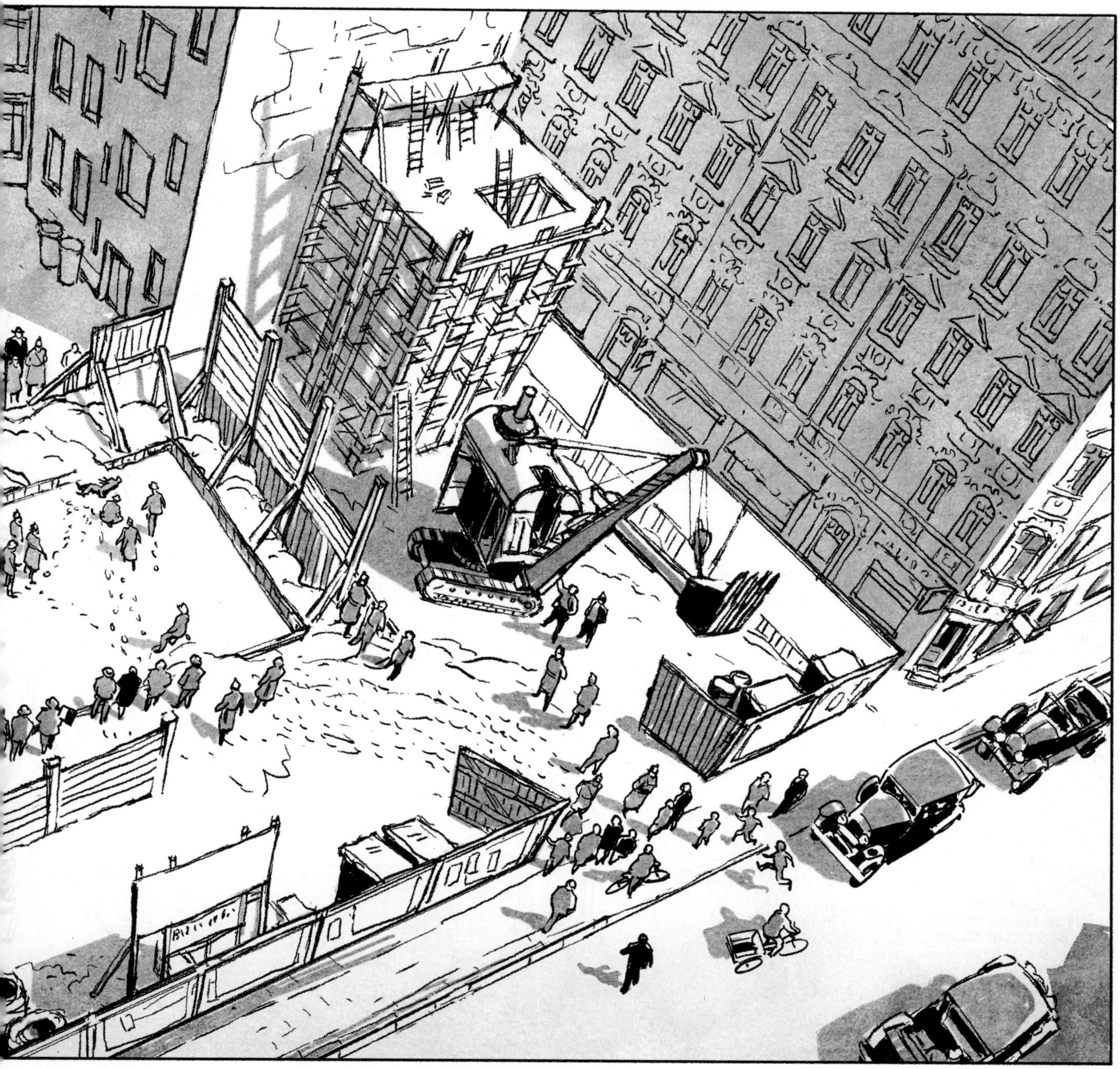

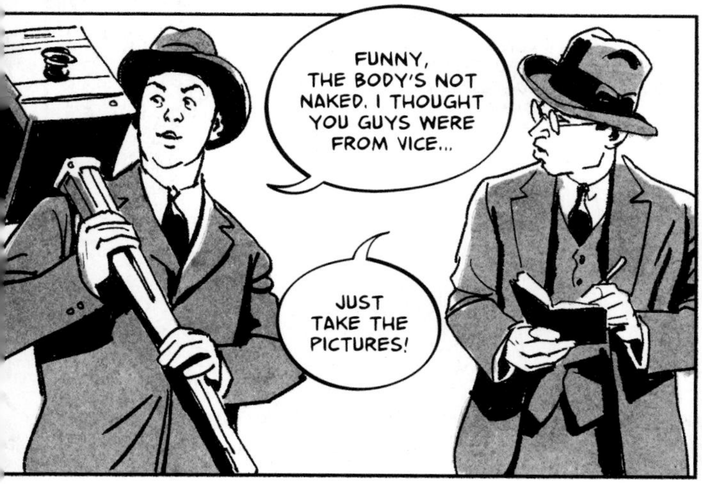
FUNNY, THE BODY'S NOT NAKED. I THOUGHT YOU GUYS WERE FROM VICE...
JUST TAKE THE PICTURES!

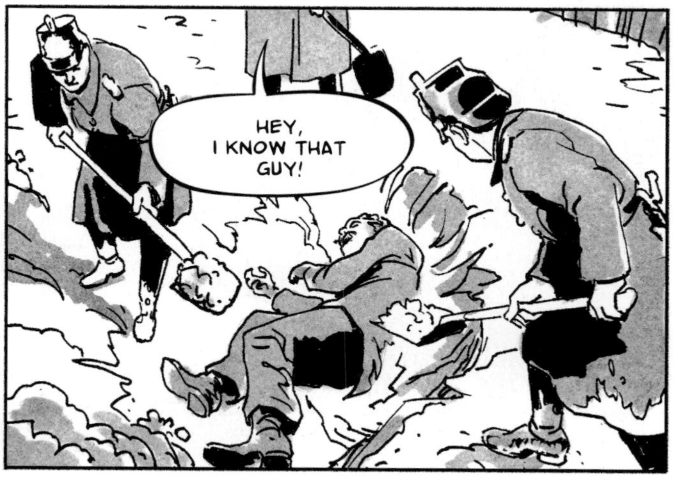
HEY, I KNOW THAT GUY!

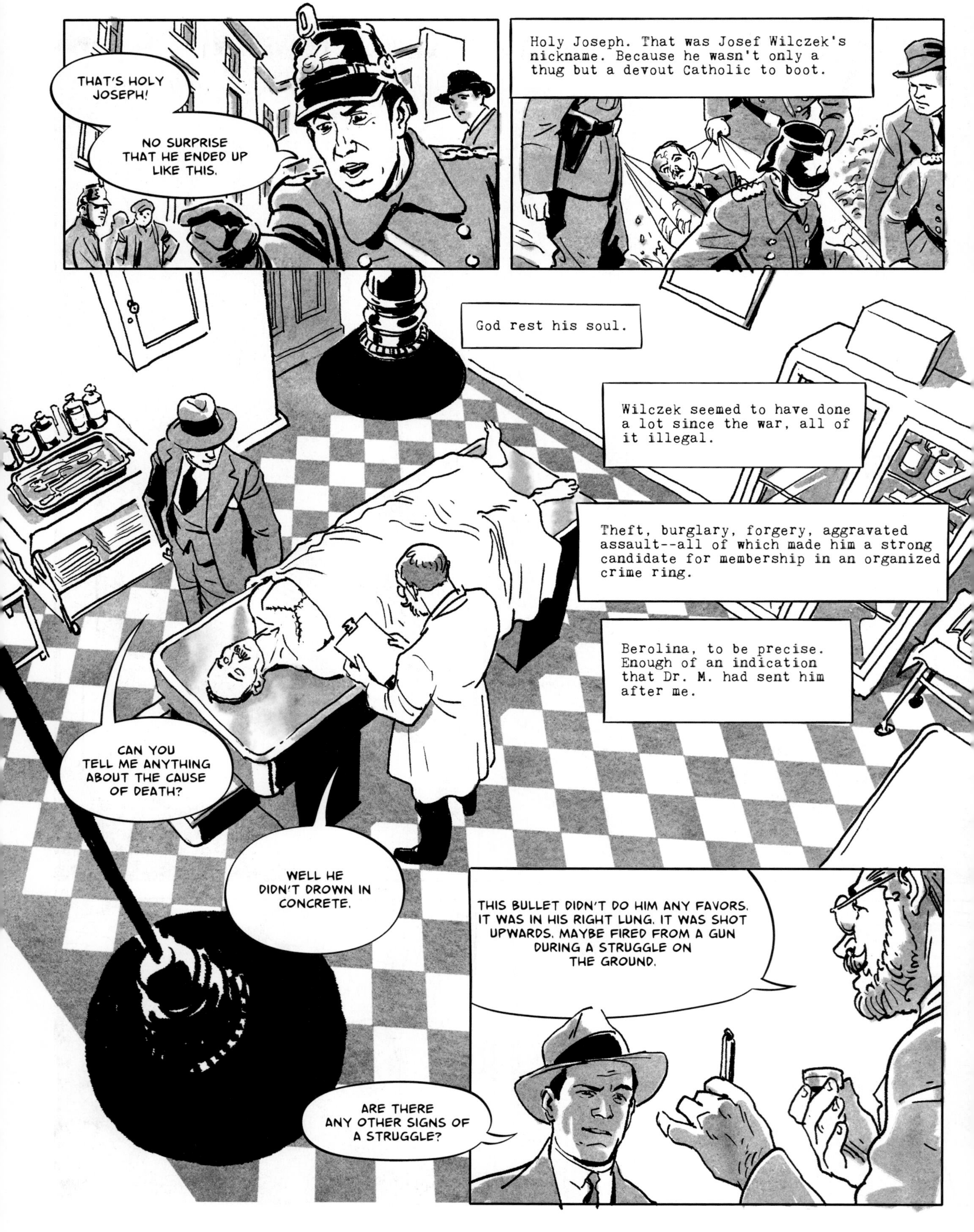
THAT'S HOLY JOSEPH!
NO SURPRISE THAT HE ENDED UP LIKE THIS.
Holy Joseph. That was Josef Wilczek's nickname. Because he wasn't only a thug but a devout Catholic to boot.
God rest his soul.
Wilczek seemed to have done a lot since the war, all of it illegal.
Theft, burglary, forgery, aggravated assault--all of which made him a strong candidate for membership in an organized crime ring.
Berolina, to be precise. Enough of an indication that Dr. M. had sent him after me.
CAN YOU TELL ME ANYTHING ABOUT THE CAUSE OF DEATH?
WELL HE DIDN'T DROWN IN CONCRETE.
THIS BULLET DIDN'T DO HIM ANY FAVORS. IT WAS IN HIS RIGHT LUNG. IT WAS SHOT UPWARDS. MAYBE FIRED FROM A GUN DURING A STRUGGLE ON THE GROUND.
ARE THERE ANY OTHER SIGNS OF A STRUGGLE?

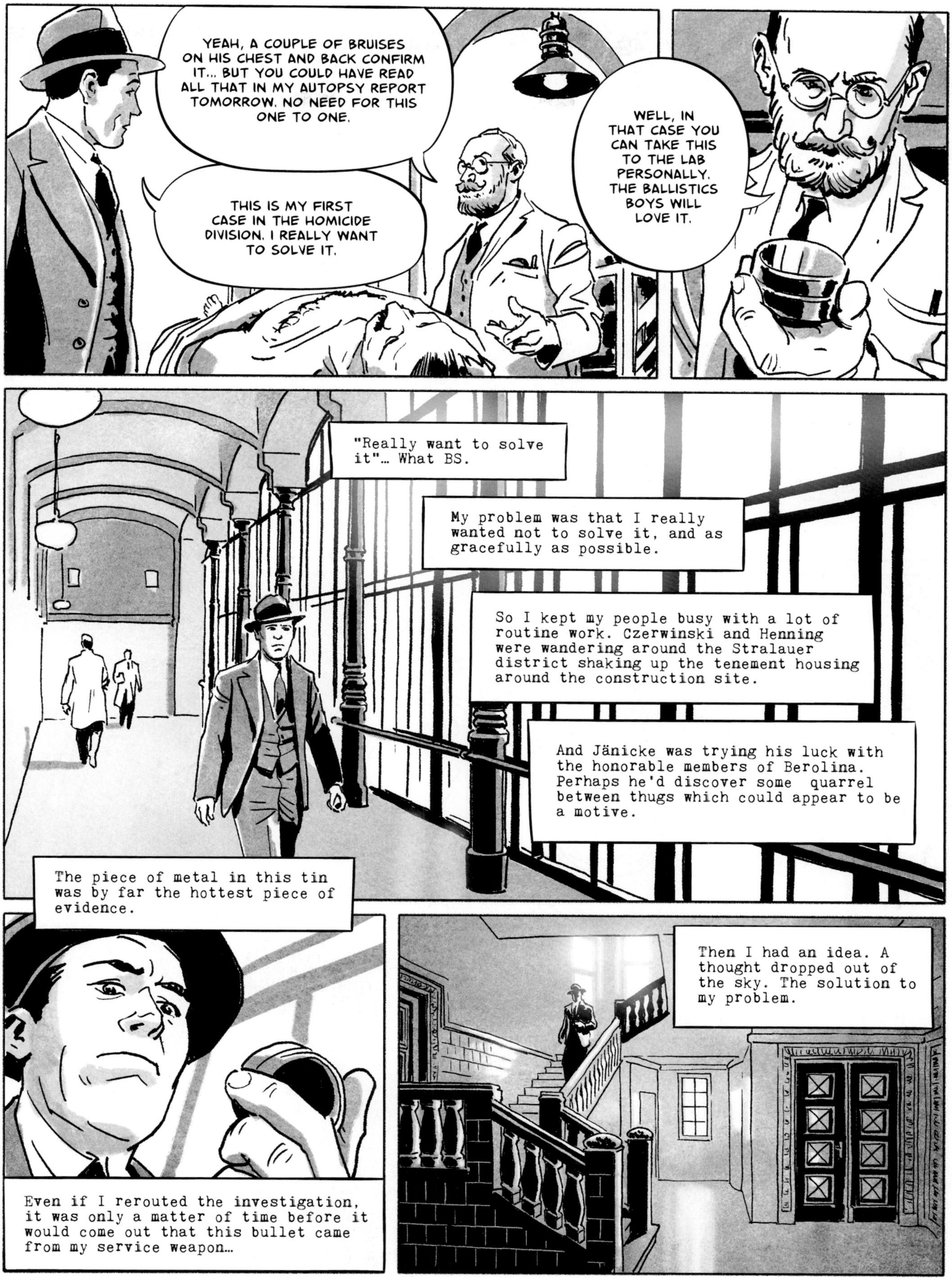
THIS IS MY FIRST CASE IN THE HOMICIDE DIVISION. I REALLY WANT TO SOLVE IT.
YEAH, A COUPLE OF BRUISES ON HIS CHEST AND BACK CONFIRM IT... BUT YOU COULD HAVE READ ALL THAT IN MY AUTOPSY REPORT TOMORROW. NO NEED FOR THIS ONE TO ONE.
WELL, IN THAT CASE YOU CAN TAKE THIS TO THE LAB PERSONALLY. THE BALLISTICS BOYS WILL LOVE IT.
"Really want to solve it"... What BS.
My problem was that I really wanted not to solve it, and as gracefully as possible.
So I kept my people busy with a lot of routine work. Czerwinski and Henning were wandering around the Stralauer district shaking up the tenement housing around the construction site.
And Jänicke was trying his luck with the honorable members of Berolina. Perhaps he'd discover some quarrel between thugs which could appear to be a motive.
The piece of metal in this tin was by far the hottest piece of evidence.
Even if I rerouted the investigation, it was only a matter of time before it would come out that this bullet came from my service weapon...
Then I had an idea. A thought dropped out of the sky. The solution to my problem.

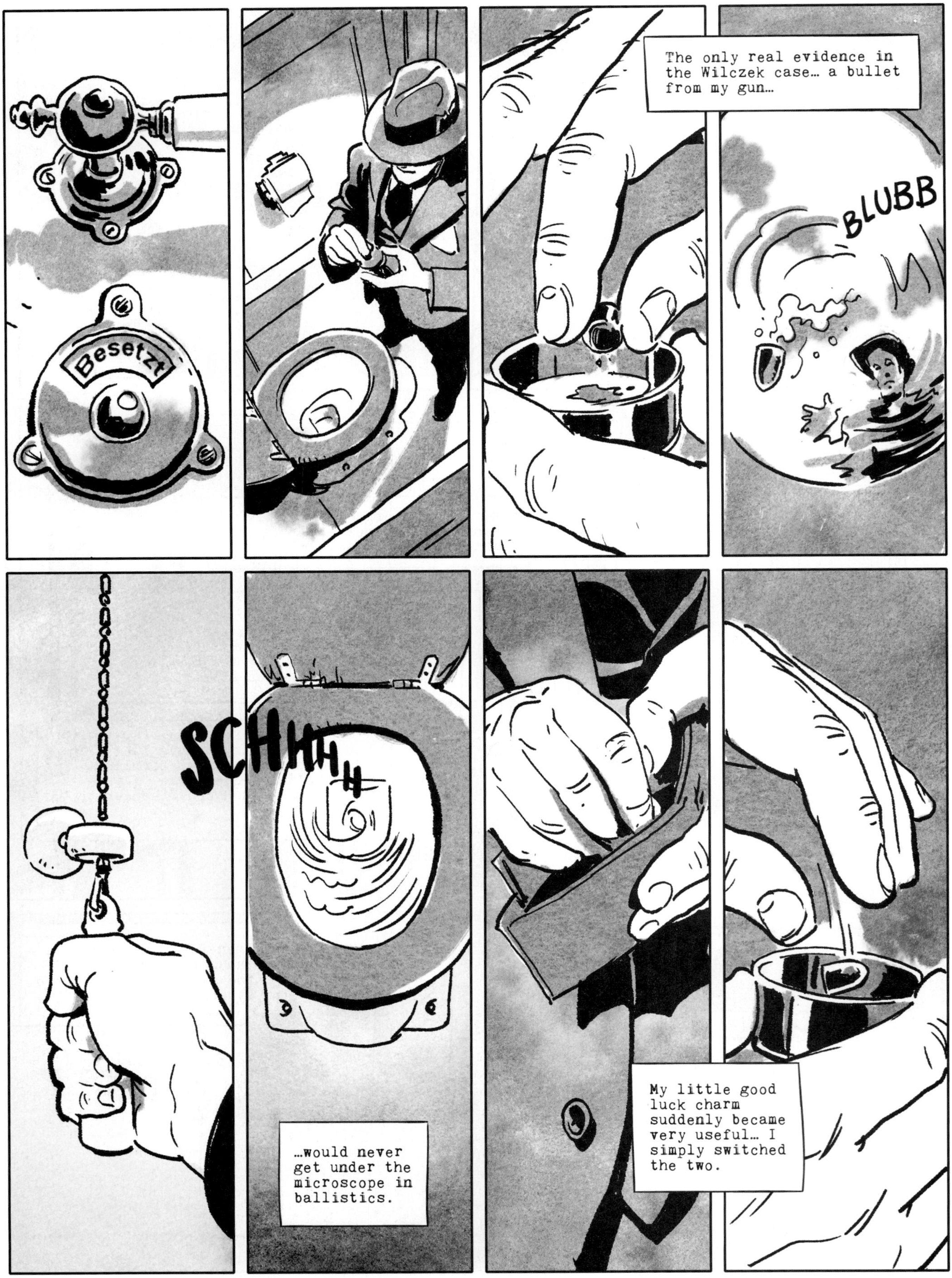
Besetzt
The only real evidence in the Wilczek case… a bullet from my gun…
BLUBB
SCHHHHH
…would never get under the microscope in ballistics.
My little good luck charm suddenly became very useful… I simply switched the two.

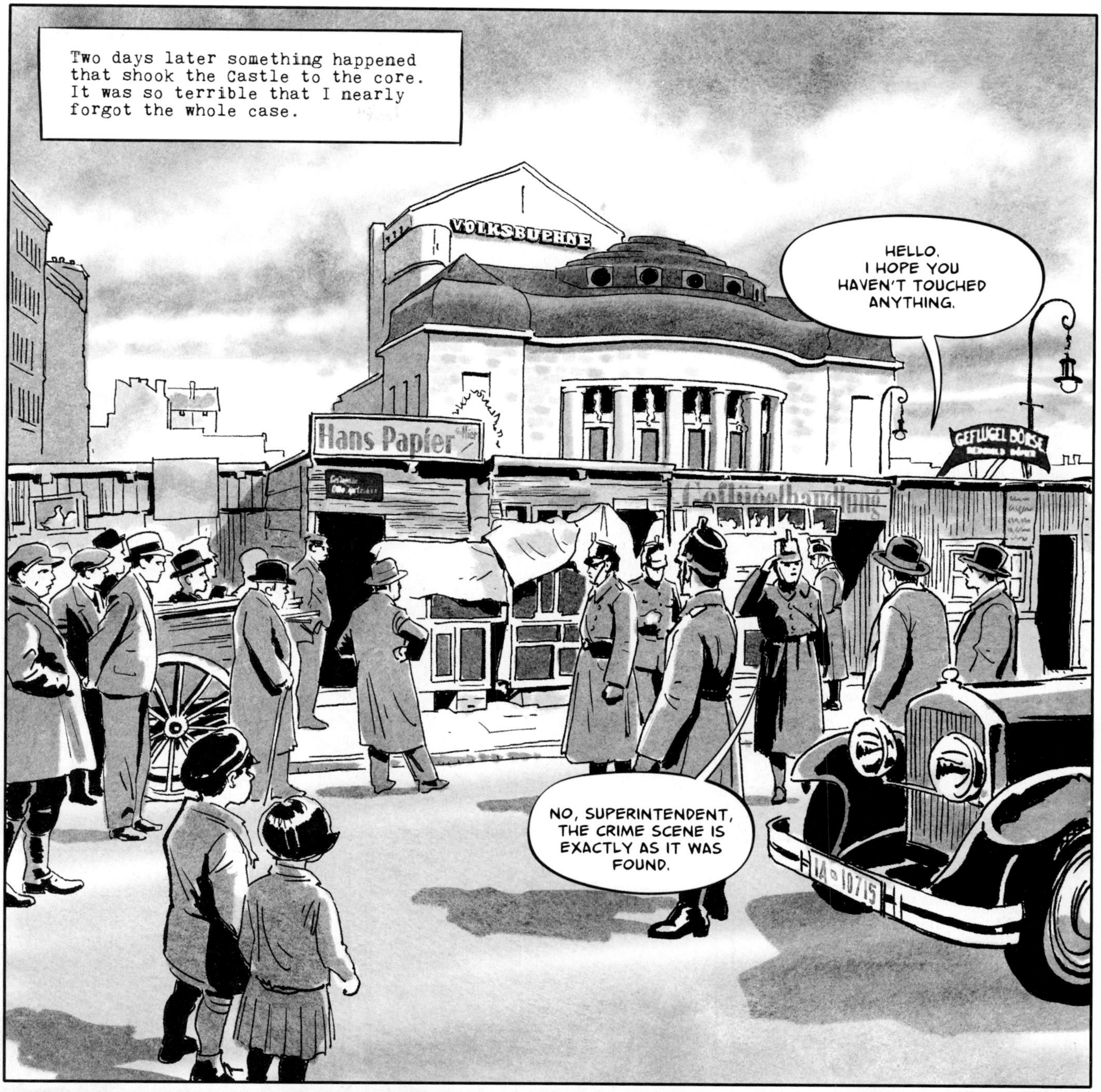
Two days later something happened that shook the Castle to the core. It was so terrible that I nearly forgot the whole case.
VOLKSBUEHNE
Hans Papier
HELLO. I HOPE YOU HAVEN'T TOUCHED ANYTHING.
NO, SUPERINTENDENT, THE CRIME SCENE IS EXACTLY AS IT WAS FOUND.

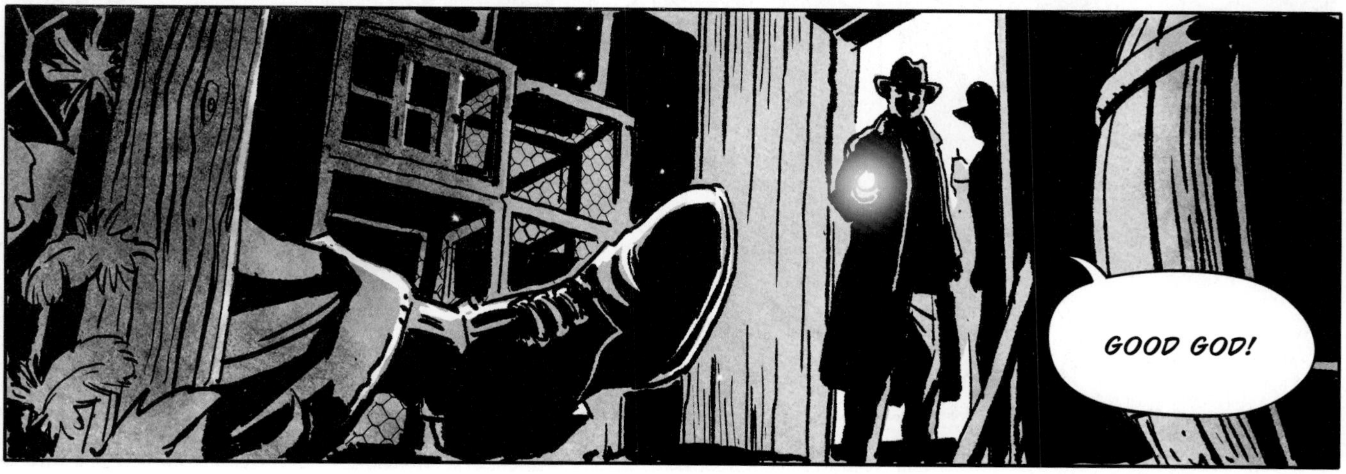
GOOD GOD!

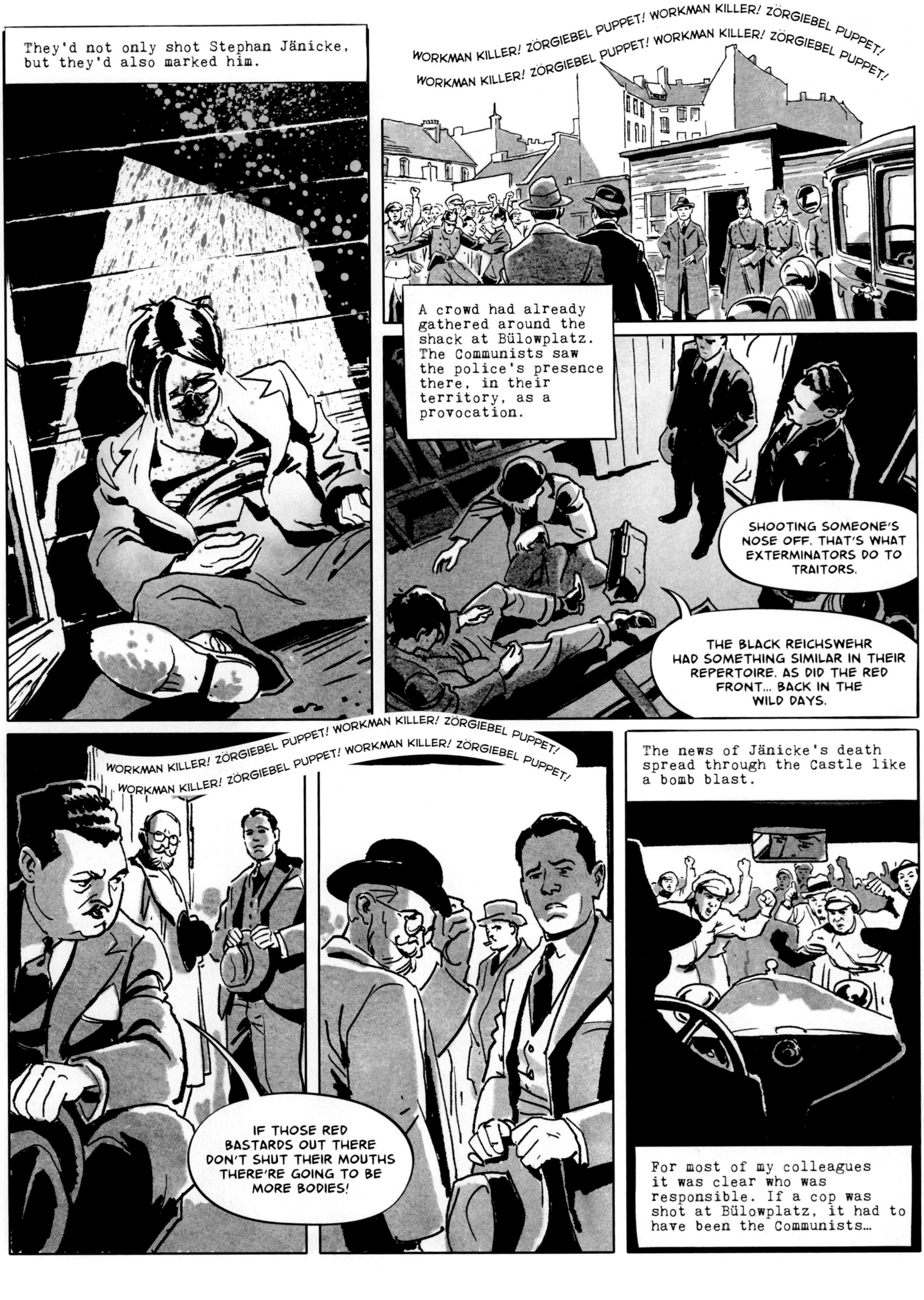
They'd not only shot Stephan Jänicke, but they'd also marked him.
WORKMAN KILLER! ZÖRGIEBEL PUPPET! WORKMAN KILLER! ZÖRGIEBEL PUPPET!
WORKMAN KILLER! ZÖRGIEBEL PUPPET! WORKMAN KILLER! ZÖRGIEBEL PUPPET!
A crowd had already gathered around the shack at Bülowplatz. The Communists saw the police's presence there, in their territory, as a provocation.
SHOOTING SOMEONE'S NOSE OFF. THAT'S WHAT EXTERMINATORS DO TO TRAITORS.
THE BLACK REICHSWEHR HAD SOMETHING SIMILAR IN THEIR REPERTOIRE. AS DID THE RED FRONT... BACK IN THE WILD DAYS.
WORKMAN KILLER! ZÖRGIEBEL PUPPET! WORKMAN KILLER! ZÖRGIEBEL PUPPET!
WORKMAN KILLER! ZÖRGIEBEL PUPPET! WORKMAN KILLER! ZÖRGIEBEL PUPPET!
IF THOSE RED BASTARDS OUT THERE DON'T SHUT THEIR MOUTHS THERE'RE GOING TO BE MORE BODIES!
The news of Jänicke's death spread through the Castle like a bomb blast.
For most of my colleagues it was clear who was responsible. If a cop was shot at Bülowplatz, it had to have been the Communists...

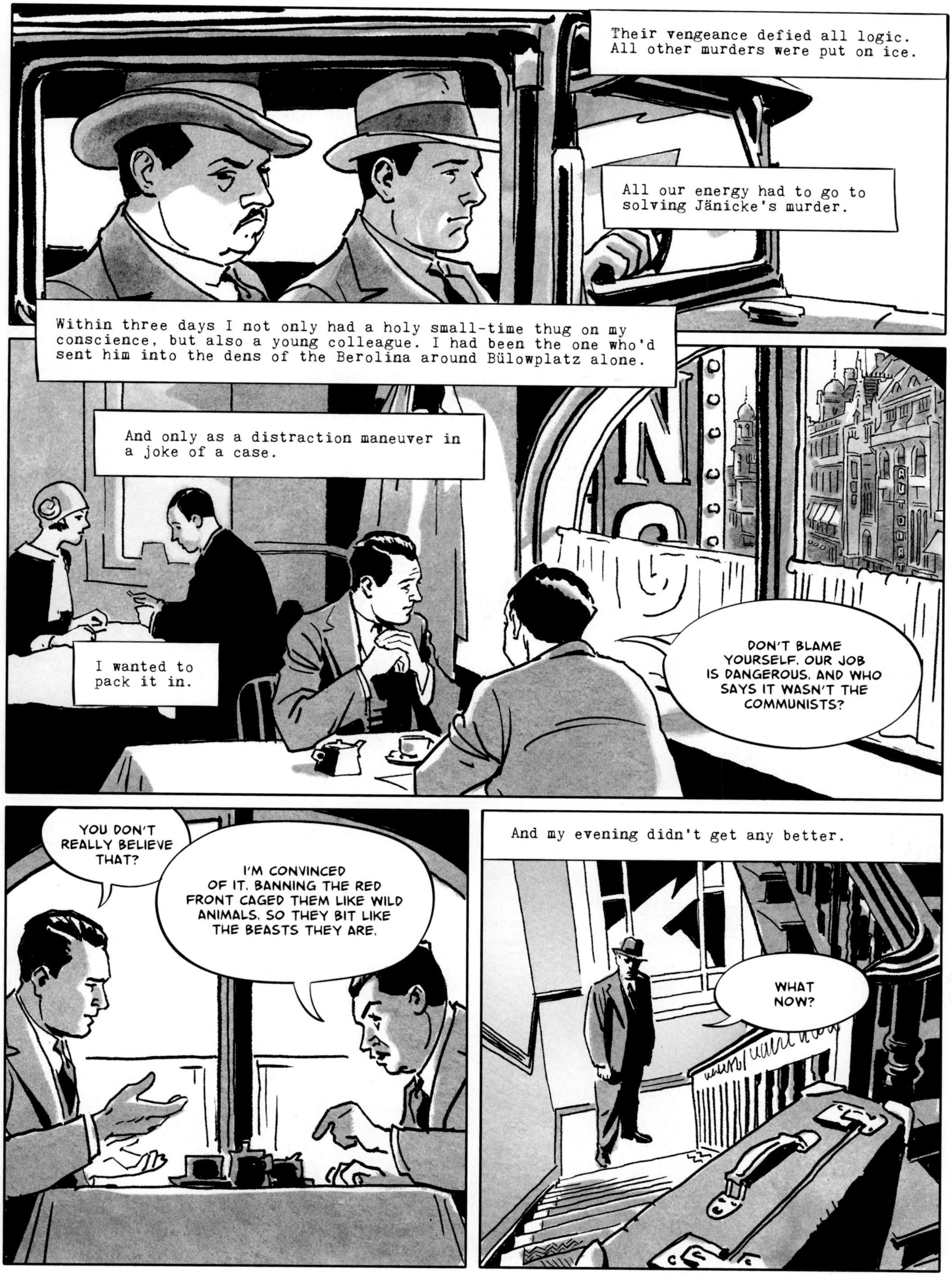
Their vengeance defied all logic. All other murders were put on ice.
All our energy had to go to solving Jänicke's murder.
Within three days I not only had a holy small-time thug on my conscience, but also a young colleague. I had been the one who'd sent him into the dens of the Berolina around Bülowplatz alone.
And only as a distraction maneuver in a joke of a case.
I wanted to pack it in.
DON'T BLAME YOURSELF. OUR JOB IS DANGEROUS. AND WHO SAYS IT WASN'T THE COMMUNISTS?
YOU DON'T REALLY BELIEVE THAT?
I'M CONVINCED OF IT. BANNING THE RED FRONT CAGED THEM LIKE WILD ANIMALS. SO THEY BIT LIKE THE BEASTS THEY ARE.
And my evening didn't get any better.
WHAT NOW?

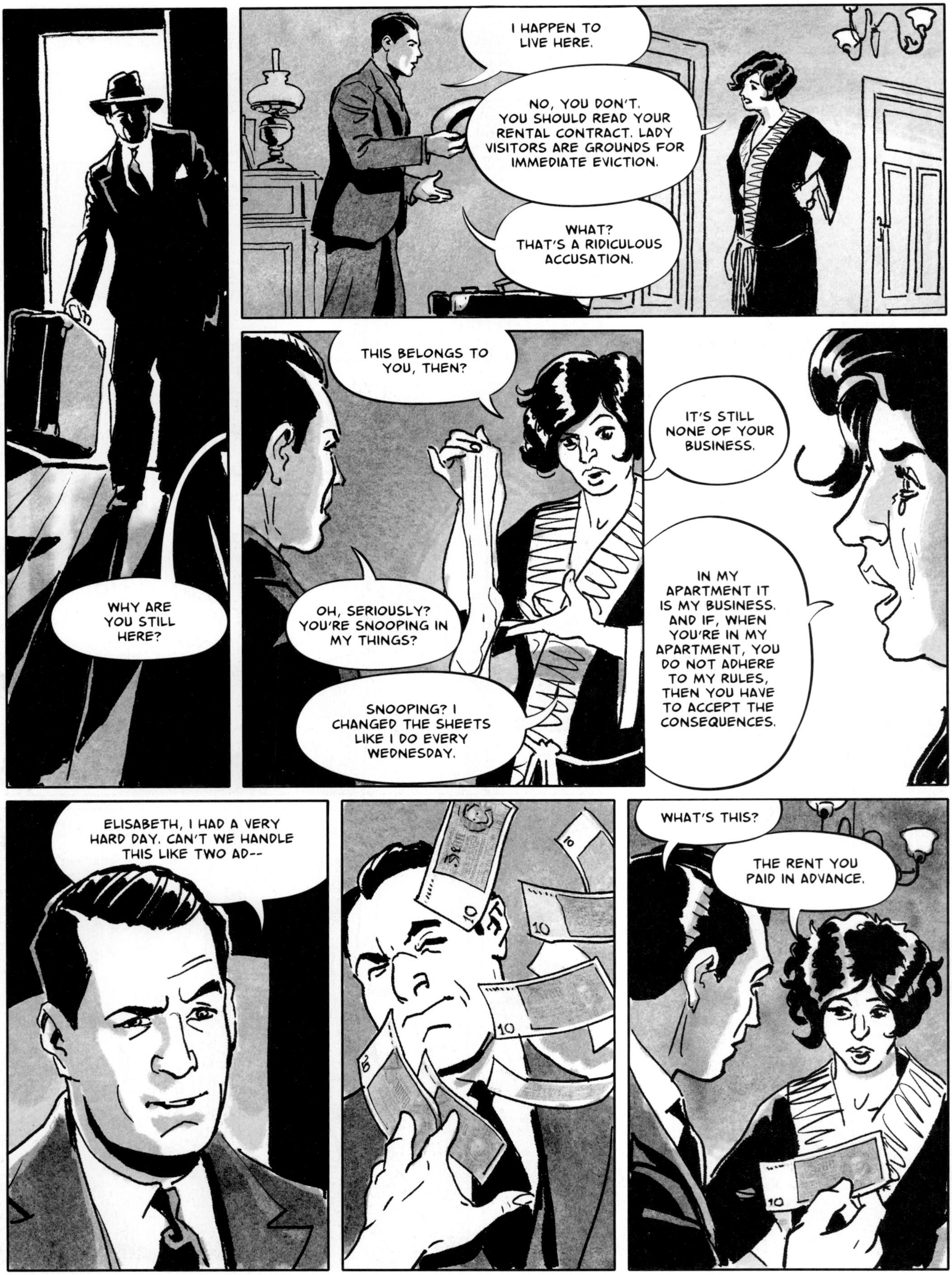
WHY ARE YOU STILL HERE?
I HAPPEN TO LIVE HERE.
NO, YOU DON'T. YOU SHOULD READ YOUR RENTAL CONTRACT. LADY VISITORS ARE GROUNDS FOR IMMEDIATE EVICTION.
WHAT? THAT'S A RIDICULOUS ACCUSATION.
THIS BELONGS TO YOU, THEN?
OH, SERIOUSLY? YOU'RE SNOOPING IN MY THINGS?
SNOOPING? I CHANGED THE SHEETS LIKE I DO EVERY WEDNESDAY.
IT'S STILL NONE OF YOUR BUSINESS.
IN MY APARTMENT IT IS MY BUSINESS. AND IF, WHEN YOU'RE IN MY APARTMENT, YOU DO NOT ADHERE TO MY RULES, THEN YOU HAVE TO ACCEPT THE CONSEQUENCES.
ELISABETH, I HAD A VERY HARD DAY. CAN'T WE HANDLE THIS LIKE TWO AD--
WHAT'S THIS?
THE RENT YOU PAID IN ADVANCE.

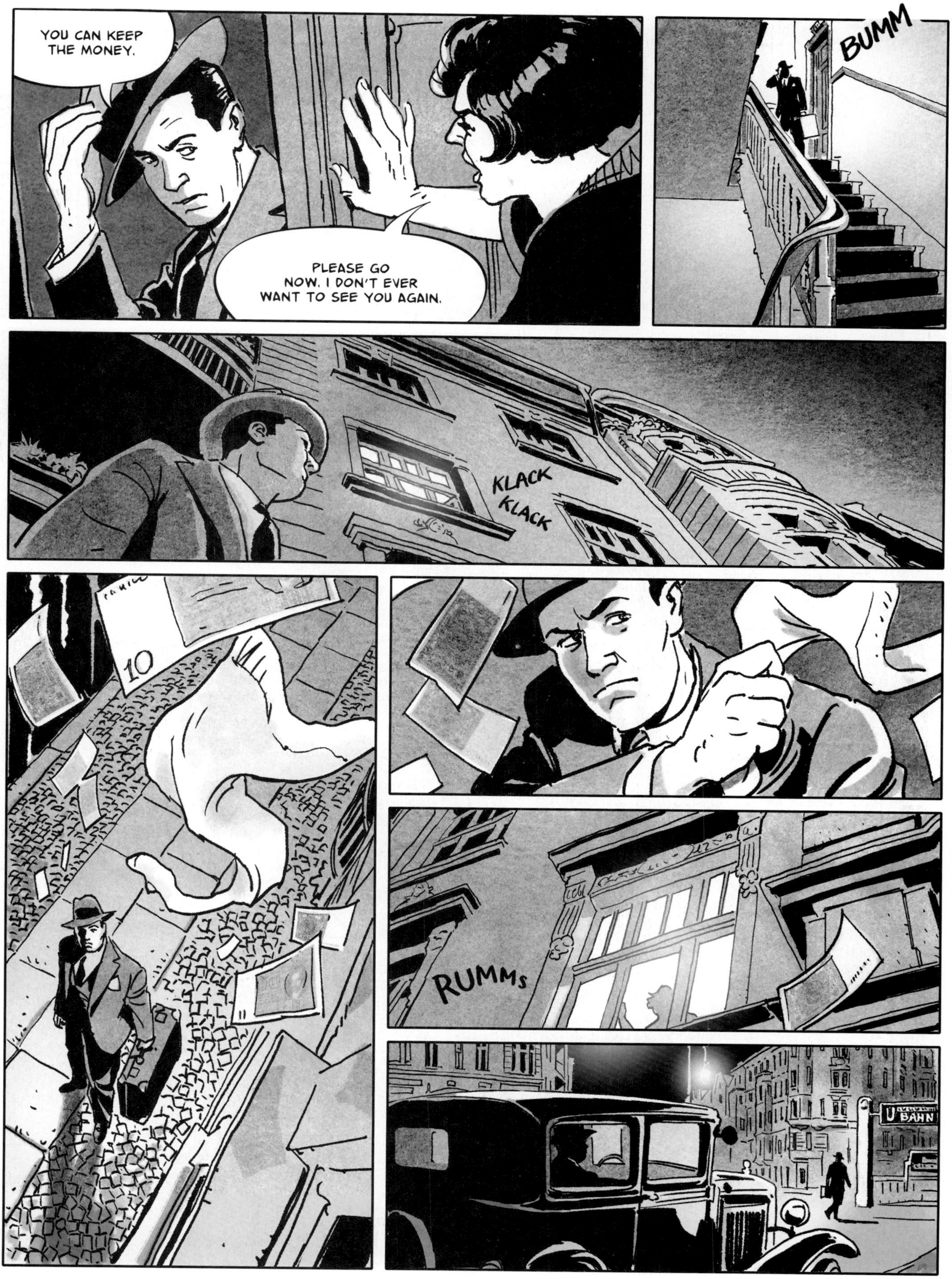
YOU CAN KEEP THE MONEY.
PLEASE GO NOW. I DON'T EVER WANT TO SEE YOU AGAIN.
BUMM
KLACK
KLACK
10
RUMMs
U BAHN

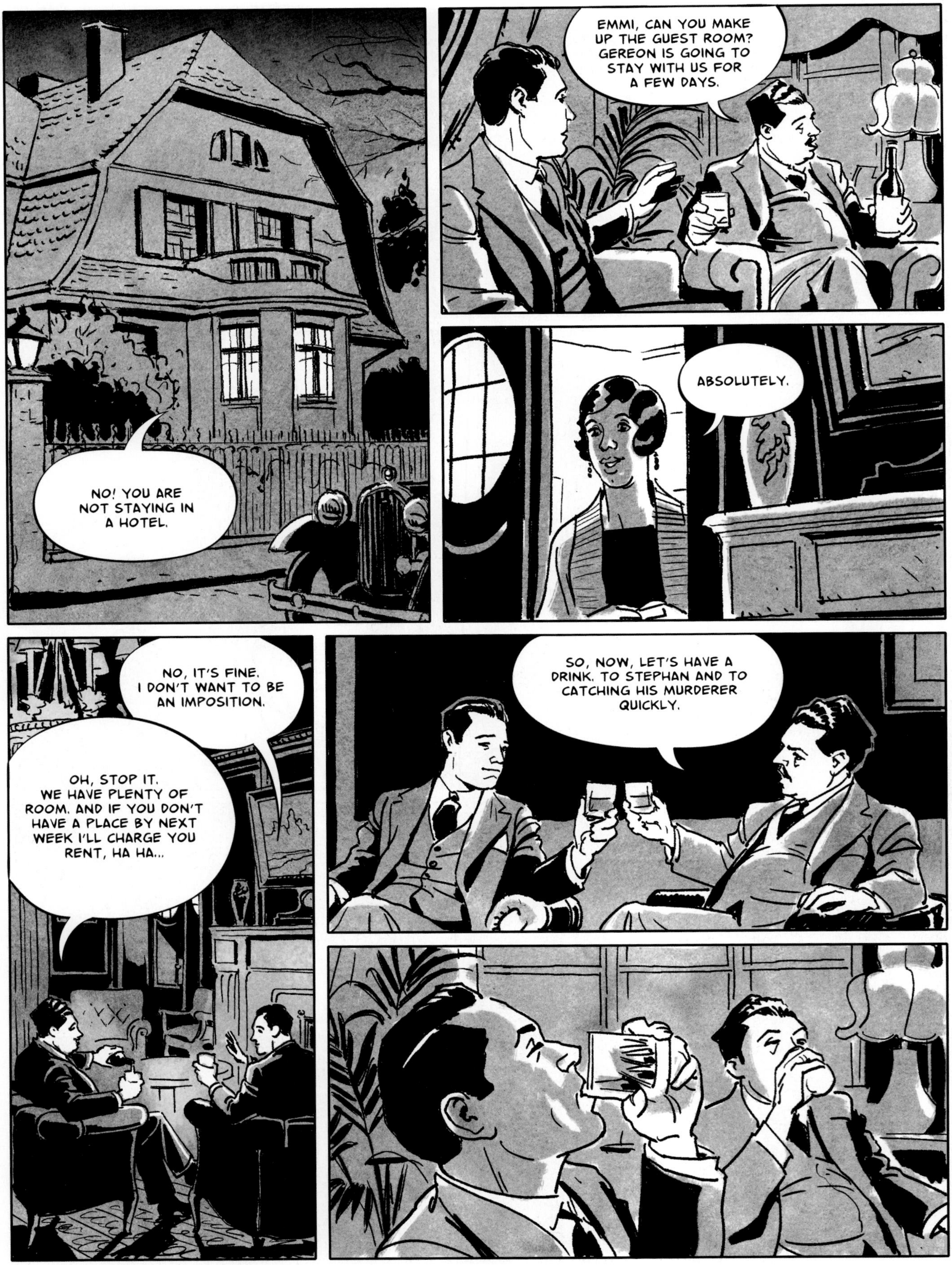
NO! YOU ARE NOT STAYING IN A HOTEL.
EMMI, CAN YOU MAKE UP THE GUEST ROOM? GEREON IS GOING TO STAY WITH US FOR A FEW DAYS.
ABSOLUTELY.
NO, IT'S FINE. I DON'T WANT TO BE AN IMPOSITION.
OH, STOP IT. WE HAVE PLENTY OF ROOM. AND IF YOU DON'T HAVE A PLACE BY NEXT WEEK I'LL CHARGE YOU RENT, HA HA...
SO, NOW, LET'S HAVE A DRINK. TO STEPHAN AND TO CATCHING HIS MURDERER QUICKLY.

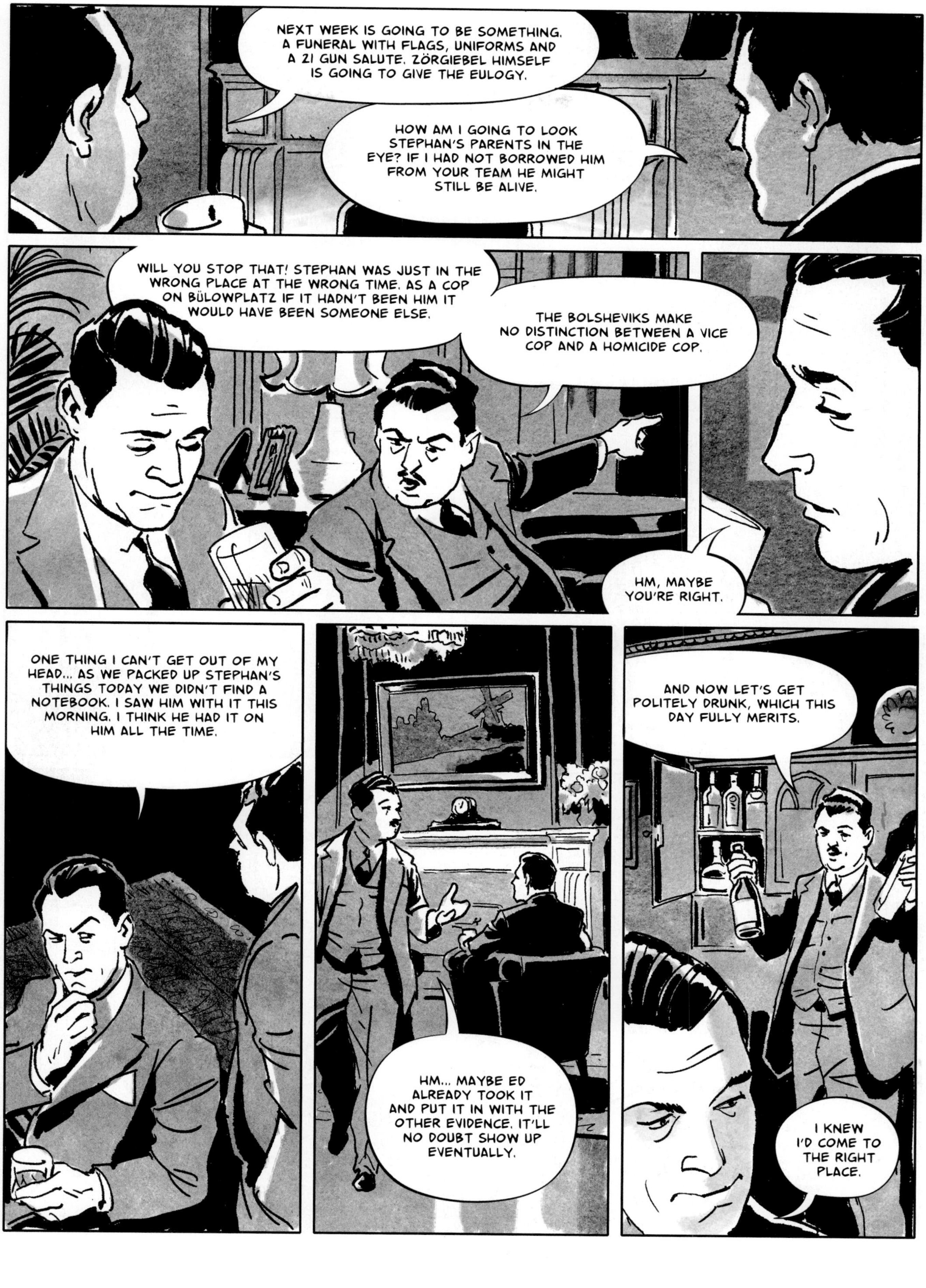
NEXT WEEK IS GOING TO BE SOMETHING. A FUNERAL WITH FLAGS, UNIFORMS AND A 21 GUN SALUTE. ZÖRGIEBEL HIMSELF IS GOING TO GIVE THE EULOGY.
HOW AM I GOING TO LOOK STEPHAN'S PARENTS IN THE EYE? IF I HAD NOT BORROWED HIM FROM YOUR TEAM HE MIGHT STILL BE ALIVE.
WILL YOU STOP THAT! STEPHAN WAS JUST IN THE WRONG PLACE AT THE WRONG TIME. AS A COP ON BÜLOWPLATZ IF IT HADN'T BEEN HIM IT WOULD HAVE BEEN SOMEONE ELSE.
THE BOLSHEVIKS MAKE NO DISTINCTION BETWEEN A VICE COP AND A HOMICIDE COP.
HM, MAYBE YOU'RE RIGHT.
ONE THING I CAN'T GET OUT OF MY HEAD... AS WE PACKED UP STEPHAN'S THINGS TODAY WE DIDN'T FIND A NOTEBOOK. I SAW HIM WITH IT THIS MORNING. I THINK HE HAD IT ON HIM ALL THE TIME.
HM... MAYBE ED ALREADY TOOK IT AND PUT IT IN WITH THE OTHER EVIDENCE. IT'LL NO DOUBT SHOW UP EVENTUALLY.
AND NOW LET'S GET POLITELY DRUNK, WHICH THIS DAY FULLY MERITS.
I KNEW I'D COME TO THE RIGHT PLACE.

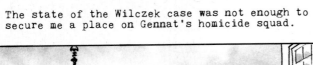

The state of the Wilczek case was not enough to secure me a place on Gennat's homicide squad.

But I still had a trump card up my sleeve--the Möckern Bridge lead.

INSPECTOR RATH, MR. ZÖRGIEBEL CAN SEE YOU NOW.

MY DEAR MR. RATH. IT'S GOOD TO SEE YOU. PLEASE, TAKE A SEAT. I HOPE YOUR DEAR FATHER IS WELL?

YOU PROBABLY KNOW MORE THAN I DO. WE DON'T SPEAK THAT OFTEN.

SO THEN, WHAT CAN I DO FOR YOU?

I'M HOPING I CAN DO SOMETHING FOR YOU, CHIEF. THROUGH SHEER COINCIDENCE I HAVE A NEW LEAD ON THE MÖCKERN BRIDGE CASE THAT COULD HELP A LOT.

THE MÖCKERN BRIDGE CASE? THAT'S GENNAT'S. WHY ARE YOU COMING TO ME WITH THIS? AND WHY DO YOU HAVE INFORMATION ON A CASE THAT YOU ARE NOT INVESTIGATING?

THAT'S A LONG STORY. I JUST THOUGHT IT WAS BETTER TO GO TO THE TOP. THEN YOU, SIR, COULD DECIDE HOW TO PROCEED.

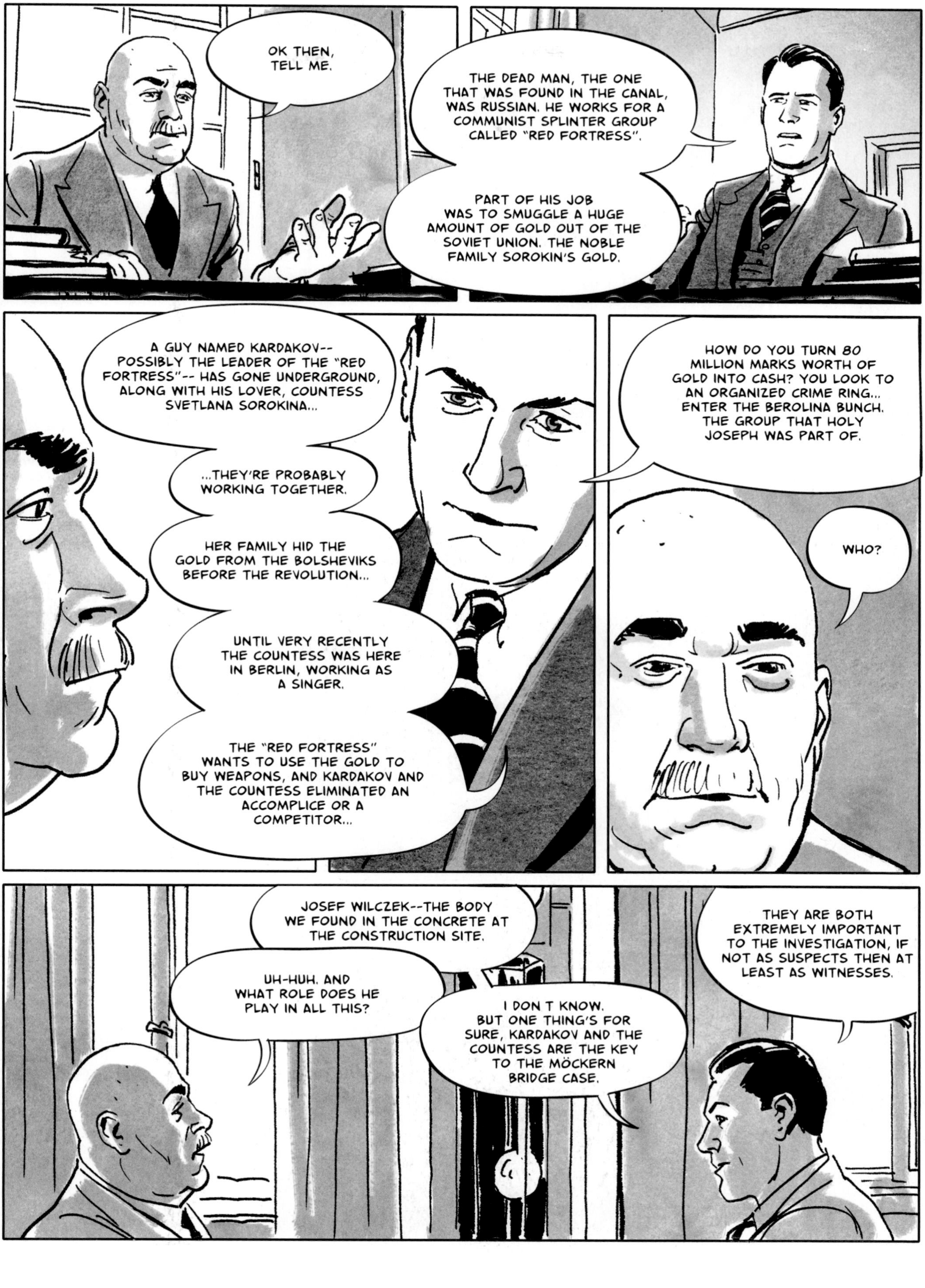
OK THEN, TELL ME.
THE DEAD MAN, THE ONE THAT WAS FOUND IN THE CANAL, WAS RUSSIAN. HE WORKS FOR A COMMUNIST SPLINTER GROUP CALLED "RED FORTRESS".
PART OF HIS JOB WAS TO SMUGGLE A HUGE AMOUNT OF GOLD OUT OF THE SOVIET UNION. THE NOBLE FAMILY SOROKIN'S GOLD.
A GUY NAMED KARDAKOV-- POSSIBLY THE LEADER OF THE "RED FORTRESS"-- HAS GONE UNDERGROUND, ALONG WITH HIS LOVER, COUNTESS SVETLANA SOROKINA...
...THEY'RE PROBABLY WORKING TOGETHER.
HER FAMILY HID THE GOLD FROM THE BOLSHEVIKS BEFORE THE REVOLUTION...
UNTIL VERY RECENTLY THE COUNTESS WAS HERE IN BERLIN, WORKING AS A SINGER.
THE "RED FORTRESS" WANTS TO USE THE GOLD TO BUY WEAPONS, AND KARDAKOV AND THE COUNTESS ELIMINATED AN ACCOMPLICE OR A COMPETITOR...
HOW DO YOU TURN 80 MILLION MARKS WORTH OF GOLD INTO CASH? YOU LOOK TO AN ORGANIZED CRIME RING... ENTER THE BEROLINA BUNCH. THE GROUP THAT HOLY JOSEPH WAS PART OF.
WHO?
JOSEF WILCZEK--THE BODY WE FOUND IN THE CONCRETE AT THE CONSTRUCTION SITE.
UH-HUH. AND WHAT ROLE DOES HE PLAY IN ALL THIS?
I DON T KNOW. BUT ONE THING'S FOR SURE, KARDAKOV AND THE COUNTESS ARE THE KEY TO THE MÖCKERN BRIDGE CASE.
THEY ARE BOTH EXTREMELY IMPORTANT TO THE INVESTIGATION, IF NOT AS SUSPECTS THEN AT LEAST AS WITNESSES.

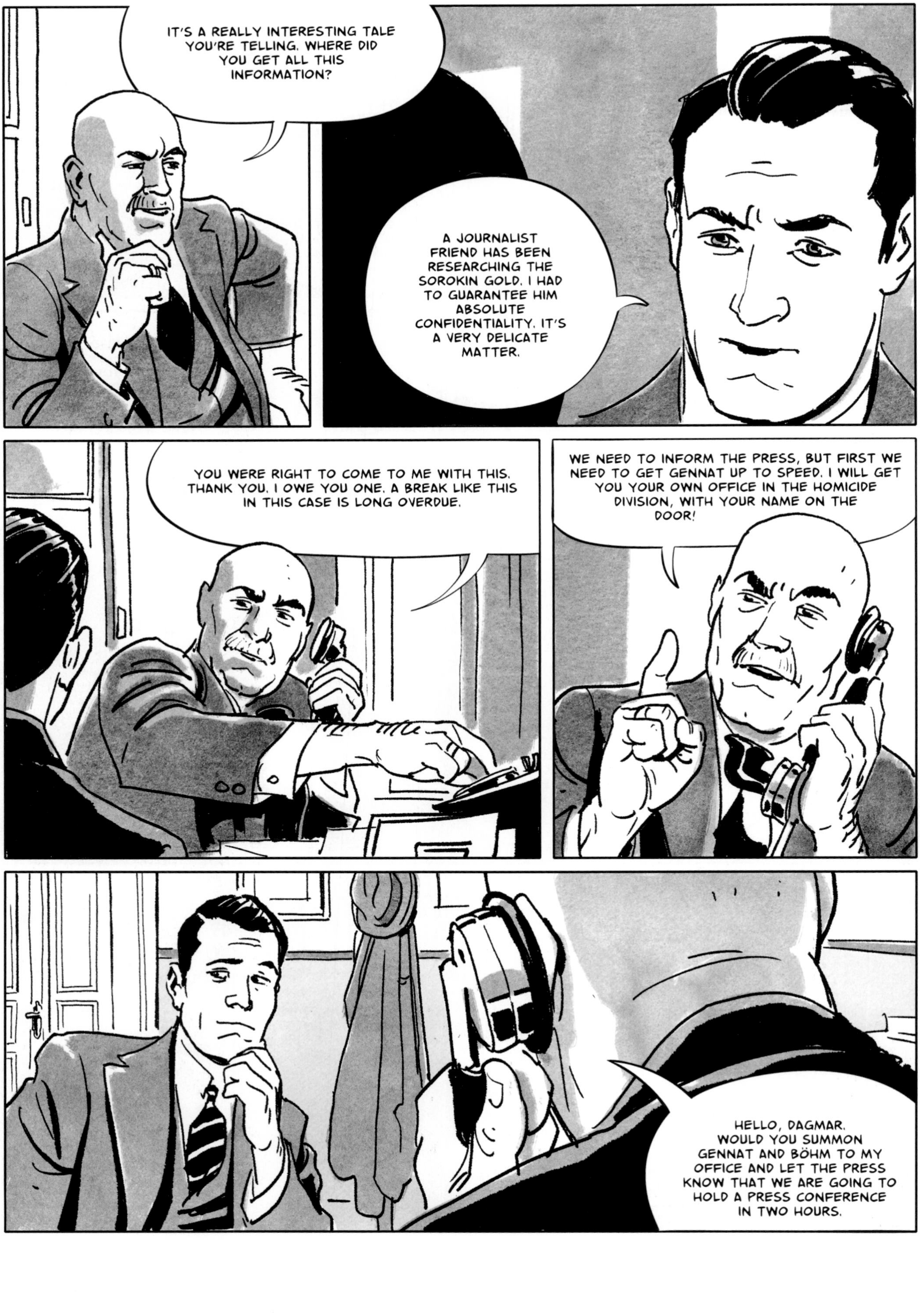
IT'S A REALLY INTERESTING TALE YOU'RE TELLING. WHERE DID YOU GET ALL THIS INFORMATION?
A JOURNALIST FRIEND HAS BEEN RESEARCHING THE SOROKIN GOLD. I HAD TO GUARANTEE HIM ABSOLUTE CONFIDENTIALITY. IT'S A VERY DELICATE MATTER.
YOU WERE RIGHT TO COME TO ME WITH THIS. THANK YOU. I OWE YOU ONE. A BREAK LIKE THIS IN THIS CASE IS LONG OVERDUE.
WE NEED TO INFORM THE PRESS, BUT FIRST WE NEED TO GET GENNAT UP TO SPEED. I WILL GET YOU YOUR OWN OFFICE IN THE HOMICIDE DIVISION, WITH YOUR NAME ON THE DOOR!
HELLO, DAGMAR. WOULD YOU SUMMON GENNAT AND BÖHM TO MY OFFICE AND LET THE PRESS KNOW THAT WE ARE GOING TO HOLD A PRESS CONFERENCE IN TWO HOURS.

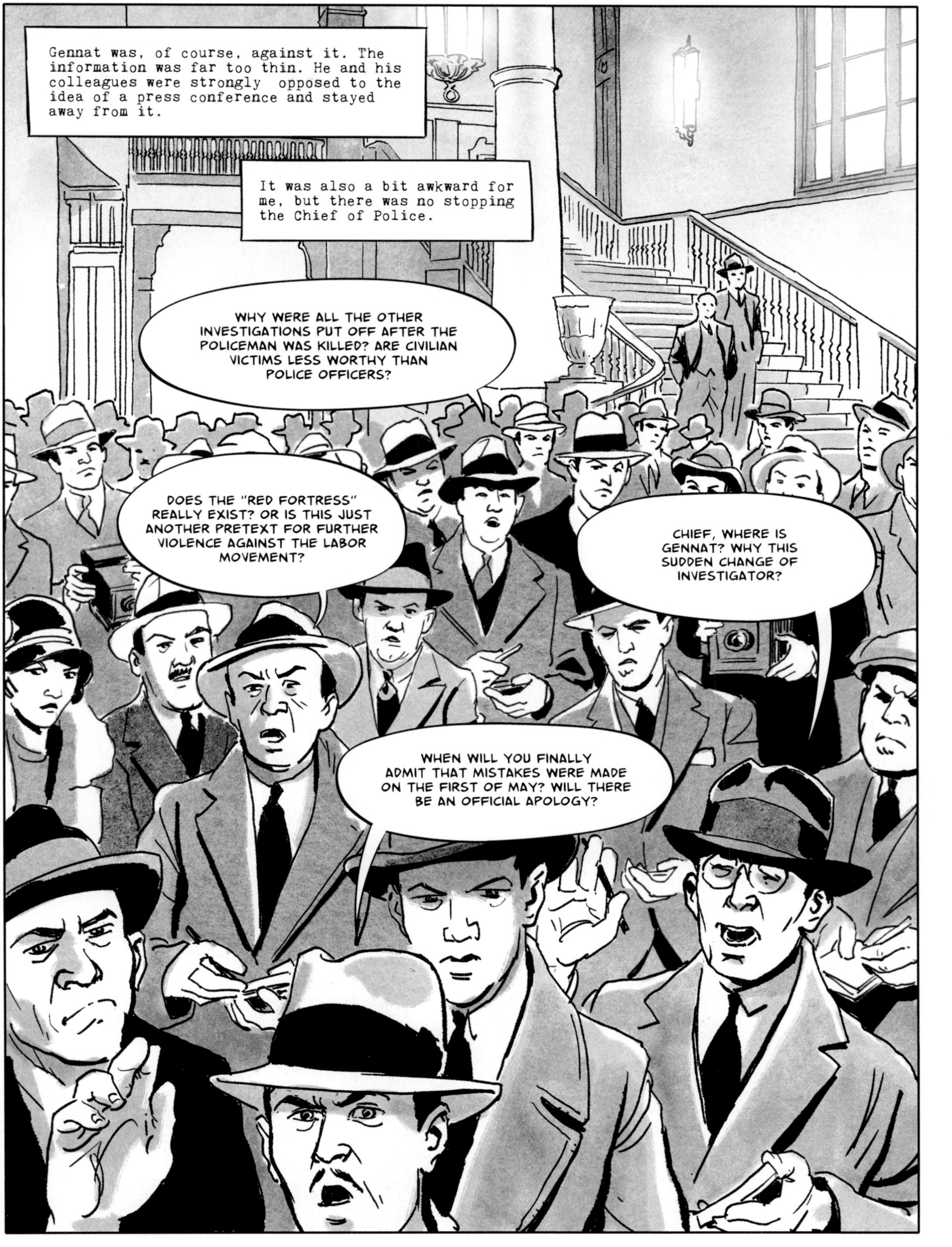

Gennat was, of course, against it. The information was far too thin. He and his colleagues were strongly opposed to the idea of a press conference and stayed away from it.
It was also a bit awkward for me, but there was no stopping the Chief of Police.
WHY WERE ALL THE OTHER INVESTIGATIONS PUT OFF AFTER THE POLICEMAN WAS KILLED? ARE CIVILIAN VICTIMS LESS WORTHY THAN POLICE OFFICERS?
DOES THE "RED FORTRESS" REALLY EXIST? OR IS THIS JUST ANOTHER PRETEXT FOR FURTHER VIOLENCE AGAINST THE LABOR MOVEMENT?
CHIEF, WHERE IS GENNAT? WHY THIS SUDDEN CHANGE OF INVESTIGATOR?
WHEN WILL YOU FINALLY ADMIT THAT MISTAKES WERE MADE ON THE FIRST OF MAY? WILL THERE BE AN OFFICIAL APOLOGY?

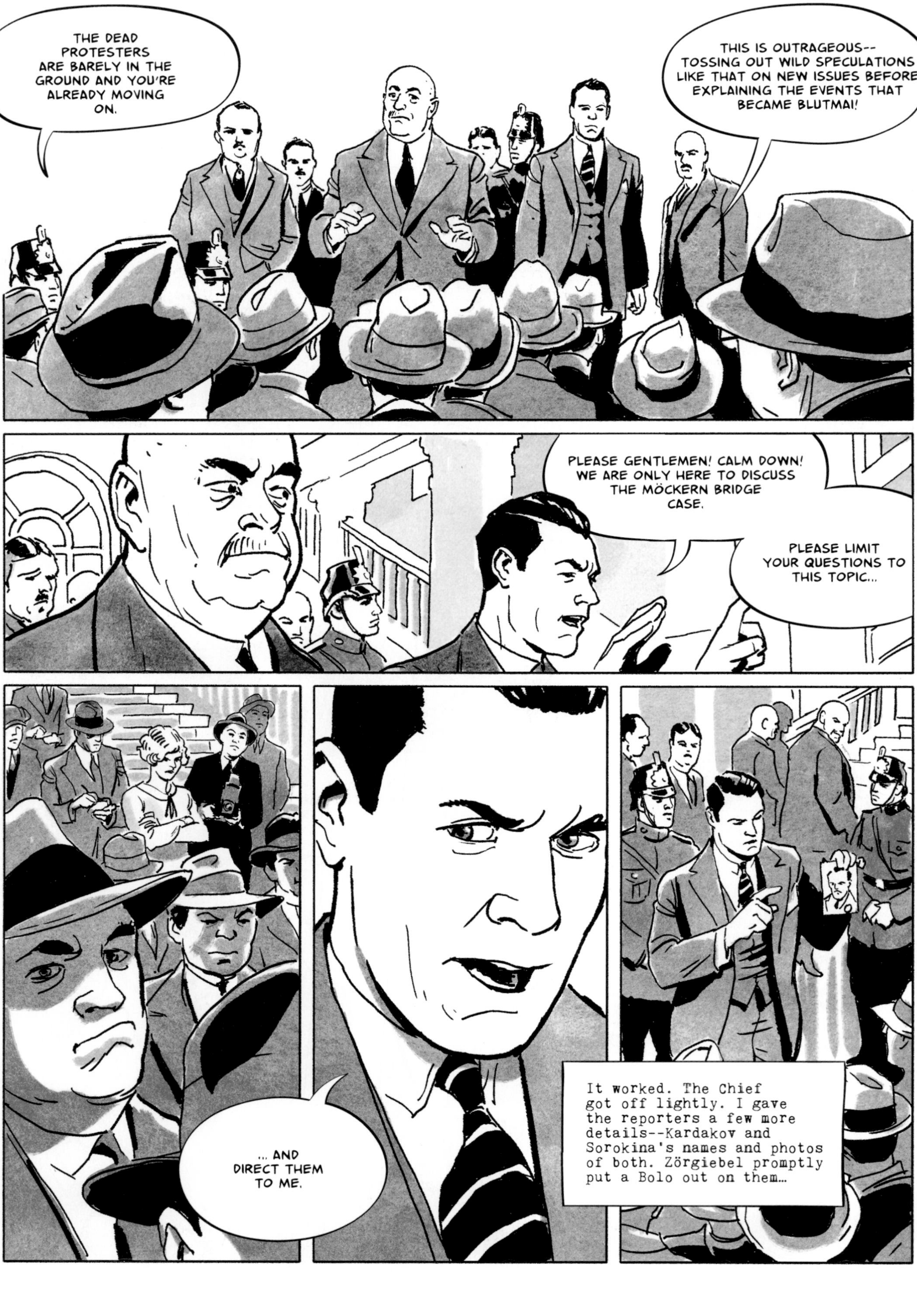
THE DEAD PROTESTERS ARE BARELY IN THE GROUND AND YOU'RE ALREADY MOVING ON.
THIS IS OUTRAGEOUS-- TOSSING OUT WILD SPECULATIONS LIKE THAT ON NEW ISSUES BEFORE EXPLAINING THE EVENTS THAT BECAME BLUTMAI!
PLEASE GENTLEMEN! CALM DOWN! WE ARE ONLY HERE TO DISCUSS THE MÖCKERN BRIDGE CASE.
PLEASE LIMIT YOUR QUESTIONS TO THIS TOPIC...
... AND DIRECT THEM TO ME.
It worked. The Chief got off lightly. I gave the reporters a few more details--Kardakov and Sorokina's names and photos of both. Zörgiebel promptly put a Bolo out on them...

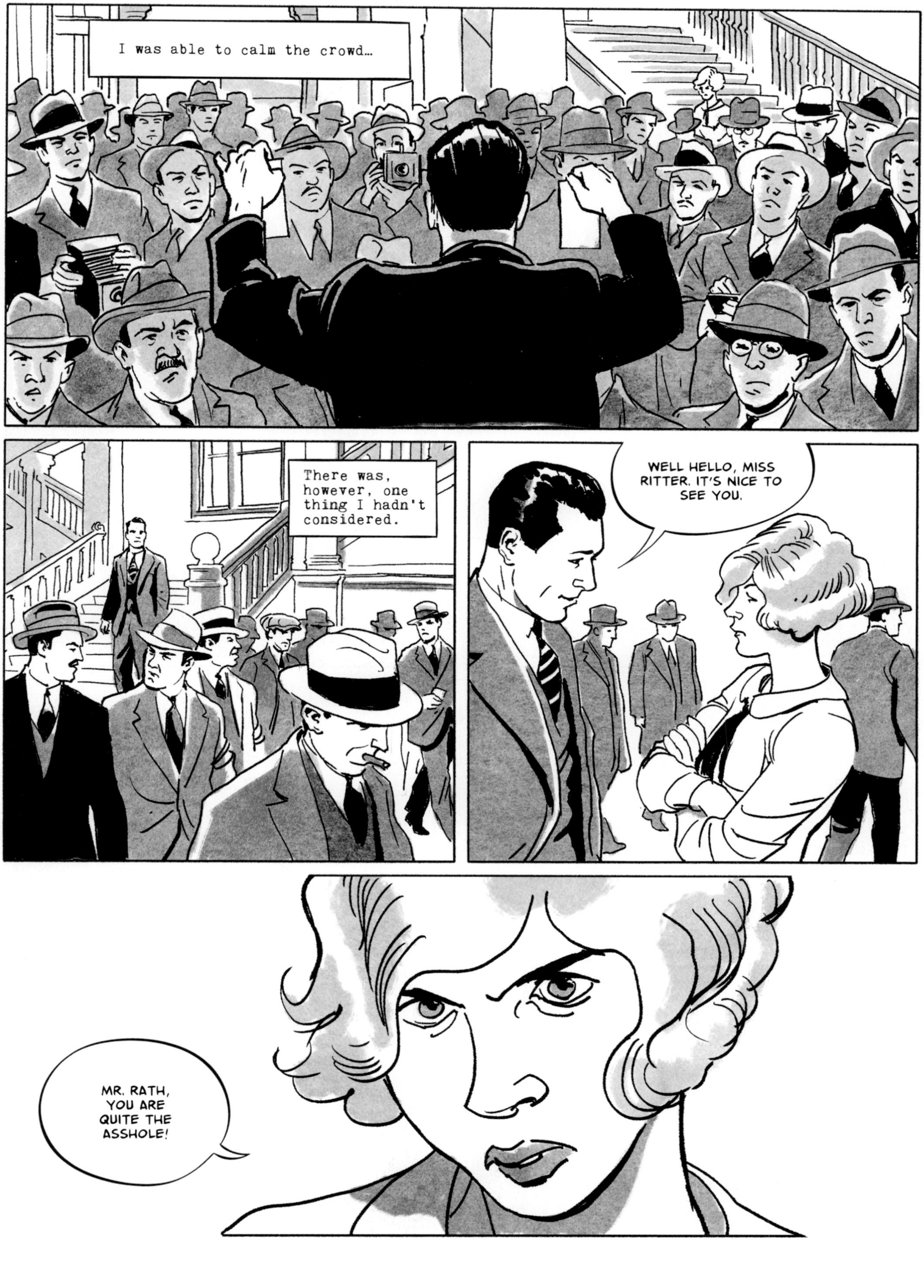
I was able to calm the crowd…
There was, however, one thing I hadn't considered.
WELL HELLO, MISS RITTER. IT'S NICE TO SEE YOU.
MR. RATH, YOU ARE QUITE THE ASSHOLE!

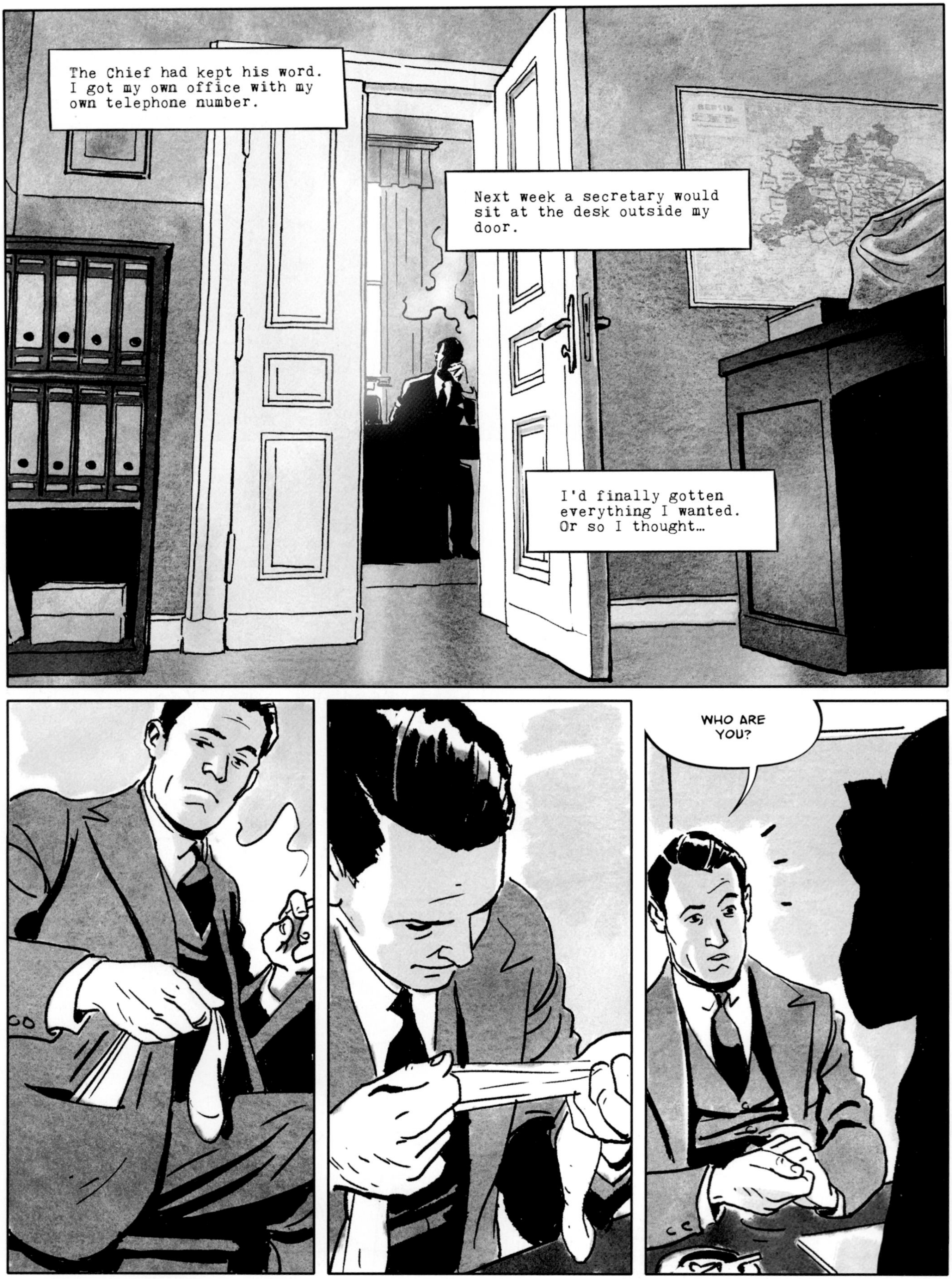
The Chief had kept his word. I got my own office with my own telephone number.
Next week a secretary would sit at the desk outside my door.
I'd finally gotten everything I wanted. Or so I thought...
WHO ARE YOU?

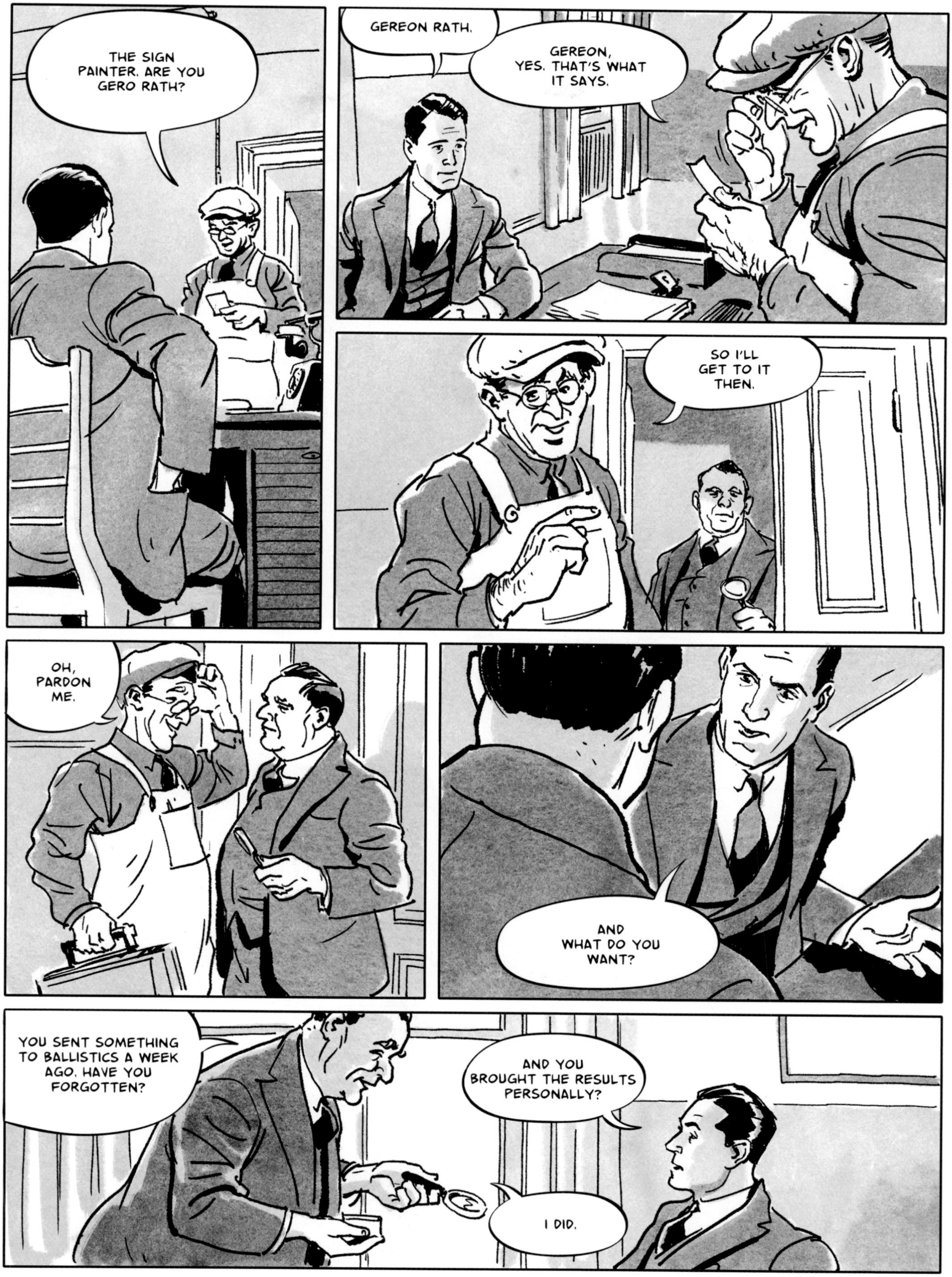
THE SIGN PAINTER. ARE YOU GERO RATH?
GEREON RATH.
GEREON, YES. THAT'S WHAT IT SAYS.
SO I'LL GET TO IT THEN.
OH, PARDON ME.
AND WHAT DO YOU WANT?
YOU SENT SOMETHING TO BALLISTICS A WEEK AGO. HAVE YOU FORGOTTEN?
AND YOU BROUGHT THE RESULTS PERSONALLY?
I DID.

SEE FOR YOURSELF.

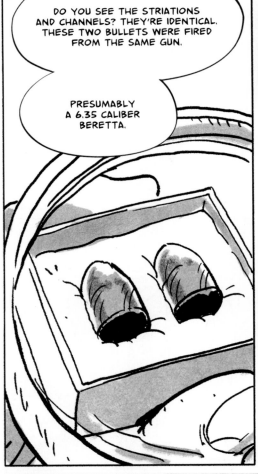

DO YOU SEE THE STRIATIONS AND CHANNELS? THEY'RE IDENTICAL. THESE TWO BULLETS WERE FIRED FROM THE SAME GUN.

PRESUMABLY A 6.35 CALIBER BERETTA.

AND WHERE IS THE SECOND BULLET FROM?

THE ONE ON THE LEFT IS THE ONE YOU BROUGHT IN. THE ONE THAT KILLED WILCZEK.

AND THE OTHER ONE WE EXAMINED LAST WEEK. IT WAS A RUSH JOB, YOU KNOW, FROM THE TOP.

IT'S THE ONE THAT KILLED THE YOUNG CRIME DIVISION ASSISTANT, JÄNICKE.

WHAT?

INSPECT

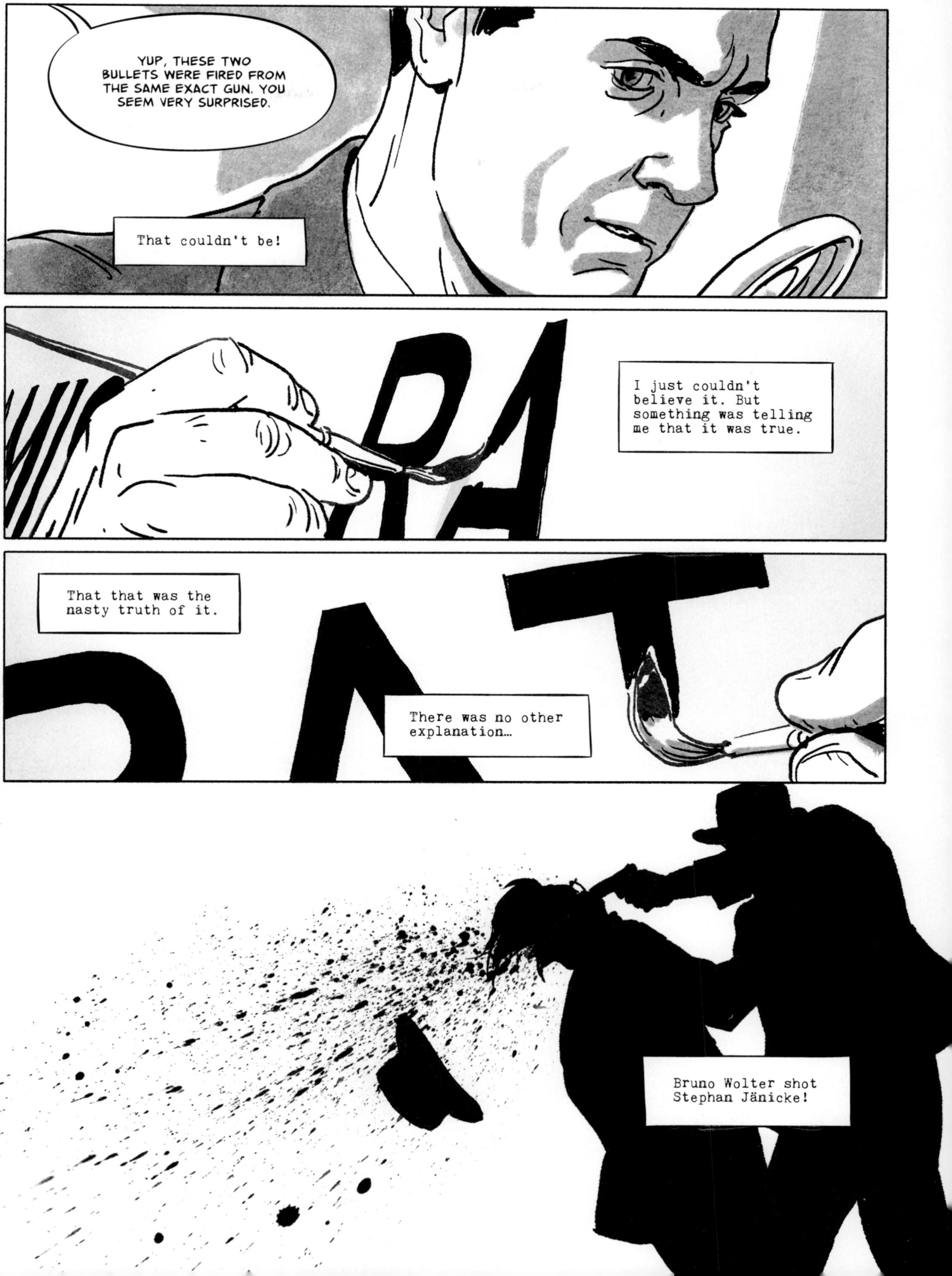
YUP, THESE TWO BULLETS WERE FIRED FROM THE SAME EXACT GUN. YOU SEEM VERY SURPRISED.
That couldn't be!
I just couldn't believe it. But something was telling me that it was true.
That that was the nasty truth of it.
There was no other explanation…
Bruno Wolter shot Stephan Jänicke!

PART III
The Whole Truth

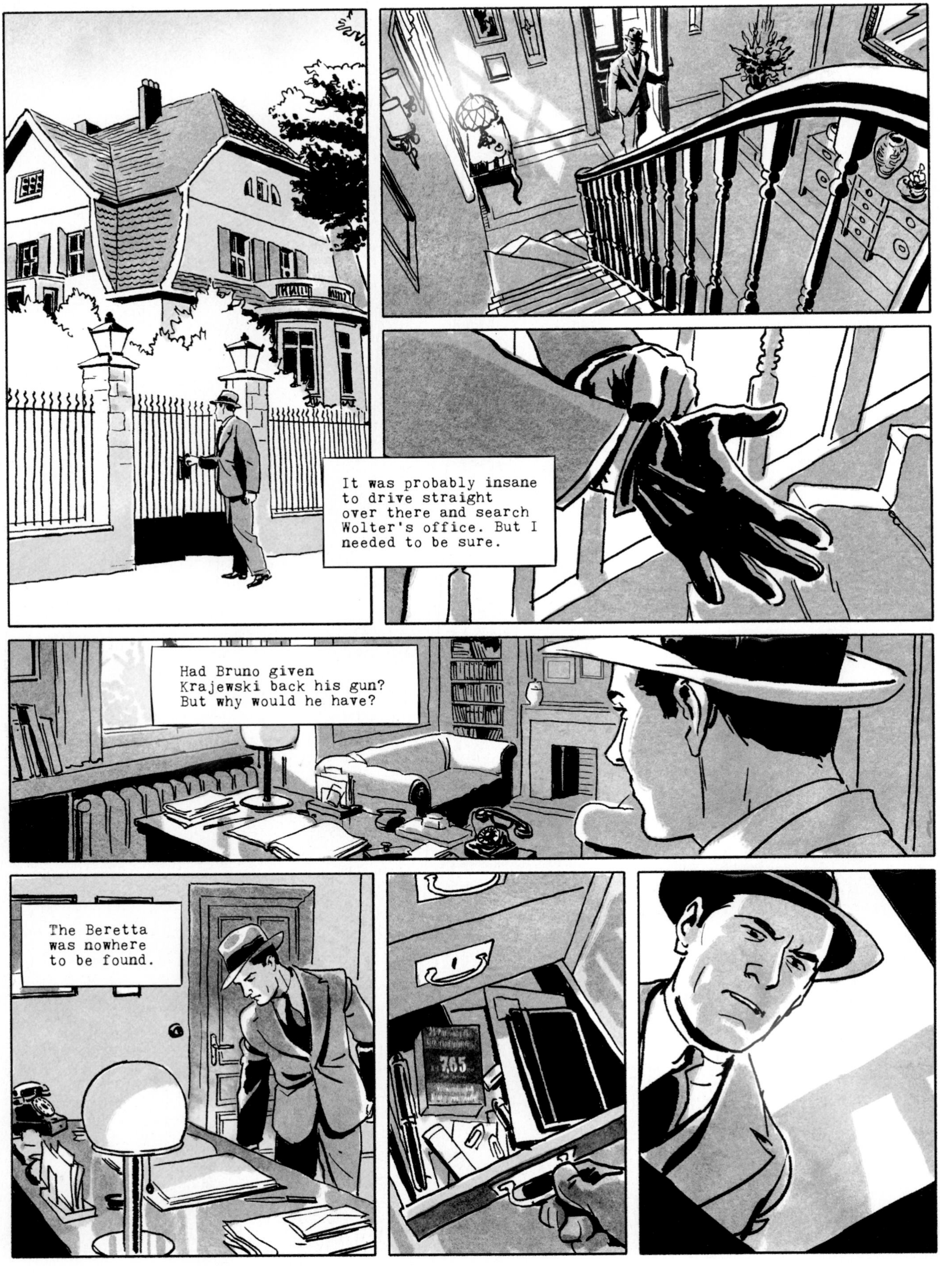

It was probably insane to drive straight over there and search Wolter's office. But I needed to be sure.
Had Bruno given Krajewski back his gun? But why would he have?
The Beretta was nowhere to be found.
7,65

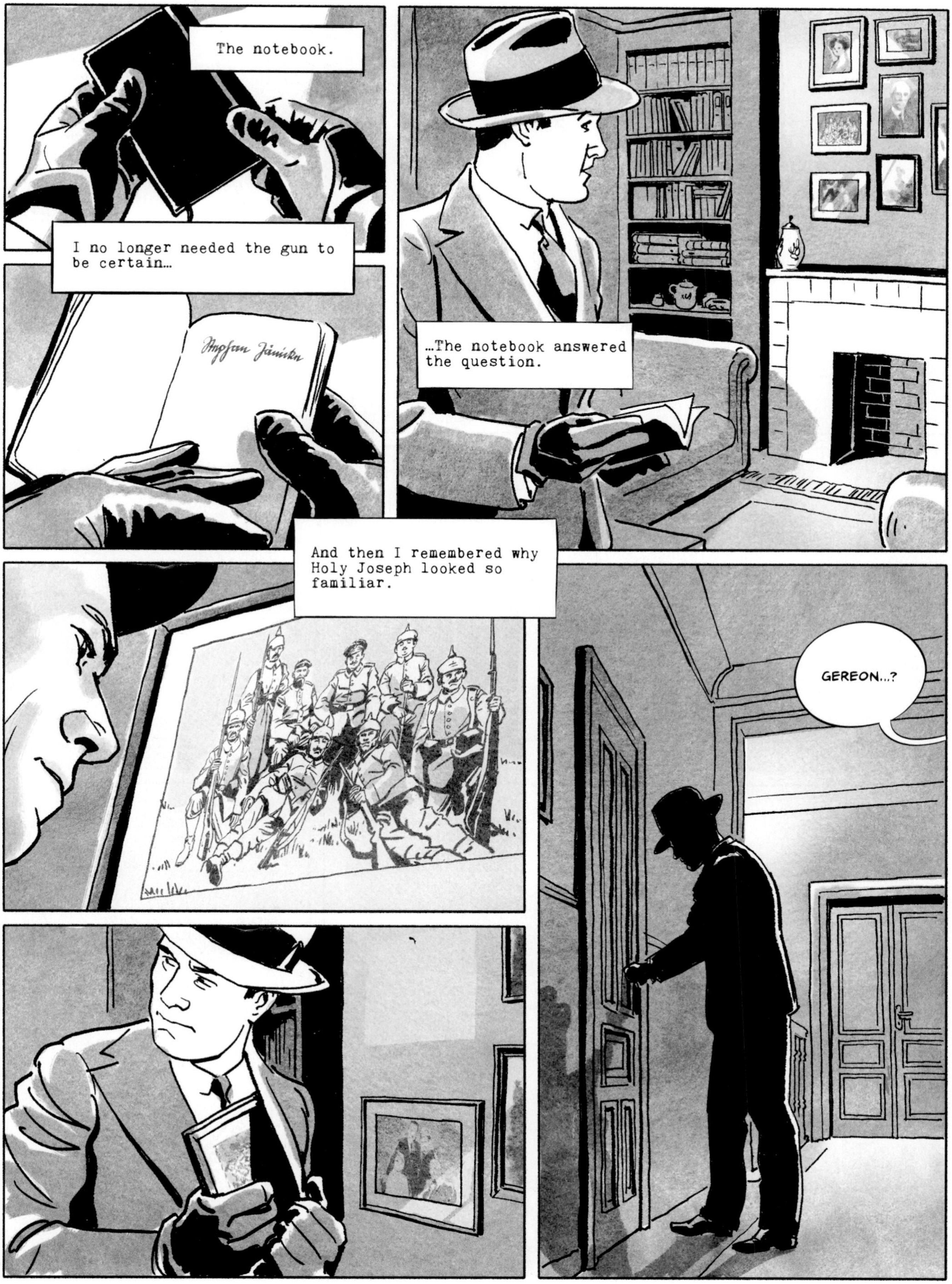
The notebook.
I no longer needed the gun to be certain...
...The notebook answered the question.
And then I remembered why Holy Joseph looked so familiar.
GEREON...?

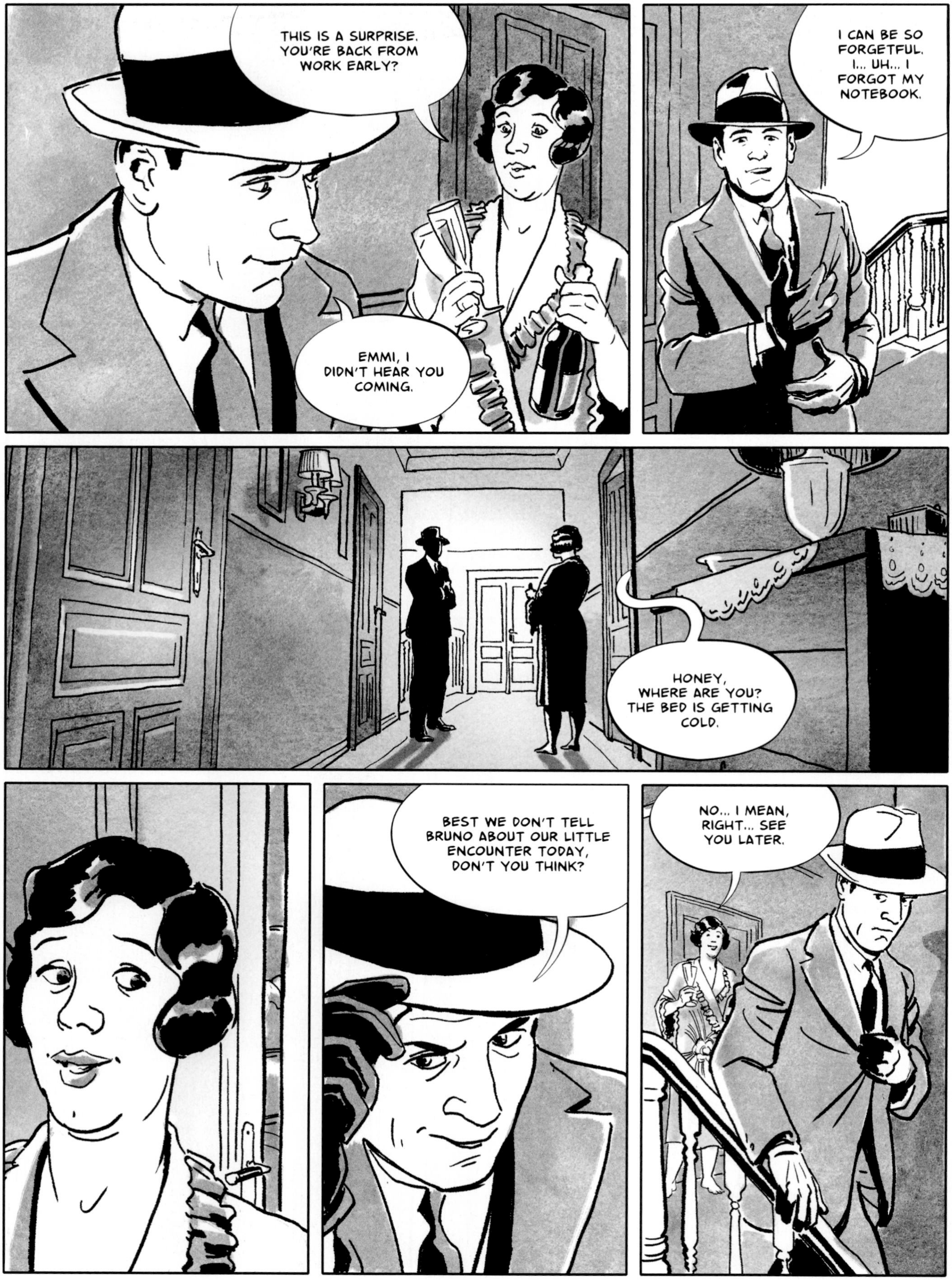
THIS IS A SURPRISE. YOU'RE BACK FROM WORK EARLY?
EMMI, I DIDN'T HEAR YOU COMING.
I CAN BE SO FORGETFUL. I... UH... I FORGOT MY NOTEBOOK.
HONEY, WHERE ARE YOU? THE BED IS GETTING COLD.
BEST WE DON'T TELL BRUNO ABOUT OUR LITTLE ENCOUNTER TODAY, DON'T YOU THINK?
NO... I MEAN, RIGHT... SEE YOU LATER.

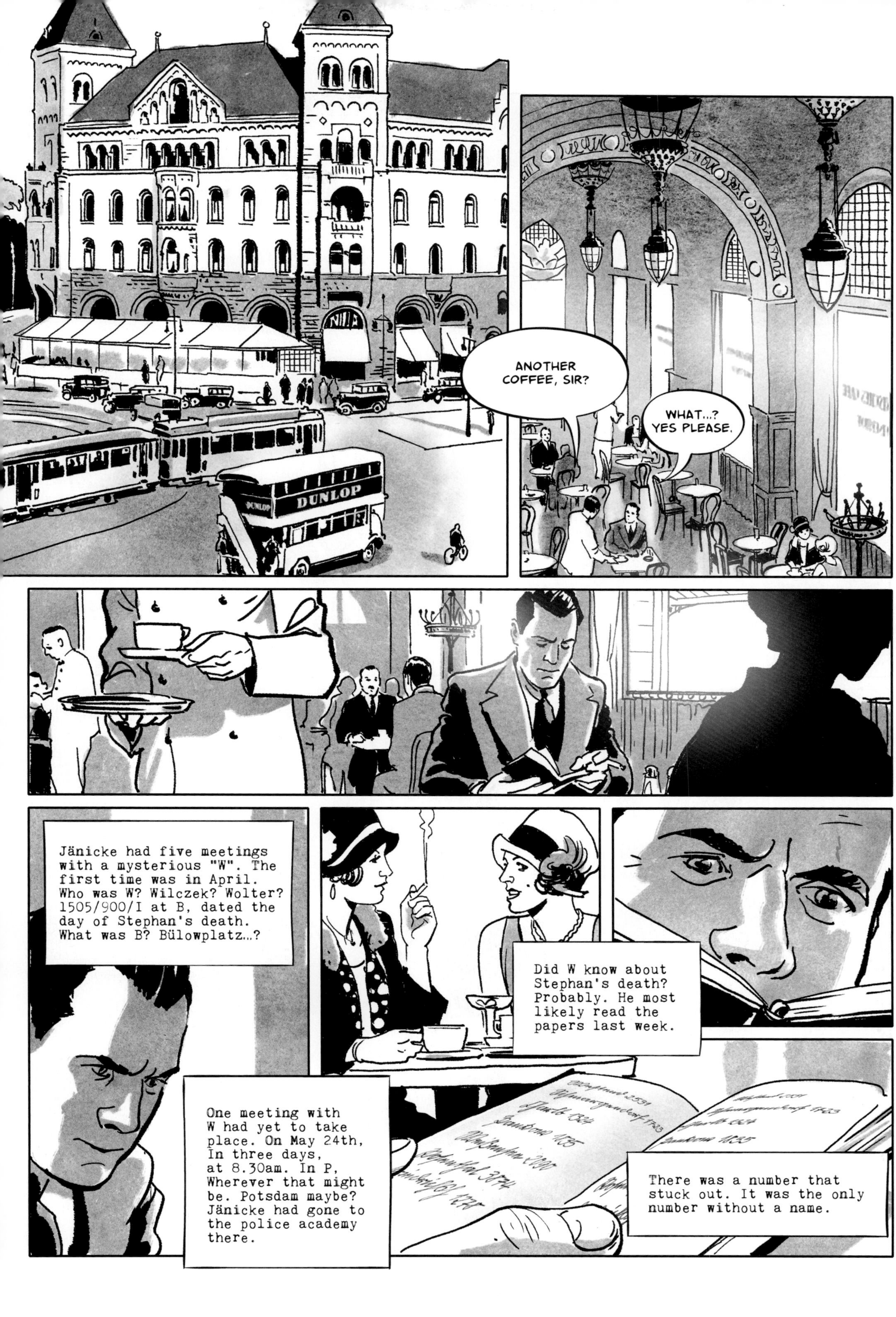
ANOTHER COFFEE, SIR?
WHAT...? YES PLEASE.
Jänicke had five meetings with a mysterious "W". The first time was in April. Who was W? Wilczek? Wolter? 1505/900/I at B, dated the day of Stephan's death. What was B? Bülowplatz...?
Did W know about Stephan's death? Probably. He most likely read the papers last week.
One meeting with W had yet to take place. On May 24th, In three days, at 8.30am. In P, Wherever that might be. Potsdam maybe? Jänicke had gone to the police academy there.
There was a number that stuck out. It was the only number without a name.

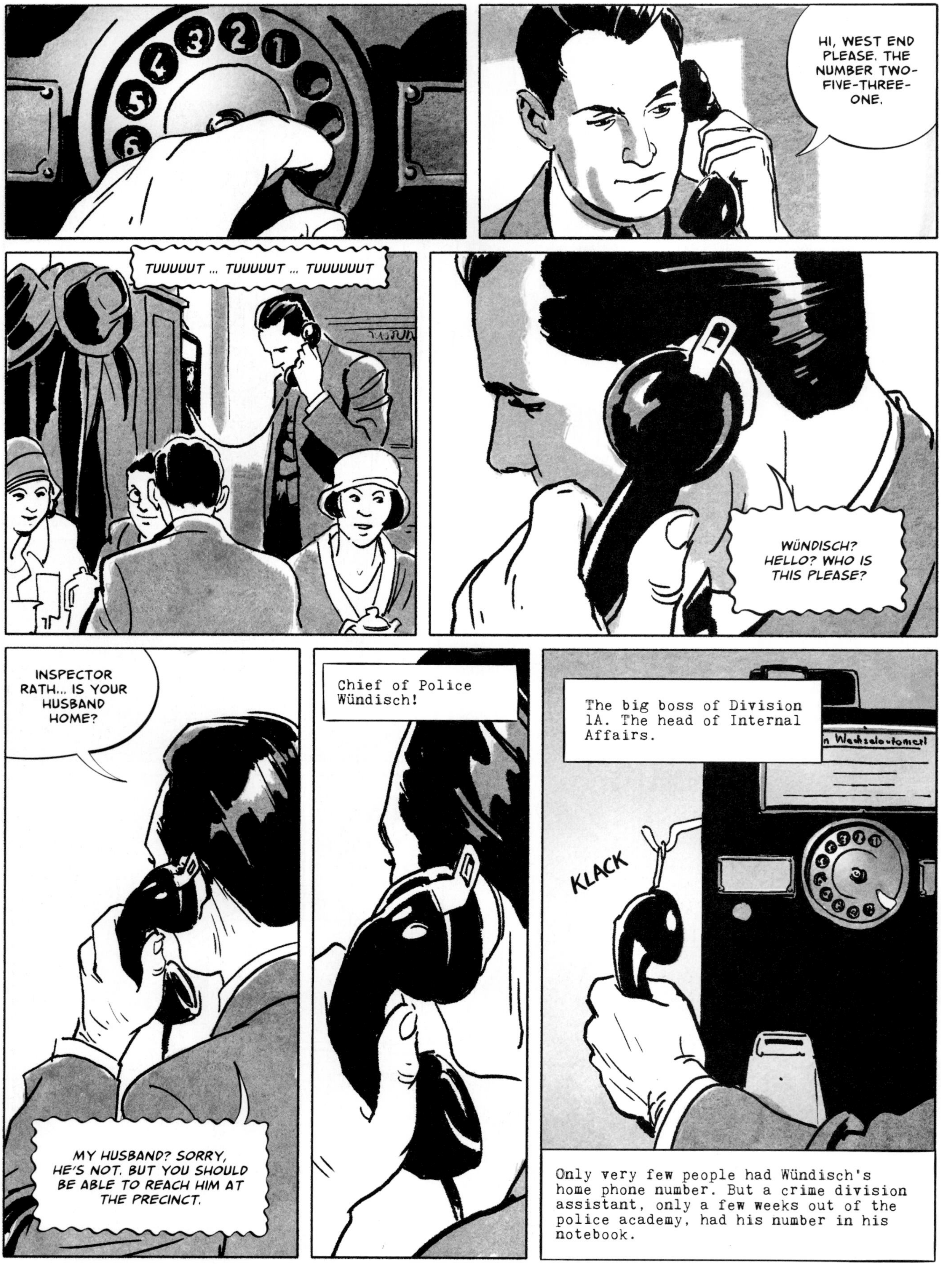
HI, WEST END PLEASE. THE NUMBER TWO-FIVE-THREE-ONE.
TUUUUUT ... TUUUUUT ... TUUUUUUT
WÜNDISCH? HELLO? WHO IS THIS PLEASE?
INSPECTOR RATH... IS YOUR HUSBAND HOME?
MY HUSBAND? SORRY, HE'S NOT. BUT YOU SHOULD BE ABLE TO REACH HIM AT THE PRECINCT.
Chief of Police Wündisch!
The big boss of Division 1A. The head of Internal Affairs.
KLACK
Only very few people had Wündisch's home phone number. But a crime division assistant, only a few weeks out of the police academy, had his number in his notebook.

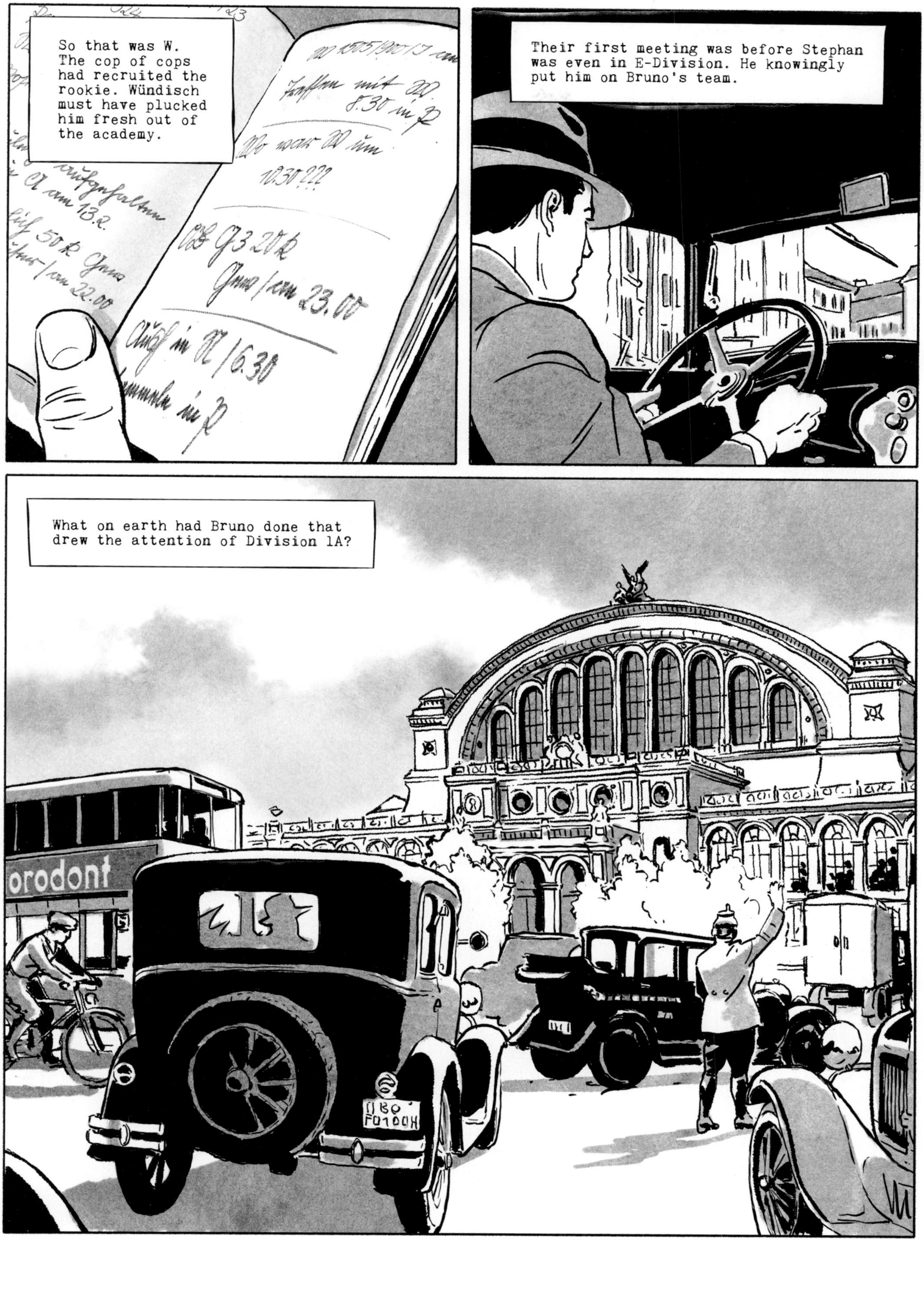
So that was W. The cop of cops had recruited the rookie. Wündisch must have plucked him fresh out of the academy.
Their first meeting was before Stephan was even in E-Division. He knowingly put him on Bruno's team.
What on earth had Bruno done that drew the attention of Division 1A?
orodont

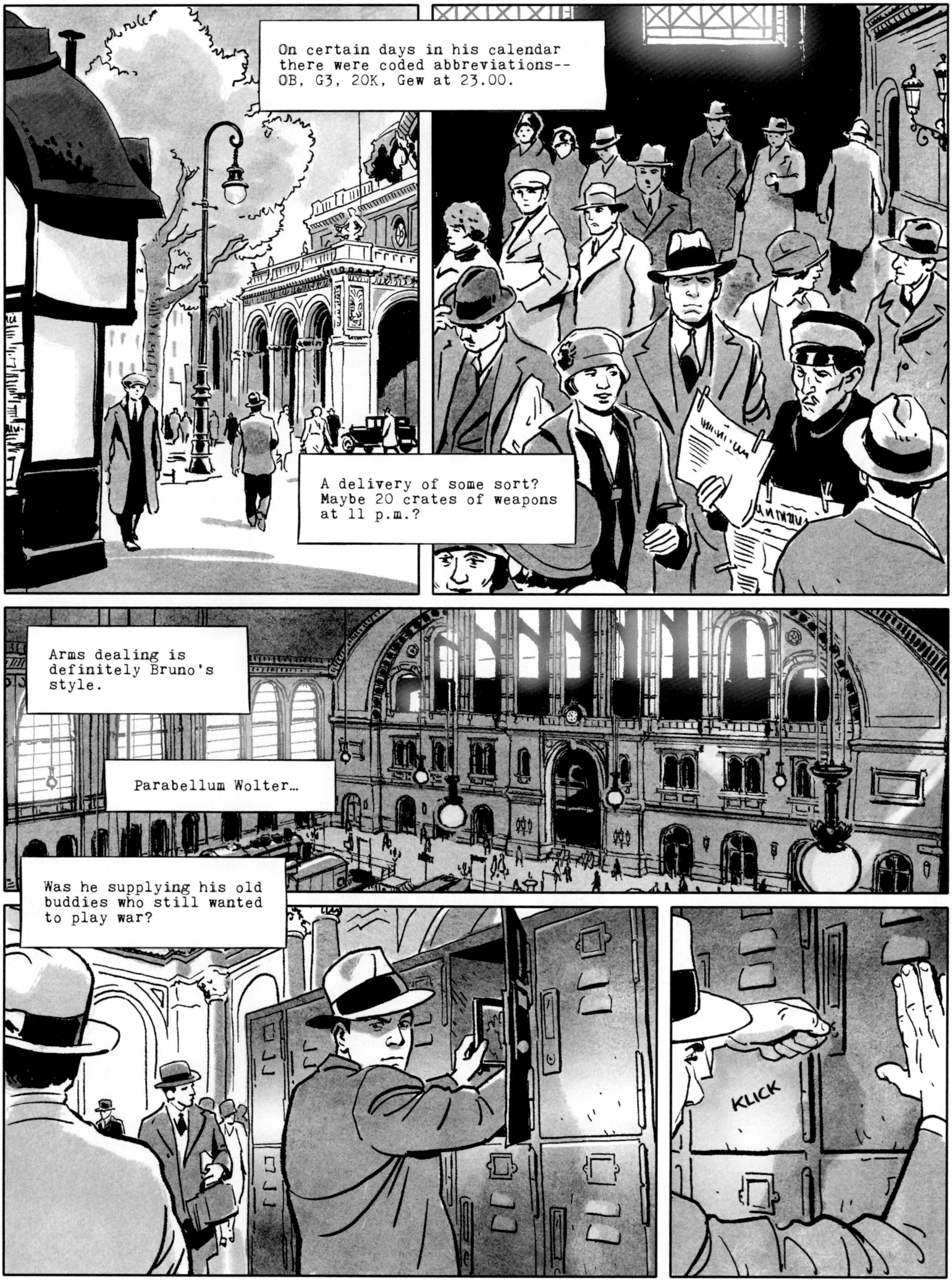
On certain days in his calendar there were coded abbreviations-- OB, G3, 20K, Gew at 23.00.
A delivery of some sort? Maybe 20 crates of weapons at 11 p.m.?
Arms dealing is definitely Bruno's style.
Parabellum Wolter...
Was he supplying his old buddies who still wanted to play war?
KLICK

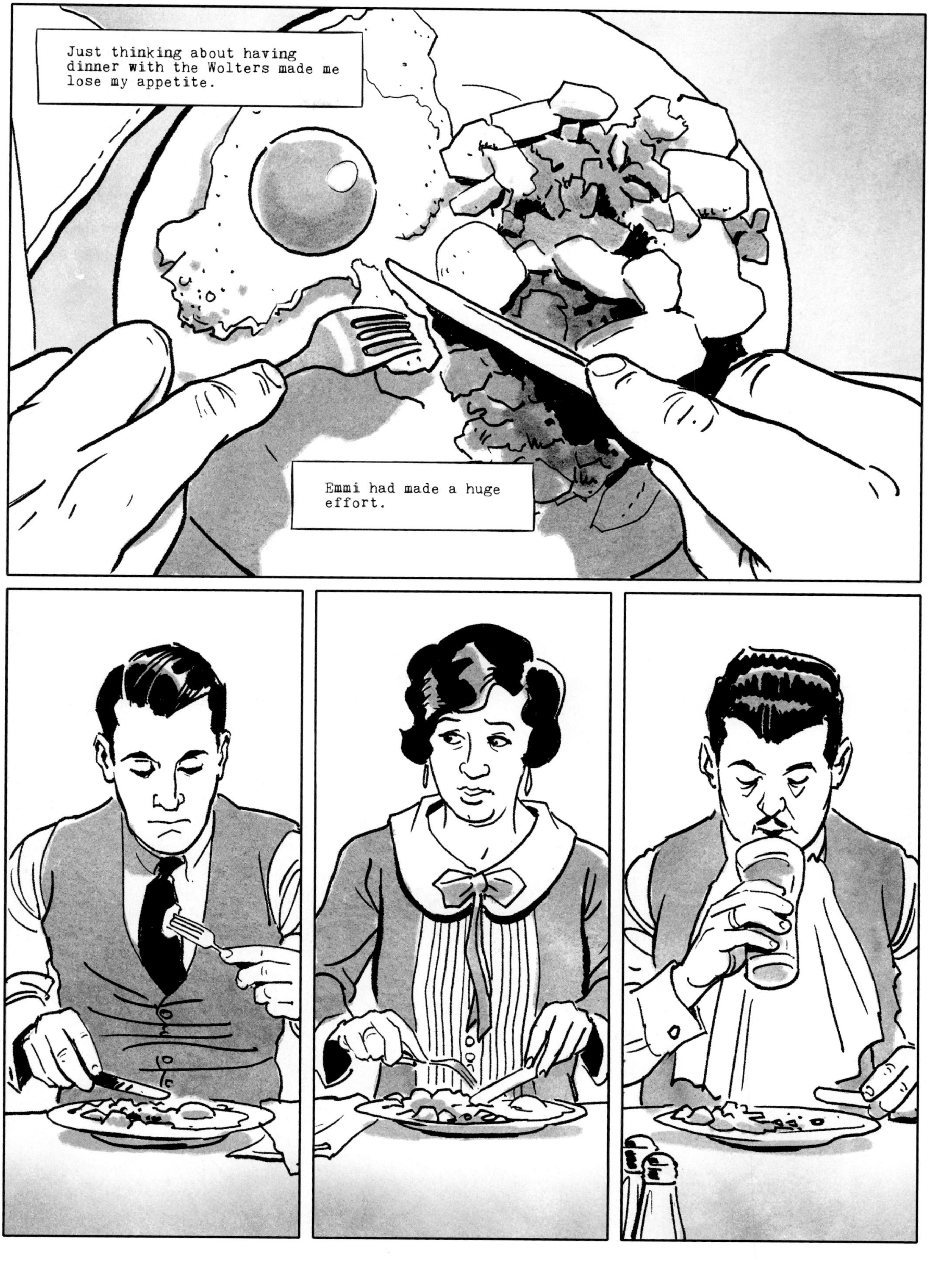
Just thinking about having dinner with the Wolters made me lose my appetite.
Emmi had made a huge effort.

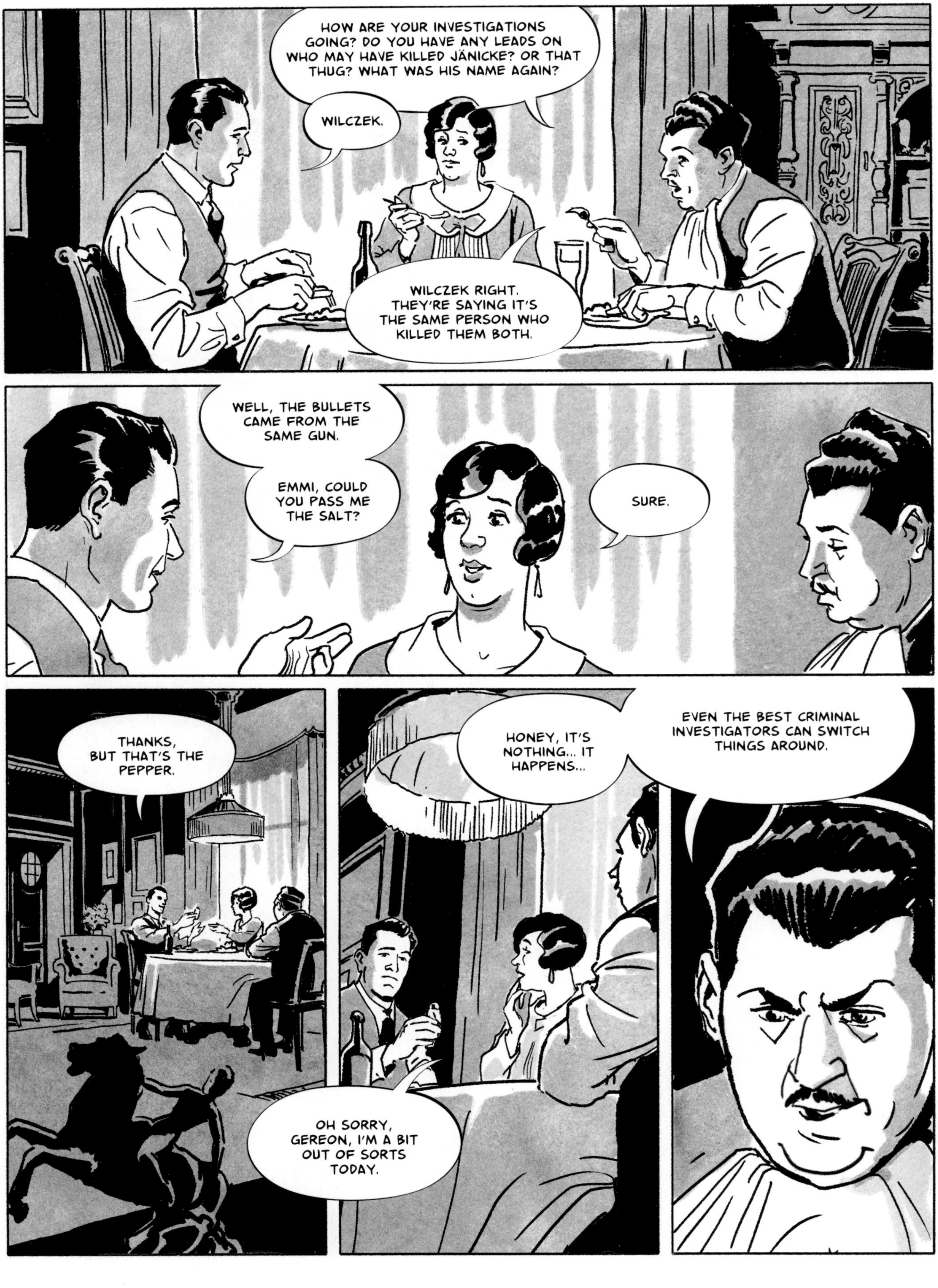
HOW ARE YOUR INVESTIGATIONS GOING? DO YOU HAVE ANY LEADS ON WHO MAY HAVE KILLED JÄNICKE? OR THAT THUG? WHAT WAS HIS NAME AGAIN?
WILCZEK.
WILCZEK RIGHT. THEY'RE SAYING IT'S THE SAME PERSON WHO KILLED THEM BOTH.
WELL, THE BULLETS CAME FROM THE SAME GUN.
EMMI, COULD YOU PASS ME THE SALT?
SURE.
THANKS, BUT THAT'S THE PEPPER.
OH SORRY, GEREON, I'M A BIT OUT OF SORTS TODAY.
HONEY, IT'S NOTHING... IT HAPPENS...
EVEN THE BEST CRIMINAL INVESTIGATORS CAN SWITCH THINGS AROUND.

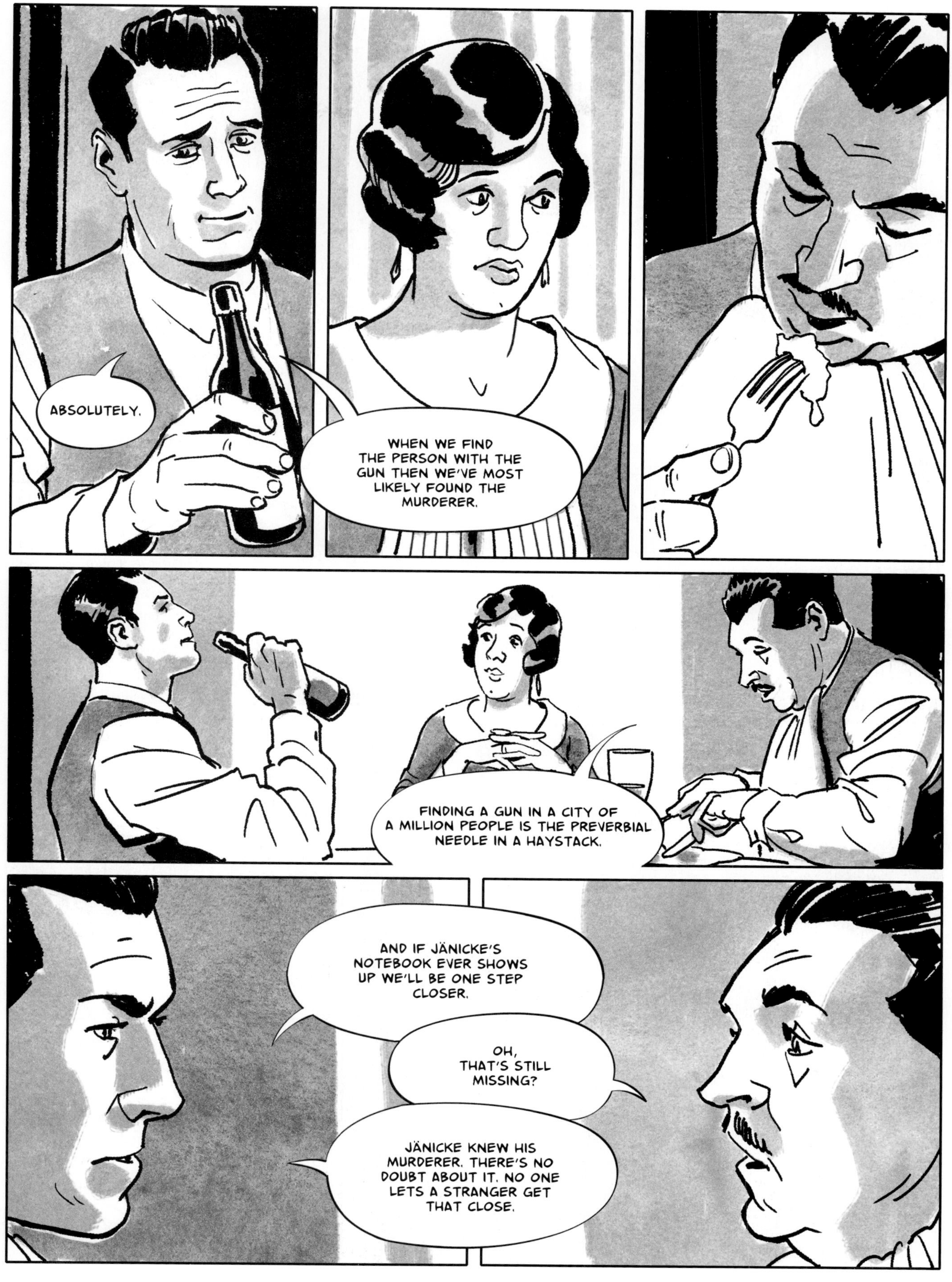
ABSOLUTELY.
WHEN WE FIND THE PERSON WITH THE GUN THEN WE'VE MOST LIKELY FOUND THE MURDERER.
FINDING A GUN IN A CITY OF A MILLION PEOPLE IS THE PREVERBIAL NEEDLE IN A HAYSTACK.
AND IF JÄNICKE'S NOTEBOOK EVER SHOWS UP WE'LL BE ONE STEP CLOSER.
OH, THAT'S STILL MISSING?
JÄNICKE KNEW HIS MURDERER. THERE'S NO DOUBT ABOUT IT. NO ONE LETS A STRANGER GET THAT CLOSE.

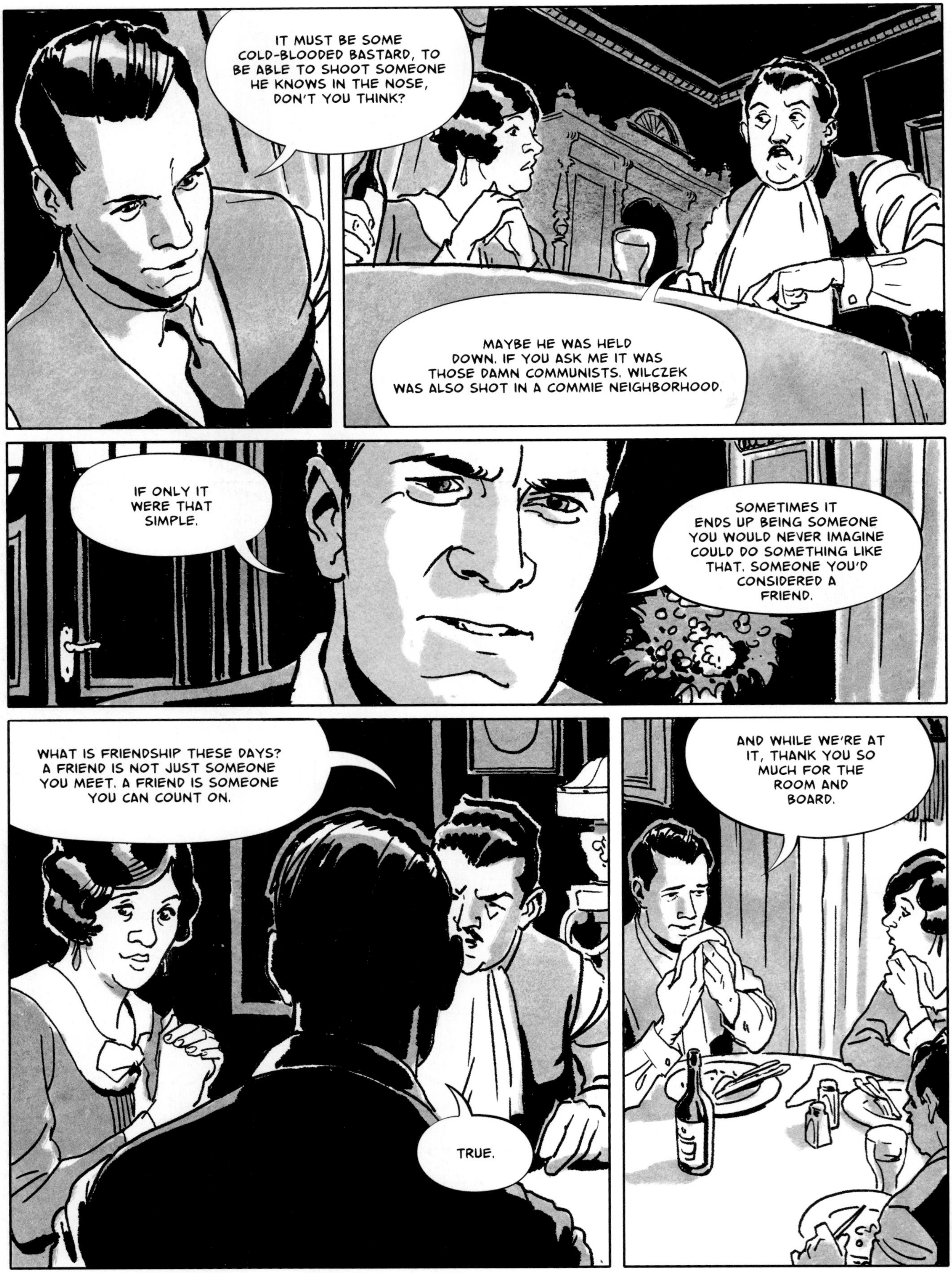
IT MUST BE SOME COLD-BLOODED BASTARD, TO BE ABLE TO SHOOT SOMEONE HE KNOWS IN THE NOSE, DON'T YOU THINK?
MAYBE HE WAS HELD DOWN. IF YOU ASK ME IT WAS THOSE DAMN COMMUNISTS. WILCZEK WAS ALSO SHOT IN A COMMIE NEIGHBORHOOD.
IF ONLY IT WERE THAT SIMPLE.
SOMETIMES IT ENDS UP BEING SOMEONE YOU WOULD NEVER IMAGINE COULD DO SOMETHING LIKE THAT. SOMEONE YOU'D CONSIDERED A FRIEND.
WHAT IS FRIENDSHIP THESE DAYS? A FRIEND IS NOT JUST SOMEONE YOU MEET. A FRIEND IS SOMEONE YOU CAN COUNT ON.
TRUE.
AND WHILE WE'RE AT IT, THANK YOU SO MUCH FOR THE ROOM AND BOARD.

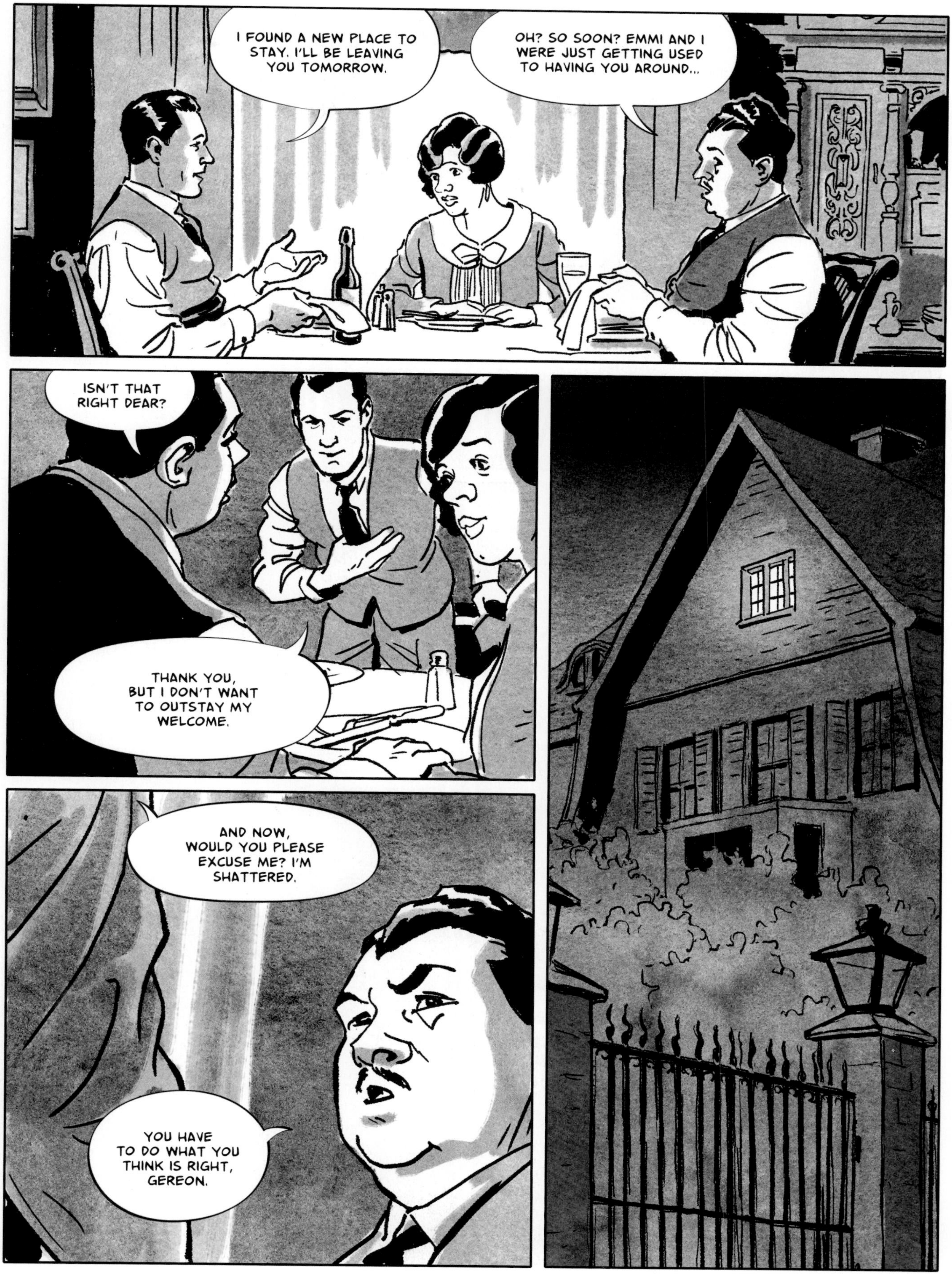
I FOUND A NEW PLACE TO STAY. I'LL BE LEAVING YOU TOMORROW.
OH? SO SOON? EMMI AND I WERE JUST GETTING USED TO HAVING YOU AROUND...
ISN'T THAT RIGHT DEAR?
THANK YOU, BUT I DON'T WANT TO OUTSTAY MY WELCOME.
AND NOW, WOULD YOU PLEASE EXCUSE ME? I'M SHATTERED.
YOU HAVE TO DO WHAT YOU THINK IS RIGHT, GEREON.

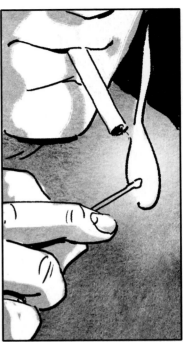

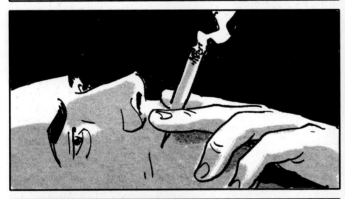

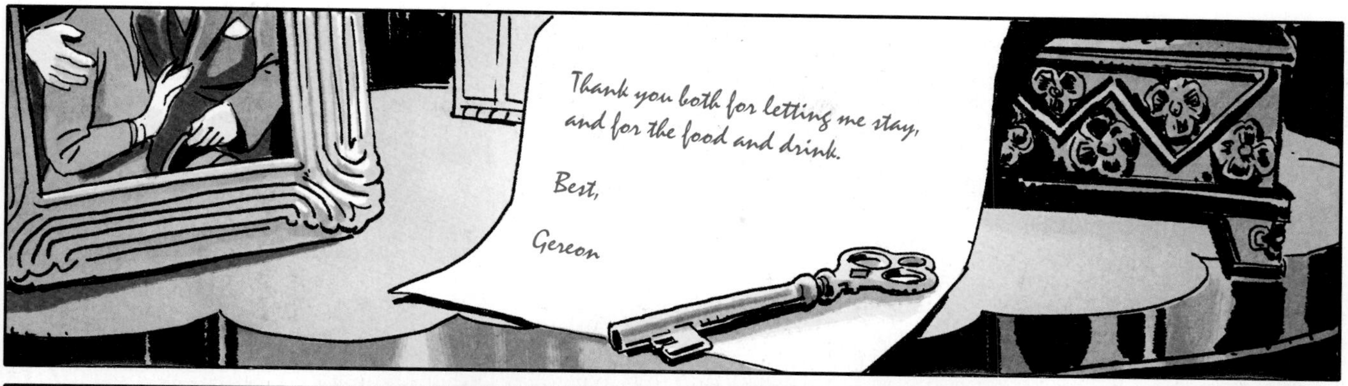
Thank you both for letting me stay, and for the food and drink.
Best,
Gereon

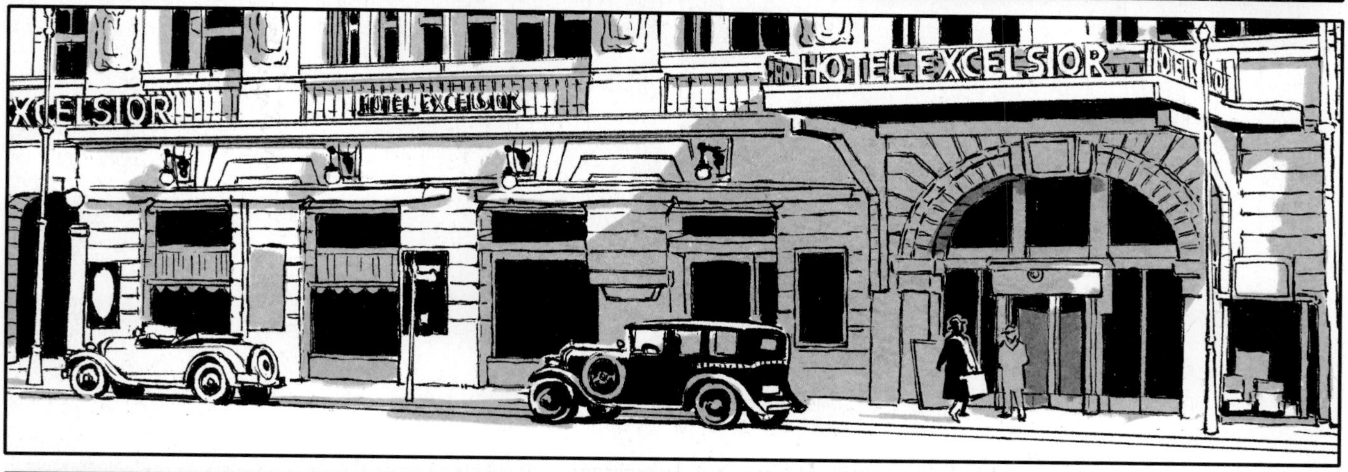
EXCELSIOR
HOTEL EXCELSIOR
HOTEL EXCELSIOR

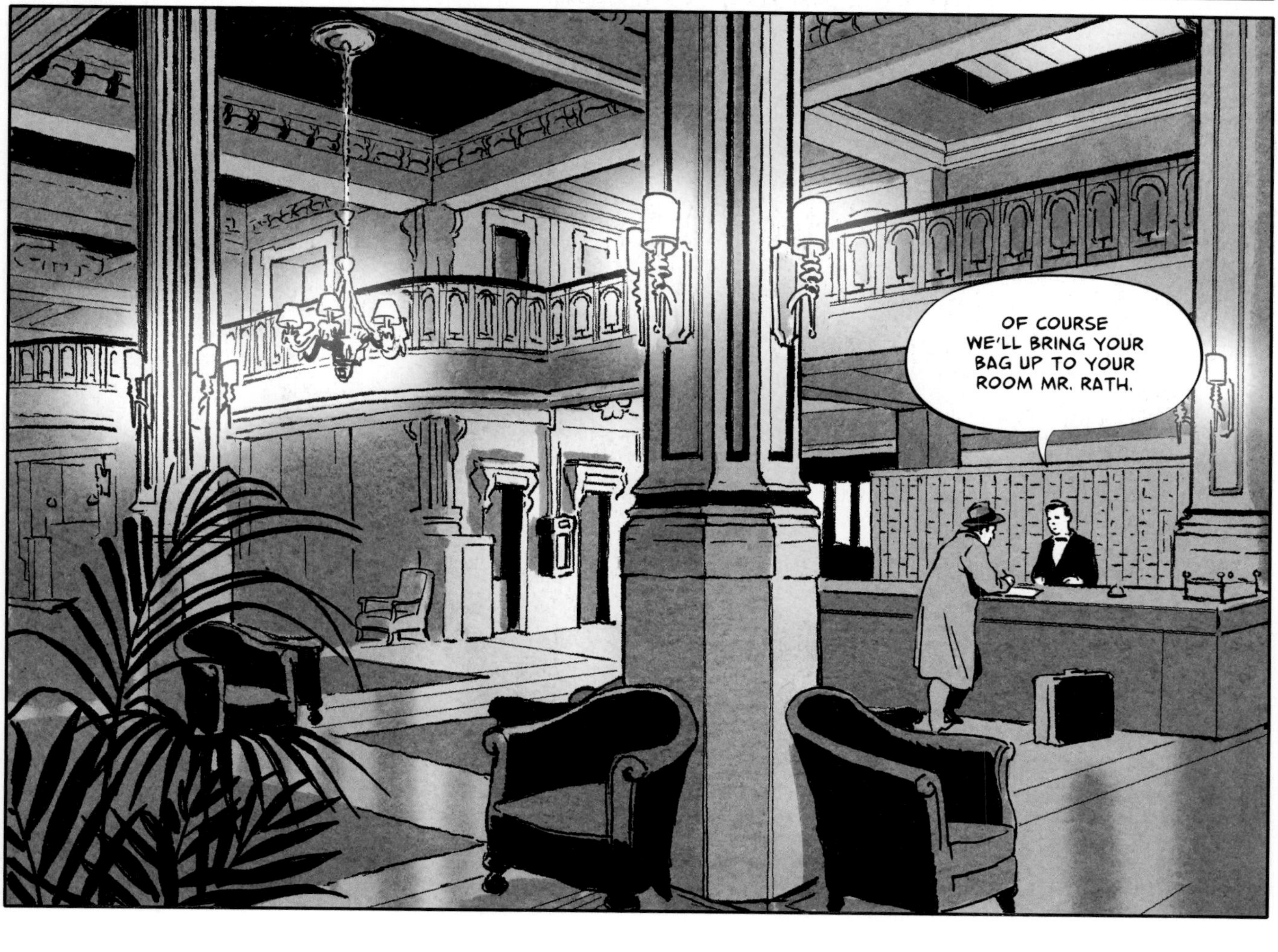
OF COURSE WE'LL BRING YOUR BAG UP TO YOUR ROOM MR. RATH.

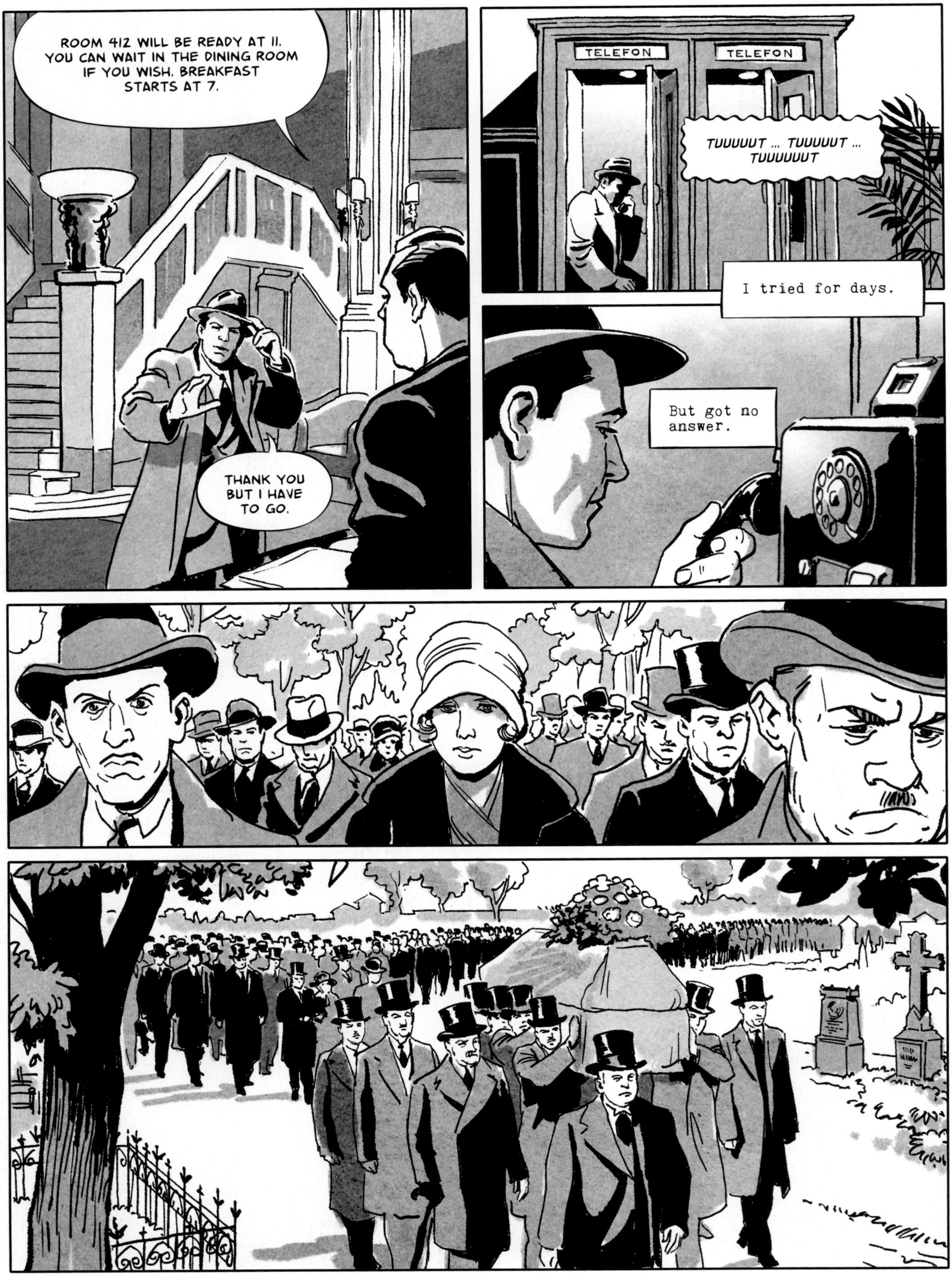
ROOM 412 WILL BE READY AT 11. YOU CAN WAIT IN THE DINING ROOM IF YOU WISH. BREAKFAST STARTS AT 7.
THANK YOU BUT I HAVE TO GO.
TELEFON
TELEFON
TUUUUUT ... TUUUUUT ... TUUUUUUT
I tried for days.
But got no answer.

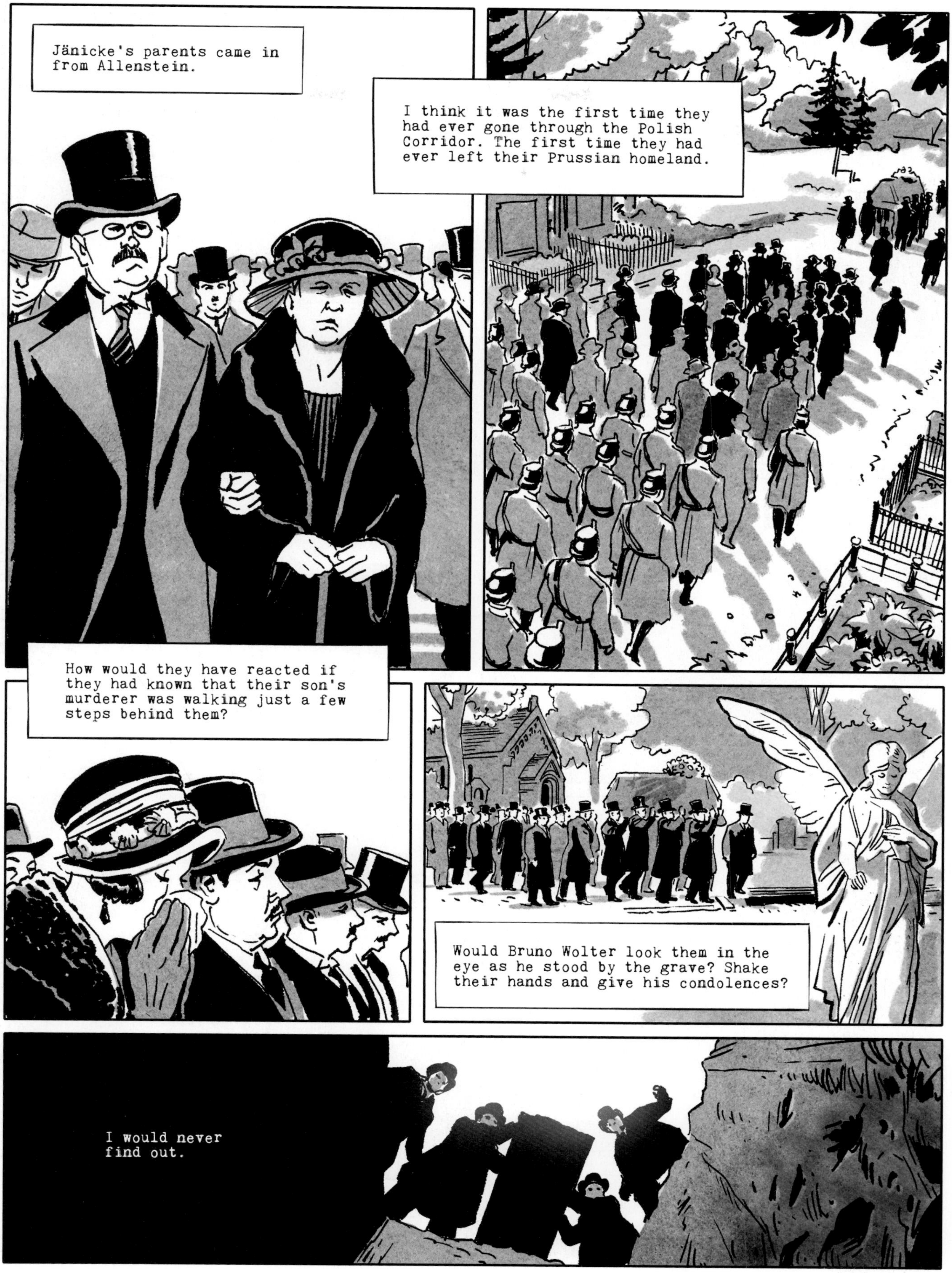
Jänicke's parents came in from Allenstein.
I think it was the first time they had ever gone through the Polish Corridor. The first time they had ever left their Prussian homeland.
How would they have reacted if they had known that their son's murderer was walking just a few steps behind them?
Would Bruno Wolter look them in the eye as he stood by the grave? Shake their hands and give his condolences?
I would never find out.

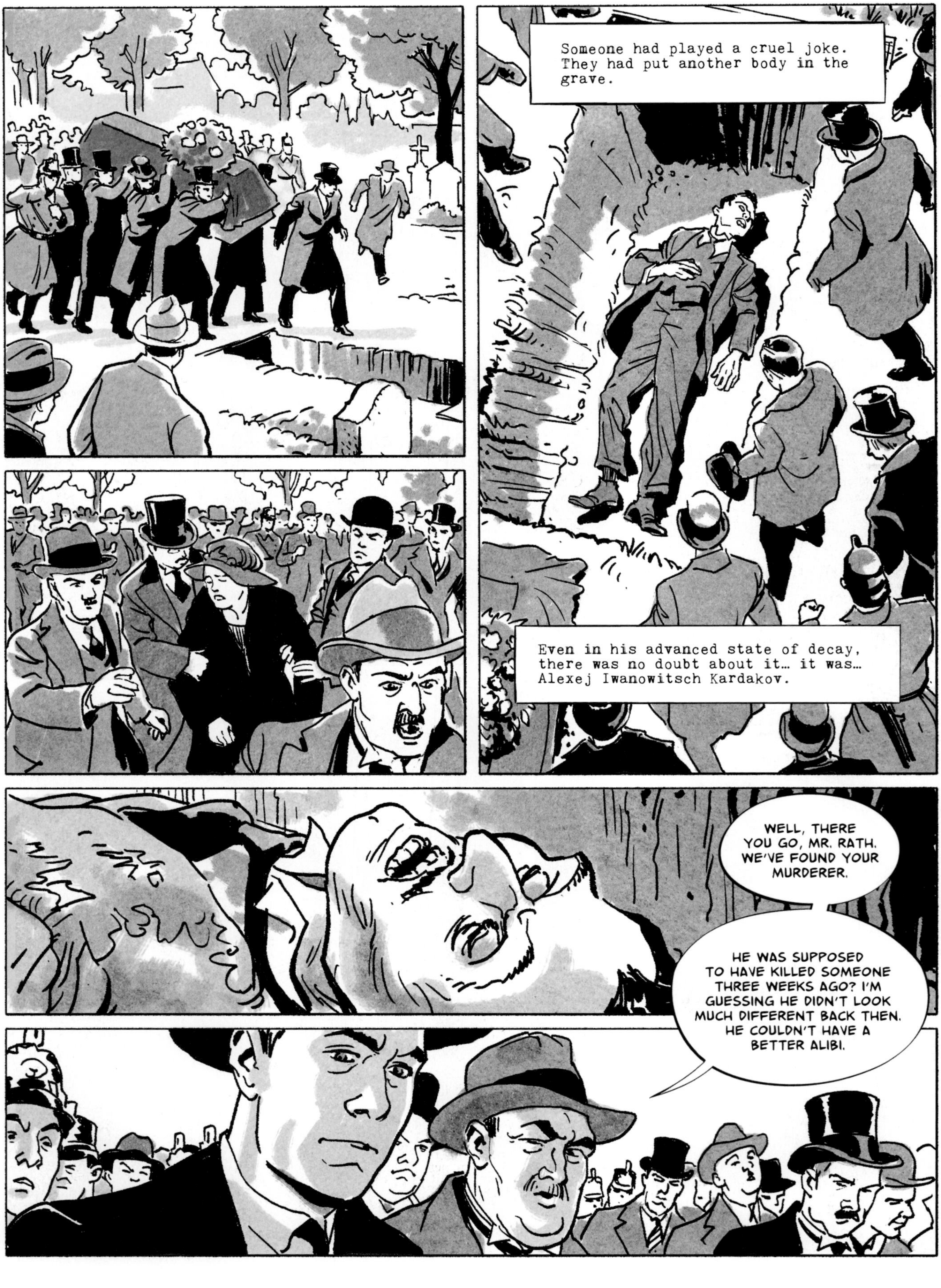
Someone had played a cruel joke. They had put another body in the grave.
Even in his advanced state of decay, there was no doubt about it… it was… Alexej Iwanowitsch Kardakov.
WELL, THERE YOU GO, MR. RATH. WE'VE FOUND YOUR MURDERER.
HE WAS SUPPOSED TO HAVE KILLED SOMEONE THREE WEEKS AGO? I'M GUESSING HE DIDN'T LOOK MUCH DIFFERENT BACK THEN. HE COULDN'T HAVE A BETTER ALIBI.

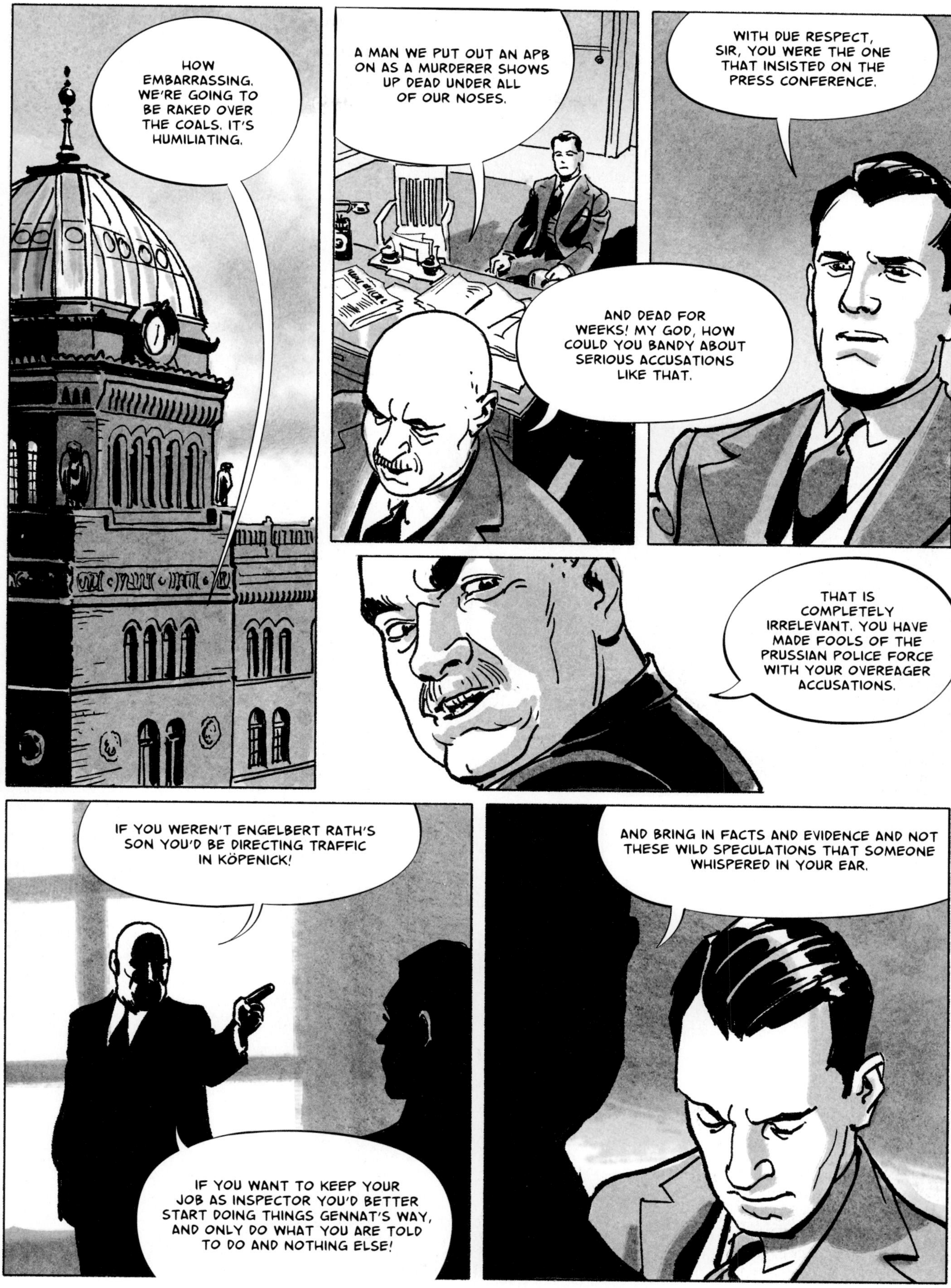
HOW EMBARRASSING. WE'RE GOING TO BE RAKED OVER THE COALS. IT'S HUMILIATING.
A MAN WE PUT OUT AN APB ON AS A MURDERER SHOWS UP DEAD UNDER ALL OF OUR NOSES.
AND DEAD FOR WEEKS! MY GOD, HOW COULD YOU BANDY ABOUT SERIOUS ACCUSATIONS LIKE THAT.
WITH DUE RESPECT, SIR, YOU WERE THE ONE THAT INSISTED ON THE PRESS CONFERENCE.
THAT IS COMPLETELY IRRELEVANT. YOU HAVE MADE FOOLS OF THE PRUSSIAN POLICE FORCE WITH YOUR OVEREAGER ACCUSATIONS.
IF YOU WEREN'T ENGELBERT RATH'S SON YOU'D BE DIRECTING TRAFFIC IN KÖPENICK!
IF YOU WANT TO KEEP YOUR JOB AS INSPECTOR YOU'D BETTER START DOING THINGS GENNAT'S WAY, AND ONLY DO WHAT YOU ARE TOLD TO DO AND NOTHING ELSE!
AND BRING IN FACTS AND EVIDENCE AND NOT THESE WILD SPECULATIONS THAT SOMEONE WHISPERED IN YOUR EAR.

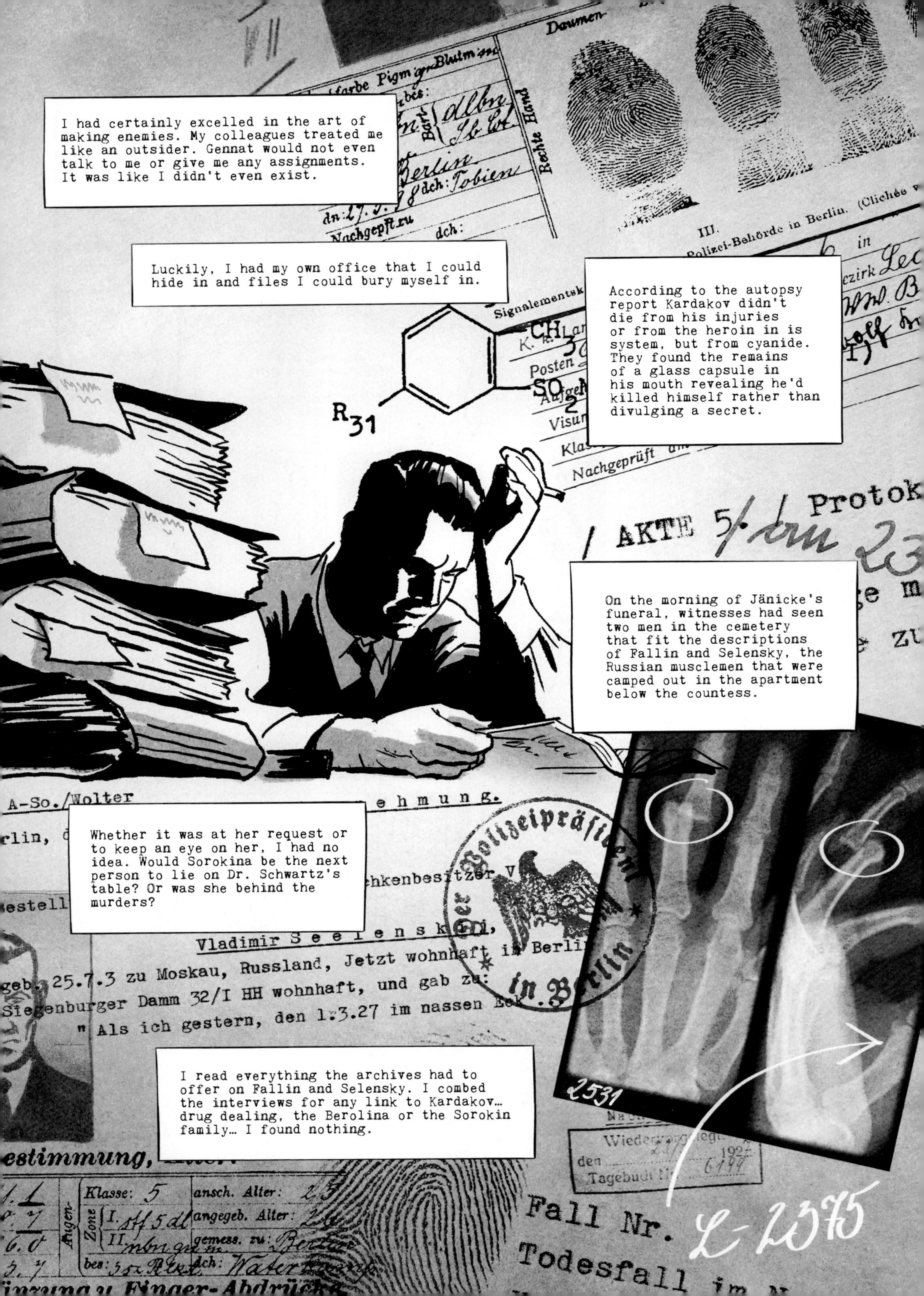
I had certainly excelled in the art of making enemies. My colleagues treated me like an outsider. Gennat would not even talk to me or give me any assignments. It was like I didn't even exist.
Luckily, I had my own office that I could hide in and files I could bury myself in.
According to the autopsy report Kardakov didn't die from his injuries or from the heroin in is system, but from cyanide. They found the remains of a glass capsule in his mouth revealing he'd killed himself rather than divulging a secret.
On the morning of Jänicke's funeral, witnesses had seen two men in the cemetery that fit the descriptions of Fallin and Selensky, the Russian musclemen that were camped out in the apartment below the countess.
Whether it was at her request or to keep an eye on her, I had no idea. Would Sorokina be the next person to lie on Dr. Schwartz's table? Or was she behind the murders?
I read everything the archives had to offer on Fallin and Selensky. I combed the interviews for any link to Kardakov… drug dealing, the Berolina or the Sorokin family… I found nothing.

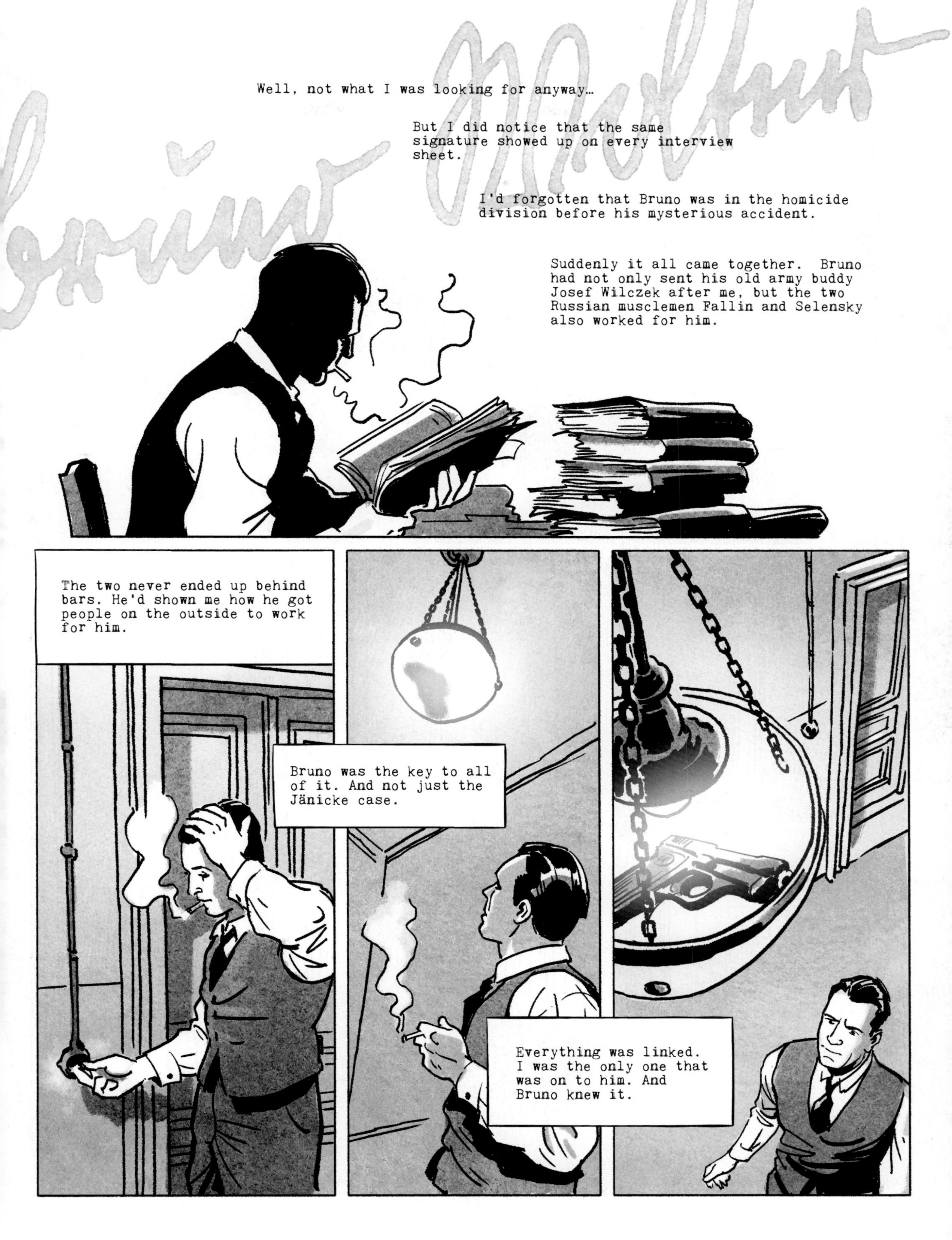
Well, not what I was looking for anyway…
But I did notice that the same signature showed up on every interview sheet.
I'd forgotten that Bruno was in the homicide division before his mysterious accident.
Suddenly it all came together. Bruno had not only sent his old army buddy Josef Wilczek after me, but the two Russian musclemen Fallin and Selensky also worked for him.
The two never ended up behind bars. He'd shown me how he got people on the outside to work for him.
Bruno was the key to all of it. And not just the Jänicke case.
Everything was linked. I was the only one that was on to him. And Bruno knew it.

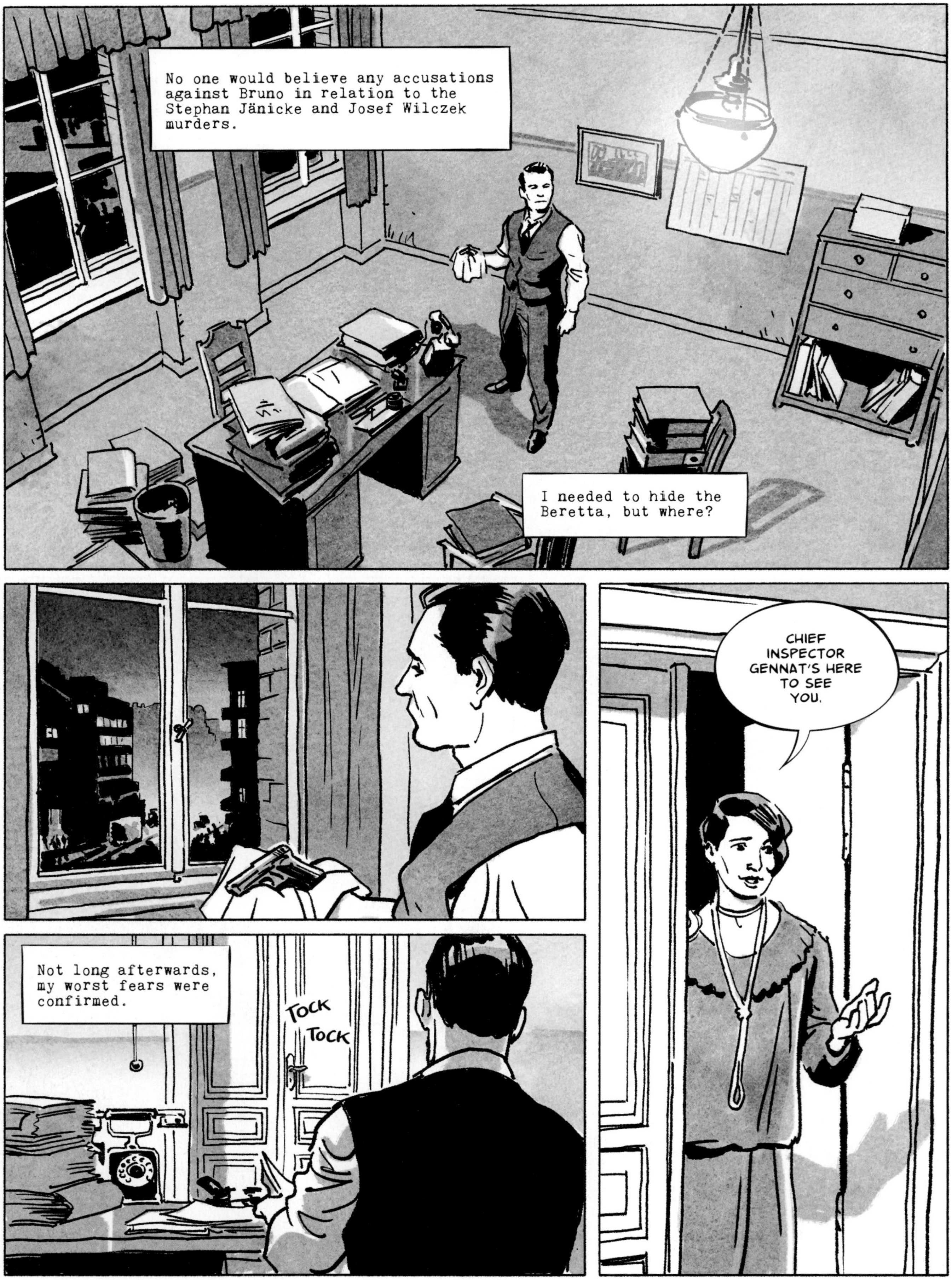

No one would believe any accusations against Bruno in relation to the Stephan Jänicke and Josef Wilczek murders.
I needed to hide the Beretta, but where?
CHIEF INSPECTOR GENNAT'S HERE TO SEE YOU.
Not long afterwards, my worst fears were confirmed.
TOCK
TOCK

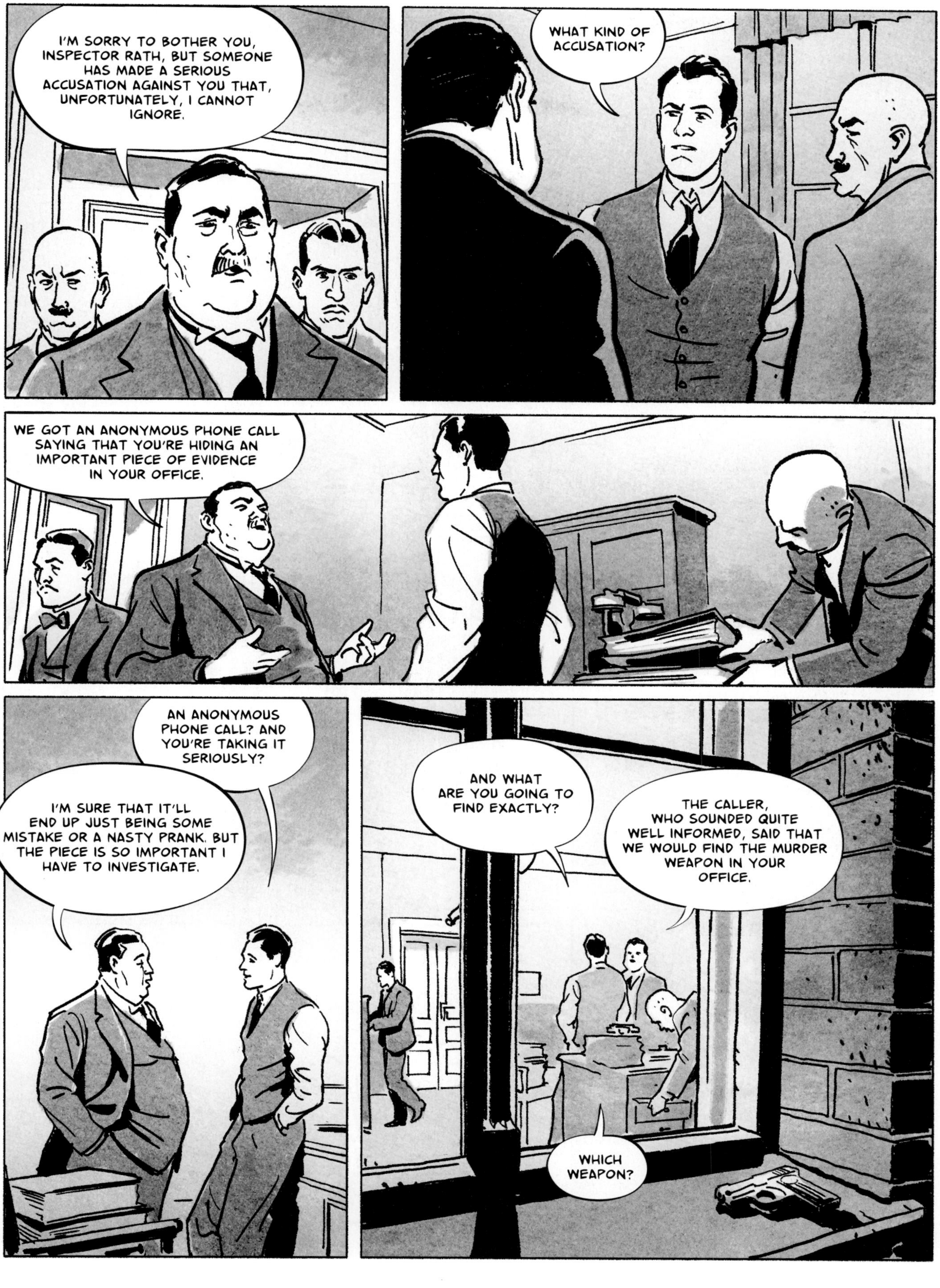
I'M SORRY TO BOTHER YOU, INSPECTOR RATH, BUT SOMEONE HAS MADE A SERIOUS ACCUSATION AGAINST YOU THAT, UNFORTUNATELY, I CANNOT IGNORE.
WHAT KIND OF ACCUSATION?
WE GOT AN ANONYMOUS PHONE CALL SAYING THAT YOU'RE HIDING AN IMPORTANT PIECE OF EVIDENCE IN YOUR OFFICE.
AN ANONYMOUS PHONE CALL? AND YOU'RE TAKING IT SERIOUSLY?
I'M SURE THAT IT'LL END UP JUST BEING SOME MISTAKE OR A NASTY PRANK. BUT THE PIECE IS SO IMPORTANT I HAVE TO INVESTIGATE.
AND WHAT ARE YOU GOING TO FIND EXACTLY?
THE CALLER, WHO SOUNDED QUITE WELL INFORMED, SAID THAT WE WOULD FIND THE MURDER WEAPON IN YOUR OFFICE.
WHICH WEAPON?

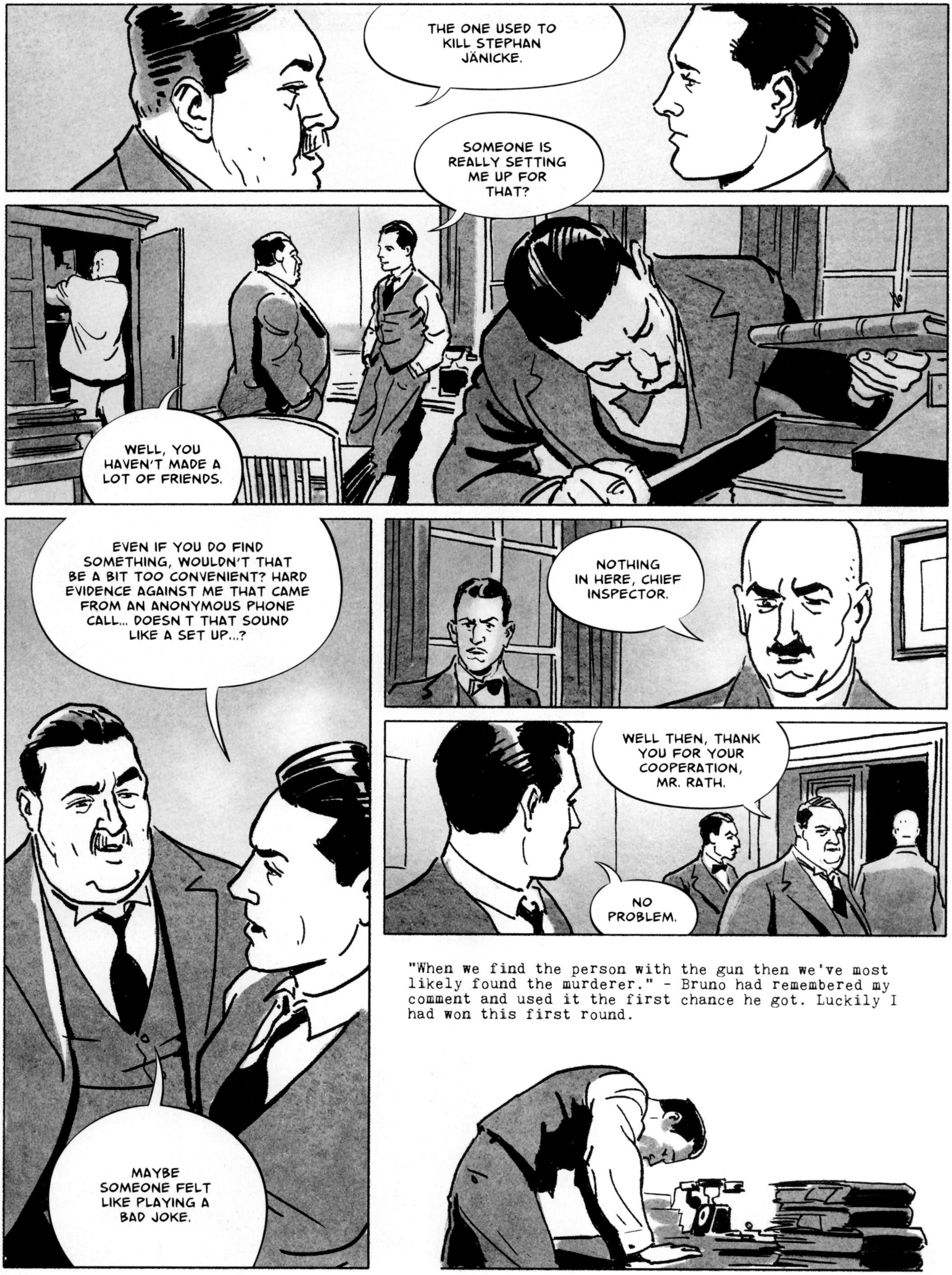
THE ONE USED TO KILL STEPHAN JÄNICKE.
SOMEONE IS REALLY SETTING ME UP FOR THAT?
WELL, YOU HAVEN'T MADE A LOT OF FRIENDS.
EVEN IF YOU DO FIND SOMETHING, WOULDN'T THAT BE A BIT TOO CONVENIENT? HARD EVIDENCE AGAINST ME THAT CAME FROM AN ANONYMOUS PHONE CALL... DOESN T THAT SOUND LIKE A SET UP...?
MAYBE SOMEONE FELT LIKE PLAYING A BAD JOKE.
NOTHING IN HERE, CHIEF INSPECTOR.
WELL THEN, THANK YOU FOR YOUR COOPERATION, MR. RATH.
NO PROBLEM.
"When we find the person with the gun then we've most likely found the murderer." - Bruno had remembered my comment and used it the first chance he got. Luckily I had won this first round.

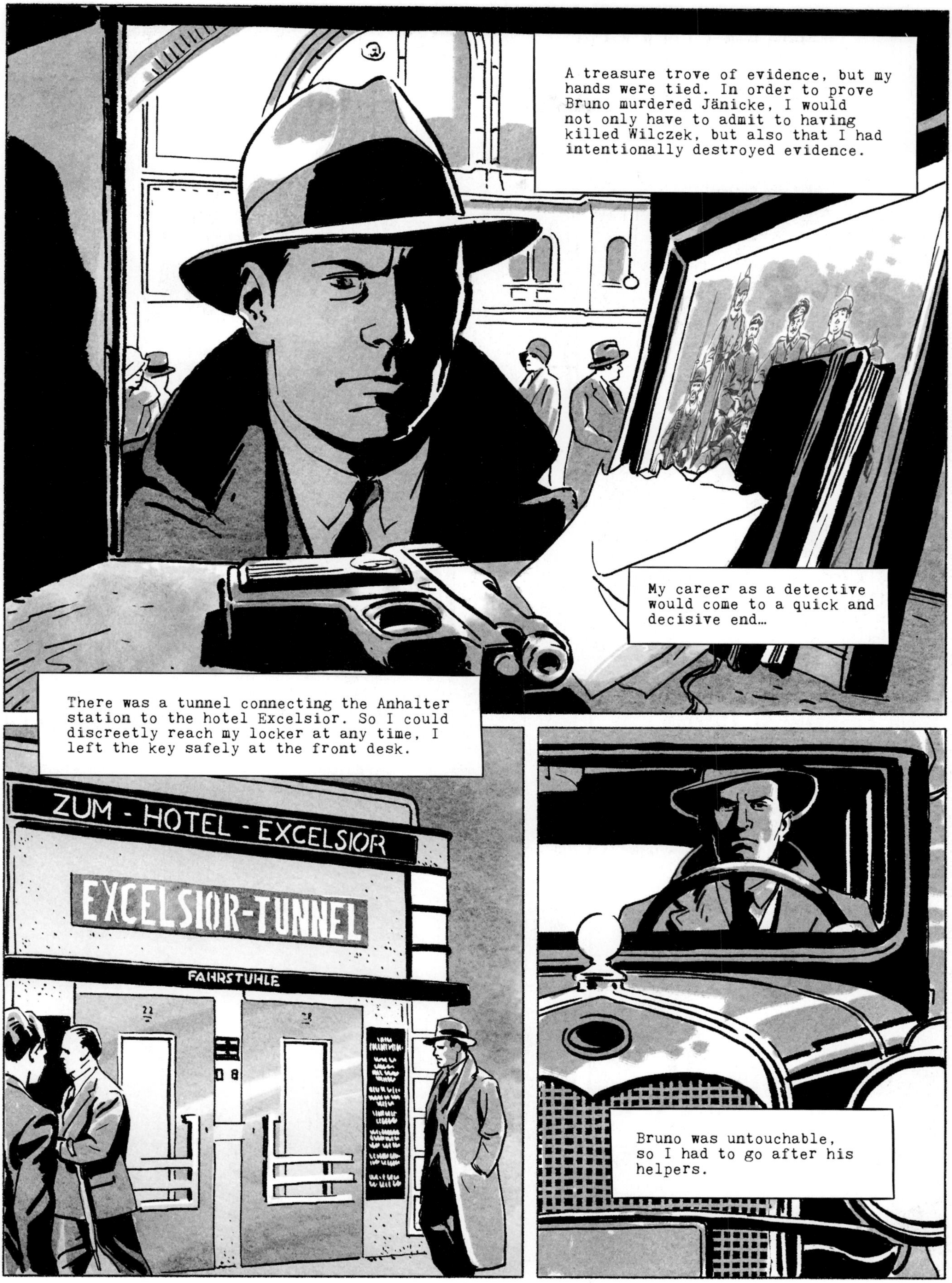
A treasure trove of evidence, but my hands were tied. In order to prove Bruno murdered Jänicke, I would not only have to admit to having killed Wilczek, but also that I had intentionally destroyed evidence.
My career as a detective would come to a quick and decisive end…
There was a tunnel connecting the Anhalter station to the hotel Excelsior. So I could discreetly reach my locker at any time, I left the key safely at the front desk.
ZUM - HOTEL - EXCELSIOR
EXCELSIOR-TUNNEL
FAHRSTUHLE
Bruno was untouchable, so I had to go after his helpers.

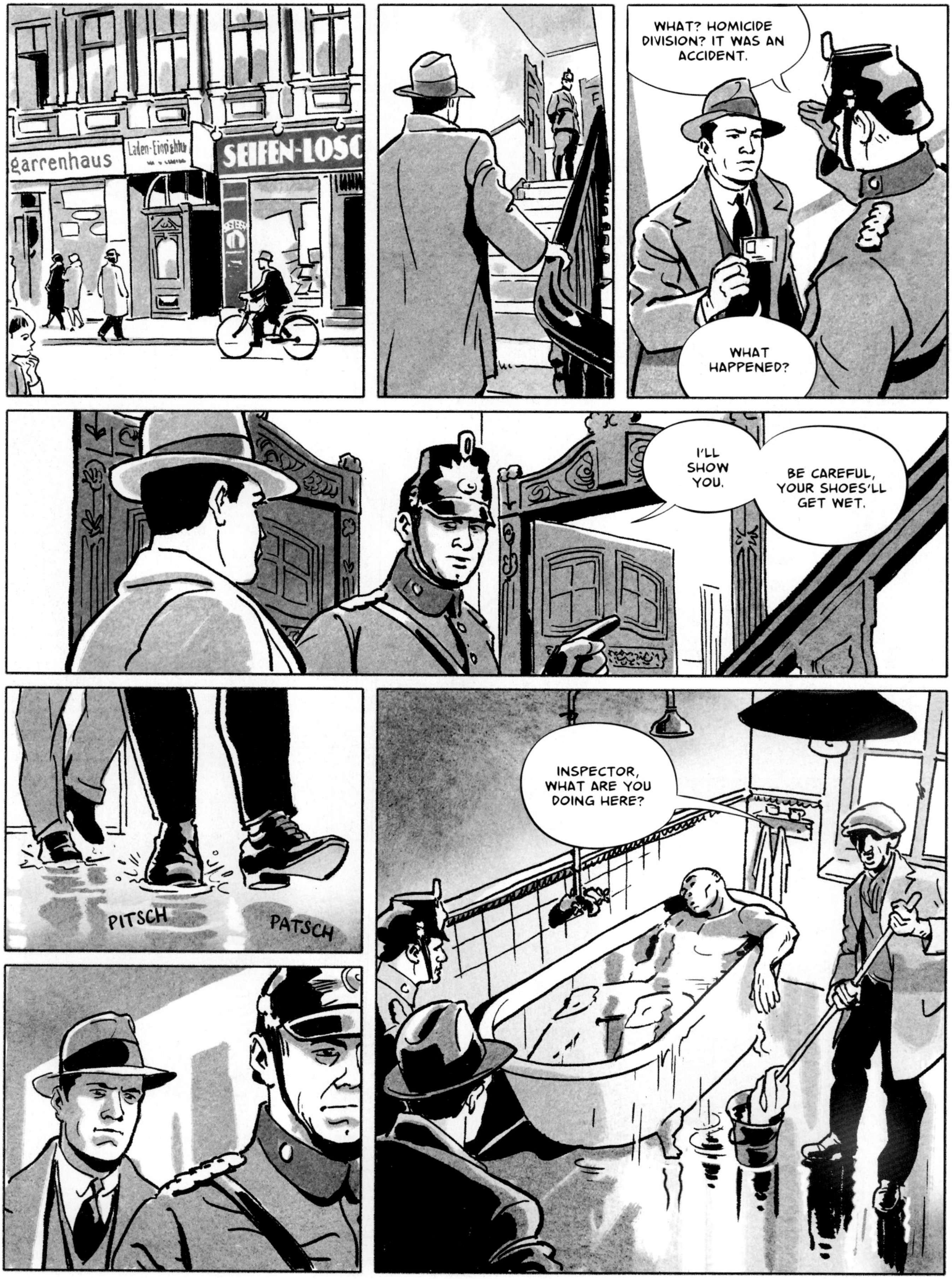
garrenhaus
Laden-Einrichtun
SEIFEN-LOSC
WHAT? HOMICIDE DIVISION? IT WAS AN ACCIDENT.
WHAT HAPPENED?
I'LL SHOW YOU.
BE CAREFUL, YOUR SHOES'LL GET WET.
PITSCH
PATSCH
INSPECTOR, WHAT ARE YOU DOING HERE?

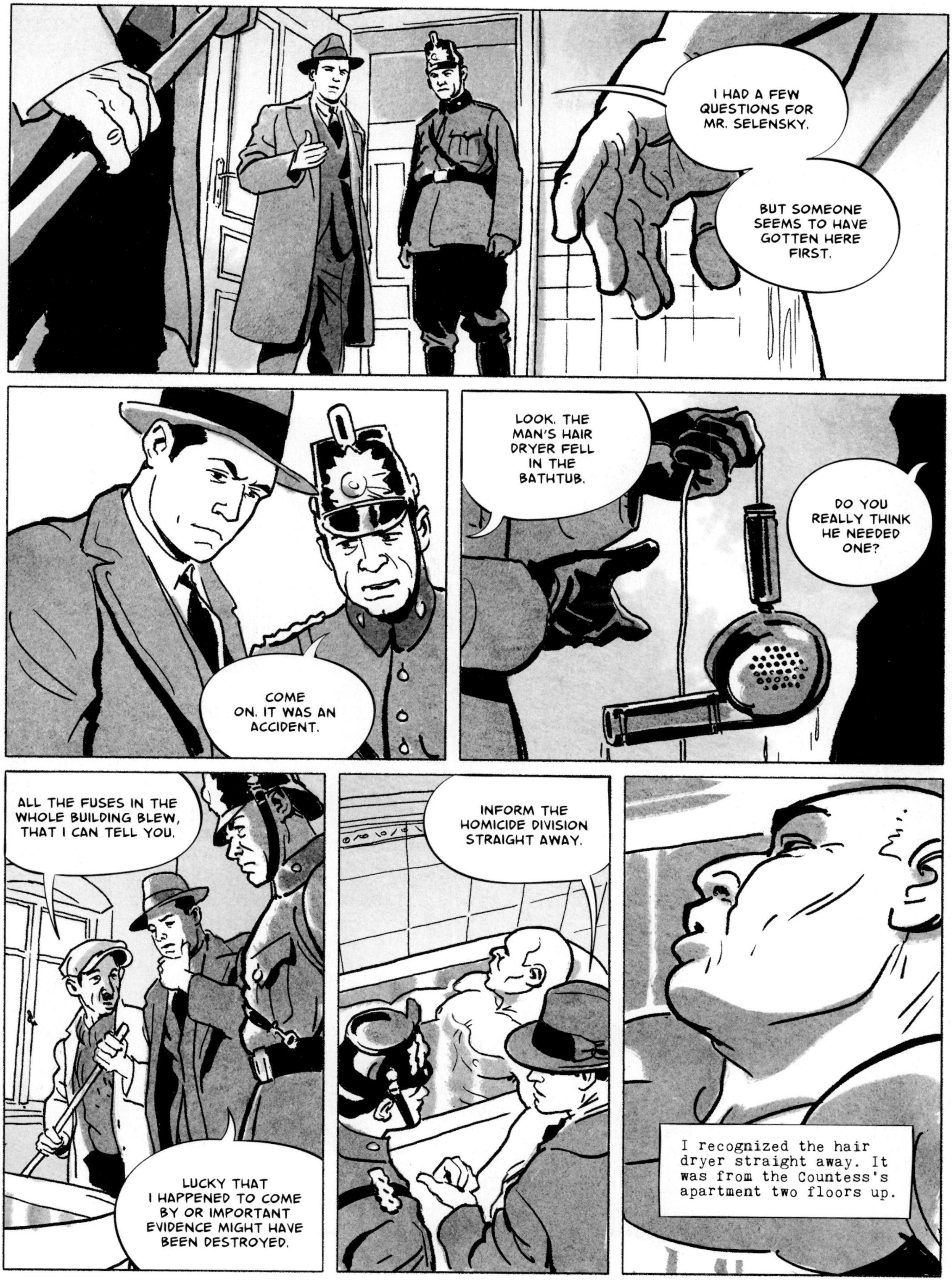
I HAD A FEW QUESTIONS FOR MR. SELENSKY.
BUT SOMEONE SEEMS TO HAVE GOTTEN HERE FIRST.
COME ON. IT WAS AN ACCIDENT.
LOOK. THE MAN'S HAIR DRYER FELL IN THE BATHTUB.
DO YOU REALLY THINK HE NEEDED ONE?
ALL THE FUSES IN THE WHOLE BUILDING BLEW, THAT I CAN TELL YOU.
LUCKY THAT I HAPPENED TO COME BY OR IMPORTANT EVIDENCE MIGHT HAVE BEEN DESTROYED.
INFORM THE HOMICIDE DIVISION STRAIGHT AWAY.
I recognized the hair dryer straight away. It was from the Countess's apartment two floors up.

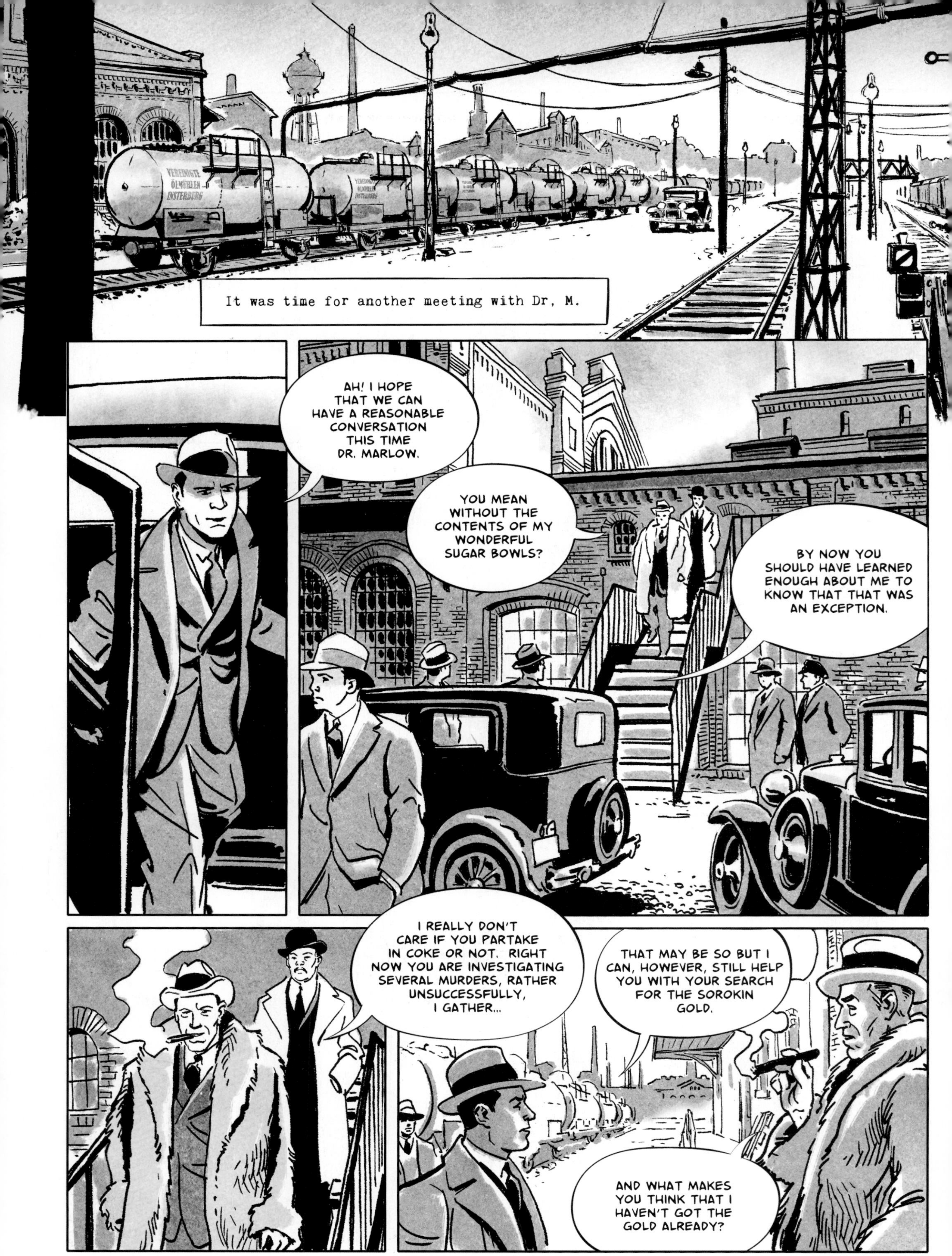

VEREINIGTE ÖLMÜHLEN INSTERBURG
It was time for another meeting with Dr, M.
AH! I HOPE THAT WE CAN HAVE A REASONABLE CONVERSATION THIS TIME DR. MARLOW.
YOU MEAN WITHOUT THE CONTENTS OF MY WONDERFUL SUGAR BOWLS?
BY NOW YOU SHOULD HAVE LEARNED ENOUGH ABOUT ME TO KNOW THAT THAT WAS AN EXCEPTION.
I REALLY DON'T CARE IF YOU PARTAKE IN COKE OR NOT. RIGHT NOW YOU ARE INVESTIGATING SEVERAL MURDERS, RATHER UNSUCCESSFULLY, I GATHER...
THAT MAY BE SO BUT I CAN, HOWEVER, STILL HELP YOU WITH YOUR SEARCH FOR THE SOROKIN GOLD.
AND WHAT MAKES YOU THINK THAT I HAVEN'T GOT THE GOLD ALREADY?

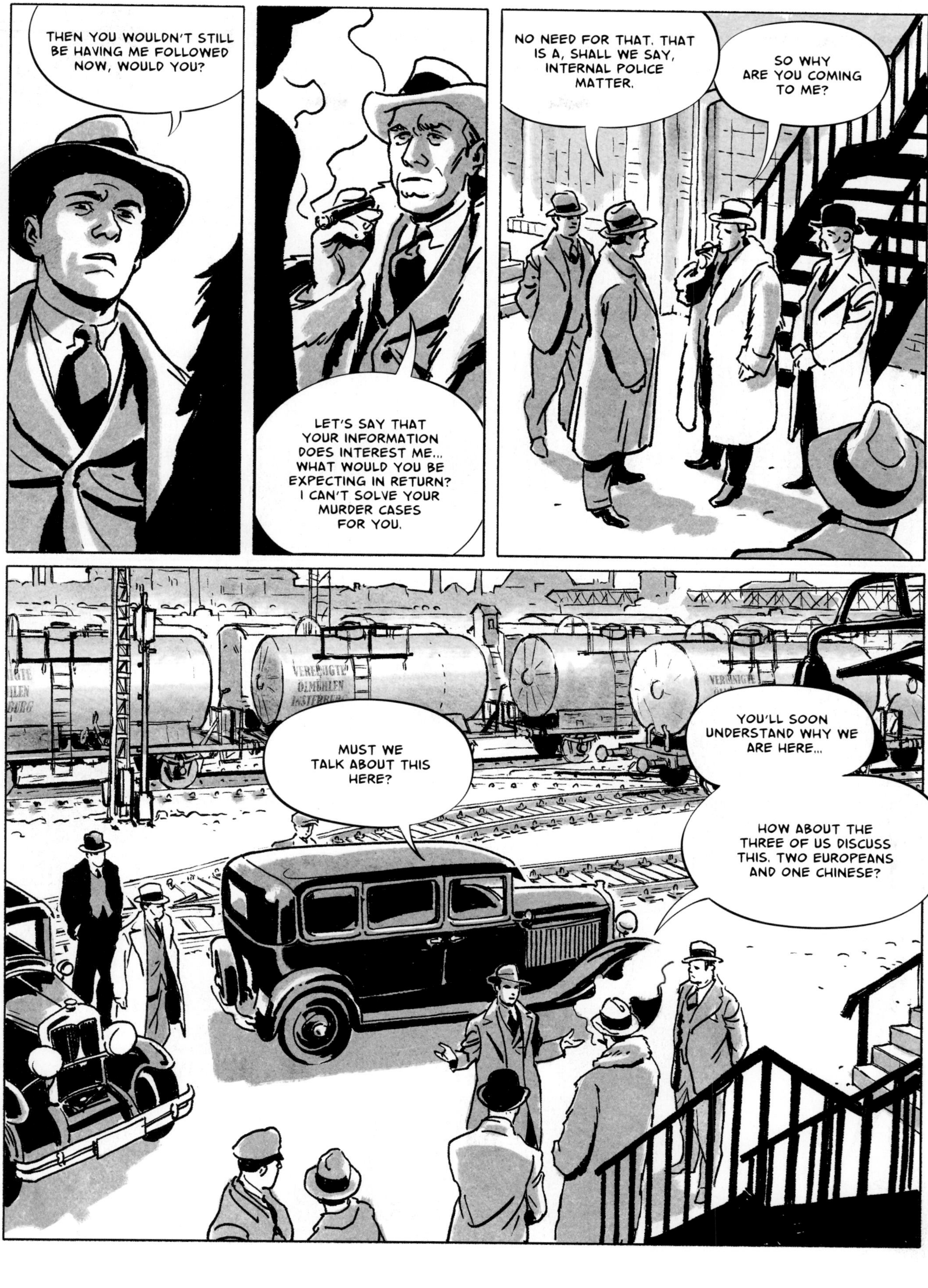
THEN YOU WOULDN'T STILL BE HAVING ME FOLLOWED NOW, WOULD YOU?
LET'S SAY THAT YOUR INFORMATION DOES INTEREST ME... WHAT WOULD YOU BE EXPECTING IN RETURN? I CAN'T SOLVE YOUR MURDER CASES FOR YOU.
NO NEED FOR THAT. THAT IS A, SHALL WE SAY, INTERNAL POLICE MATTER.
SO WHY ARE YOU COMING TO ME?
VEREINIGTE OLMÜHLEN INSTERBURG
MUST WE TALK ABOUT THIS HERE?
YOU'LL SOON UNDERSTAND WHY WE ARE HERE...
HOW ABOUT THE THREE OF US DISCUSS THIS. TWO EUROPEANS AND ONE CHINESE?

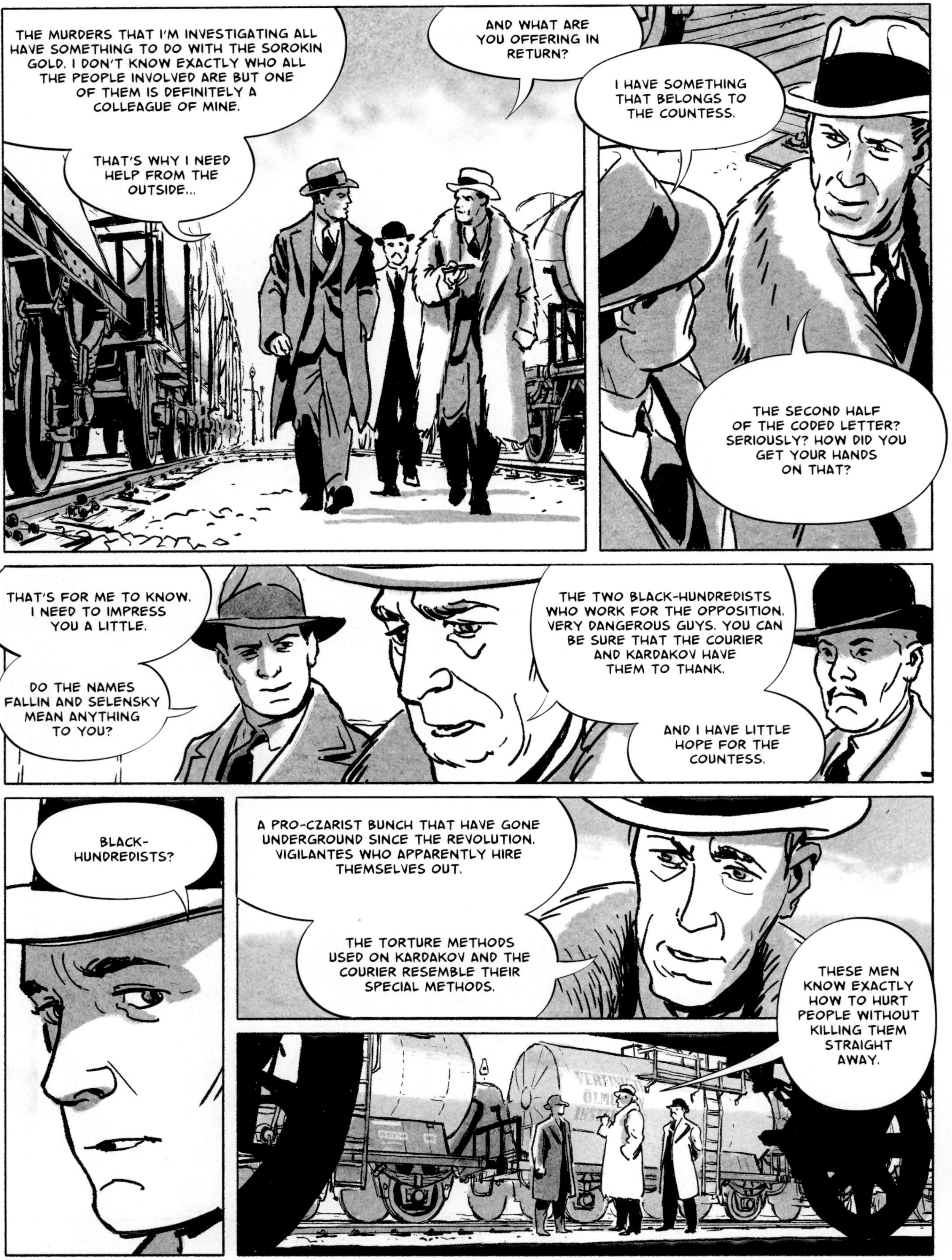
THE MURDERS THAT I'M INVESTIGATING ALL HAVE SOMETHING TO DO WITH THE SOROKIN GOLD. I DON'T KNOW EXACTLY WHO ALL THE PEOPLE INVOLVED ARE BUT ONE OF THEM IS DEFINITELY A COLLEAGUE OF MINE.
THAT'S WHY I NEED HELP FROM THE OUTSIDE...
AND WHAT ARE YOU OFFERING IN RETURN?
I HAVE SOMETHING THAT BELONGS TO THE COUNTESS.
THE SECOND HALF OF THE CODED LETTER? SERIOUSLY? HOW DID YOU GET YOUR HANDS ON THAT?
THAT'S FOR ME TO KNOW. I NEED TO IMPRESS YOU A LITTLE.
DO THE NAMES FALLIN AND SELENSKY MEAN ANYTHING TO YOU?
THE TWO BLACK-HUNDREDISTS WHO WORK FOR THE OPPOSITION. VERY DANGEROUS GUYS. YOU CAN BE SURE THAT THE COURIER AND KARDAKOV HAVE THEM TO THANK.
AND I HAVE LITTLE HOPE FOR THE COUNTESS.
BLACK-HUNDREDISTS?
A PRO-CZARIST BUNCH THAT HAVE GONE UNDERGROUND SINCE THE REVOLUTION. VIGILANTES WHO APPARENTLY HIRE THEMSELVES OUT.
THE TORTURE METHODS USED ON KARDAKOV AND THE COURIER RESEMBLE THEIR SPECIAL METHODS.
THESE MEN KNOW EXACTLY HOW TO HURT PEOPLE WITHOUT KILLING THEM STRAIGHT AWAY.

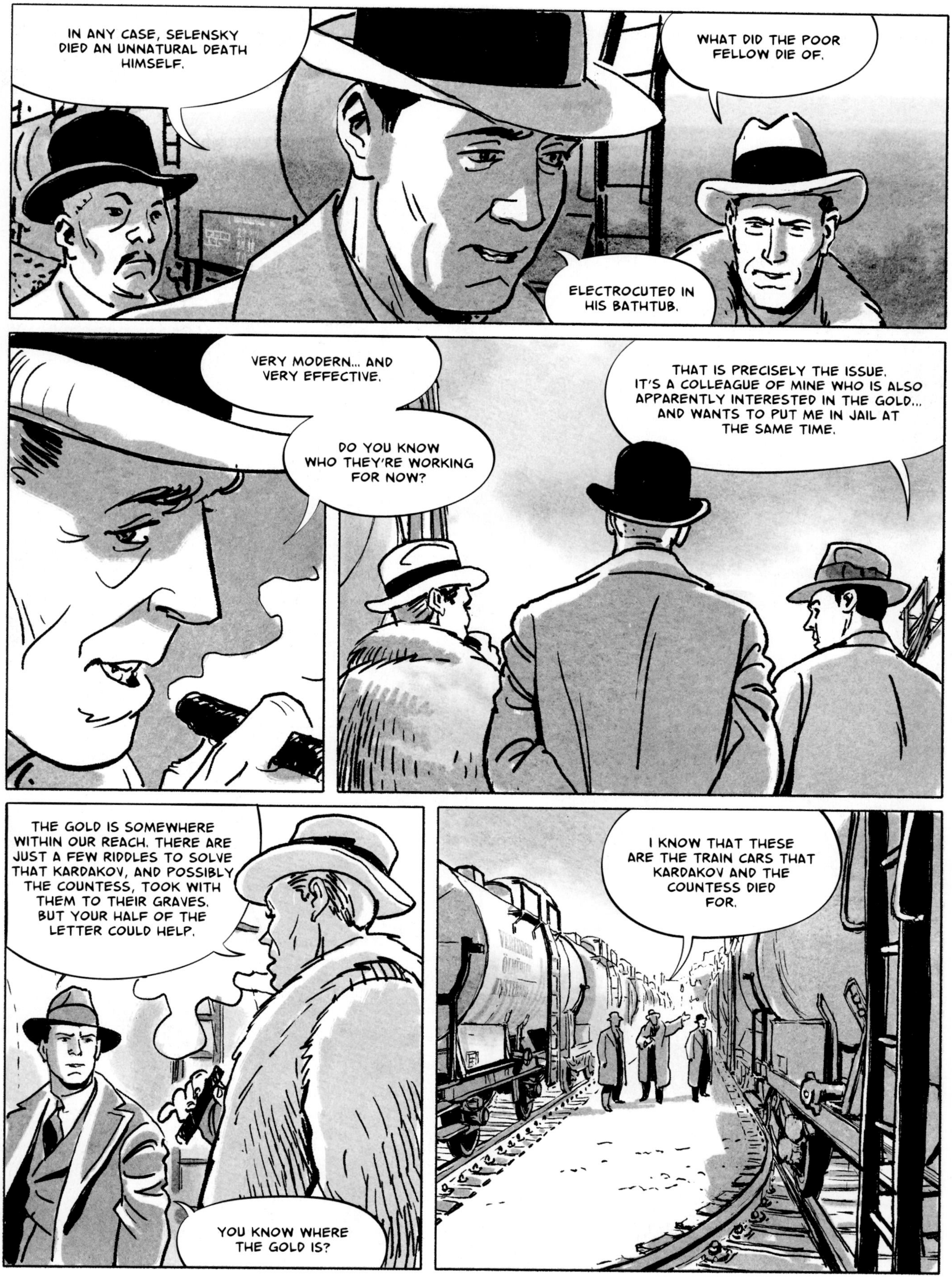
IN ANY CASE, SELENSKY DIED AN UNNATURAL DEATH HIMSELF.
WHAT DID THE POOR FELLOW DIE OF.
ELECTROCUTED IN HIS BATHTUB.
VERY MODERN... AND VERY EFFECTIVE.
DO YOU KNOW WHO THEY'RE WORKING FOR NOW?
THAT IS PRECISELY THE ISSUE. IT'S A COLLEAGUE OF MINE WHO IS ALSO APPARENTLY INTERESTED IN THE GOLD... AND WANTS TO PUT ME IN JAIL AT THE SAME TIME.
THE GOLD IS SOMEWHERE WITHIN OUR REACH. THERE ARE JUST A FEW RIDDLES TO SOLVE THAT KARDAKOV, AND POSSIBLY THE COUNTESS, TOOK WITH THEM TO THEIR GRAVES. BUT YOUR HALF OF THE LETTER COULD HELP.
YOU KNOW WHERE THE GOLD IS?
I KNOW THAT THESE ARE THE TRAIN CARS THAT KARDAKOV AND THE COUNTESS DIED FOR.

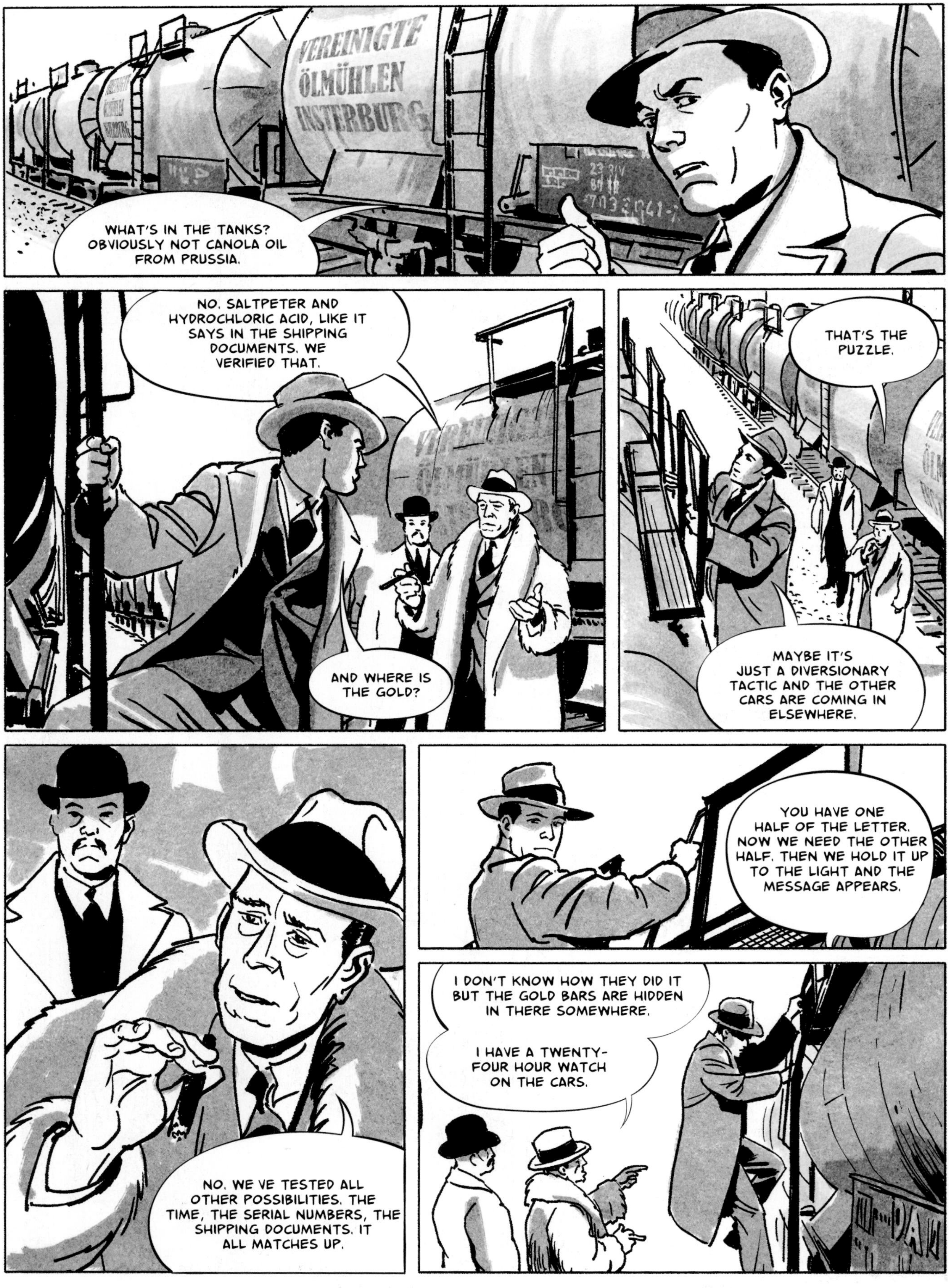

VEREINIGTE ÖLMÜHLEN INSTERBURG
WHAT'S IN THE TANKS? OBVIOUSLY NOT CANOLA OIL FROM PRUSSIA.
NO. SALTPETER AND HYDROCHLORIC ACID, LIKE IT SAYS IN THE SHIPPING DOCUMENTS. WE VERIFIED THAT.
AND WHERE IS THE GOLD?
THAT'S THE PUZZLE.
MAYBE IT'S JUST A DIVERSIONARY TACTIC AND THE OTHER CARS ARE COMING IN ELSEWHERE.
NO. WE'VE TESTED ALL OTHER POSSIBILITIES. THE TIME, THE SERIAL NUMBERS, THE SHIPPING DOCUMENTS. IT ALL MATCHES UP.
YOU HAVE ONE HALF OF THE LETTER. NOW WE NEED THE OTHER HALF. THEN WE HOLD IT UP TO THE LIGHT AND THE MESSAGE APPEARS.
I DON'T KNOW HOW THEY DID IT BUT THE GOLD BARS ARE HIDDEN IN THERE SOMEWHERE.
I HAVE A TWENTY-FOUR HOUR WATCH ON THE CARS.

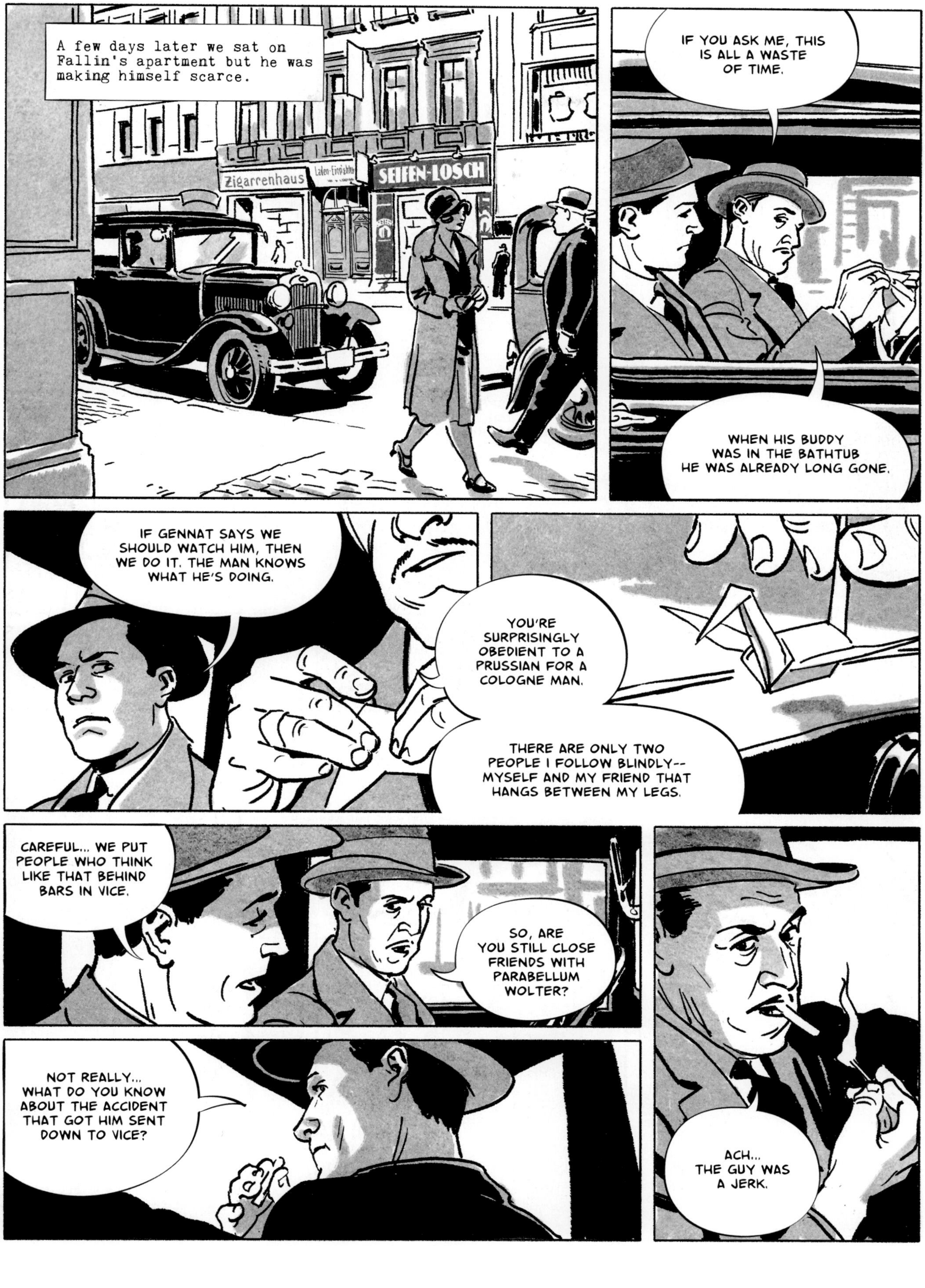
A few days later we sat on Fallin's apartment but he was making himself scarce.
Zigarrenhaus
SEIFEN-LOSCH
IF YOU ASK ME, THIS IS ALL A WASTE OF TIME.
WHEN HIS BUDDY WAS IN THE BATHTUB HE WAS ALREADY LONG GONE.
IF GENNAT SAYS WE SHOULD WATCH HIM, THEN WE DO IT. THE MAN KNOWS WHAT HE'S DOING.
YOU'RE SURPRISINGLY OBEDIENT TO A PRUSSIAN FOR A COLOGNE MAN.
THERE ARE ONLY TWO PEOPLE I FOLLOW BLINDLY-- MYSELF AND MY FRIEND THAT HANGS BETWEEN MY LEGS.
CAREFUL... WE PUT PEOPLE WHO THINK LIKE THAT BEHIND BARS IN VICE.
SO, ARE YOU STILL CLOSE FRIENDS WITH PARABELLUM WOLTER?
NOT REALLY... WHAT DO YOU KNOW ABOUT THE ACCIDENT THAT GOT HIM SENT DOWN TO VICE?
ACH... THE GUY WAS A JERK.

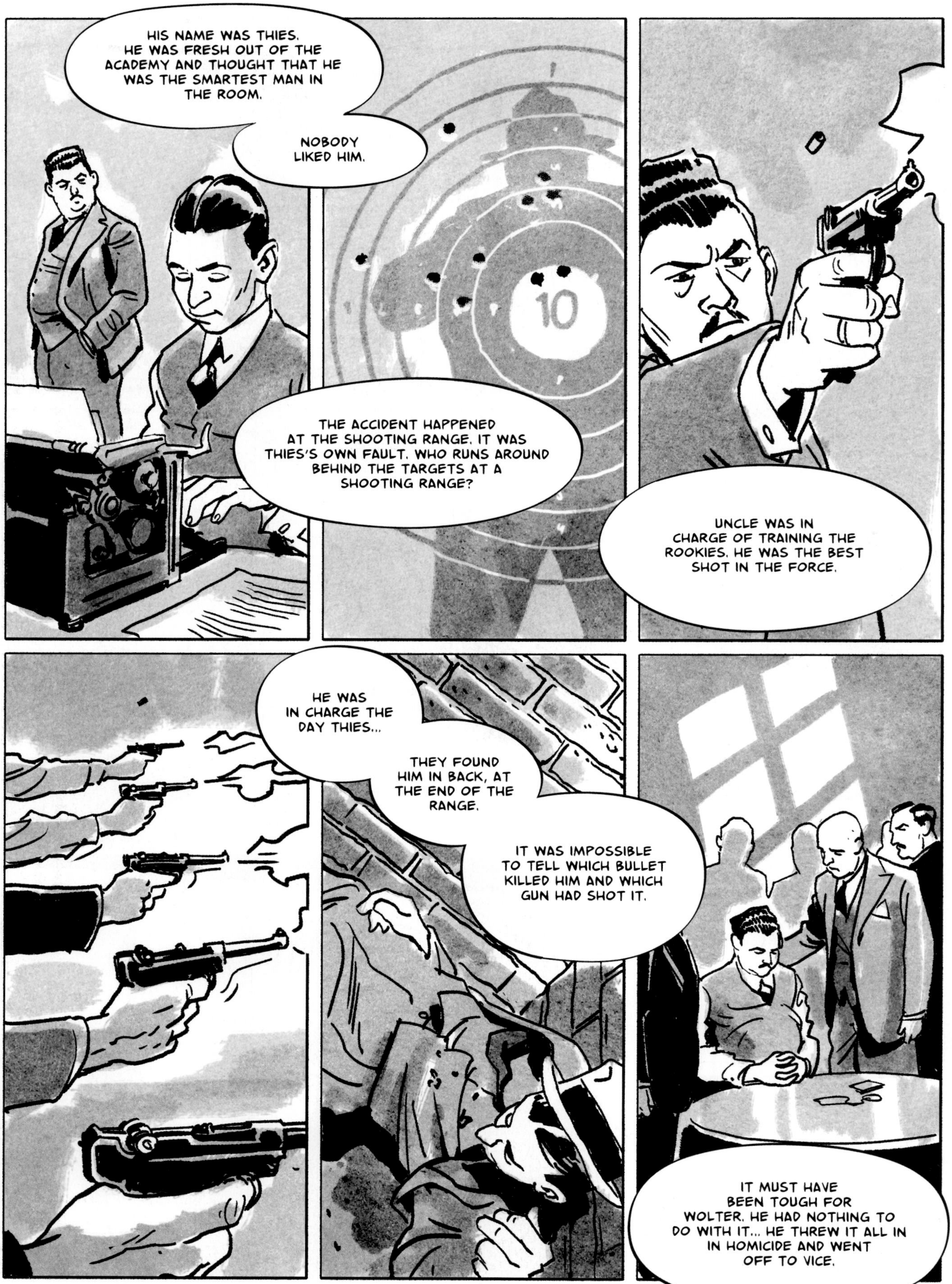
HIS NAME WAS THIES. HE WAS FRESH OUT OF THE ACADEMY AND THOUGHT THAT HE WAS THE SMARTEST MAN IN THE ROOM.
NOBODY LIKED HIM.
THE ACCIDENT HAPPENED AT THE SHOOTING RANGE. IT WAS THIES'S OWN FAULT. WHO RUNS AROUND BEHIND THE TARGETS AT A SHOOTING RANGE?
10
UNCLE WAS IN CHARGE OF TRAINING THE ROOKIES. HE WAS THE BEST SHOT IN THE FORCE.
HE WAS IN CHARGE THE DAY THIES...
THEY FOUND HIM IN BACK, AT THE END OF THE RANGE.
IT WAS IMPOSSIBLE TO TELL WHICH BULLET KILLED HIM AND WHICH GUN HAD SHOT IT.
IT MUST HAVE BEEN TOUGH FOR WOLTER. HE HAD NOTHING TO DO WITH IT... HE THREW IT ALL IN IN HOMICIDE AND WENT OFF TO VICE.

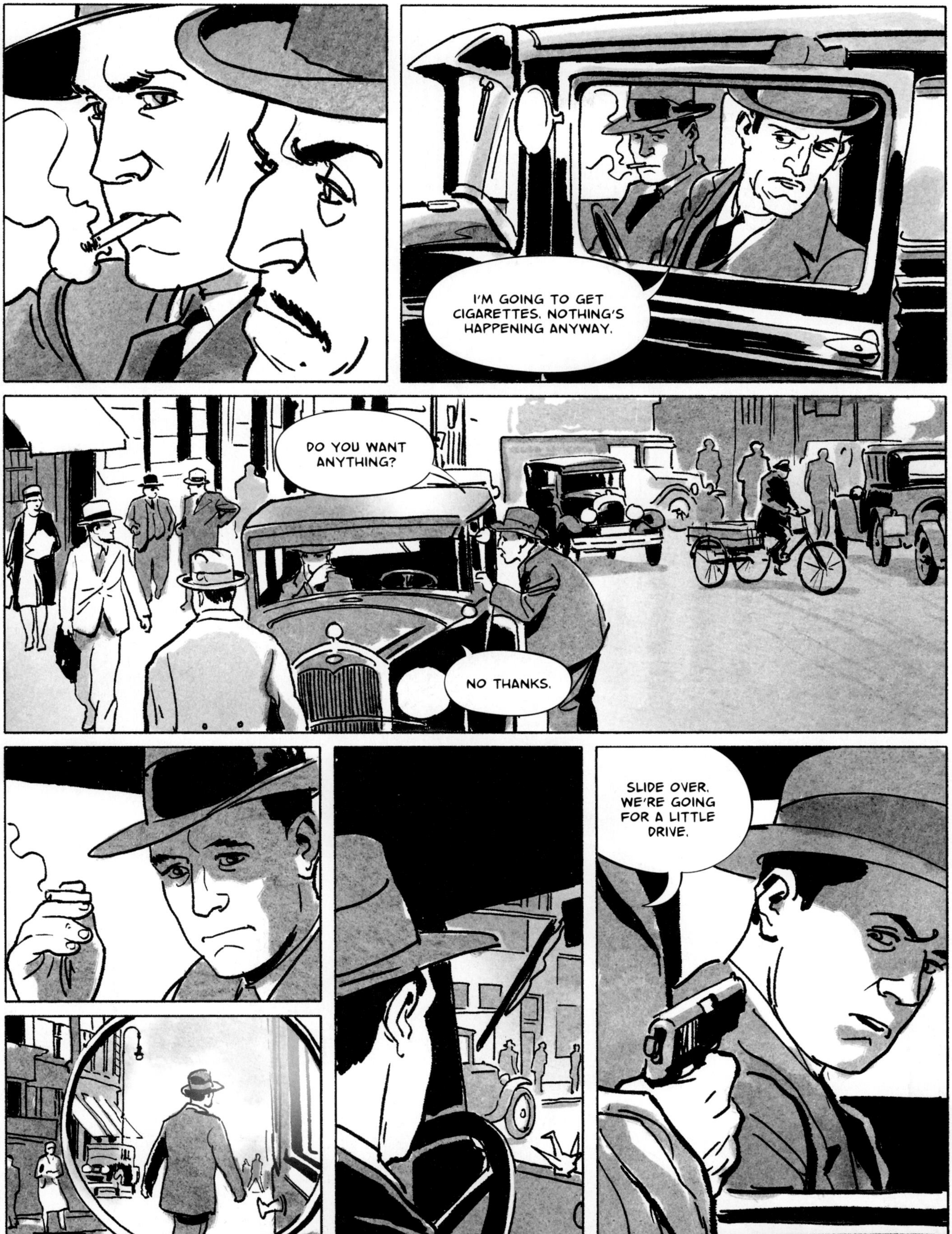

I'M GOING TO GET CIGARETTES. NOTHING'S HAPPENING ANYWAY.
DO YOU WANT ANYTHING?
NO THANKS.
SLIDE OVER. WE'RE GOING FOR A LITTLE DRIVE.

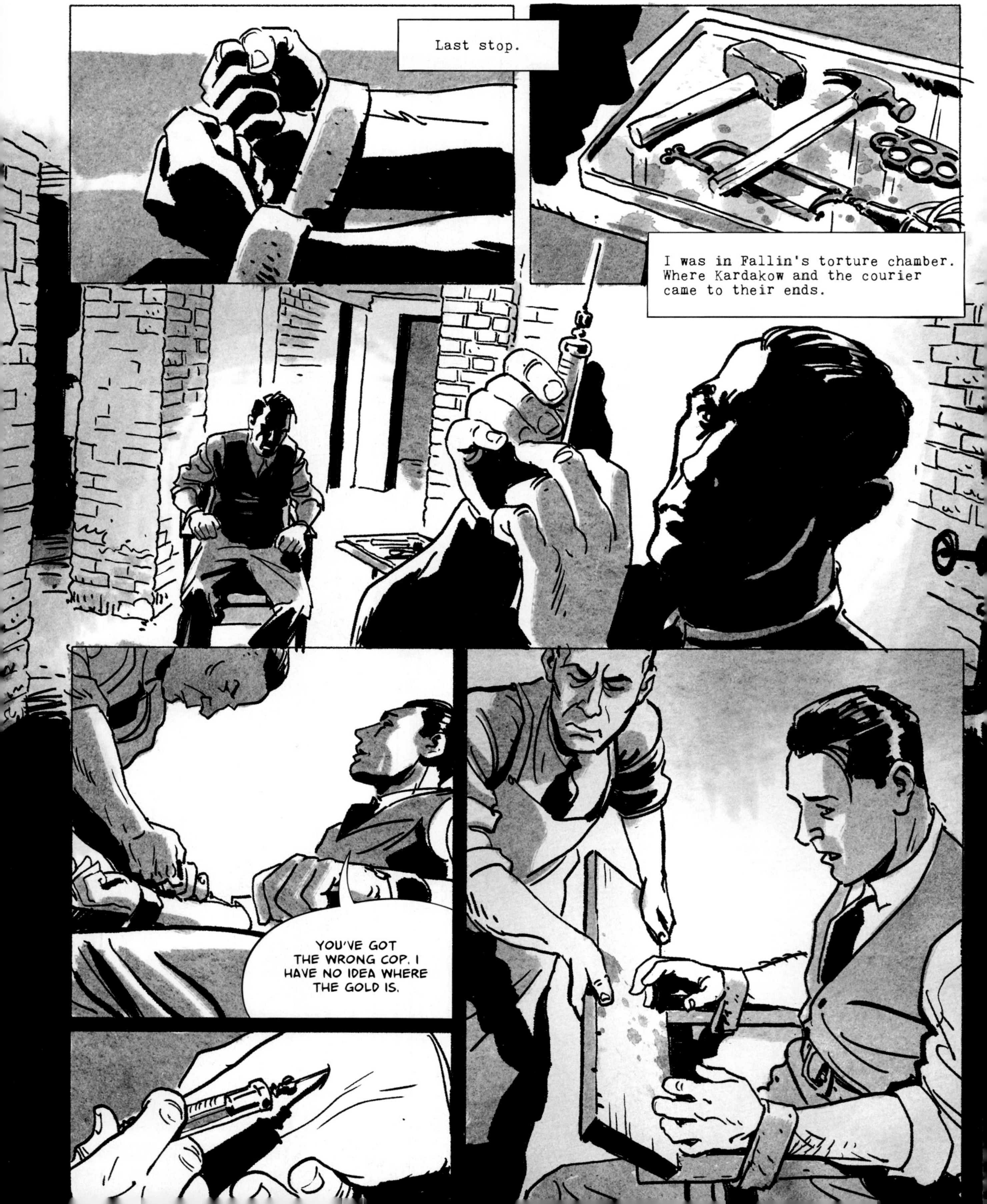

Last stop.
I was in Fallin's torture chamber. Where Kardakow and the courier came to their ends.
YOU'VE GOT THE WRONG COP. I HAVE NO IDEA WHERE THE GOLD IS.

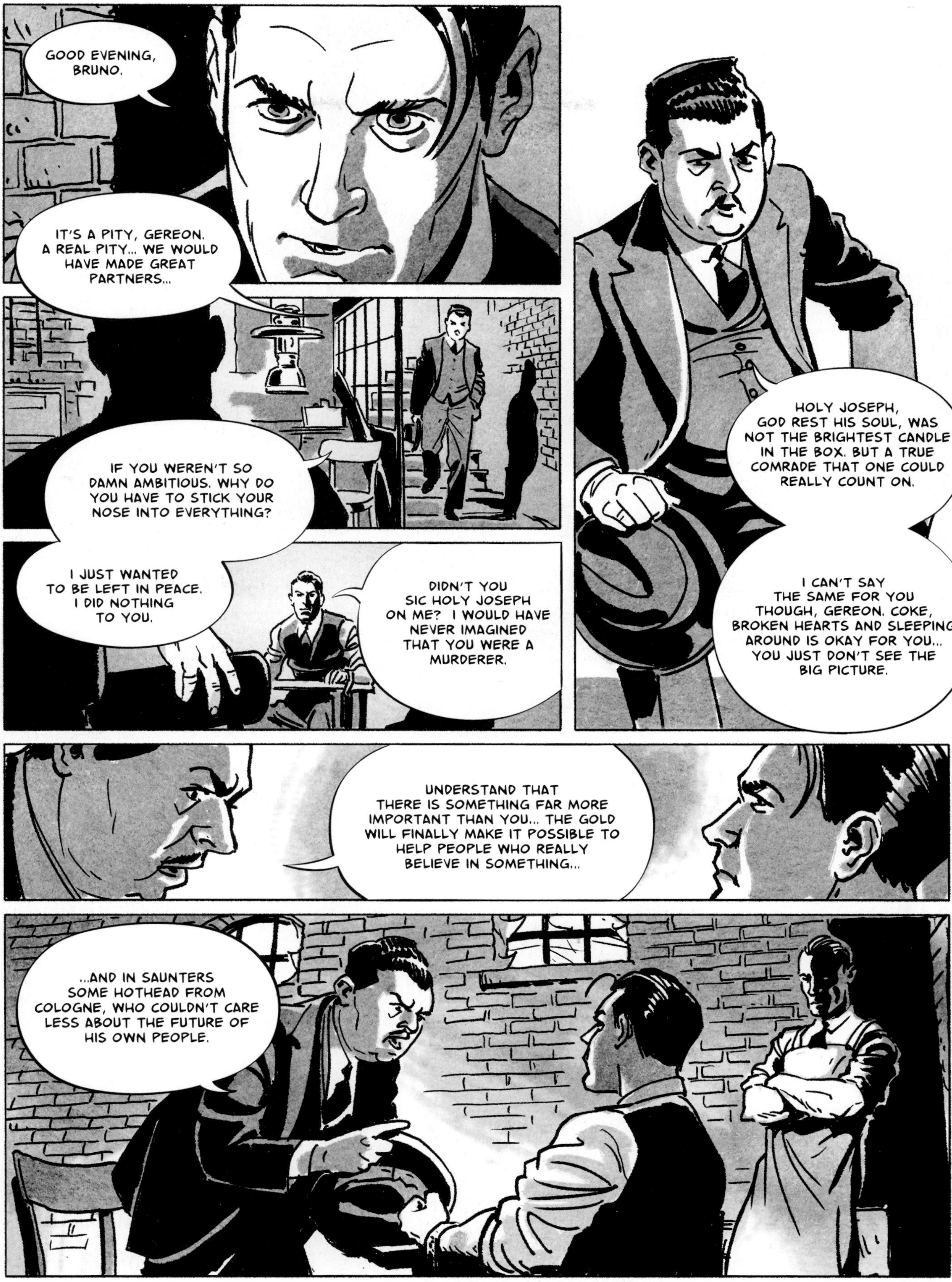
GOOD EVENING, BRUNO.
IT'S A PITY, GEREON. A REAL PITY... WE WOULD HAVE MADE GREAT PARTNERS...
IF YOU WEREN'T SO DAMN AMBITIOUS. WHY DO YOU HAVE TO STICK YOUR NOSE INTO EVERYTHING?
I JUST WANTED TO BE LEFT IN PEACE. I DID NOTHING TO YOU.
DIDN'T YOU SIC HOLY JOSEPH ON ME? I WOULD HAVE NEVER IMAGINED THAT YOU WERE A MURDERER.
HOLY JOSEPH, GOD REST HIS SOUL, WAS NOT THE BRIGHTEST CANDLE IN THE BOX. BUT A TRUE COMRADE THAT ONE COULD REALLY COUNT ON.
I CAN'T SAY THE SAME FOR YOU THOUGH, GEREON. COKE, BROKEN HEARTS AND SLEEPING AROUND IS OKAY FOR YOU... YOU JUST DON'T SEE THE BIG PICTURE.
UNDERSTAND THAT THERE IS SOMETHING FAR MORE IMPORTANT THAN YOU... THE GOLD WILL FINALLY MAKE IT POSSIBLE TO HELP PEOPLE WHO REALLY BELIEVE IN SOMETHING...
...AND IN SAUNTERS SOME HOTHEAD FROM COLOGNE, WHO COULDN'T CARE LESS ABOUT THE FUTURE OF HIS OWN PEOPLE.

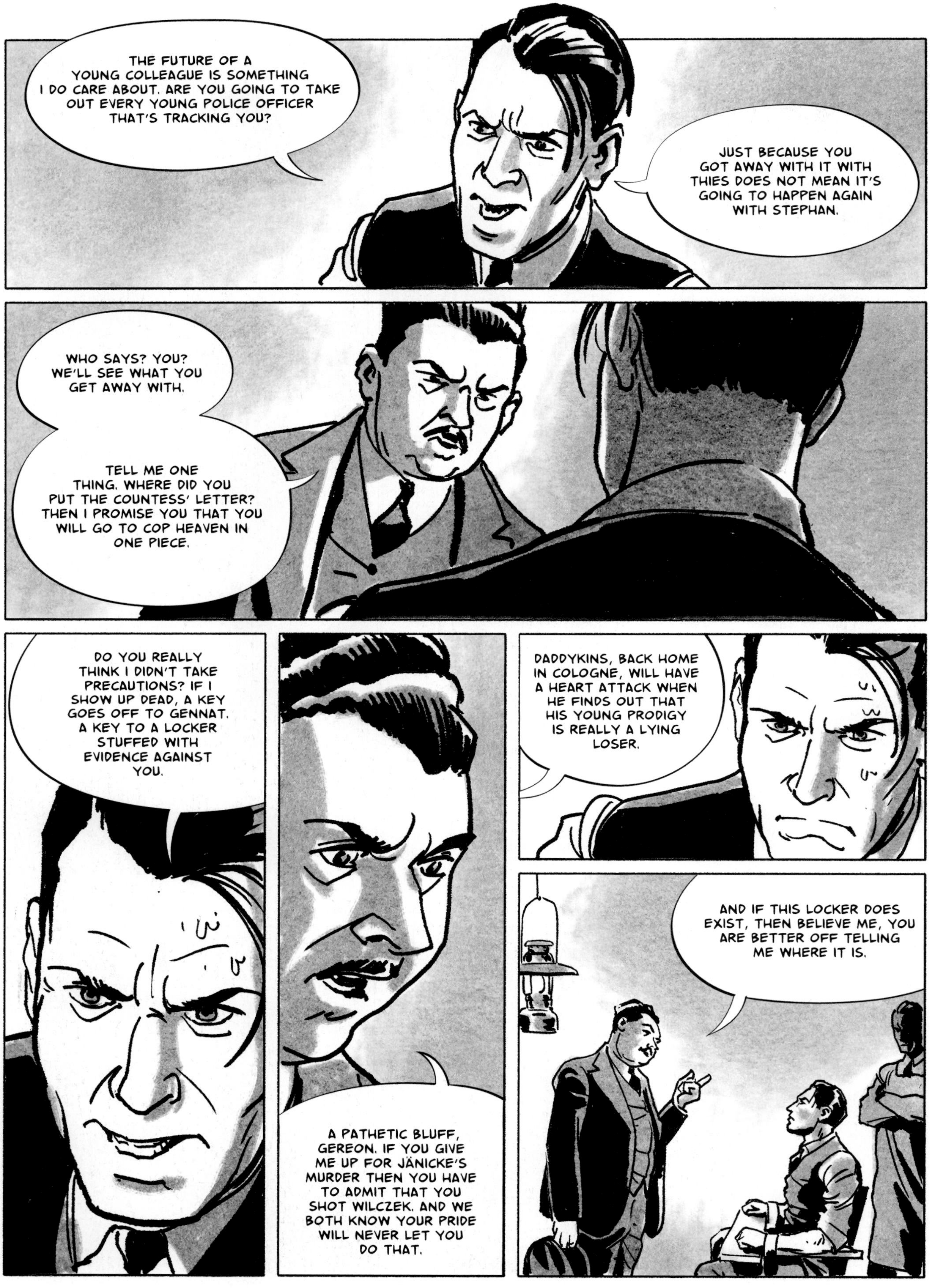
THE FUTURE OF A YOUNG COLLEAGUE IS SOMETHING I DO CARE ABOUT. ARE YOU GOING TO TAKE OUT EVERY YOUNG POLICE OFFICER THAT'S TRACKING YOU?
JUST BECAUSE YOU GOT AWAY WITH IT WITH THIES DOES NOT MEAN IT'S GOING TO HAPPEN AGAIN WITH STEPHAN.
WHO SAYS? YOU? WE'LL SEE WHAT YOU GET AWAY WITH.
TELL ME ONE THING. WHERE DID YOU PUT THE COUNTESS' LETTER? THEN I PROMISE YOU THAT YOU WILL GO TO COP HEAVEN IN ONE PIECE.
DO YOU REALLY THINK I DIDN'T TAKE PRECAUTIONS? IF I SHOW UP DEAD, A KEY GOES OFF TO GENNAT. A KEY TO A LOCKER STUFFED WITH EVIDENCE AGAINST YOU.
A PATHETIC BLUFF, GEREON. IF YOU GIVE ME UP FOR JÄNICKE'S MURDER THEN YOU HAVE TO ADMIT THAT YOU SHOT WILCZEK. AND WE BOTH KNOW YOUR PRIDE WILL NEVER LET YOU DO THAT.
DADDYKINS, BACK HOME IN COLOGNE, WILL HAVE A HEART ATTACK WHEN HE FINDS OUT THAT HIS YOUNG PRODIGY IS REALLY A LYING LOSER.
AND IF THIS LOCKER DOES EXIST, THEN BELIEVE ME, YOU ARE BETTER OFF TELLING ME WHERE IT IS.

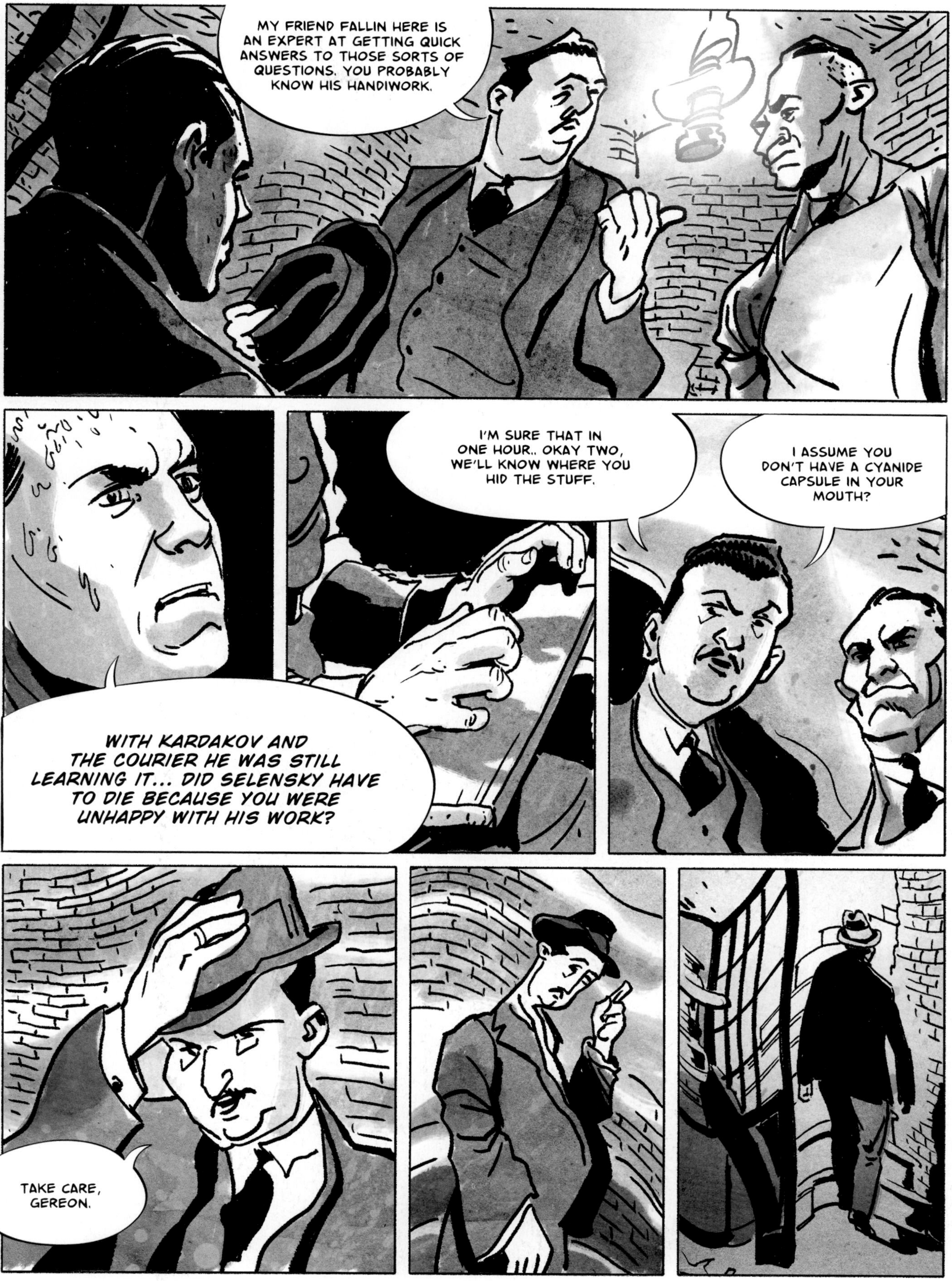
MY FRIEND FALLIN HERE IS AN EXPERT AT GETTING QUICK ANSWERS TO THOSE SORTS OF QUESTIONS. YOU PROBABLY KNOW HIS HANDIWORK.
WITH KARDAKOV AND THE COURIER HE WAS STILL LEARNING IT... DID SELENSKY HAVE TO DIE BECAUSE YOU WERE UNHAPPY WITH HIS WORK?
I'M SURE THAT IN ONE HOUR.. OKAY TWO, WE'LL KNOW WHERE YOU HID THE STUFF.
I ASSUME YOU DON'T HAVE A CYANIDE CAPSULE IN YOUR MOUTH?
TAKE CARE, GEREON.

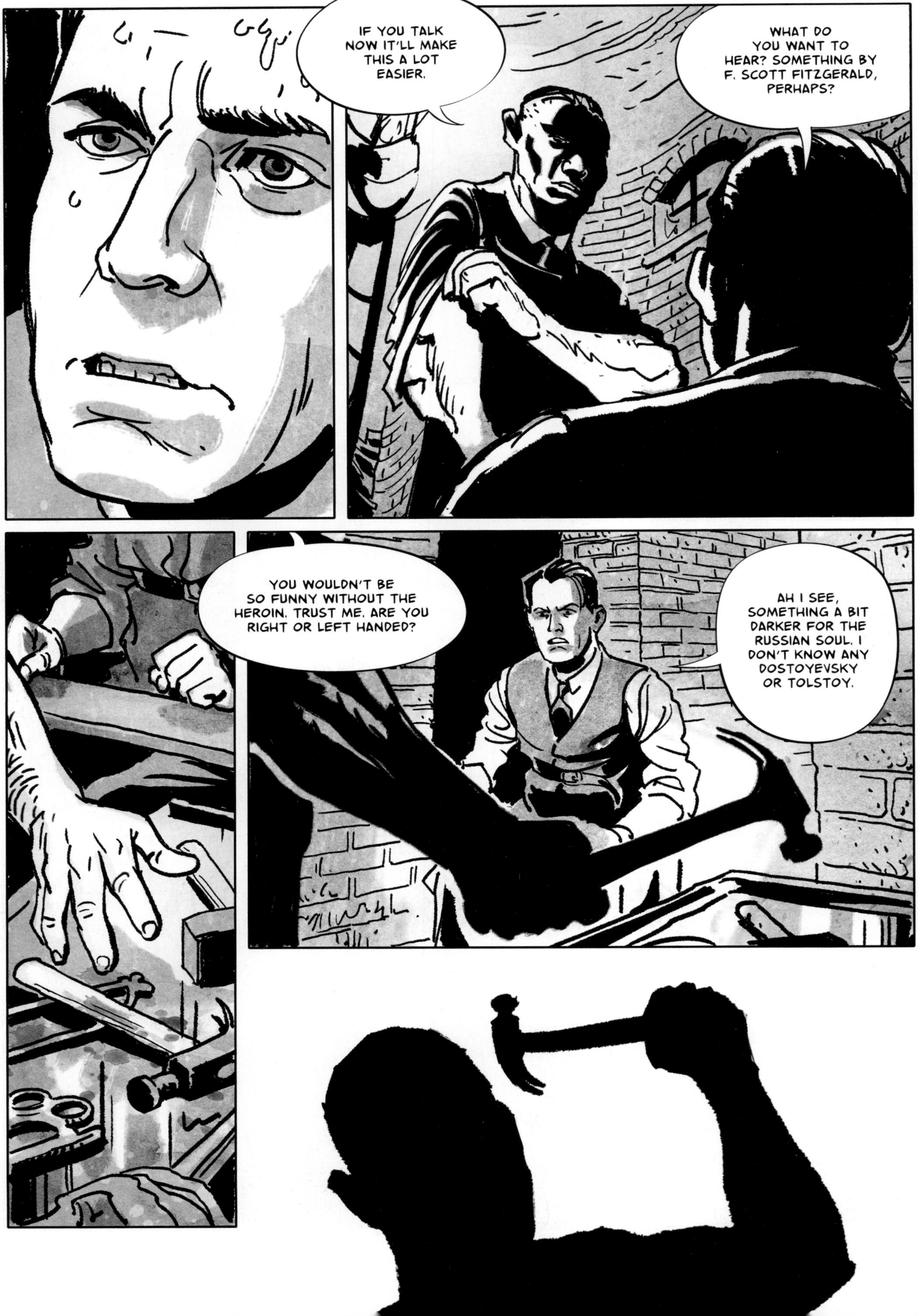
IF YOU TALK NOW IT'LL MAKE THIS A LOT EASIER.
WHAT DO YOU WANT TO HEAR? SOMETHING BY F. SCOTT FITZGERALD, PERHAPS?
YOU WOULDN'T BE SO FUNNY WITHOUT THE HEROIN. TRUST ME. ARE YOU RIGHT OR LEFT HANDED?
AH I SEE, SOMETHING A BIT DARKER FOR THE RUSSIAN SOUL. I DON'T KNOW ANY DOSTOYEVSKY OR TOLSTOY.

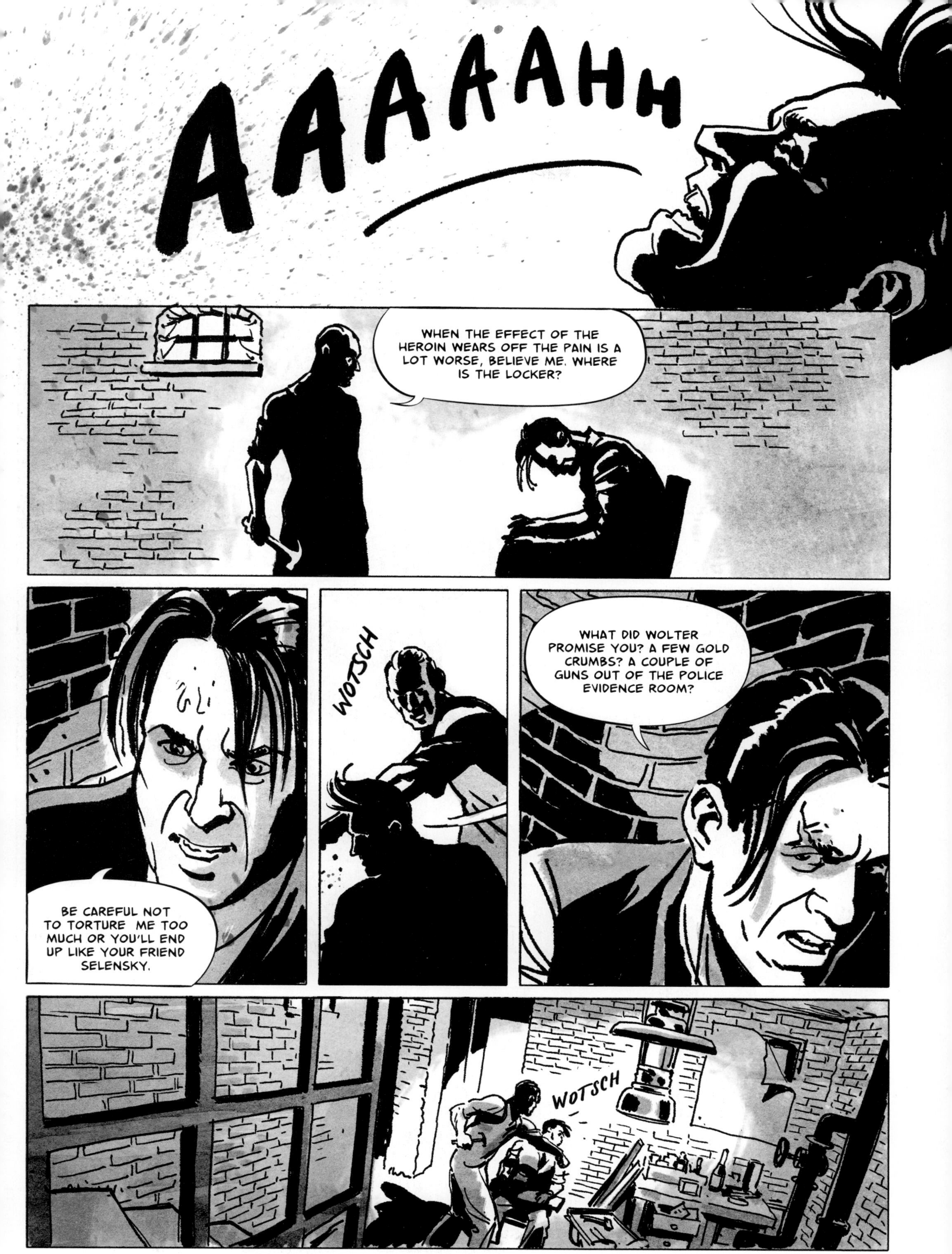
AAAAAHH
WHEN THE EFFECT OF THE HEROIN WEARS OFF THE PAIN IS A LOT WORSE, BELIEVE ME. WHERE IS THE LOCKER?
BE CAREFUL NOT TO TORTURE ME TOO MUCH OR YOU'LL END UP LIKE YOUR FRIEND SELENSKY.
WOTSCH
WHAT DID WOLTER PROMISE YOU? A FEW GOLD CRUMBS? A COUPLE OF GUNS OUT OF THE POLICE EVIDENCE ROOM?
WOTSCH

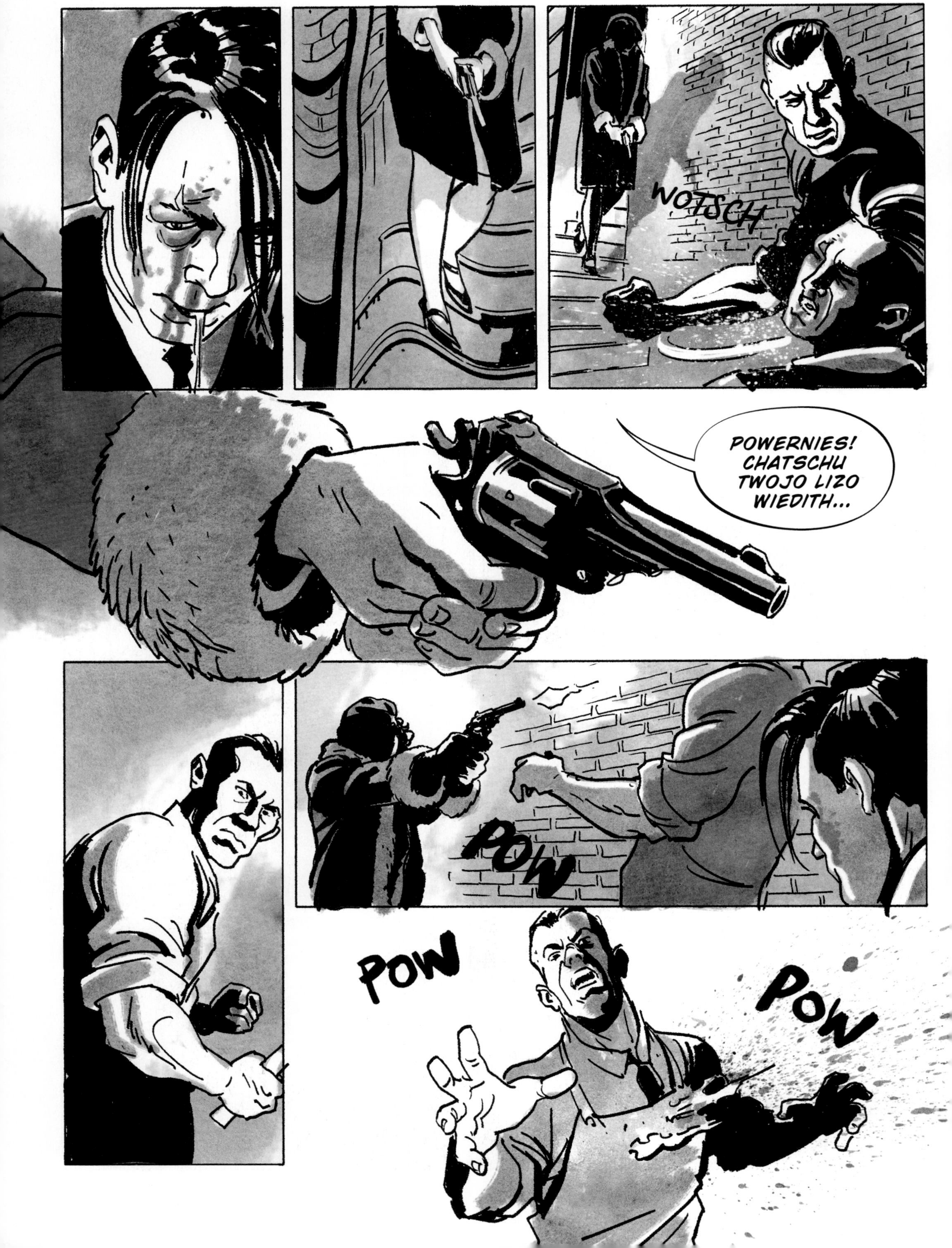
WOTSCH
POWERNIES! CHATSCHU TWOJO LIZO WIEDITH...
POW
POW
POW

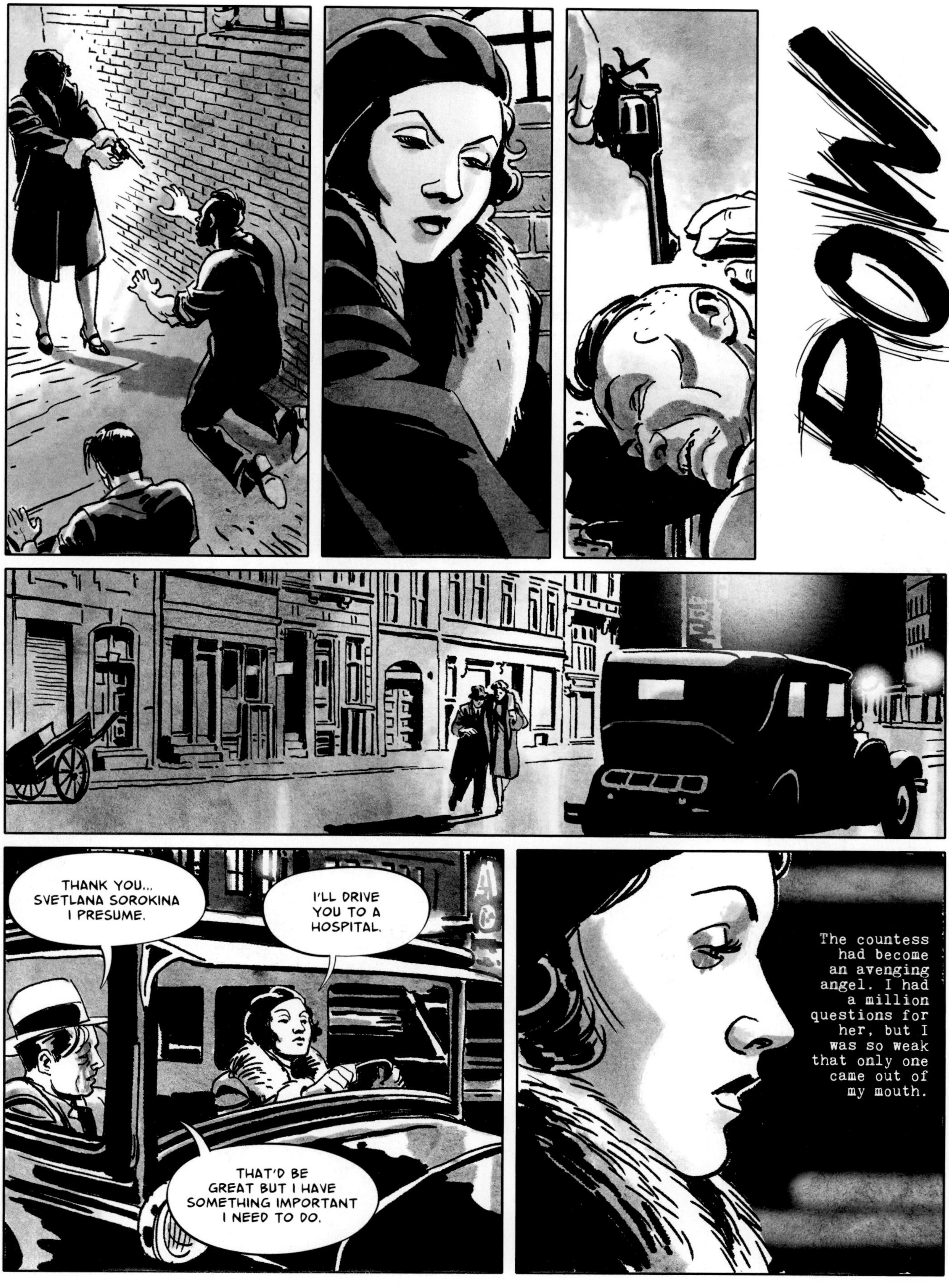
POW
THANK YOU... SVETLANA SOROKINA I PRESUME.
I'LL DRIVE YOU TO A HOSPITAL.
THAT'D BE GREAT BUT I HAVE SOMETHING IMPORTANT I NEED TO DO.
The countess had become an avenging angel. I had a million questions for her, but I was so weak that only one came out of my mouth.

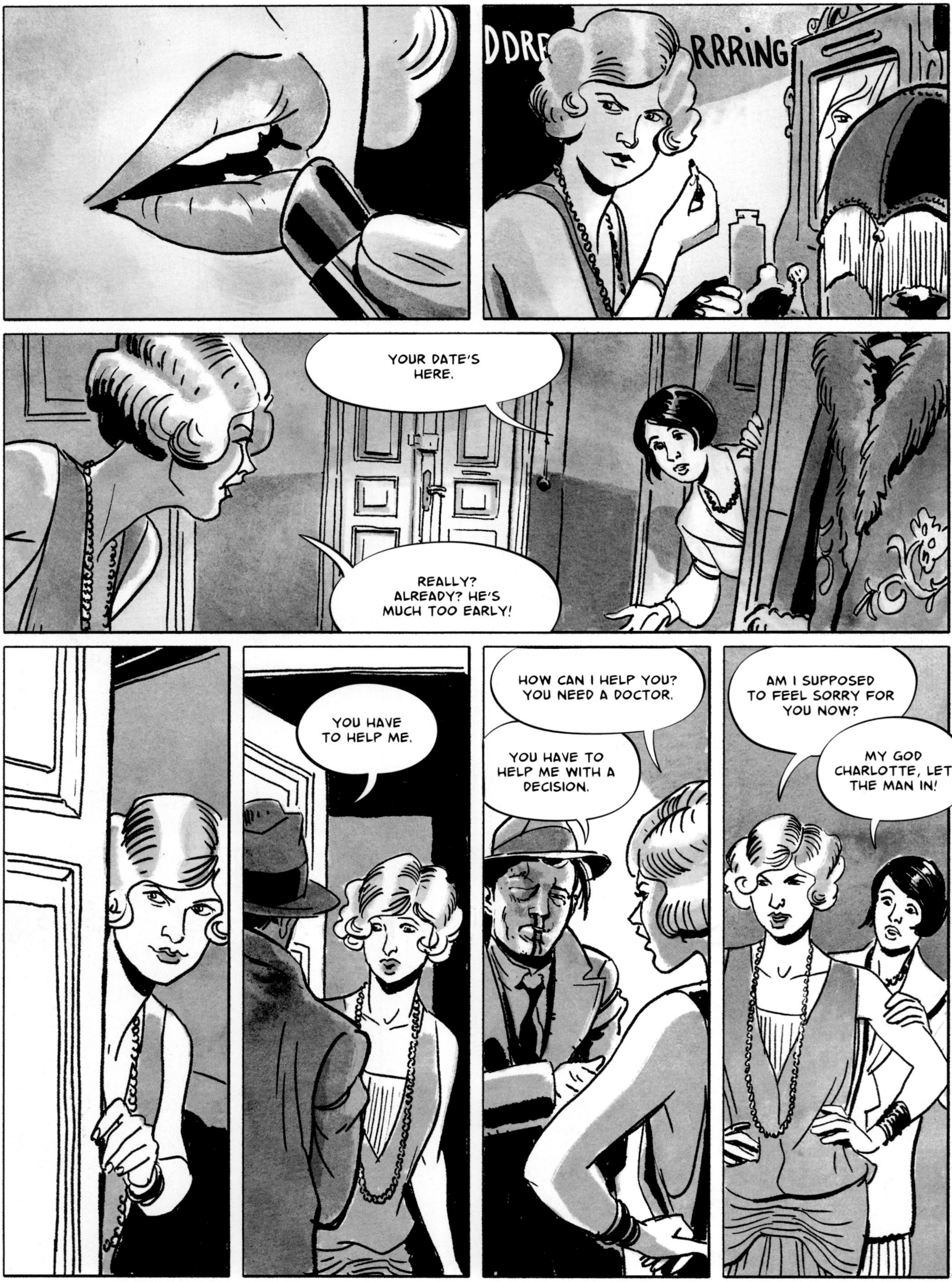
DDRE
RRRING
YOUR DATE'S HERE.
REALLY? ALREADY? HE'S MUCH TOO EARLY!
YOU HAVE TO HELP ME.
HOW CAN I HELP YOU? YOU NEED A DOCTOR.
YOU HAVE TO HELP ME WITH A DECISION.
AM I SUPPOSED TO FEEL SORRY FOR YOU NOW?
MY GOD CHARLOTTE, LET THE MAN IN!

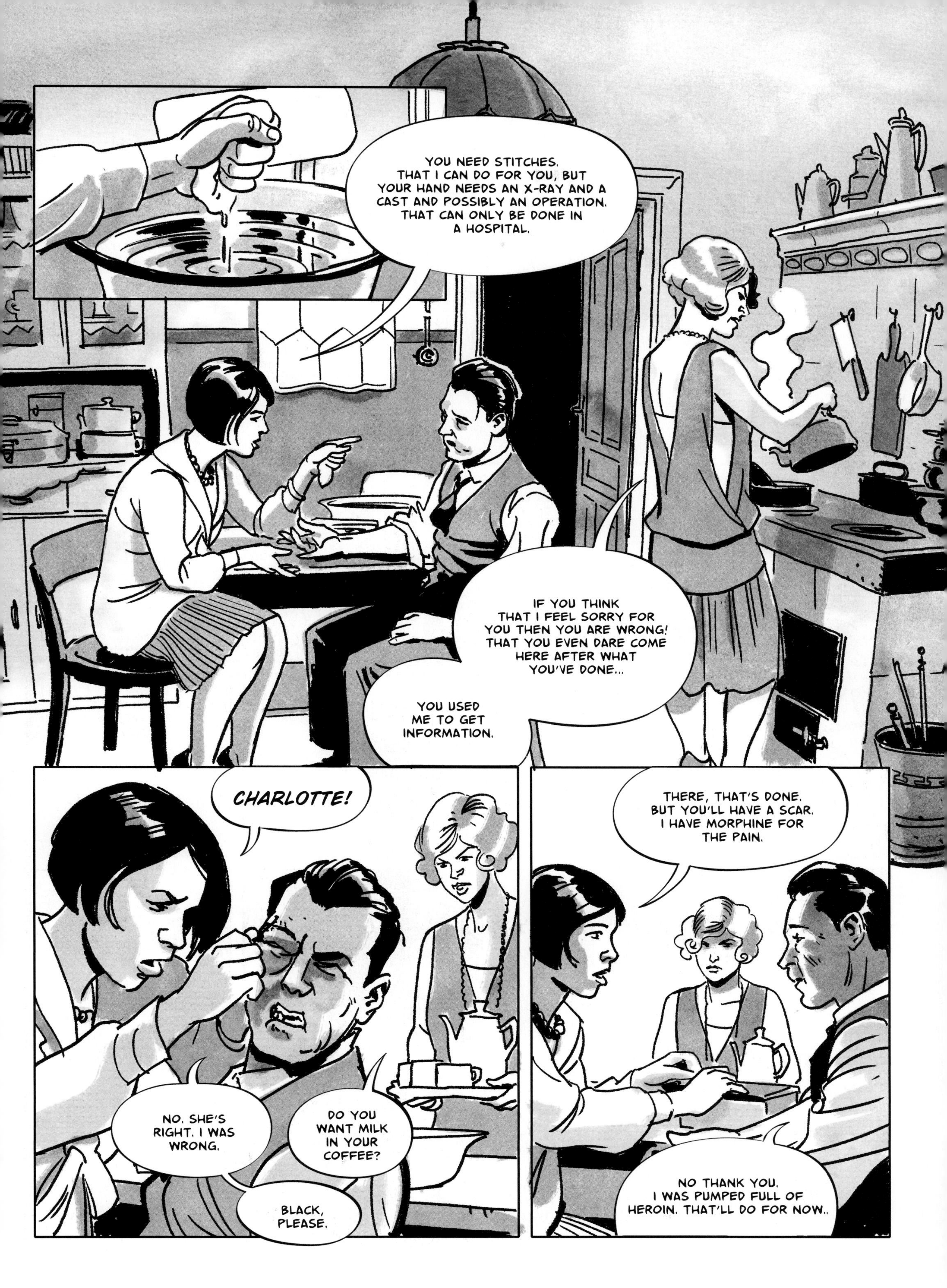
YOU NEED STITCHES. THAT I CAN DO FOR YOU, BUT YOUR HAND NEEDS AN X-RAY AND A CAST AND POSSIBLY AN OPERATION. THAT CAN ONLY BE DONE IN A HOSPITAL.
IF YOU THINK THAT I FEEL SORRY FOR YOU THEN YOU ARE WRONG! THAT YOU EVEN DARE COME HERE AFTER WHAT YOU'VE DONE...
YOU USED ME TO GET INFORMATION.
CHARLOTTE!
NO. SHE'S RIGHT. I WAS WRONG.
DO YOU WANT MILK IN YOUR COFFEE?
BLACK, PLEASE.
THERE, THAT'S DONE. BUT YOU'LL HAVE A SCAR. I HAVE MORPHINE FOR THE PAIN.
NO THANK YOU. I WAS PUMPED FULL OF HEROIN. THAT'LL DO FOR NOW..

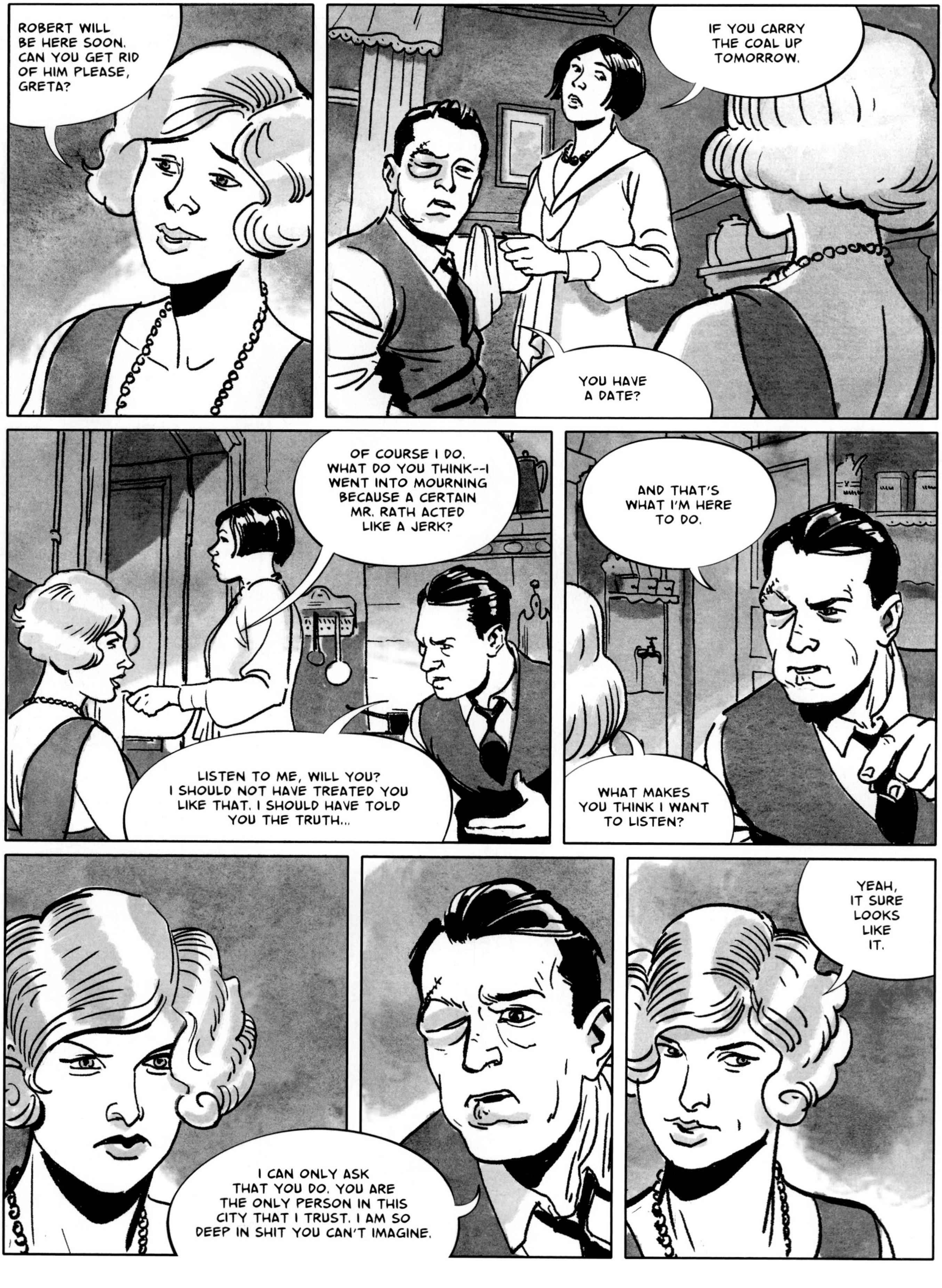

ROBERT WILL BE HERE SOON. CAN YOU GET RID OF HIM PLEASE, GRETA?
IF YOU CARRY THE COAL UP TOMORROW.
YOU HAVE A DATE?
OF COURSE I DO. WHAT DO YOU THINK--I WENT INTO MOURNING BECAUSE A CERTAIN MR. RATH ACTED LIKE A JERK?
LISTEN TO ME, WILL YOU? I SHOULD NOT HAVE TREATED YOU LIKE THAT. I SHOULD HAVE TOLD YOU THE TRUTH...
AND THAT'S WHAT I'M HERE TO DO.
WHAT MAKES YOU THINK I WANT TO LISTEN?
I CAN ONLY ASK THAT YOU DO. YOU ARE THE ONLY PERSON IN THIS CITY THAT I TRUST. I AM SO DEEP IN SHIT YOU CAN'T IMAGINE.
YEAH, IT SURE LOOKS LIKE IT.

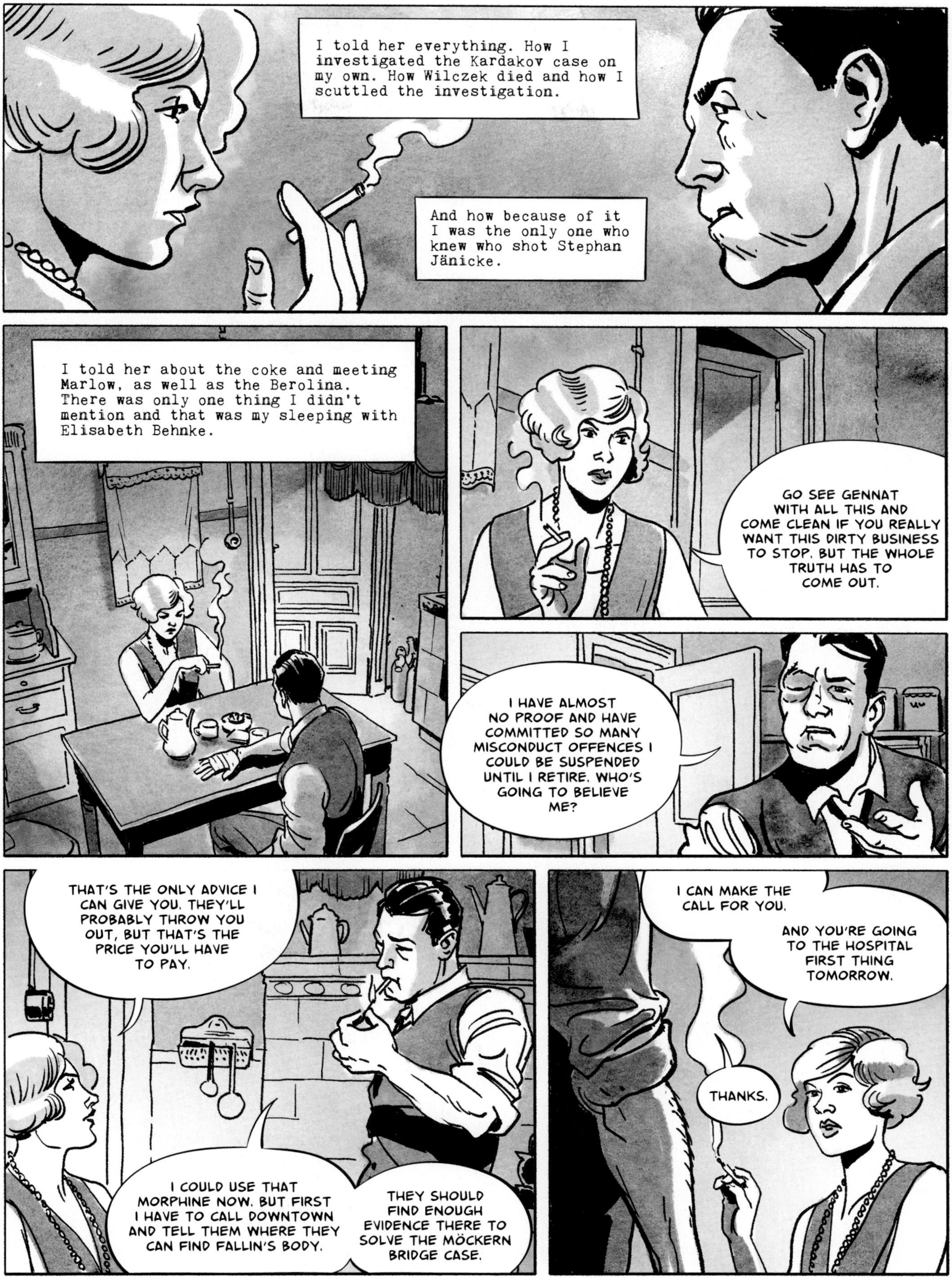
I told her everything. How I investigated the Kardakov case on my own. How Wilczek died and how I scuttled the investigation.
And how because of it I was the only one who knew who shot Stephan Jänicke.
I told her about the coke and meeting Marlow, as well as the Berolina. There was only one thing I didn't mention and that was my sleeping with Elisabeth Behnke.
GO SEE GENNAT WITH ALL THIS AND COME CLEAN IF YOU REALLY WANT THIS DIRTY BUSINESS TO STOP. BUT THE WHOLE TRUTH HAS TO COME OUT.
I HAVE ALMOST NO PROOF AND HAVE COMMITTED SO MANY MISCONDUCT OFFENCES I COULD BE SUSPENDED UNTIL I RETIRE. WHO'S GOING TO BELIEVE ME?
THAT'S THE ONLY ADVICE I CAN GIVE YOU. THEY'LL PROBABLY THROW YOU OUT, BUT THAT'S THE PRICE YOU'LL HAVE TO PAY.
I COULD USE THAT MORPHINE NOW. BUT FIRST I HAVE TO CALL DOWNTOWN AND TELL THEM WHERE THEY CAN FIND FALLIN'S BODY.
THEY SHOULD FIND ENOUGH EVIDENCE THERE TO SOLVE THE MÖCKERN BRIDGE CASE.
I CAN MAKE THE CALL FOR YOU.
AND YOU'RE GOING TO THE HOSPITAL FIRST THING TOMORROW.
THANKS.

PART IV
The Plan

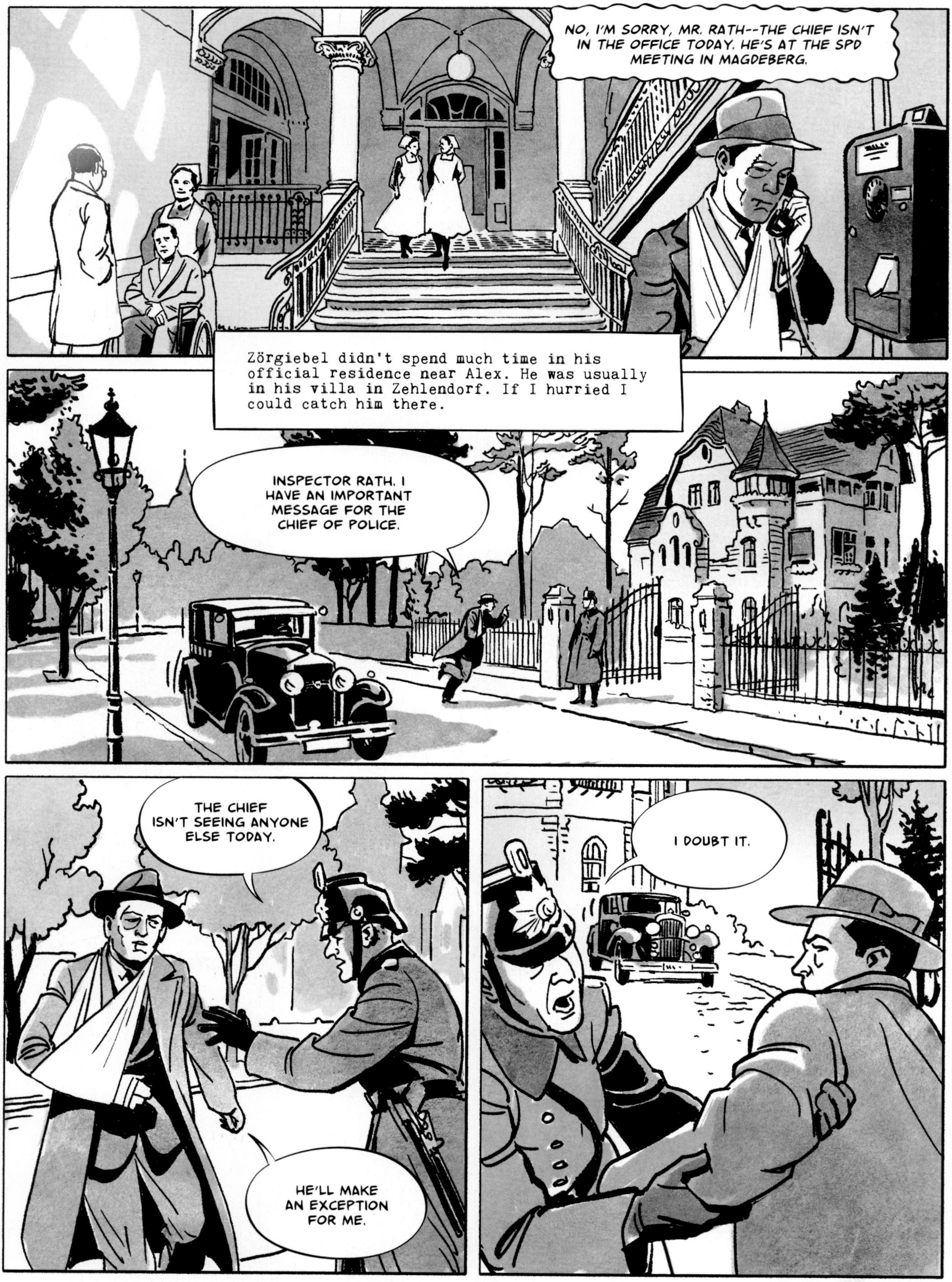
NO, I'M SORRY, MR. RATH--THE CHIEF ISN'T IN THE OFFICE TODAY. HE'S AT THE SPD MEETING IN MAGDEBERG.
Zörgiebel didn't spend much time in his official residence near Alex. He was usually in his villa in Zehlendorf. If I hurried I could catch him there.
INSPECTOR RATH. I HAVE AN IMPORTANT MESSAGE FOR THE CHIEF OF POLICE.
THE CHIEF ISN'T SEEING ANYONE ELSE TODAY.
HE'LL MAKE AN EXCEPTION FOR ME.
I DOUBT IT.

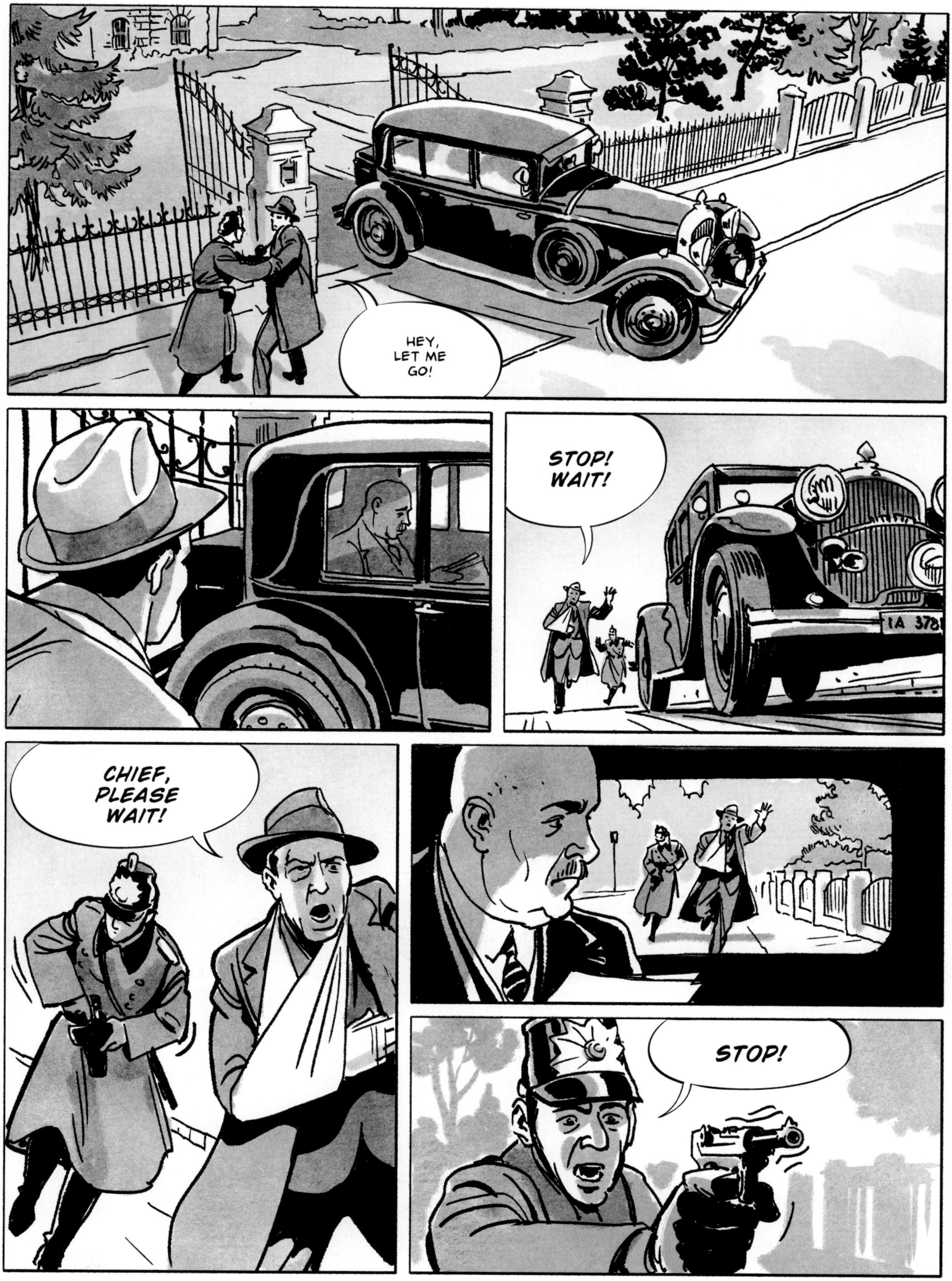
HEY, LET ME GO!
STOP! WAIT!
CHIEF, PLEASE WAIT!
STOP!

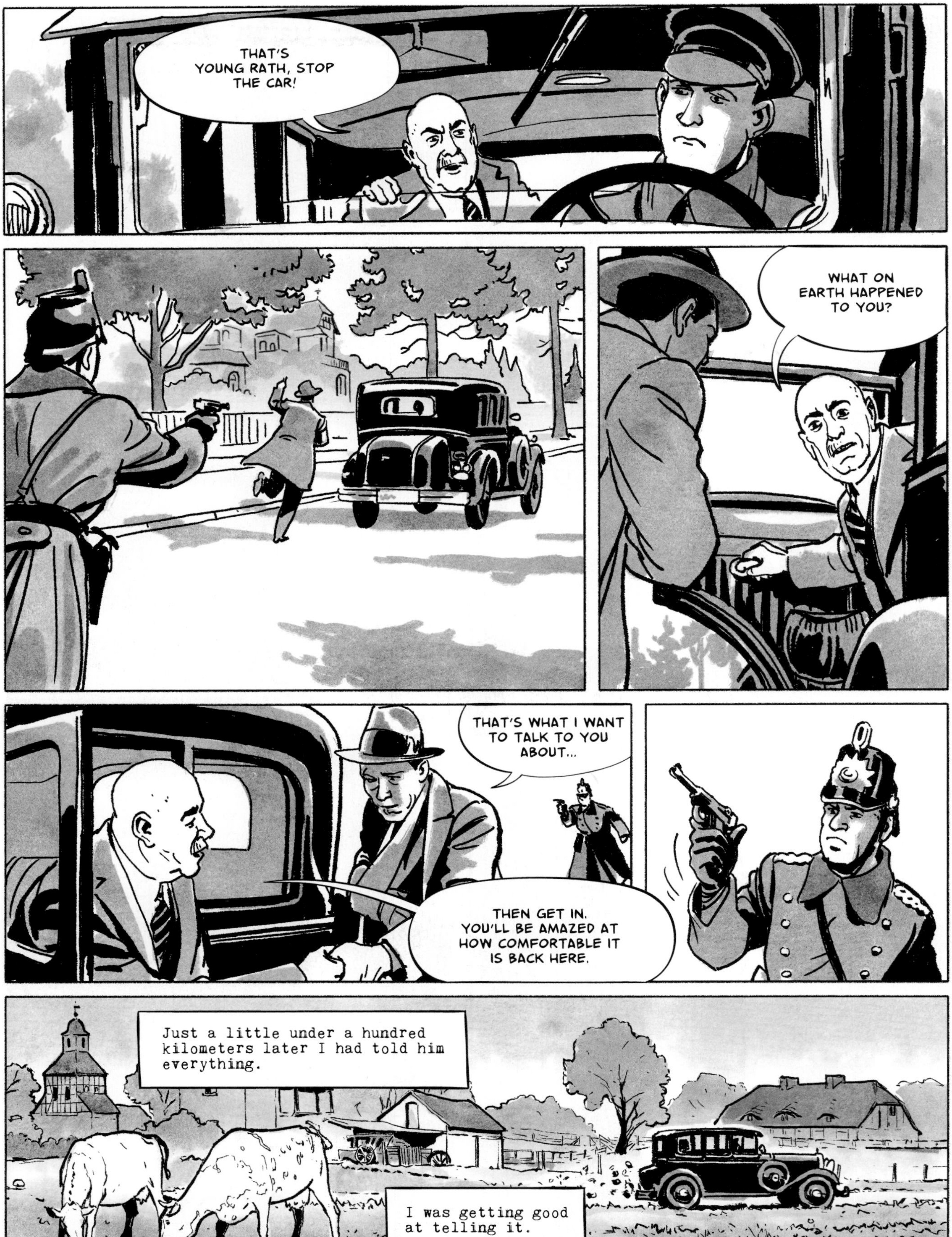
THAT'S YOUNG RATH, STOP THE CAR!
WHAT ON EARTH HAPPENED TO YOU?
THAT'S WHAT I WANT TO TALK TO YOU ABOUT...
THEN GET IN. YOU'LL BE AMAZED AT HOW COMFORTABLE IT IS BACK HERE.
Just a little under a hundred kilometers later I had told him everything.
I was getting good at telling it.

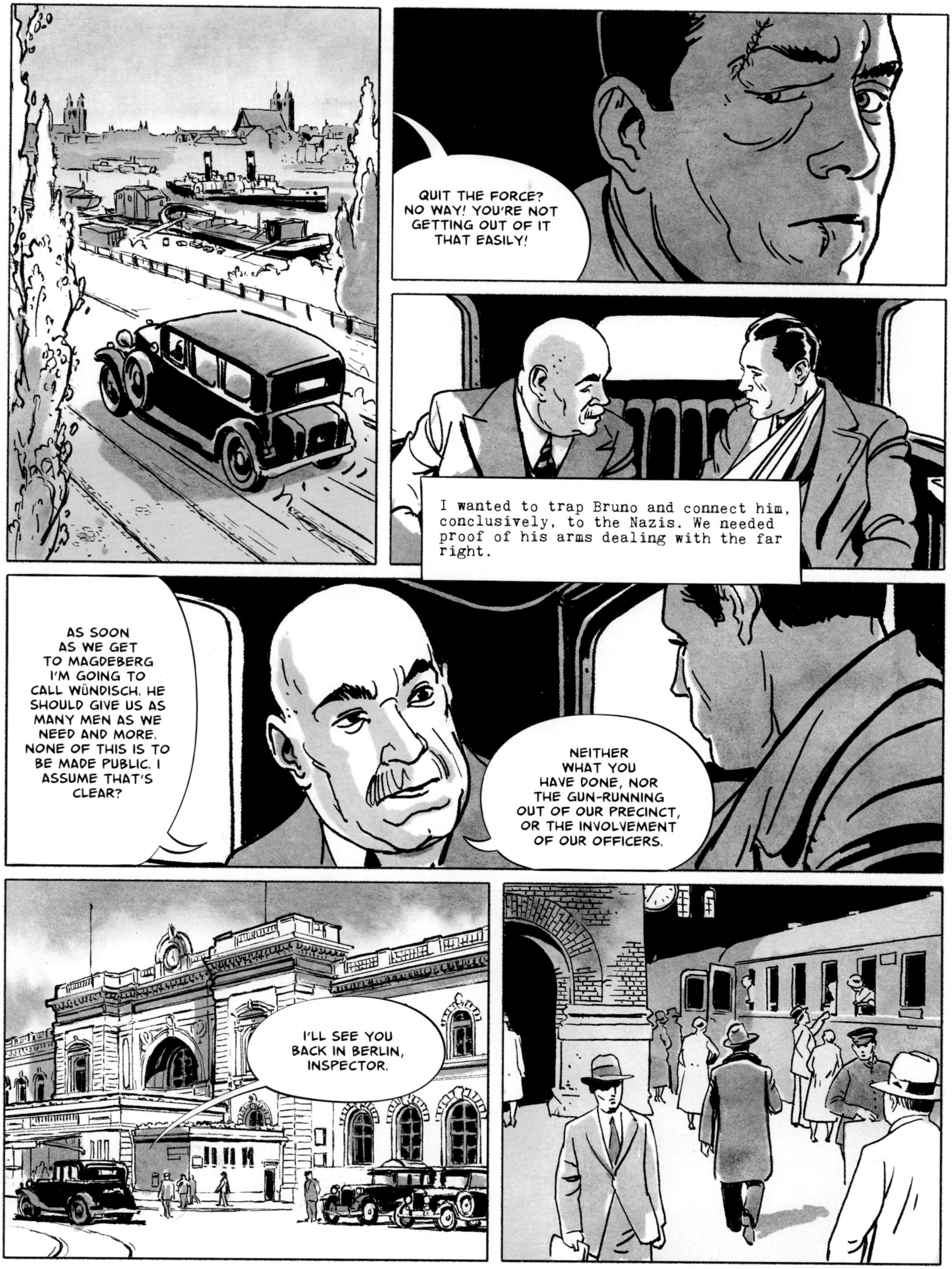
QUIT THE FORCE? NO WAY! YOU'RE NOT GETTING OUT OF IT THAT EASILY!
I wanted to trap Bruno and connect him, conclusively, to the Nazis. We needed proof of his arms dealing with the far right.
AS SOON AS WE GET TO MAGDEBERG I'M GOING TO CALL WÜNDISCH. HE SHOULD GIVE US AS MANY MEN AS WE NEED AND MORE. NONE OF THIS IS TO BE MADE PUBLIC. I ASSUME THAT'S CLEAR?
NEITHER WHAT YOU HAVE DONE, NOR THE GUN-RUNNING OUT OF OUR PRECINCT, OR THE INVOLVEMENT OF OUR OFFICERS.
I'LL SEE YOU BACK IN BERLIN, INSPECTOR.

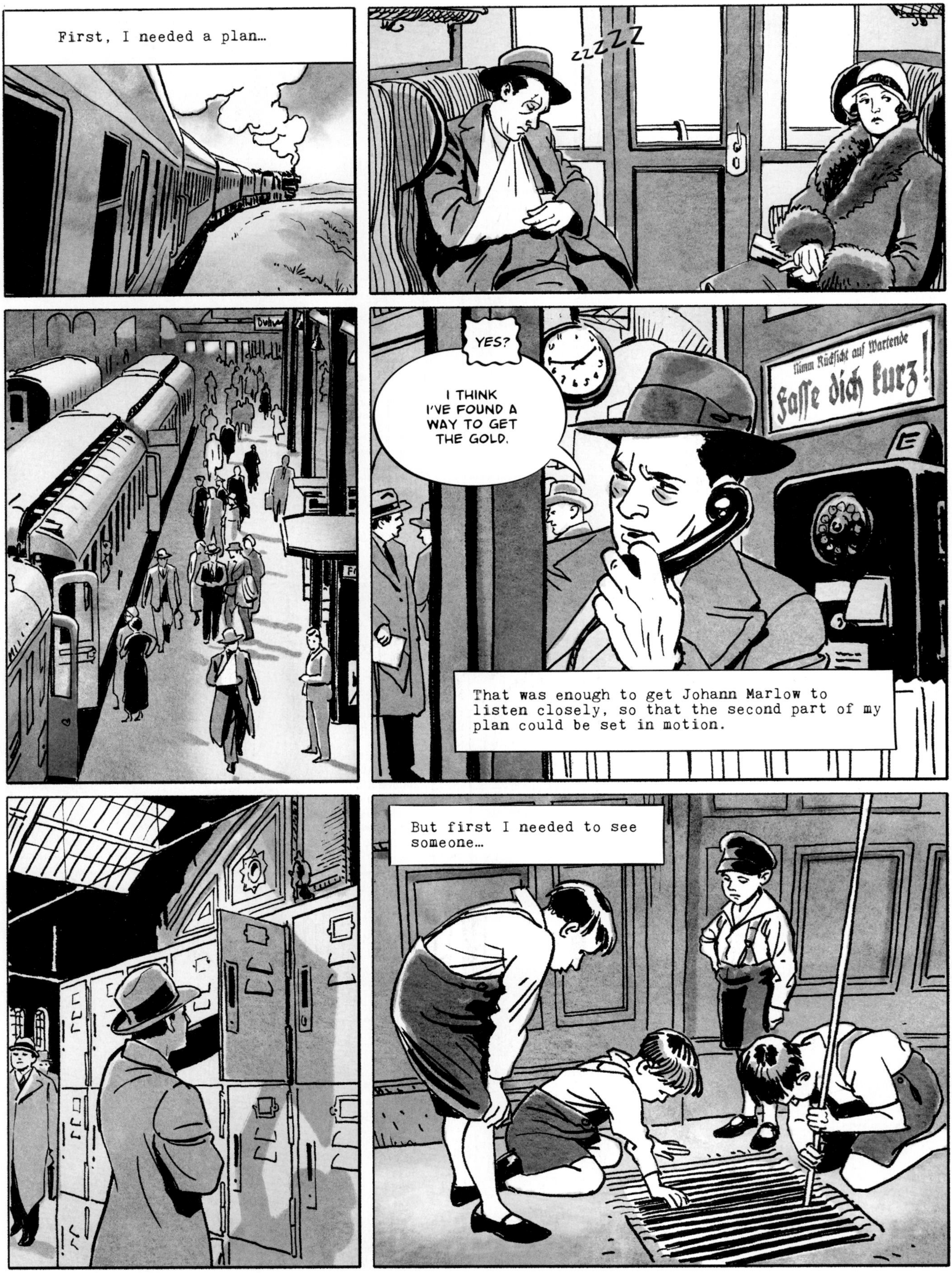
First, I needed a plan...
zzZZZ
YES?
I THINK I'VE FOUND A WAY TO GET THE GOLD.
Nimm Rücksicht auf Wartende
Fasse dich kurz!
That was enough to get Johann Marlow to listen closely, so that the second part of my plan could be set in motion.
But first I needed to see someone...

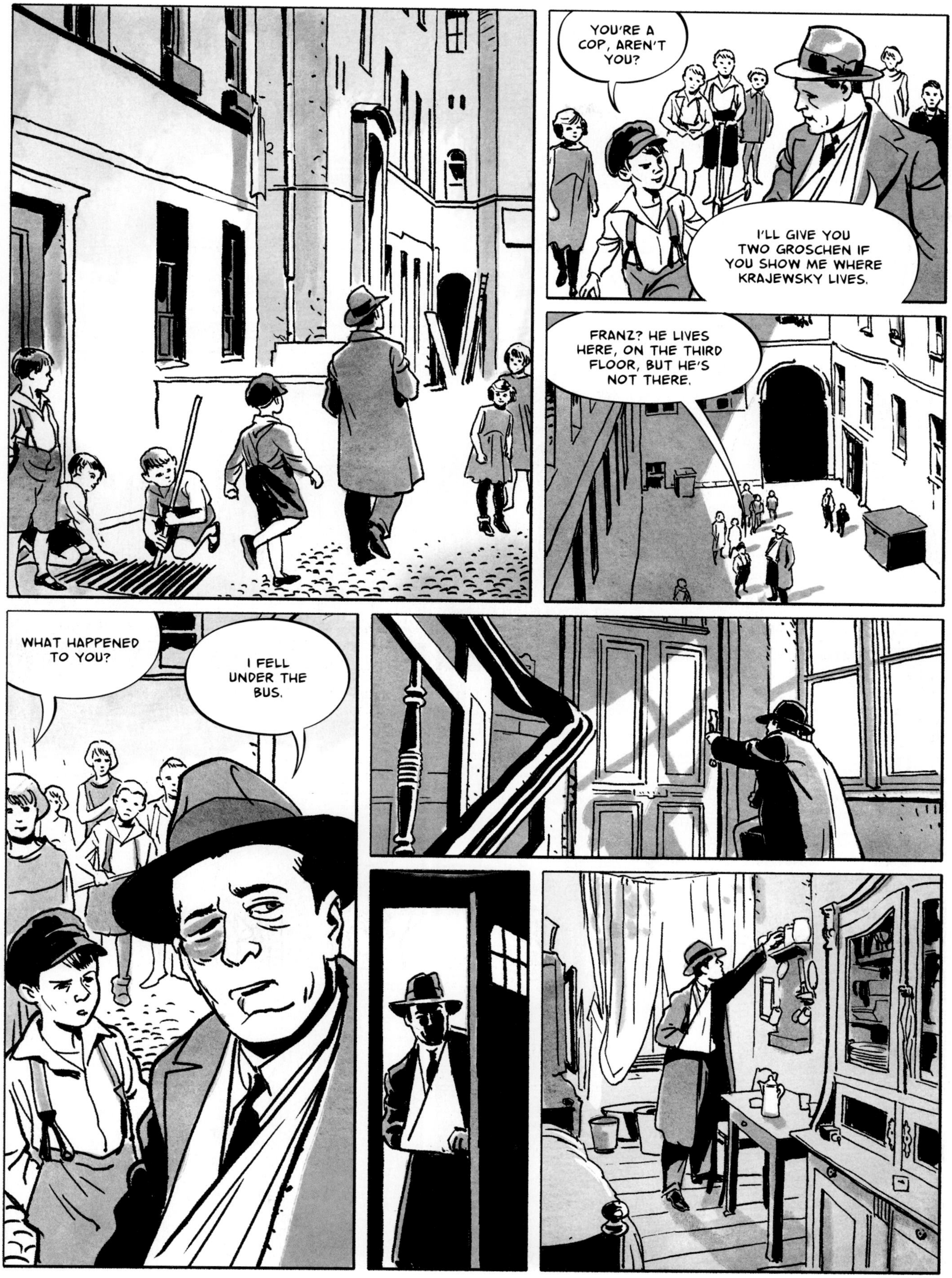
YOU'RE A COP, AREN'T YOU?
I'LL GIVE YOU TWO GROSCHEN IF YOU SHOW ME WHERE KRAJEWSKY LIVES.
FRANZ? HE LIVES HERE, ON THE THIRD FLOOR, BUT HE'S NOT THERE.
WHAT HAPPENED TO YOU?
I FELL UNDER THE BUS.

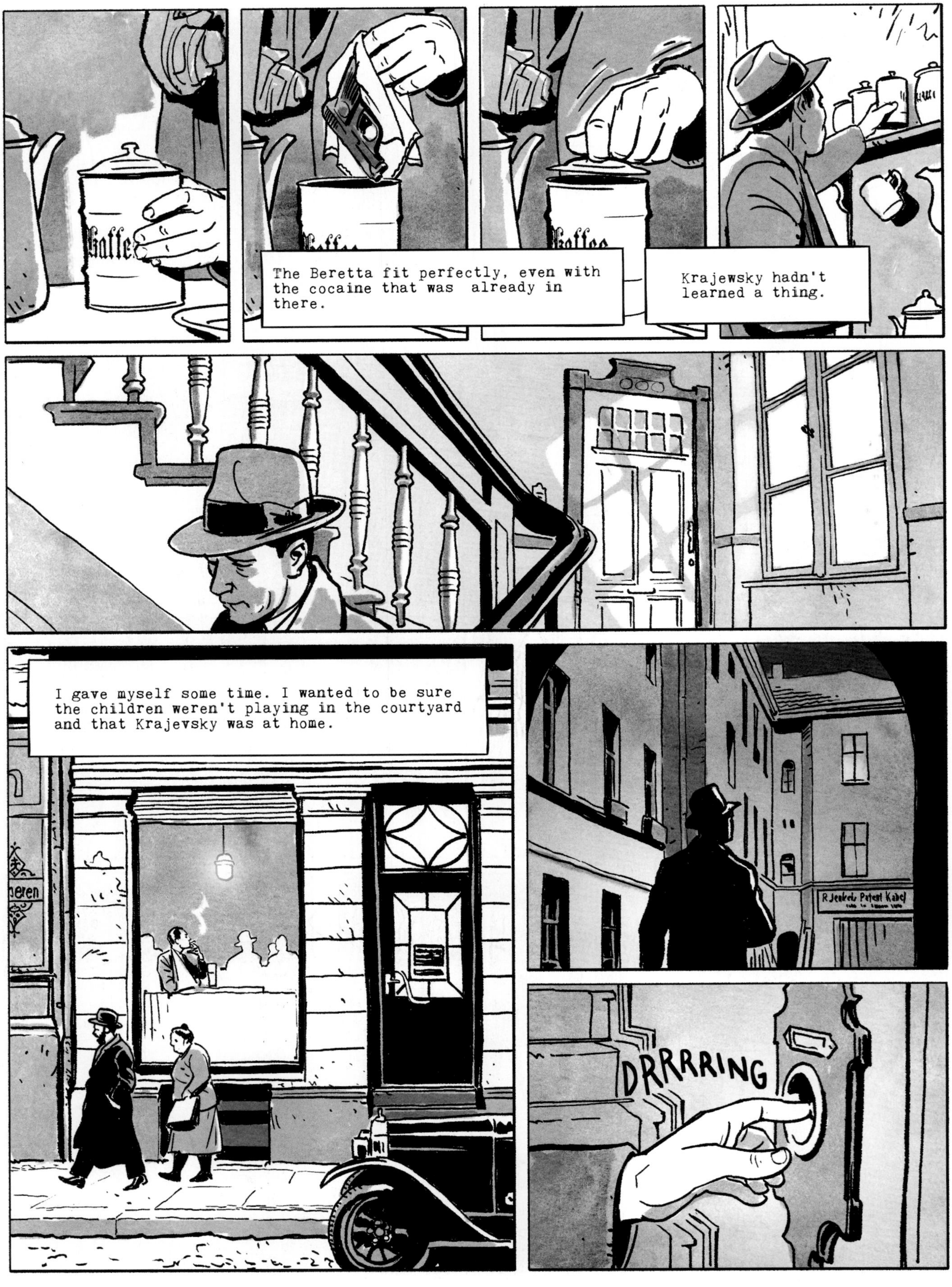
The Beretta fit perfectly, even with the cocaine that was already in there.
Krajewsky hadn't learned a thing.
I gave myself some time. I wanted to be sure the children weren't playing in the courtyard and that Krajevsky was at home.
DRRRRING

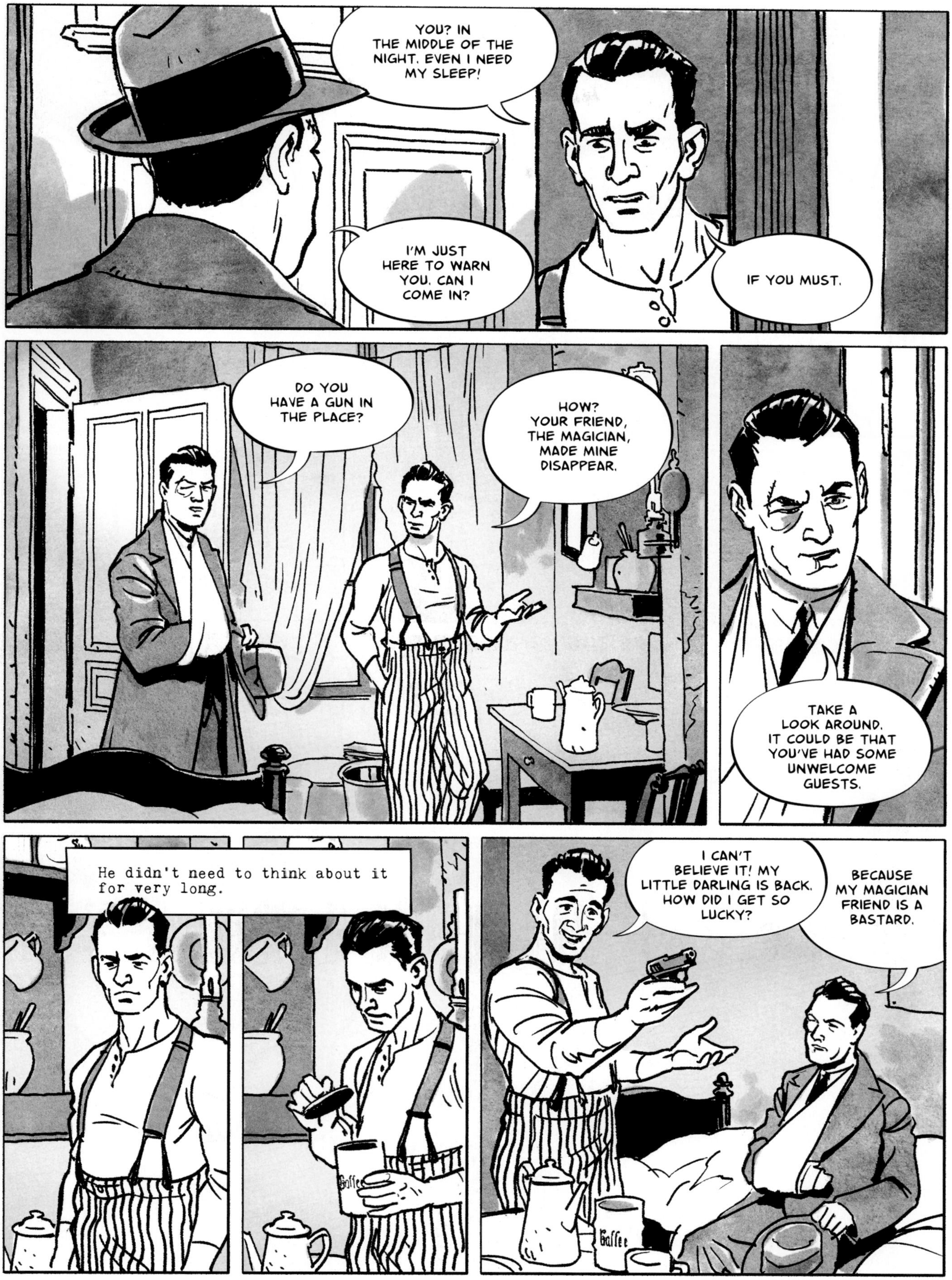
YOU? IN THE MIDDLE OF THE NIGHT. EVEN I NEED MY SLEEP!
I'M JUST HERE TO WARN YOU. CAN I COME IN?
IF YOU MUST.
DO YOU HAVE A GUN IN THE PLACE?
HOW? YOUR FRIEND, THE MAGICIAN, MADE MINE DISAPPEAR.
TAKE A LOOK AROUND. IT COULD BE THAT YOU'VE HAD SOME UNWELCOME GUESTS.
He didn't need to think about it for very long.
I CAN'T BELIEVE IT! MY LITTLE DARLING IS BACK. HOW DID I GET SO LUCKY?
BECAUSE MY MAGICIAN FRIEND IS A BASTARD.

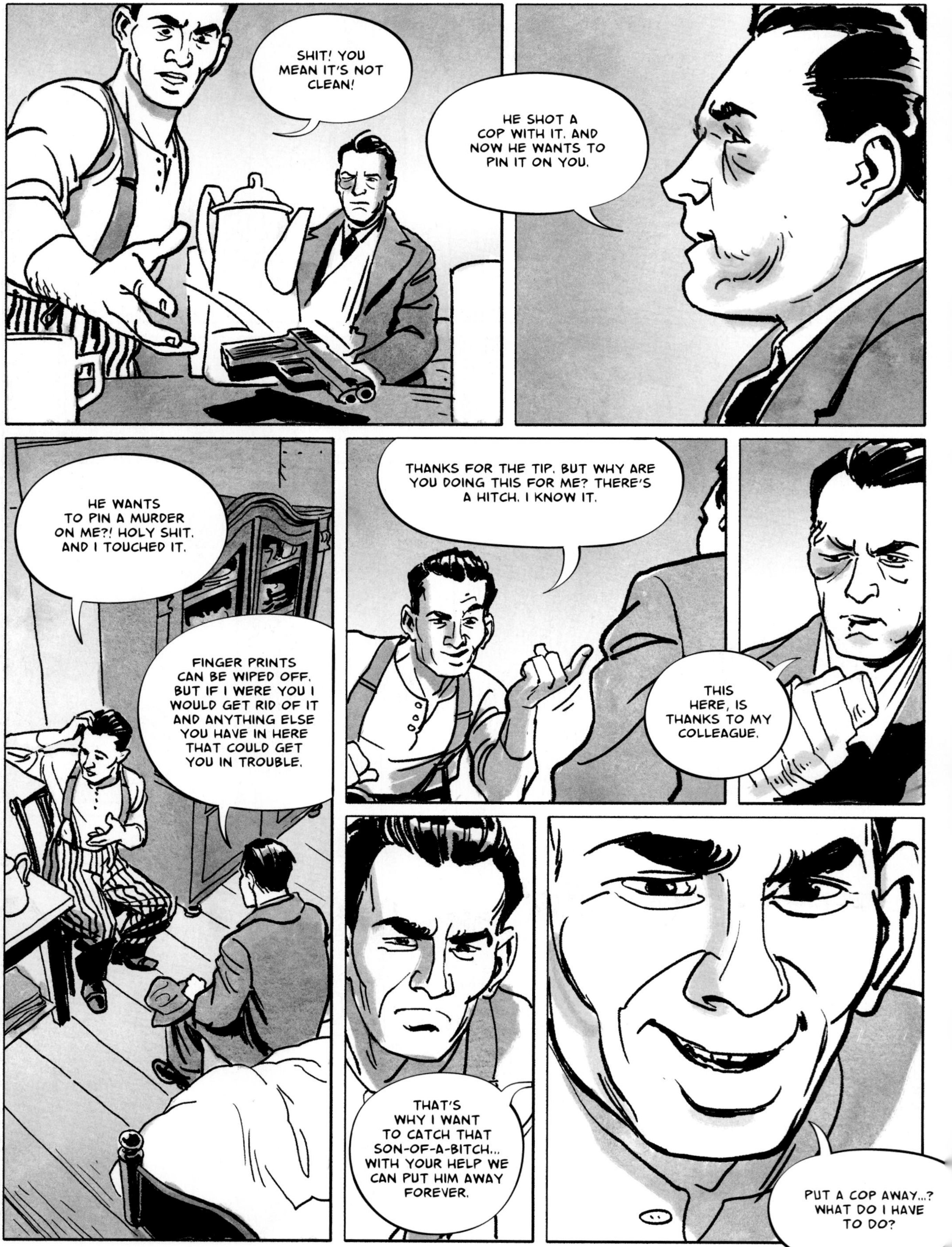
SHIT! YOU MEAN IT'S NOT CLEAN!
HE SHOT A COP WITH IT. AND NOW HE WANTS TO PIN IT ON YOU.
HE WANTS TO PIN A MURDER ON ME?! HOLY SHIT. AND I TOUCHED IT.
FINGER PRINTS CAN BE WIPED OFF. BUT IF I WERE YOU I WOULD GET RID OF IT AND ANYTHING ELSE YOU HAVE IN HERE THAT COULD GET YOU IN TROUBLE.
THANKS FOR THE TIP. BUT WHY ARE YOU DOING THIS FOR ME? THERE'S A HITCH. I KNOW IT.
THIS HERE, IS THANKS TO MY COLLEAGUE.
THAT'S WHY I WANT TO CATCH THAT SON-OF-A-BITCH... WITH YOUR HELP WE CAN PUT HIM AWAY FOREVER.
PUT A COP AWAY...? WHAT DO I HAVE TO DO?

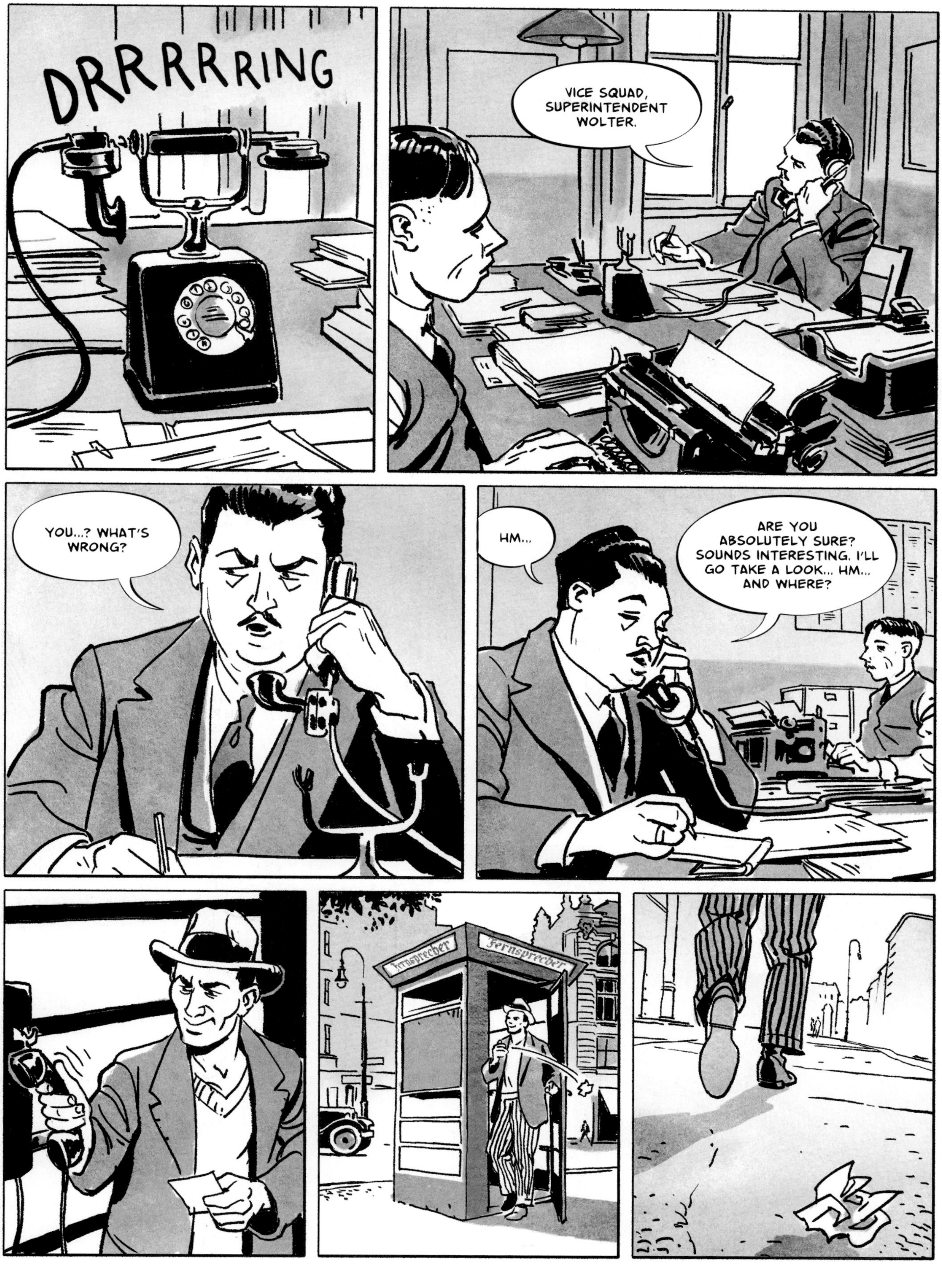
DRRRRRING
VICE SQUAD, SUPERINTENDENT WOLTER.
YOU...? WHAT'S WRONG?
HM...
ARE YOU ABSOLUTELY SURE? SOUNDS INTERESTING. I'LL GO TAKE A LOOK... HM... AND WHERE?
Fernsprecher
Fernsprecher

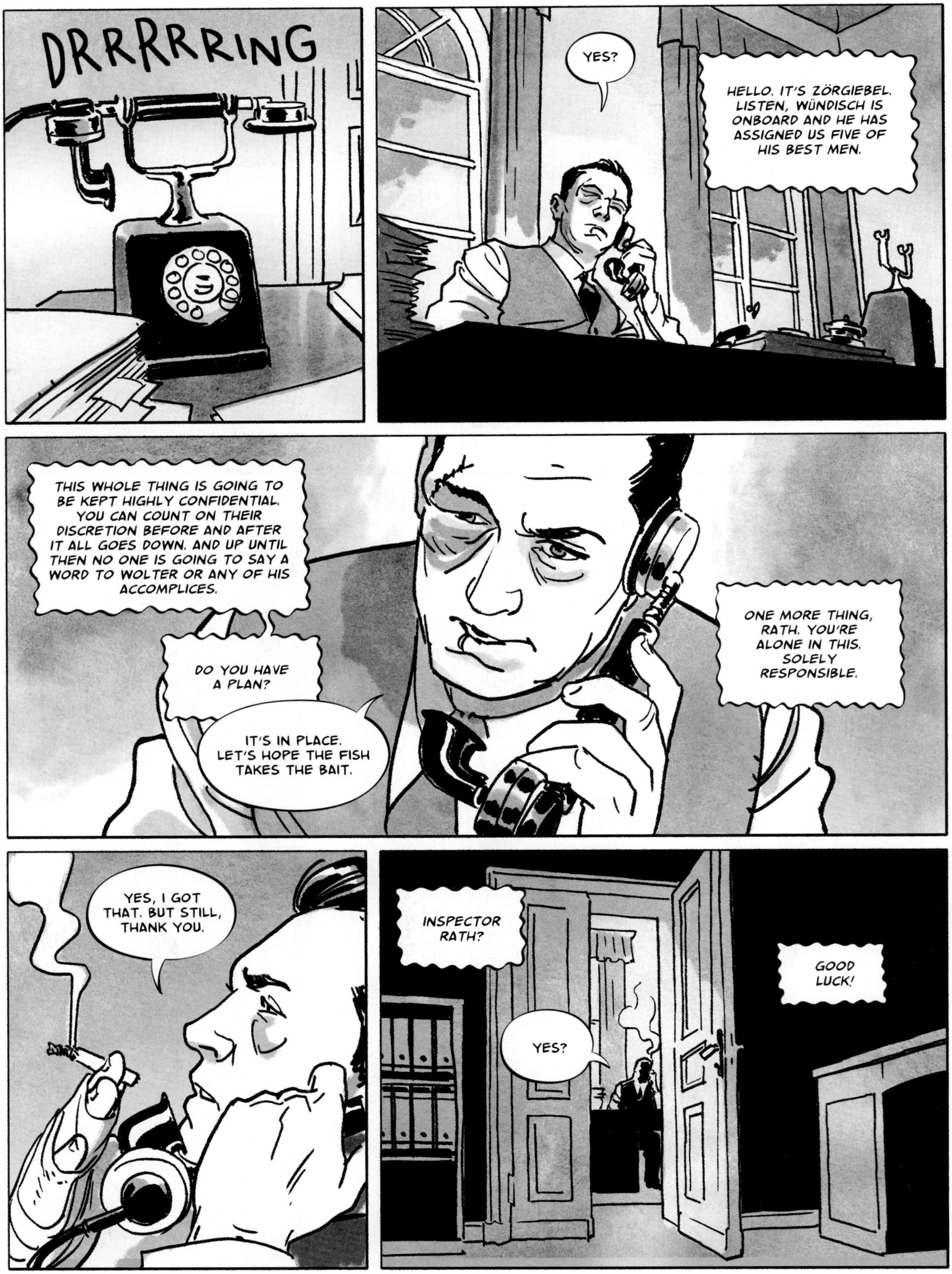

DRRRRRING
YES?
HELLO. IT'S ZÖRGIEBEL. LISTEN, WÜNDISCH IS ONBOARD AND HE HAS ASSIGNED US FIVE OF HIS BEST MEN.
THIS WHOLE THING IS GOING TO BE KEPT HIGHLY CONFIDENTIAL. YOU CAN COUNT ON THEIR DISCRETION BEFORE AND AFTER IT ALL GOES DOWN. AND UP UNTIL THEN NO ONE IS GOING TO SAY A WORD TO WOLTER OR ANY OF HIS ACCOMPLICES.
DO YOU HAVE A PLAN?
IT'S IN PLACE. LET'S HOPE THE FISH TAKES THE BAIT.
ONE MORE THING, RATH. YOU'RE ALONE IN THIS. SOLELY RESPONSIBLE.
YES, I GOT THAT. BUT STILL, THANK YOU.
INSPECTOR RATH?
GOOD LUCK!
YES?

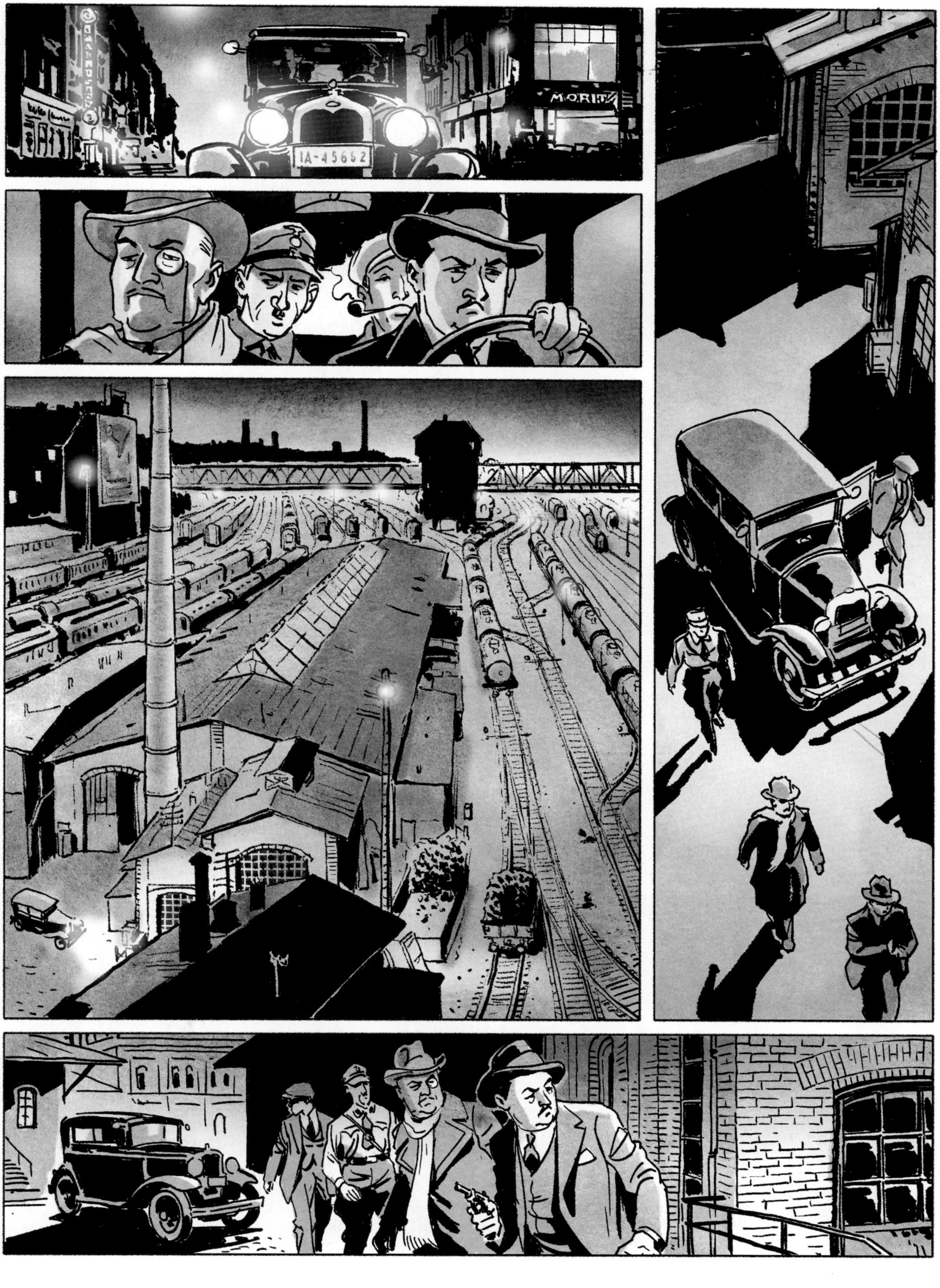
MORITZ
IA-45662

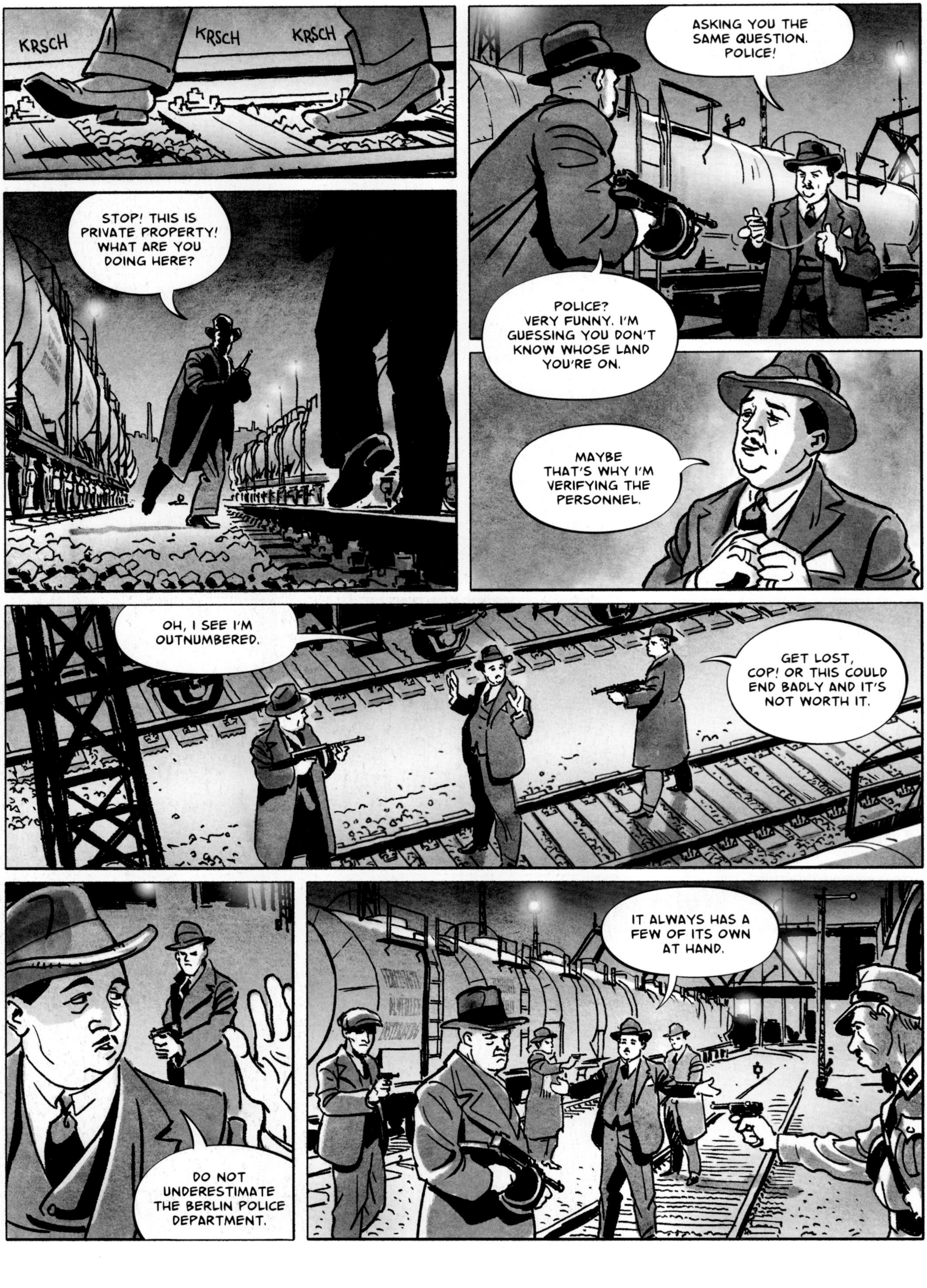
KRSCH
KRSCH
KRSCH
ASKING YOU THE SAME QUESTION. POLICE!
STOP! THIS IS PRIVATE PROPERTY! WHAT ARE YOU DOING HERE?
POLICE? VERY FUNNY. I'M GUESSING YOU DON'T KNOW WHOSE LAND YOU'RE ON.
MAYBE THAT'S WHY I'M VERIFYING THE PERSONNEL.
OH, I SEE I'M OUTNUMBERED.
GET LOST, COP! OR THIS COULD END BADLY AND IT'S NOT WORTH IT.
DO NOT UNDERESTIMATE THE BERLIN POLICE DEPARTMENT.
IT ALWAYS HAS A FEW OF ITS OWN AT HAND.

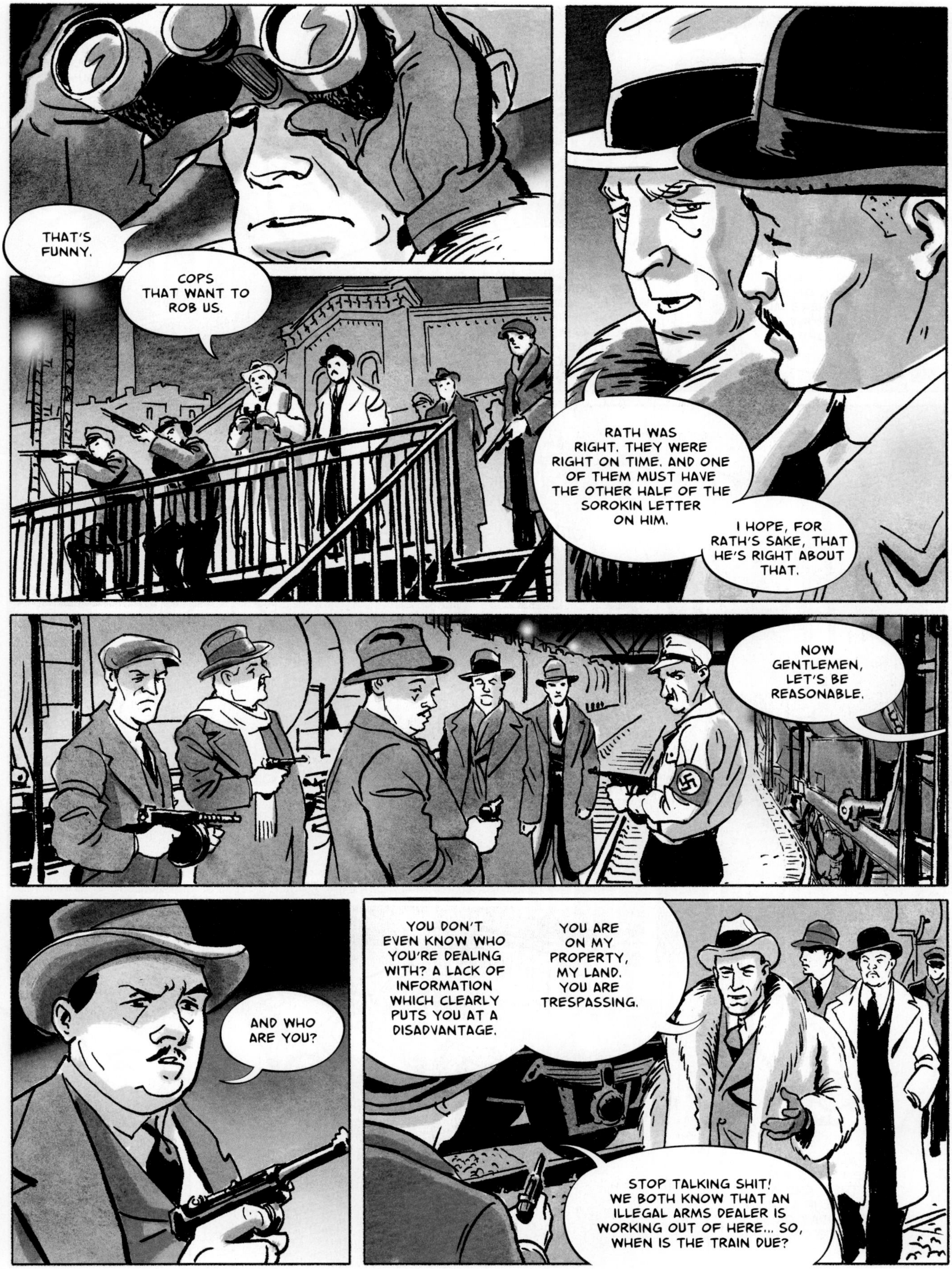
THAT'S FUNNY.
COPS THAT WANT TO ROB US.
RATH WAS RIGHT. THEY WERE RIGHT ON TIME. AND ONE OF THEM MUST HAVE THE OTHER HALF OF THE SOROKIN LETTER ON HIM.
I HOPE, FOR RATH'S SAKE, THAT HE'S RIGHT ABOUT THAT.
NOW GENTLEMEN, LET'S BE REASONABLE.
AND WHO ARE YOU?
YOU DON'T EVEN KNOW WHO YOU'RE DEALING WITH? A LACK OF INFORMATION WHICH CLEARLY PUTS YOU AT A DISADVANTAGE.
YOU ARE ON MY PROPERTY, MY LAND. YOU ARE TRESPASSING.
STOP TALKING SHIT! WE BOTH KNOW THAT AN ILLEGAL ARMS DEALER IS WORKING OUT OF HERE... SO, WHEN IS THE TRAIN DUE?

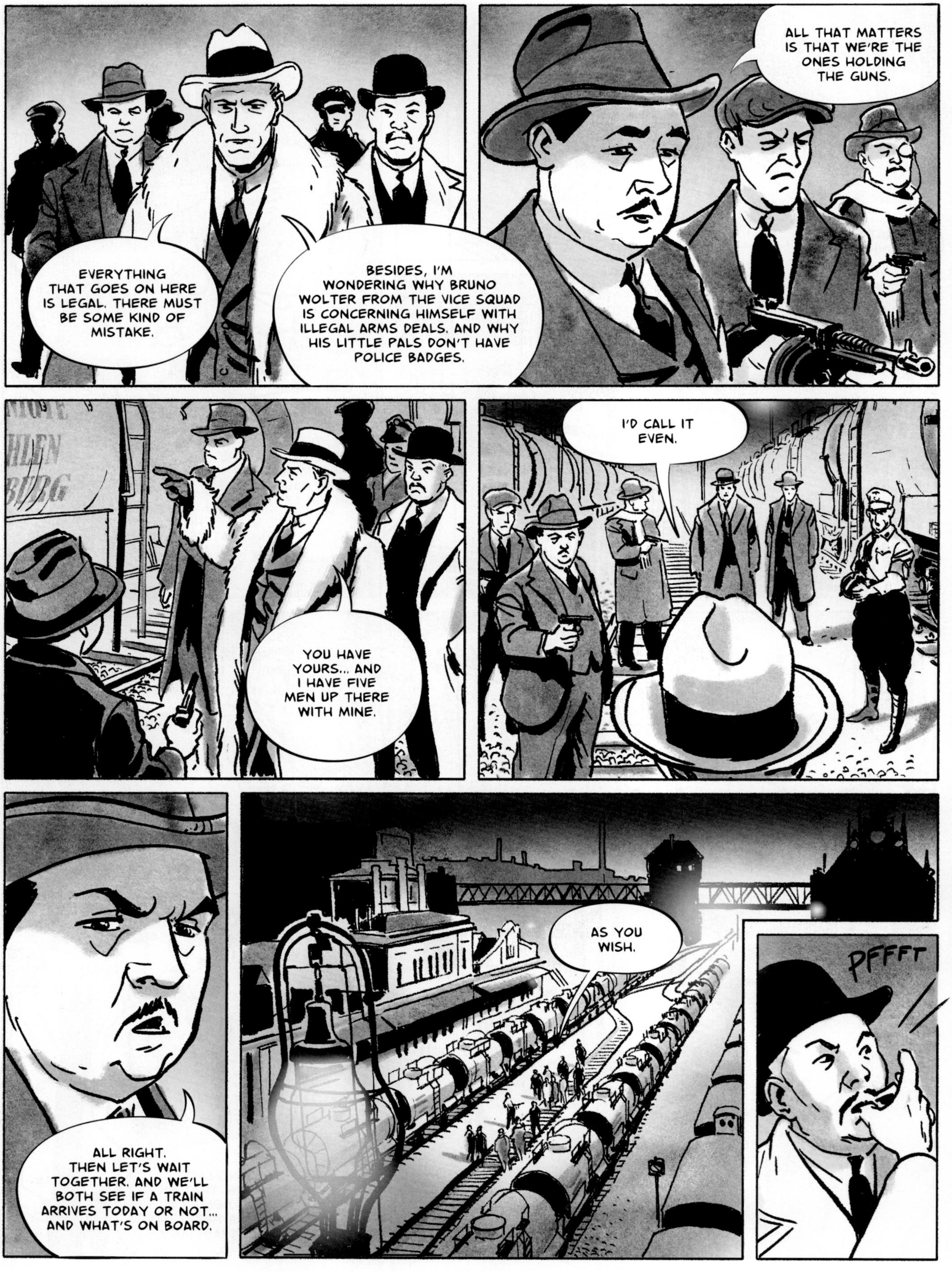
EVERYTHING THAT GOES ON HERE IS LEGAL. THERE MUST BE SOME KIND OF MISTAKE.
BESIDES, I'M WONDERING WHY BRUNO WOLTER FROM THE VICE SQUAD IS CONCERNING HIMSELF WITH ILLEGAL ARMS DEALS. AND WHY HIS LITTLE PALS DON'T HAVE POLICE BADGES.
ALL THAT MATTERS IS THAT WE'RE THE ONES HOLDING THE GUNS.
YOU HAVE YOURS... AND I HAVE FIVE MEN UP THERE WITH MINE.
I'D CALL IT EVEN.
ALL RIGHT. THEN LET'S WAIT TOGETHER. AND WE'LL BOTH SEE IF A TRAIN ARRIVES TODAY OR NOT... AND WHAT'S ON BOARD.
AS YOU WISH.
PFFFT

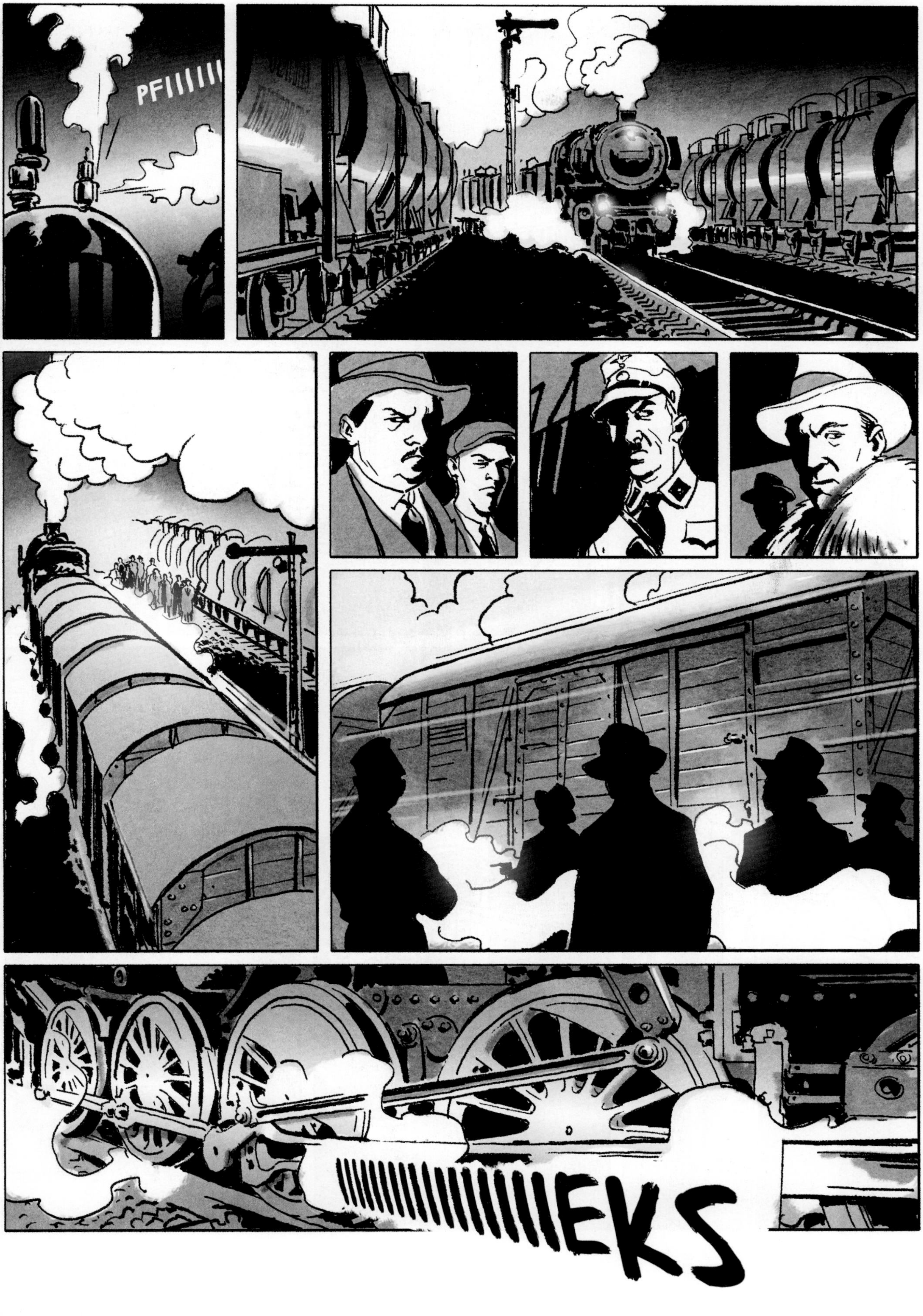
PFIIIIII
IIIIIIIIIIIIIIIIIIEKS

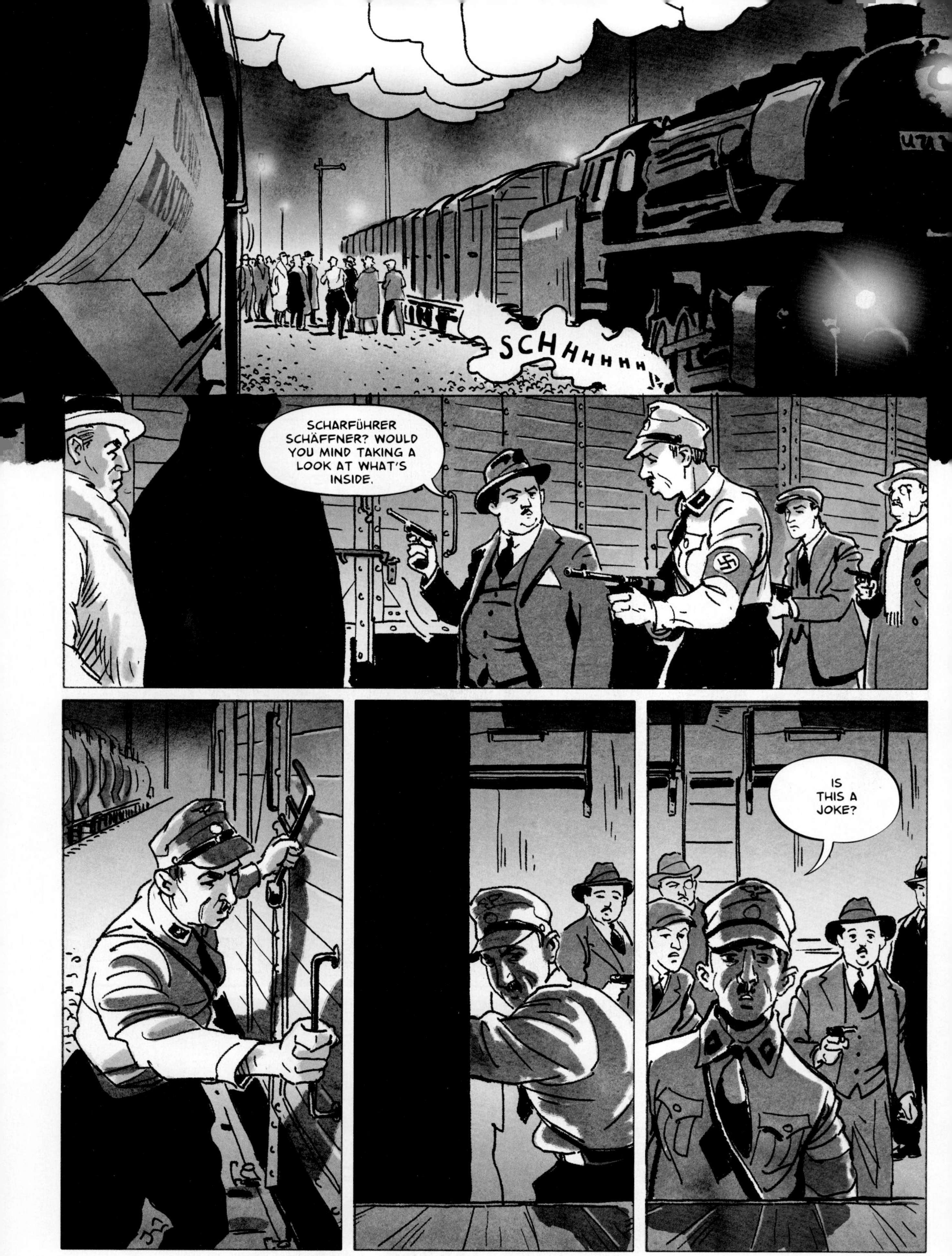
SCHHHHHH!
SCHARFÜHRER SCHÄFFNER? WOULD YOU MIND TAKING A LOOK AT WHAT'S INSIDE.
IS THIS A JOKE?

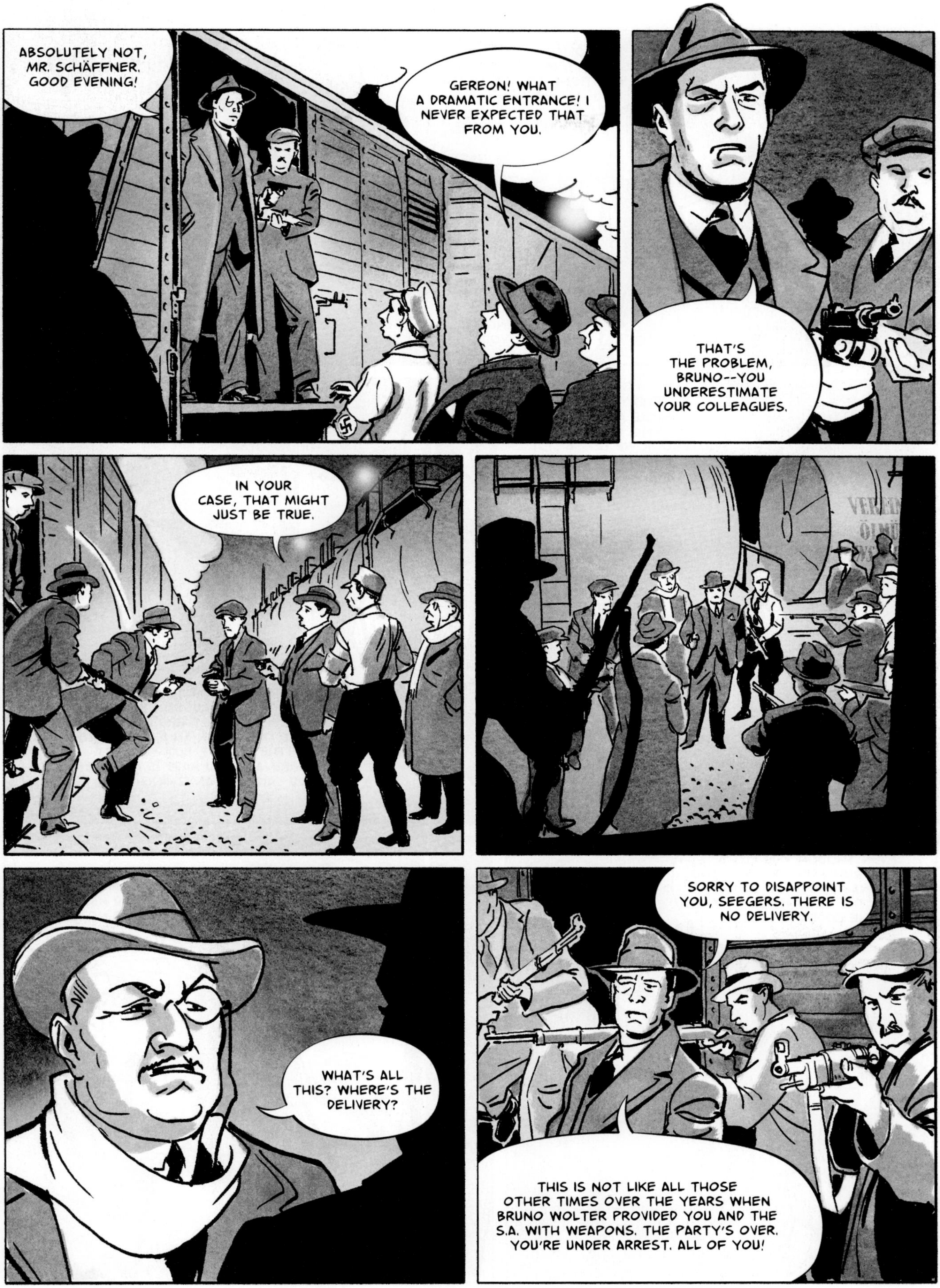
ABSOLUTELY NOT, MR. SCHÄFFNER. GOOD EVENING!
GEREON! WHAT A DRAMATIC ENTRANCE! I NEVER EXPECTED THAT FROM YOU.
THAT'S THE PROBLEM, BRUNO--YOU UNDERESTIMATE YOUR COLLEAGUES.
IN YOUR CASE, THAT MIGHT JUST BE TRUE.
WHAT'S ALL THIS? WHERE'S THE DELIVERY?
SORRY TO DISAPPOINT YOU, SEEGERS. THERE IS NO DELIVERY.
THIS IS NOT LIKE ALL THOSE OTHER TIMES OVER THE YEARS WHEN BRUNO WOLTER PROVIDED YOU AND THE S.A. WITH WEAPONS. THE PARTY'S OVER. YOU'RE UNDER ARREST. ALL OF YOU!

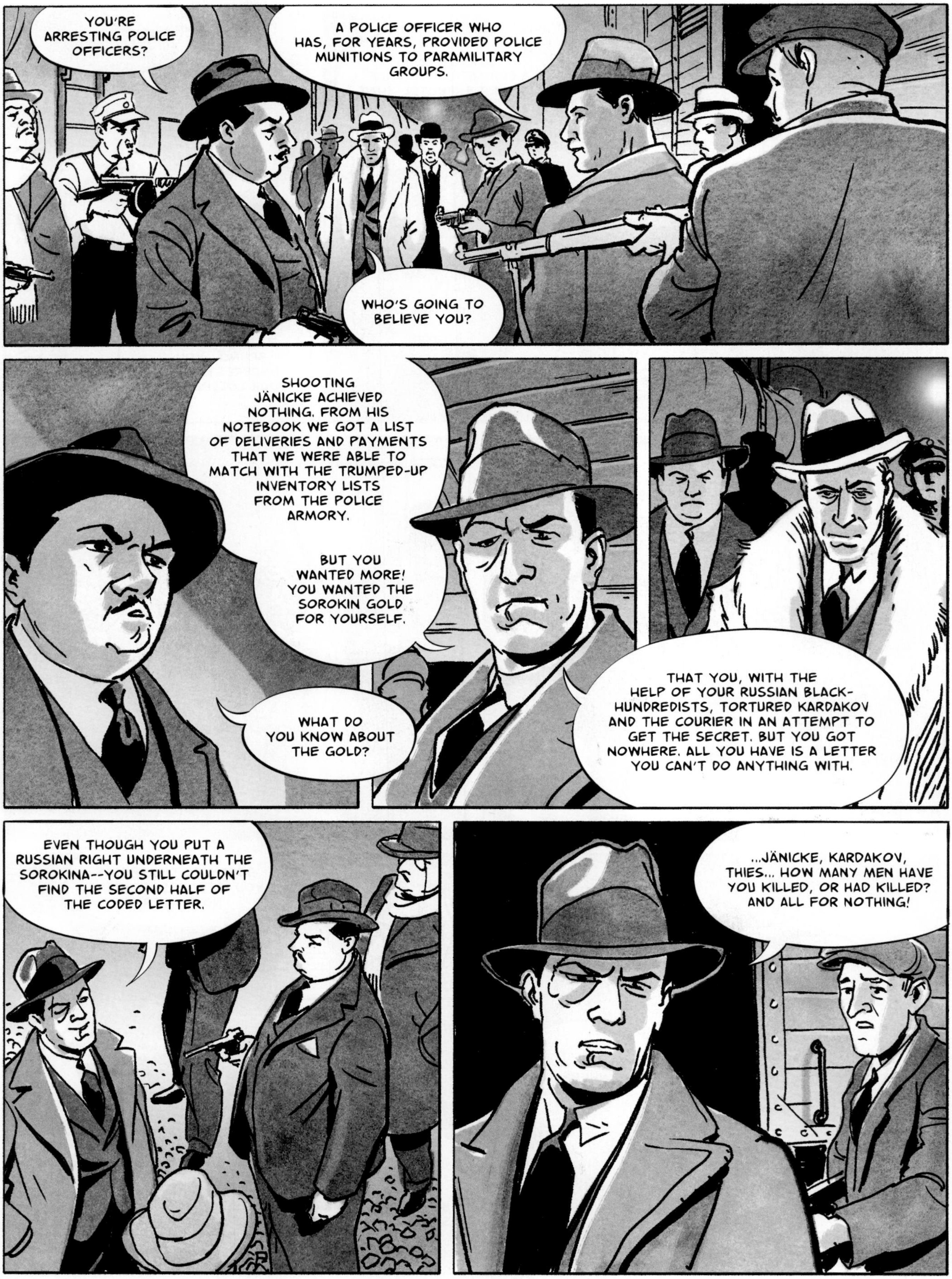
YOU'RE ARRESTING POLICE OFFICERS?
A POLICE OFFICER WHO HAS, FOR YEARS, PROVIDED POLICE MUNITIONS TO PARAMILITARY GROUPS.
WHO'S GOING TO BELIEVE YOU?
SHOOTING JÄNICKE ACHIEVED NOTHING. FROM HIS NOTEBOOK WE GOT A LIST OF DELIVERIES AND PAYMENTS THAT WE WERE ABLE TO MATCH WITH THE TRUMPED-UP INVENTORY LISTS FROM THE POLICE ARMORY.
BUT YOU WANTED MORE! YOU WANTED THE SOROKIN GOLD FOR YOURSELF.
WHAT DO YOU KNOW ABOUT THE GOLD?
THAT YOU, WITH THE HELP OF YOUR RUSSIAN BLACK-HUNDREDISTS, TORTURED KARDAKOV AND THE COURIER IN AN ATTEMPT TO GET THE SECRET. BUT YOU GOT NOWHERE. ALL YOU HAVE IS A LETTER YOU CAN'T DO ANYTHING WITH.
EVEN THOUGH YOU PUT A RUSSIAN RIGHT UNDERNEATH THE SOROKINA--YOU STILL COULDN'T FIND THE SECOND HALF OF THE CODED LETTER.
...JÄNICKE, KARDAKOV, THIES... HOW MANY MEN HAVE YOU KILLED, OR HAD KILLED? AND ALL FOR NOTHING!

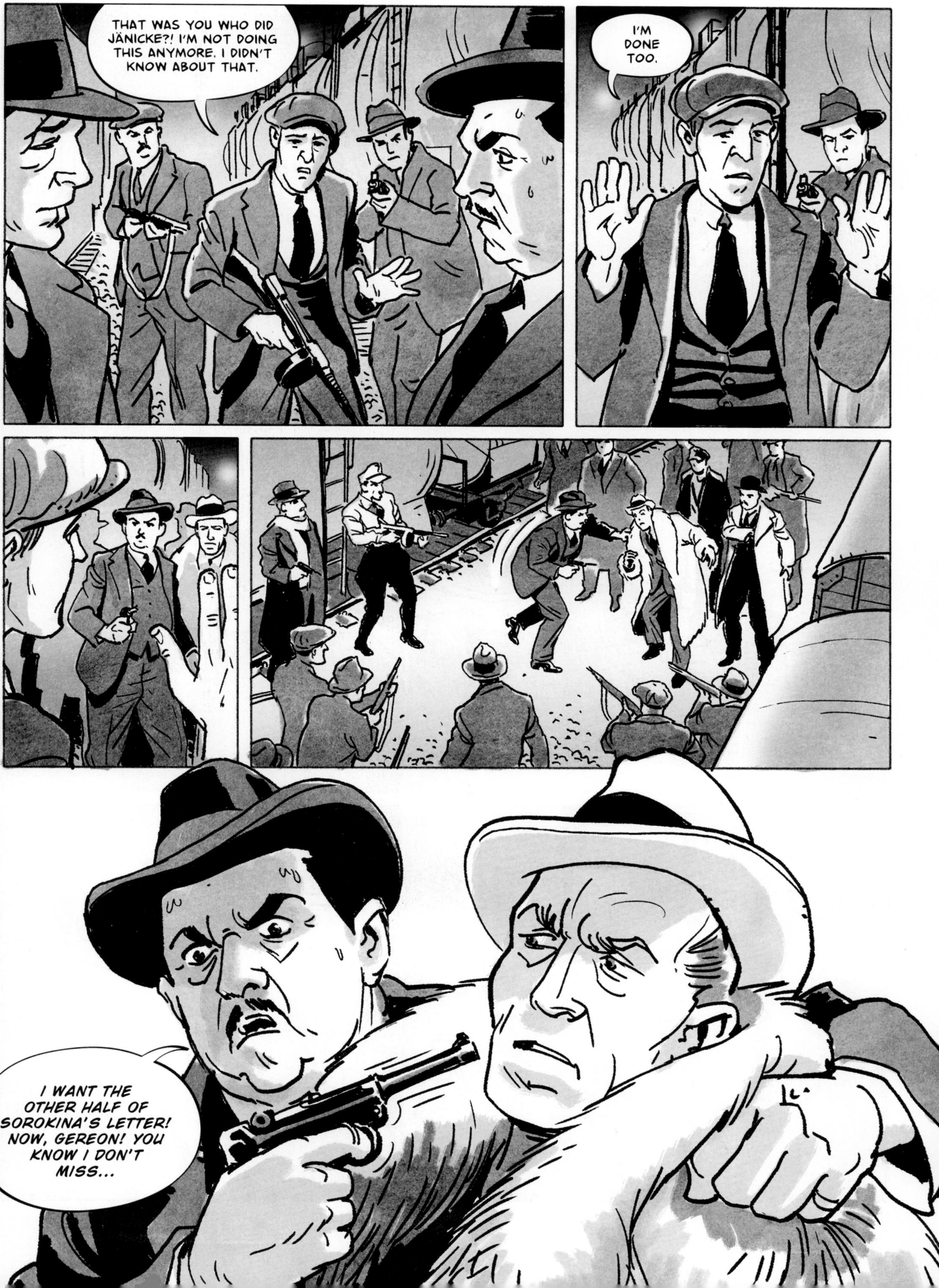
THAT WAS YOU WHO DID JÄNICKE?! I'M NOT DOING THIS ANYMORE. I DIDN'T KNOW ABOUT THAT.
I'M DONE TOO.
I WANT THE OTHER HALF OF SOROKINA'S LETTER! NOW, GEREON! YOU KNOW I DON'T MISS...

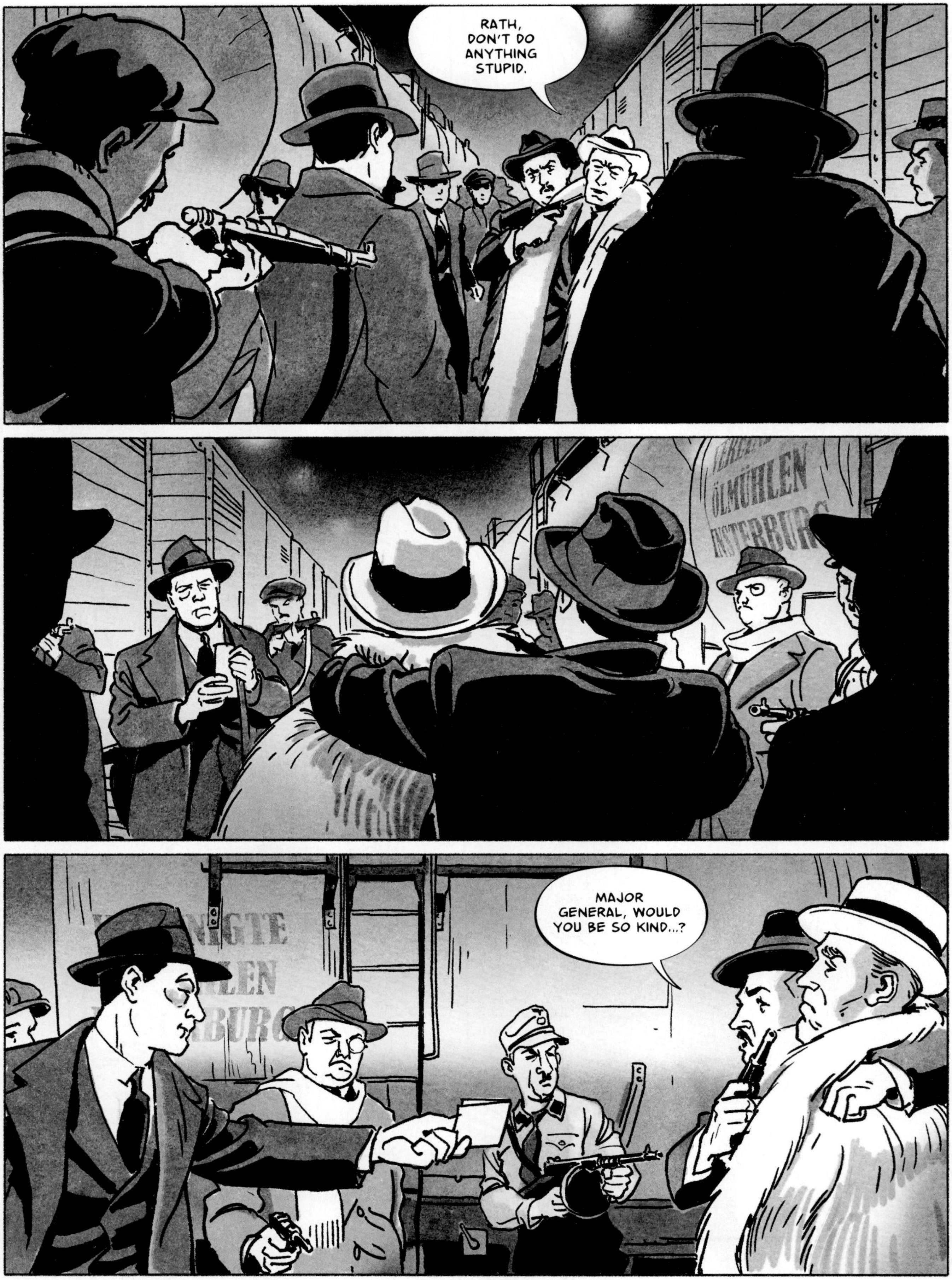
RATH, DON'T DO ANYTHING STUPID.
ÖLMÜHLEN
MAJOR GENERAL, WOULD YOU BE SO KIND...?

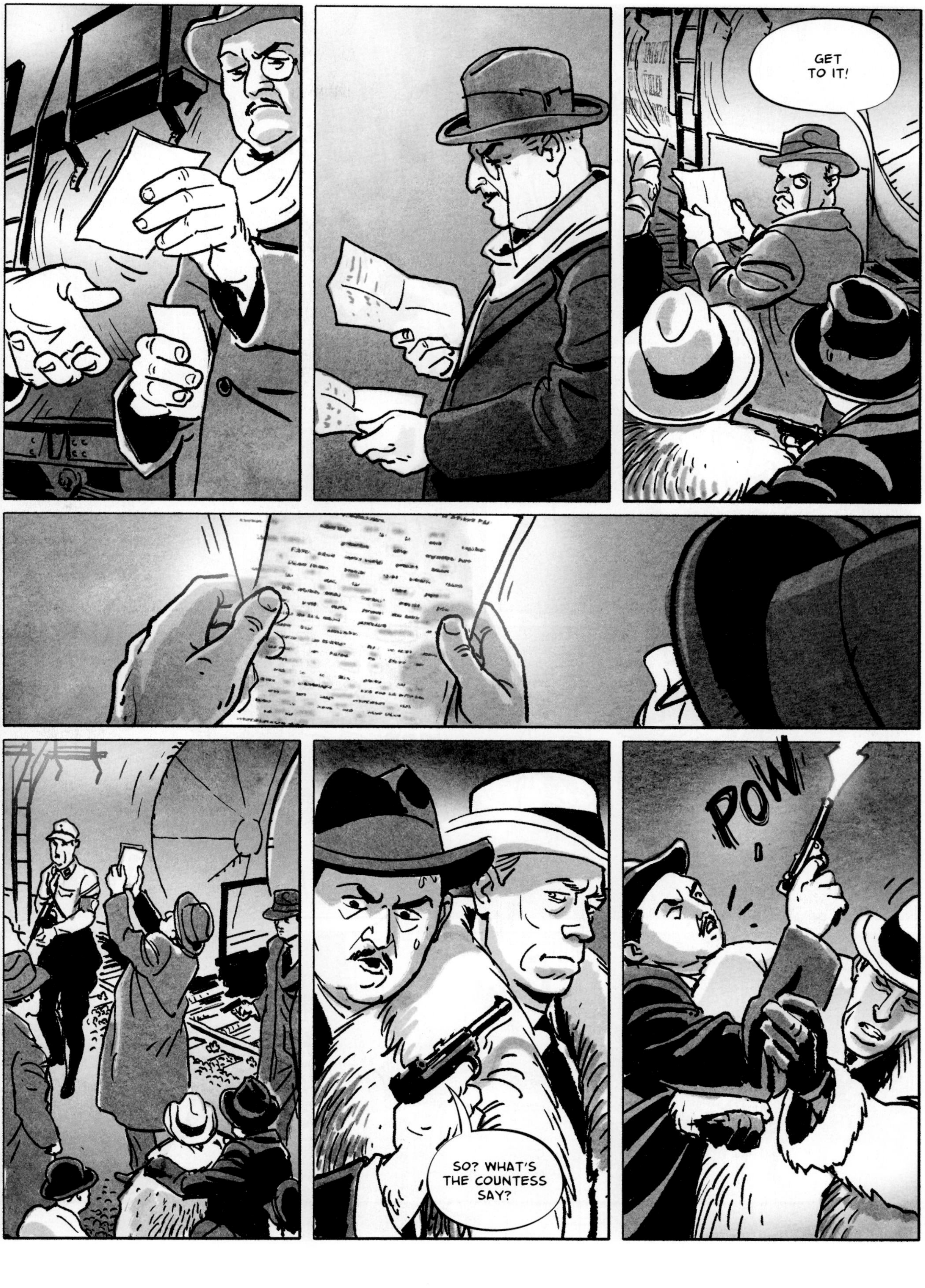
GET TO IT!
SO? WHAT'S THE COUNTESS SAY?
POW

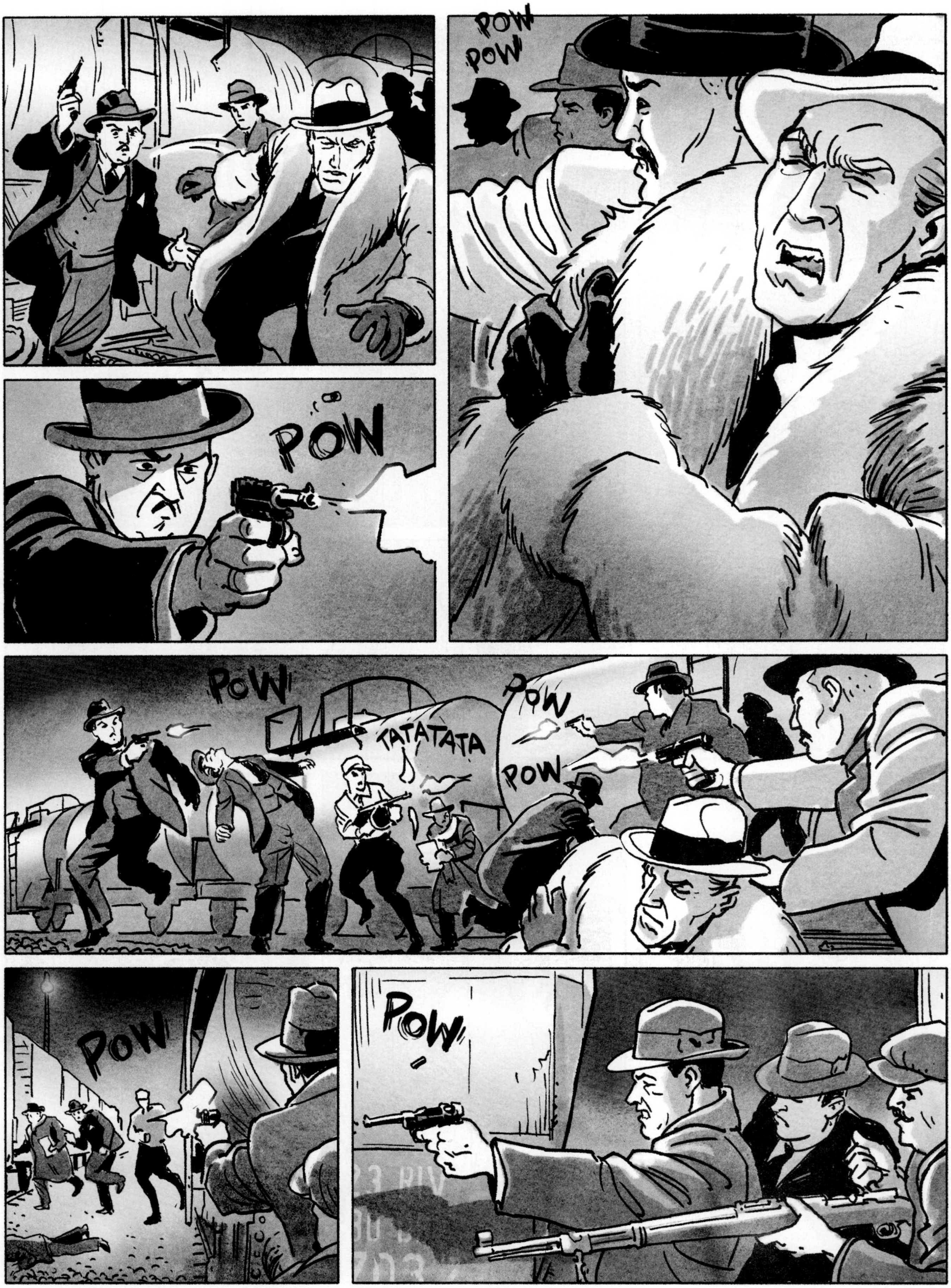
POW
POW
POW
POW
POW
TATATATA
POW
POW
POW

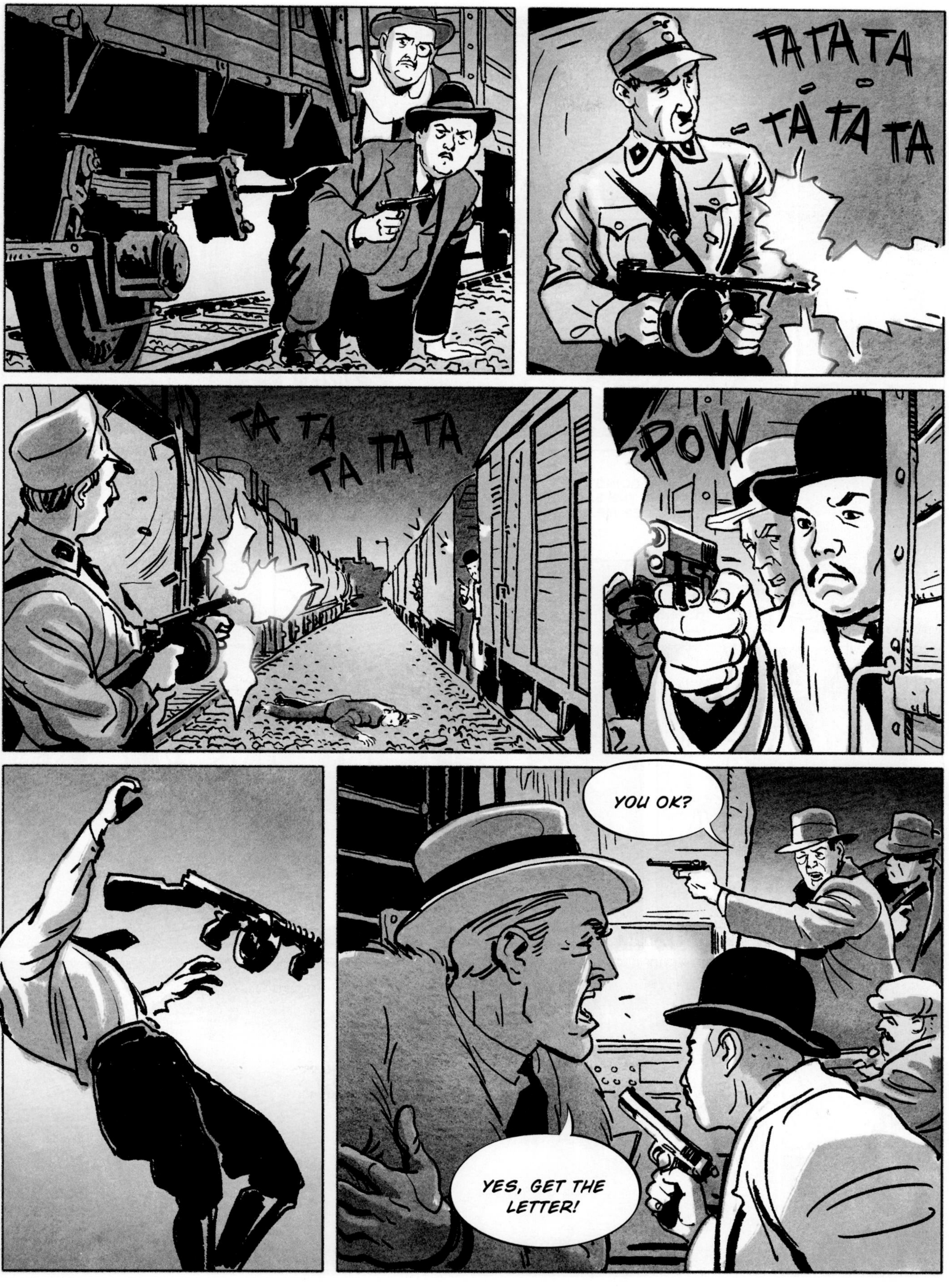
TA TA TA - - TA TA TA TA
TA TA TA TA TA TA
POW
YOU OK?
YES, GET THE LETTER!

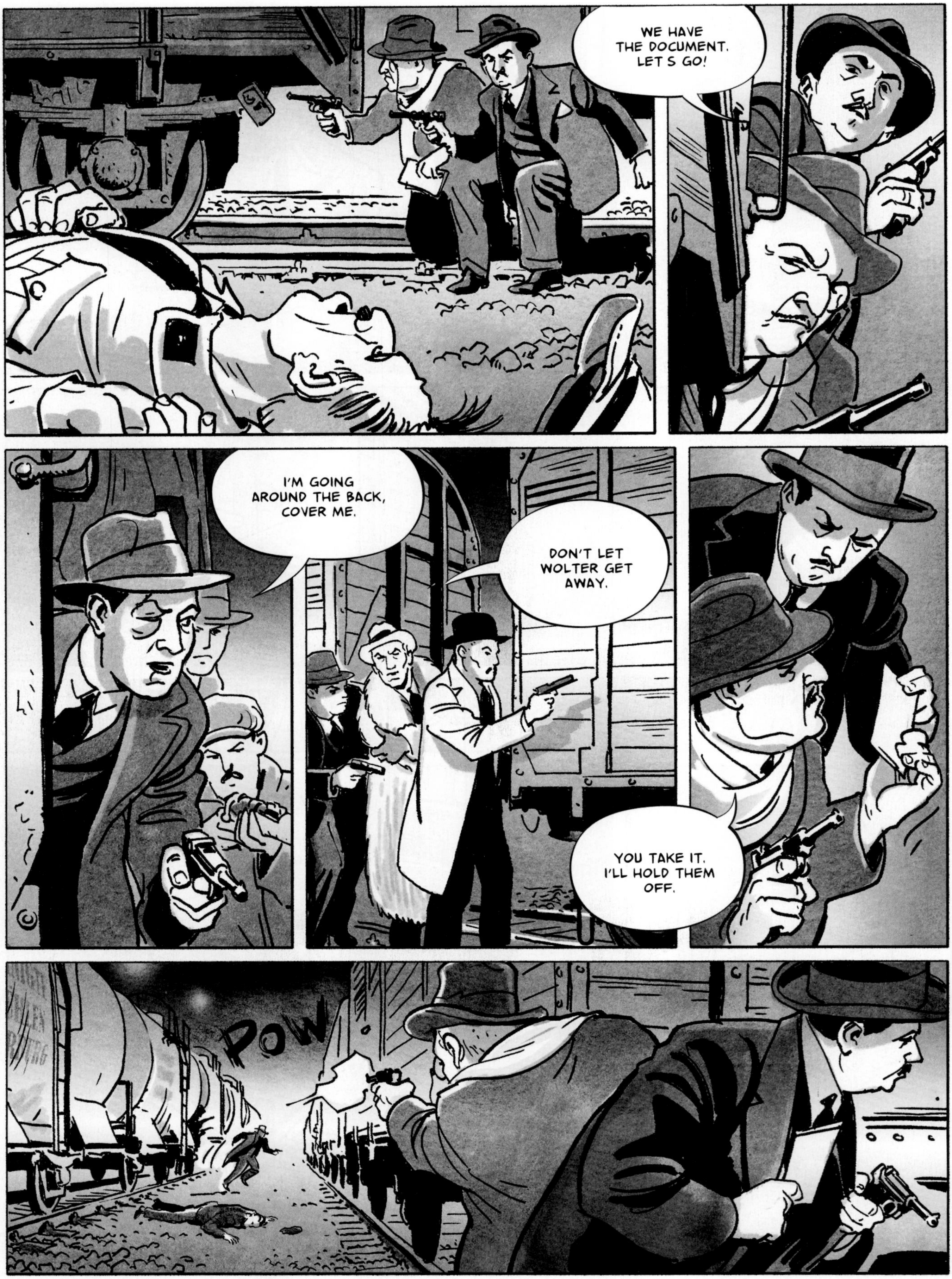
WE HAVE THE DOCUMENT. LET'S GO!
I'M GOING AROUND THE BACK, COVER ME.
DON'T LET WOLTER GET AWAY.
YOU TAKE IT. I'LL HOLD THEM OFF.
POW

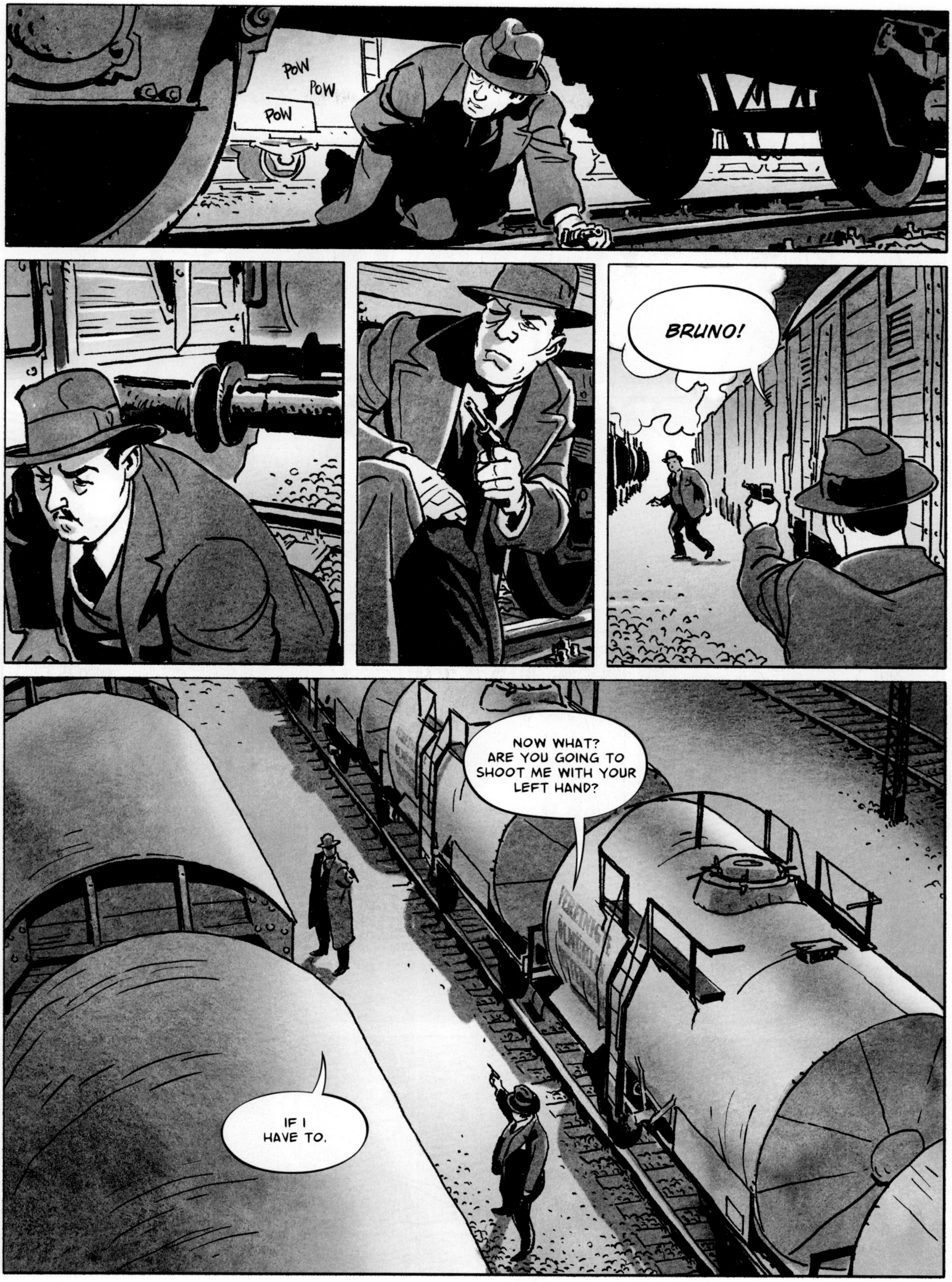
POW
POW
POW
BRUNO!
NOW WHAT? ARE YOU GOING TO SHOOT ME WITH YOUR LEFT HAND?
IF I HAVE TO.

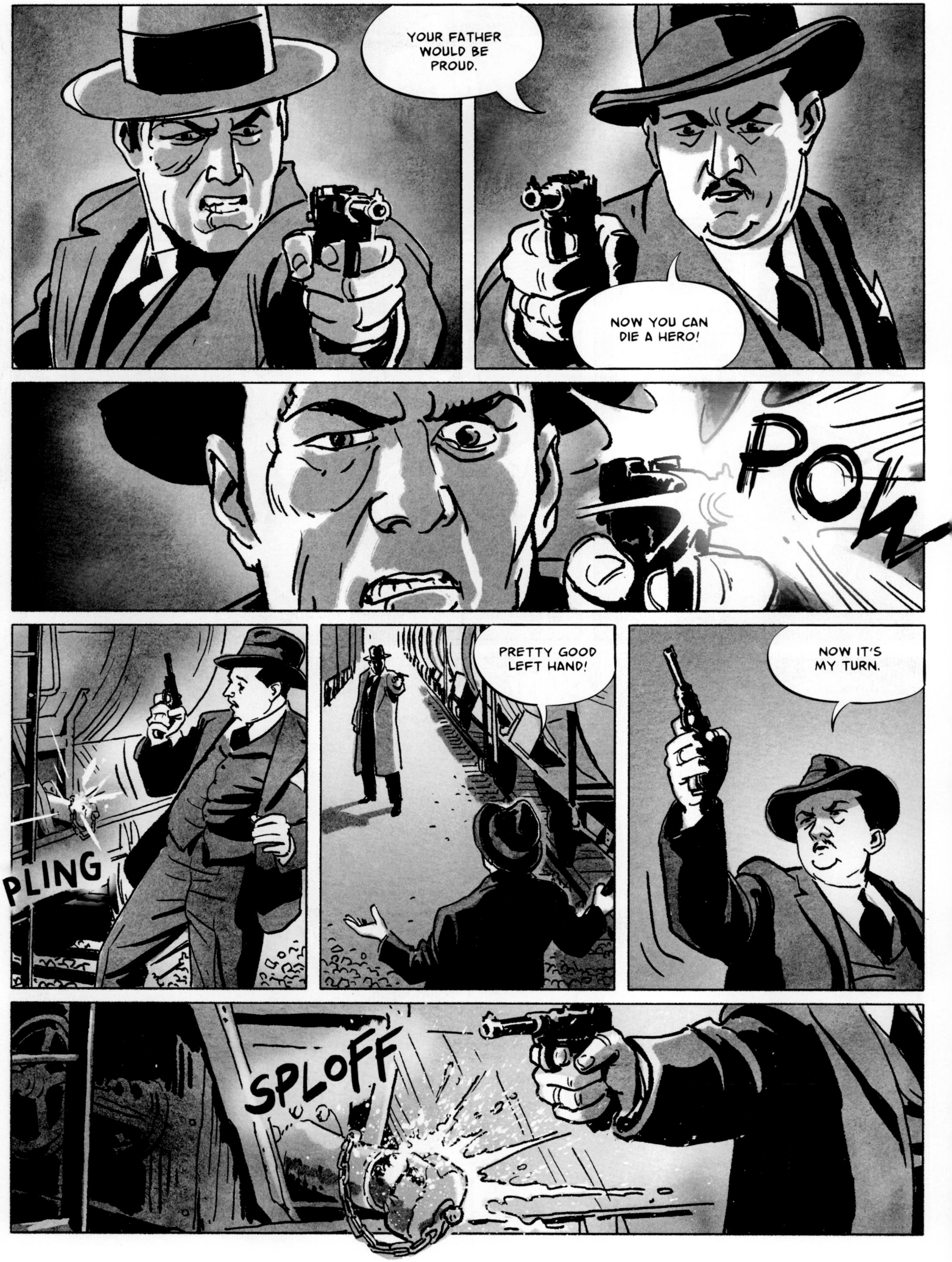
YOUR FATHER WOULD BE PROUD.
NOW YOU CAN DIE A HERO!
POW
PLING
PRETTY GOOD LEFT HAND!
NOW IT'S MY TURN.
SPLOFF

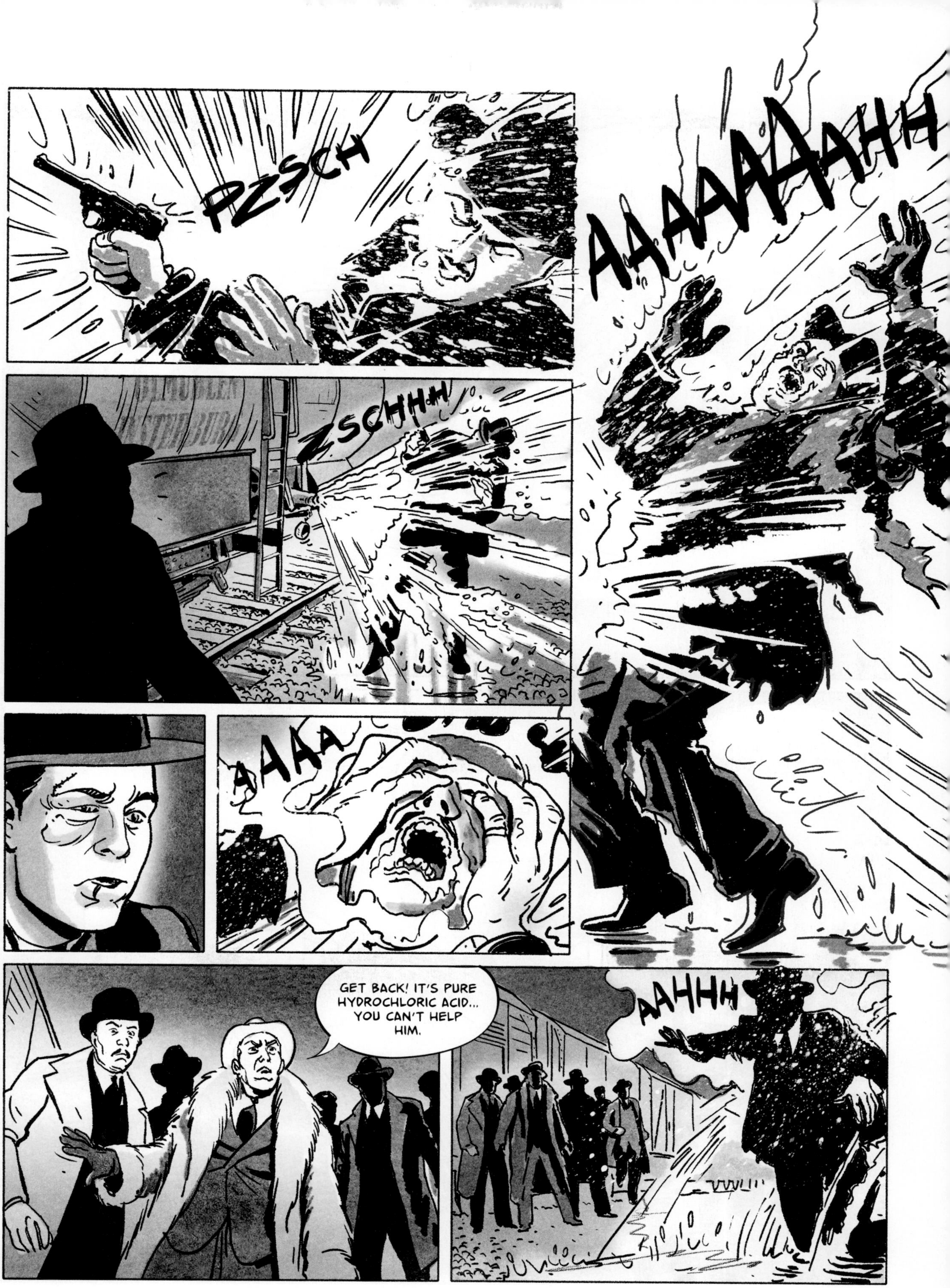
PZSCH
AAAAAAAAHH
ZSCHHH
AAAA
GET BACK! IT'S PURE HYDROCHLORIC ACID... YOU CAN'T HELP HIM.
AAHHH

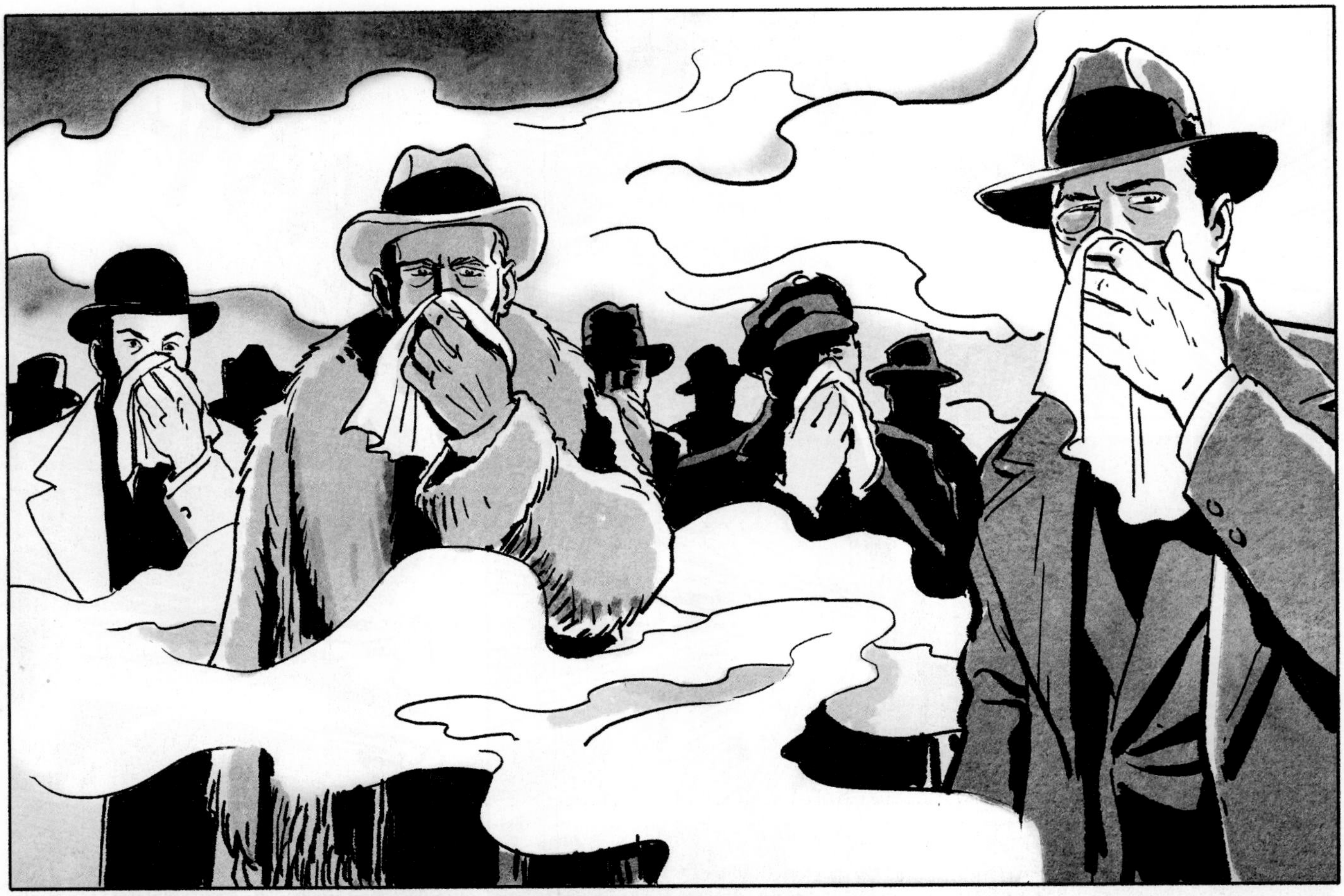

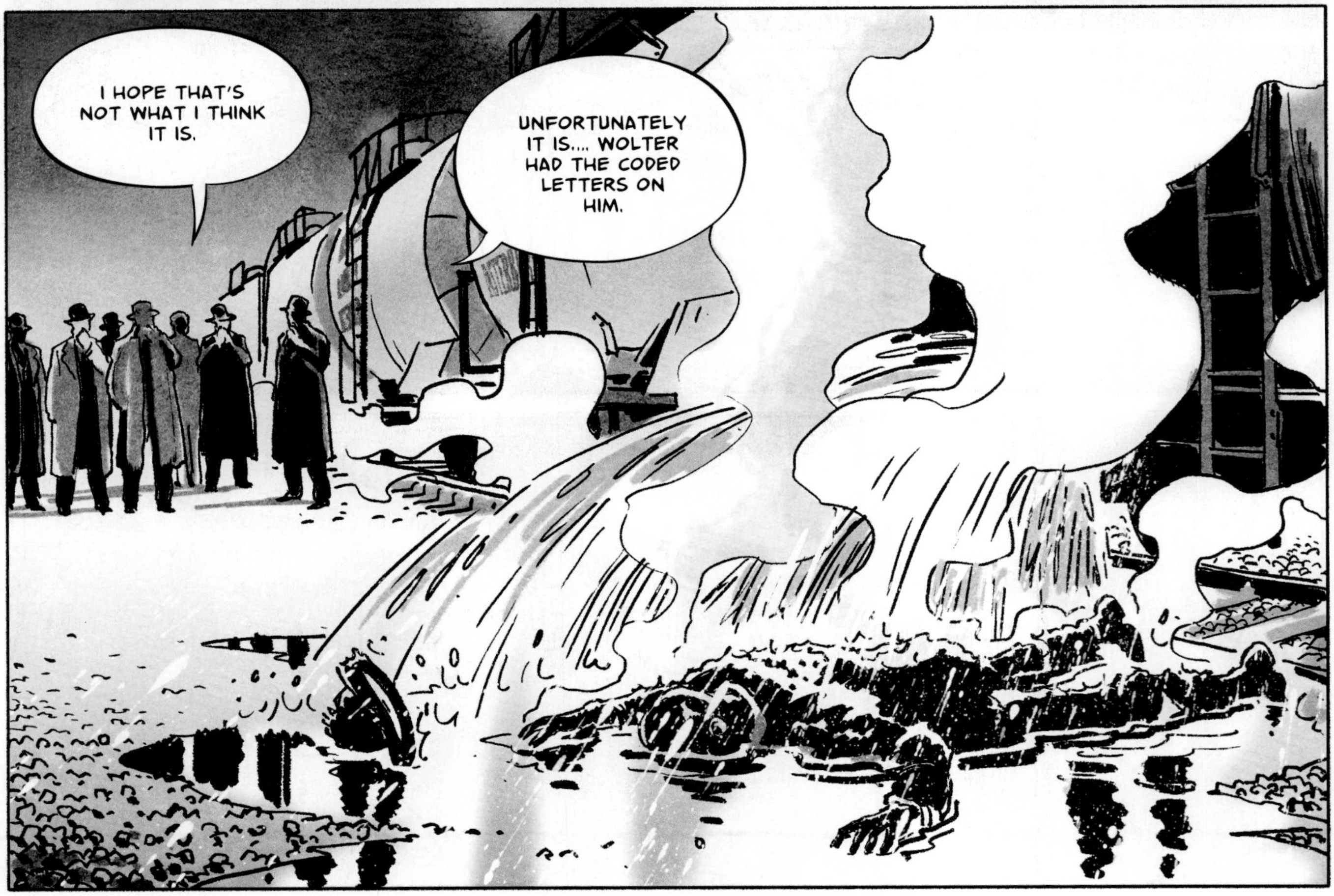
I HOPE THAT'S NOT WHAT I THINK IT IS.
UNFORTUNATELY IT IS.... WOLTER HAD THE CODED LETTERS ON HIM.

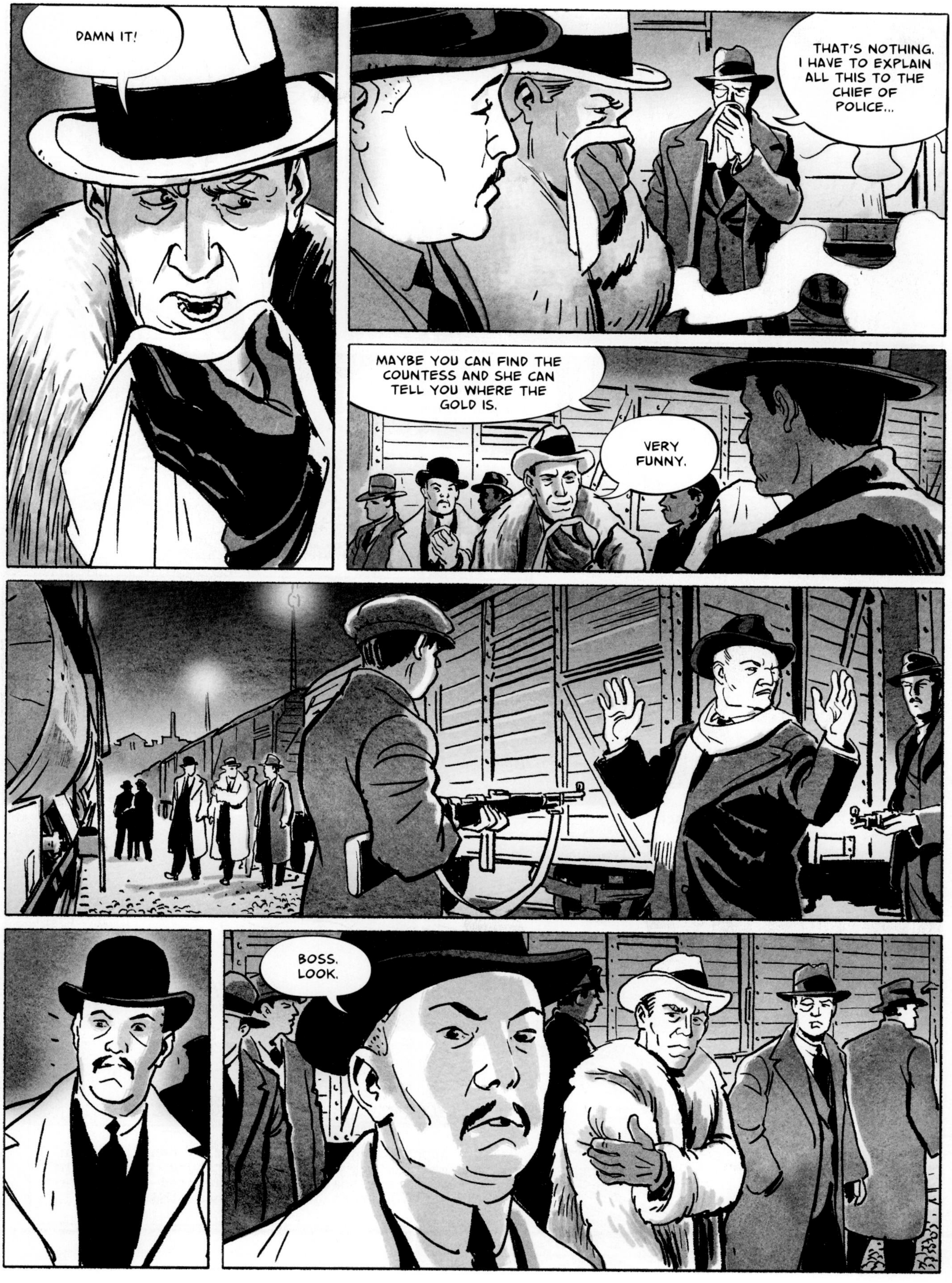
DAMN IT!
THAT'S NOTHING. I HAVE TO EXPLAIN ALL THIS TO THE CHIEF OF POLICE...
MAYBE YOU CAN FIND THE COUNTESS AND SHE CAN TELL YOU WHERE THE GOLD IS.
VERY FUNNY.
BOSS. LOOK.

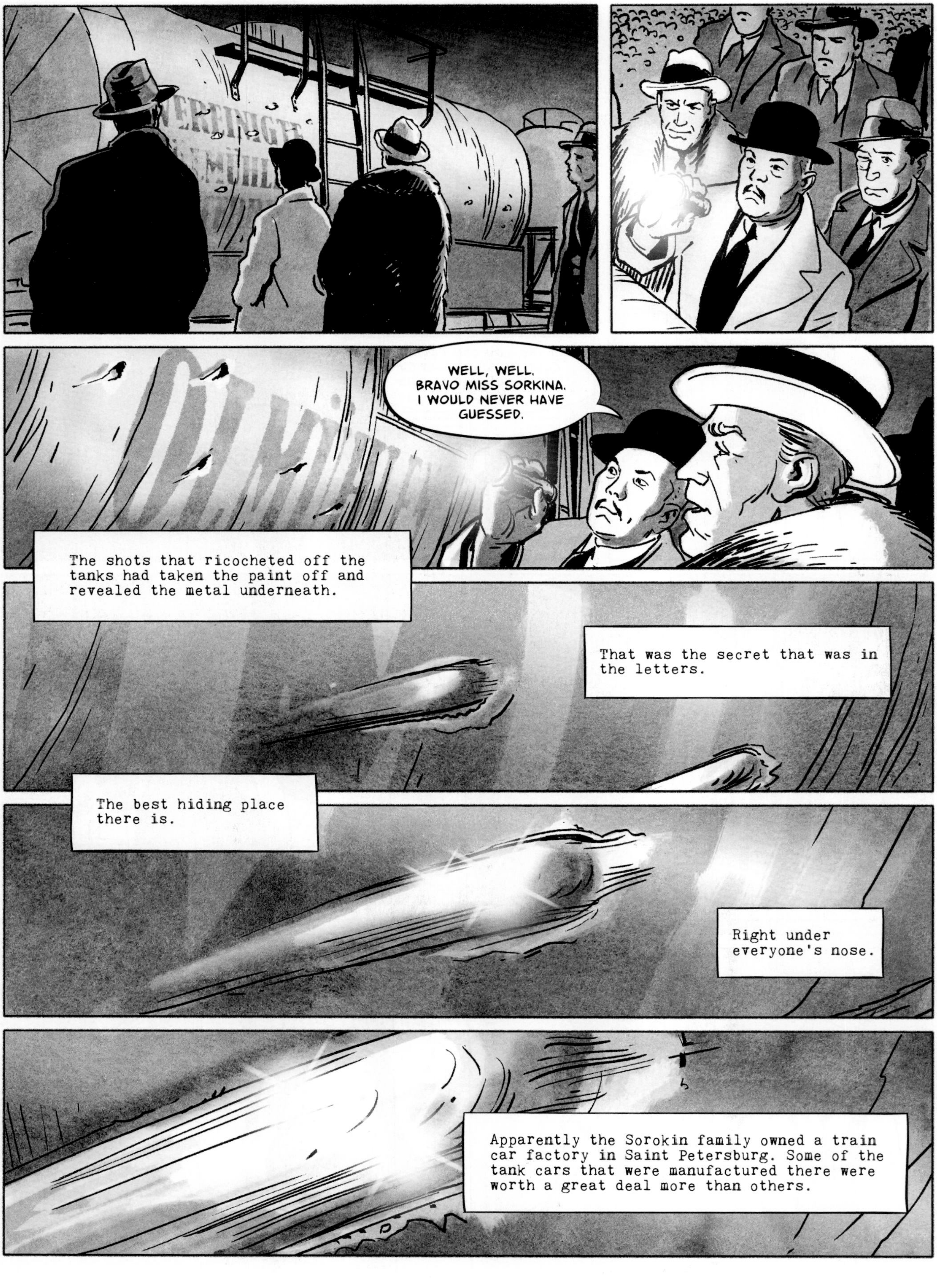
WELL, WELL. BRAVO MISS SORKINA. I WOULD NEVER HAVE GUESSED.
The shots that ricocheted off the tanks had taken the paint off and revealed the metal underneath.
That was the secret that was in the letters.
The best hiding place there is.
Right under everyone's nose.
Apparently the Sorokin family owned a train car factory in Saint Petersburg. Some of the tank cars that were manufactured there were worth a great deal more than others.

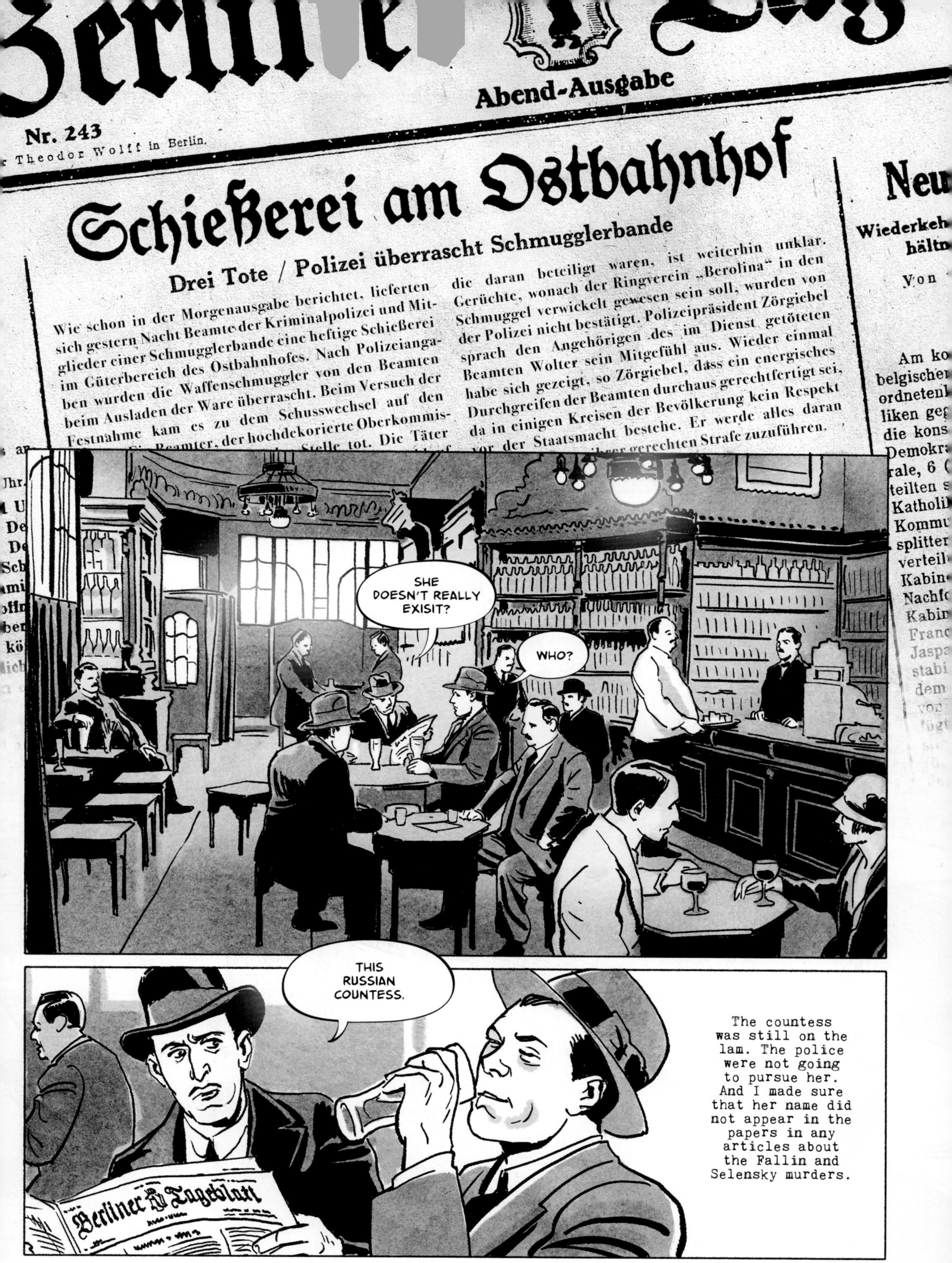
Abend-Ausgabe
Nr. 243
Theodor Wolff in Berlin.
Schießerei am Ostbahnhof
Drei Tote / Polizei überrascht Schmugglerbande
Wie schon in der Morgenausgabe berichtet, lieferten sich gestern Nacht Beamte der Kriminalpolizei und Mitglieder einer Schmugglerbande eine heftige Schießerei im Güterbereich des Ostbahnhofes. Nach Polizeiangaben wurden die Waffenschmuggler von den Beamten beim Ausladen der Ware überrascht. Beim Versuch der Festnahme kam es zu dem Schusswechsel auf den Beamter, der hochdekorierte Oberkommis-
Stelle tot. Die Täter
die daran beteiligt waren, ist weiterhin unklar. Gerüchte, wonach der Ringverein „Berolina" in den Schmuggel verwickelt gewesen sein soll, wurden von der Polizei nicht bestätigt. Polizeipräsident Zörgiebel sprach den Angehörigen des im Dienst getöteten Beamten Wolter sein Mitgefühl aus. Wieder einmal habe sich gezeigt, so Zörgiebel, dass ein energisches Durchgreifen der Beamten durchaus gerechtfertigt sei, da in einigen Kreisen der Bevölkerung kein Respekt vor der Staatsmacht bestehe. Er werde alles daran
gerechten Strafe zuzuführen.
Neu
Wiederkeh
hältn
Von
Am ko
belgischer
ordnetenl
liken geg
die kons
Demokr
rale, 6 (
teilten s
Katholi
Kommu
splitter
verteil
Kabin
Nachfo
Kabin
Franc
Jaspa
stabi
dem
SHE DOESN'T REALLY EXISIT?
WHO?
THIS RUSSIAN COUNTESS.
The countess was still on the lam. The police were not going to pursue her. And I made sure that her name did not appear in the papers in any articles about the Fallin and Selensky murders.
Berliner Tageblatt

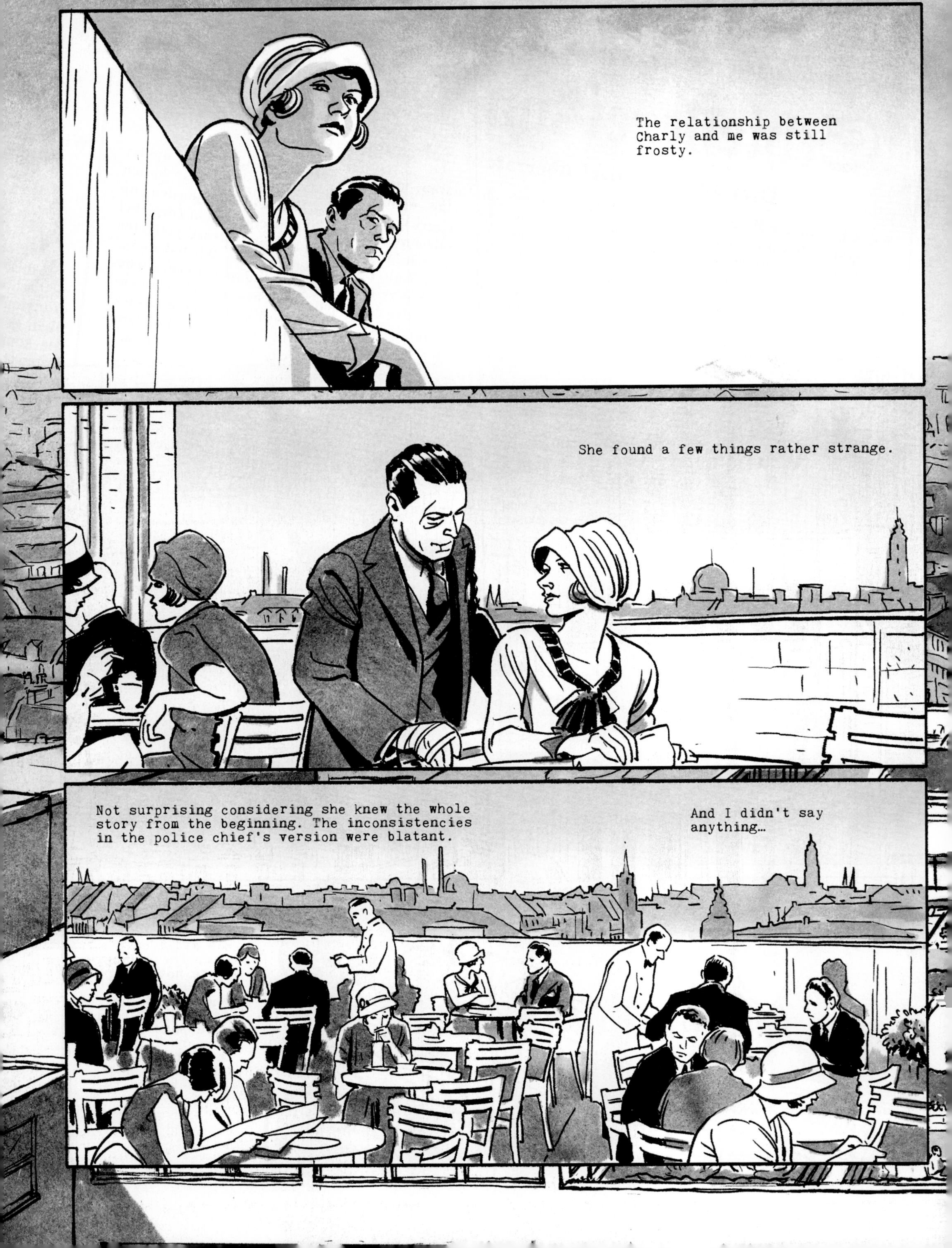
The relationship between Charly and me was still frosty.
She found a few things rather strange.
Not surprising considering she knew the whole story from the beginning. The inconsistencies in the police chief's version were blatant.
And I didn't say anything…

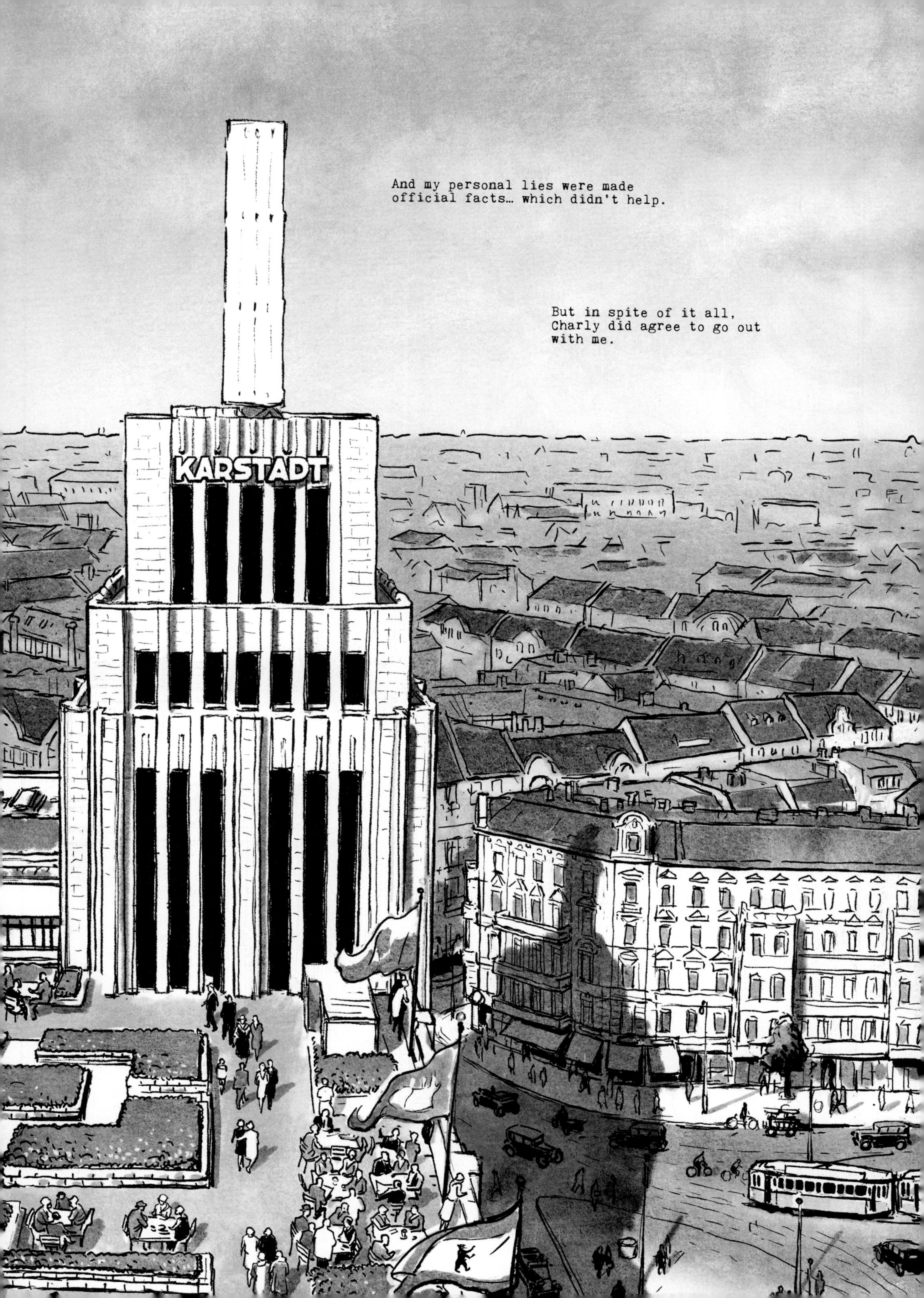
And my personal lies were made official facts… which didn't help.
But in spite of it all, Charly did agree to go out with me.
KARSTADT

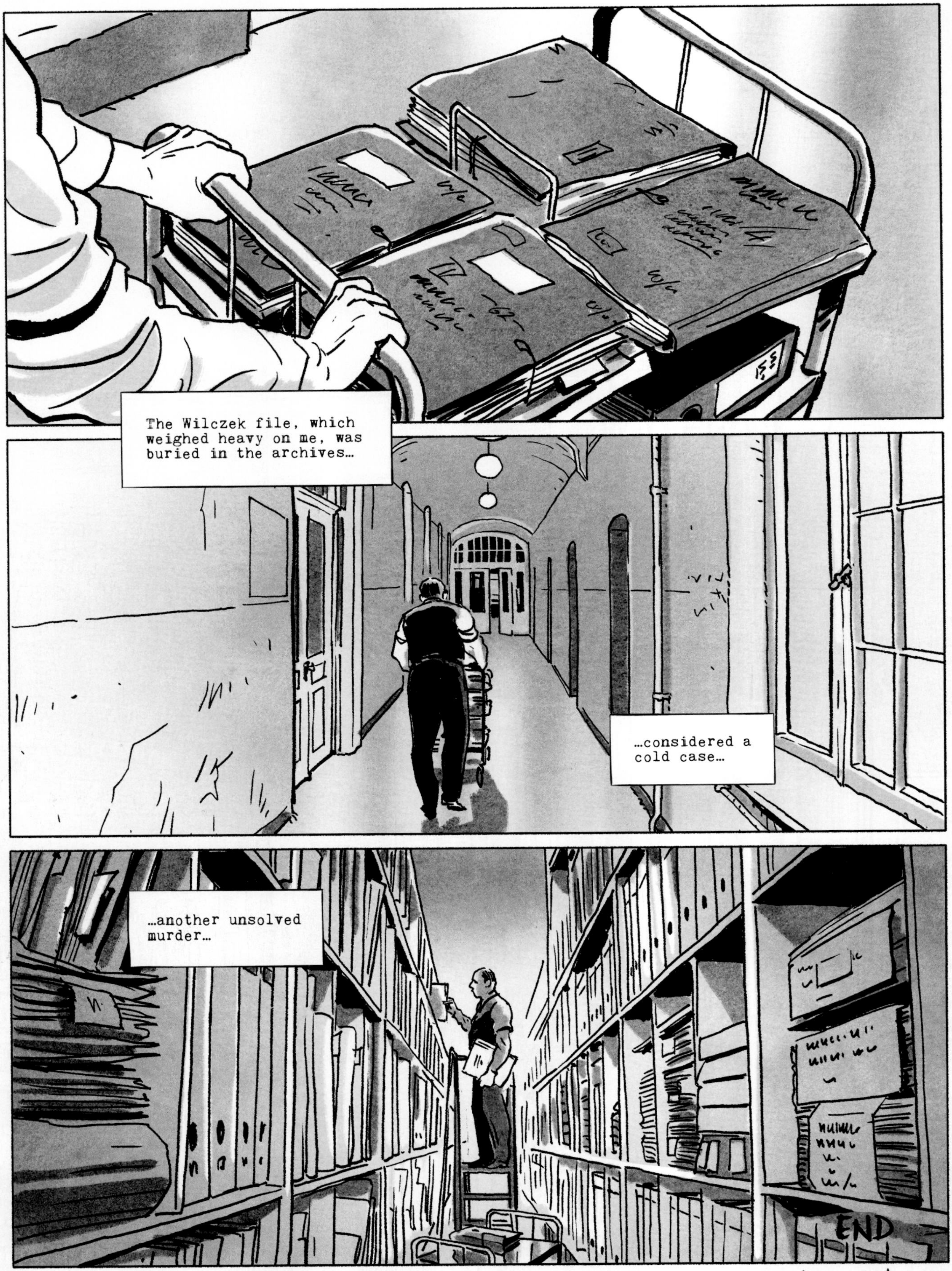
The Wilczek file, which weighed heavy on me, was buried in the archives…
…considered a cold case…
…another unsolved murder…
END
A.JYSCH/2017

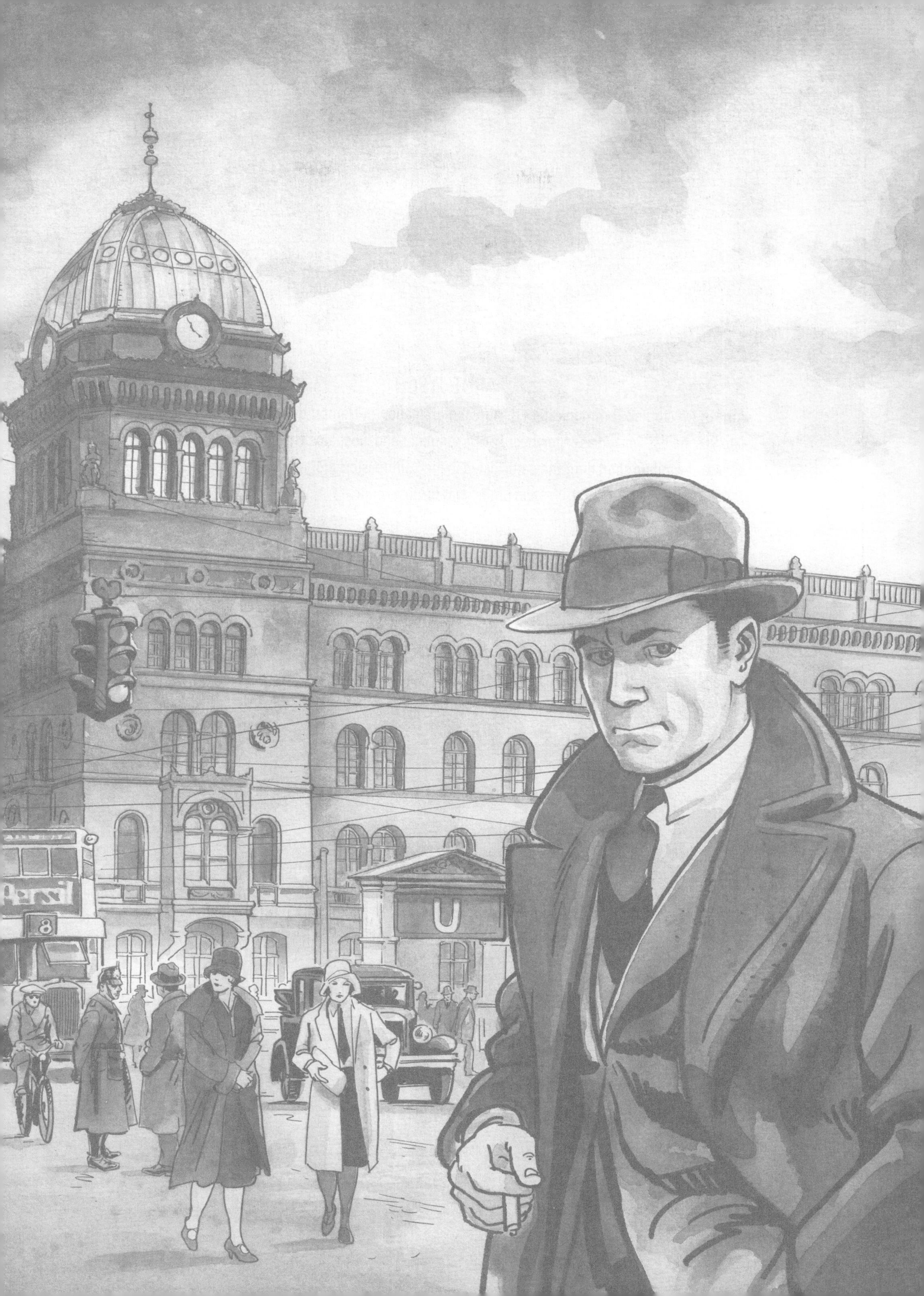

8
U

CREATORS

ARNE JYSCH

Arne Jysch studied communication design and animation in Hamburg and Potsdam. Since the late 90s, he has worked as a storyboard artist, animator and illustrator. He produced "Der Beste", an award-winning short film, and participated in the "Filmmasters Program" in Hollywood. "Wave and Smile" was his first comic.

VOLKER KUTSCHER

Volker Kutscher studied German, Philosophy and History, and worked as a newspaper editor before writing his first detective novel. *Babylon Berlin*, the first of the award-winning Gereon Rath novels, was a success in Germany and has led to a further four novels in the series. Volker Kutscher works as a full-time author and lives in Cologne.